Moura

Moura

The Dangerous Life of the Baroness Budberg

Nina Berberova

TRANSLATED BY

Marian Schwartz
and Richard D. Sylvester

NEW YORK REVIEW BOOKS

New York

Copyright © 1988 by Actes Sud

Translation copyright © 2005 by Marian Schwartz and Richard D. Sylvester

All rights reserved.

Published in the United States of America by
The New York Review of Books
1755 Broadway
New York, NY 10019
www.nyrb.com

The publishers would like to thank Andrea Lynn for her
assistance in locating many of the images in this book.

Library of Congress Cataloging-in-Publication Data

Berberova, Nina Nikolaevna.
  [Zheleznaia zhenshchina. English]
  Moura : the dangerous life of the Baroness Budberg / by Nina Berberova ; translated by Marian
Schwartz and Richard D. Sylvester.
      p. cm. — (New York Review Books classics)
  Includes bibliographical references and index.
  ISBN 1-59017-137-3 (alk. paper)
  1. Budberg, Moura. 2. Gorky, Maksim, 1868–1936. 3. Soviet Union—Biography. I. Title. II.
Series.
  CT1218.B784B4713 2005
  947.084'092—dc22

2005000248
ISBN 1-59017-137-3

Printed in the United States of America on acid-free paper.

1 3 5 7 9 10 8 6 4 2

Contents

Translators' Note

NINA BERBEROVA BEGAN work on what she referred to as the "Moura book" in Princeton, New Jersey, in September 1978, one month after her seventy-seventh birthday. (Moura is a Russian nickname for Maria: the first syllable sounds like "moor.") In her preface, Berberova says she always knew she would write a book about Moura Budberg, but she did not start in earnest until 1976, when she spent the summer at Stanford University's Hoover Institution. Richard Sylvester went with her to help sort through letters and documents relating to her former lover, the brilliant poet Vladislav Khodasevich, who had accompanied Nina on the journey from Petrograd to Berlin in 1922—a journey into permanent emigration, though neither knew it at the time.

Moura Budberg's name came up frequently in their letters, and others, too, written to Berberova in the 1920s by the artist Valentina Khodasevich (the poet's niece). In conversation with friends at Stanford and Princeton over the next two years, Nina spoke often of Moura, intriguing her listeners with the story of Moura's role in Stalin's secret acquisition of archives he used for the infamous Moscow Trials of the 1930s.

When she finished the book and published it in Russian in 1981, it bore the almost playful title *Iron Woman: The Story of the Life of*

M. I. [Maria Ignatievna] Zakrevskaya-Benckendorff-Budberg, About Her Herself, and About Her Friends. It has since been translated into several languages, retaining usually a variation of that title, though the French version, translated by Michel Niqueux (Arles: Actes Sud, 1988), is entitled *Histoire de la Baronne Boudberg.* We have decided to call it *Moura,* because that is how Nina first referred to it and how we have always thought of it while translating it into English.

We began our translation of the manuscript, at Nina's request, in 1980. A few years later, Nina sold the foreign rights to all her works to Actes Sud in France, and the book came to the attention of Jacqueline Kennedy Onassis, who was reading the French editions of Berberova's masterful works of fiction. It was, in fact, through Mrs. Onassis's efforts that Knopf published Nina's seminal collection of novellas, *The Tattered Cloak and Other Novels,* in 1991, but she never did find a home for *Moura* in English. *Moura*'s fate in Russian—and in Russia—has been altogether different. Because Nina wrote *Iron Woman* during the Soviet era, for publication she turned to the fine émigré publisher Russica, in New York City. By the time Mikhail Gorbachev declared his policy of glasnost, the book had been through a second edition and was well known among Slavists in the West. When the work was finally published in the land of Nina's birth, her joy was palpable. Not only, she explained to Marian Schwartz over the phone, was the book being serialized in two important periodicals at once (*Druzhba Narodov* and *Oktiabr'*) but it was also being published in book form by two different firms (there have been other editions since). The Western notion of protected copyright was not to her advantage in Russia—the more editions the merrier, as far as she was concerned, particularly when it meant the kind of acclaim she was receiving.

Born in 1901, Nina was only twenty-one when she emigrated to Europe with Khodasevich, a man fifteen years her senior. It was thanks to him that she found herself living, for the first three years after their emigration, under Maxim Gorky's roof and in proximity to Moura. The self-effacement that characterizes Nina's narration of Moura's story is partly a matter of principle, as she explains in her preface, but it also reflects her status in the household of Russia's most prominent living author at that time, where accomplished artists and officials in Lenin's government were frequent visitors.

Moura Budberg's life intersected with a brilliant cast of characters, the world of great events and the men who shaped them. All three of her publicly acknowledged lovers—Sir Robert Bruce Lockhart, Maxim Gorky, and H. G. Wells—either subsequently became or already were famous authors. As a young woman Moura met Kaiser Wilhelm, and later in life she had dealings with Stalin. Lockhart used her intelligence-gathering services when he worked for British intelligence between the wars; Berberova points to Moura's similarly clandestine contacts with the Soviet side. As the Russian subtitle of the book implies, Moura's life story is bound up with pivotal historical events that beg to be recounted. Thus, this is very much a "life and times" biography of someone who operated at the intersection of tradition and revolution, Russia and the Soviet Union, East and West.

Nina was aware, as were we, that her book was perhaps too long for a Western audience already familiar with the historical events that needed to be explained to a Russian reader. When Michel Niqueux undertook his excellent French translation, he and the author worked together to shorten the book by a third. We have followed their abridged version in our present translation. We have also completely revised and rewritten our original English version.

The few notes to the text are the author's. Quotes are from sources identified in the narrative and described more fully in the bibliography. We have shortened the bibliography by eliminating some Russian sources (they can all be found in the original Russian edition). Whenever possible, we have reinstated the original English wording of passages quoted from Lockhart, Wells, and others, including Foreign Office documents of the period (edited by Jane Degras) and Russian-American documents from 1917 to 1920 (edited by C. K. Cumming and Walter Pettit). Unless otherwise indicated, translations of poems are our own. Information about the large cast of characters in the book will be found in the index of names.

Our translation has been a collaborative effort throughout—a formidable challenge, but also a task of great satisfaction in knowing that we were giving Nina the chance tell her story in English, a language for which she had a writer's appreciation. According to Nina's old friend, Murl Barker, Nina kept this book by her bedside in the last few months of her life, rereading what she felt was the best book she had ever written. She would be pleased to see *Moura* in English at last.

MARIAN SCHWARTZ, *Austin, Texas*
RICHARD D. SYLVESTER, *Hamilton, New York*
December 31, 2004

Author's Preface

"WHO WAS SHE?" I was asked by friends who listened to Moura Budberg's story and encouraged me to write it down. "A Mata Hari? Another Lou Salomé?"

Yes, there was something of them both in her—the notorious adventuress who was a spy and movie heroine, and the Russian general's daughter to whom Nietzsche, Rilke, and Freud were strongly attracted. But my intention is not to evaluate or judge Moura, or to impose my opinion of her on the reader. My aim is to tell everything about her that I know. There is no one left who knew her before 1940 or even 1950. I have waited ten years for something to be written about her, but one by one those who knew her before World War II, her contemporaries, have disappeared. Those who remain know only what she told them. Of these, some still remember her and have mentioned her in their writings or told me what they know, but almost always there are the same anecdotes about her old age: that she was fat and very talkative when drunk; that she gossiped a lot, arranged the occasional liaison, and resembled at times an old clown.[1]

---

1. "Though Moura was a favorite of the Empress and well acquainted with Rasputin, she weathered the Russian Revolution and survived to become the lifelong friend of Kerensky.... She

For three years I lived under the same roof with Moura, and I saved the notes I made about her (not a diary, but calendar entries and notes of our conversations). Our relations were cordial but not intimate, without emotional overtones. In those remote years, for reasons which will be apparent, she placed much greater value on her friendship with Vladislav Khodasevich than with me (I was nine years younger than she was).

All the facts I have tried to rescue from oblivion are here. My sources are documents and books published between 1900 and 1975. They helped me discover her true origins, details of her personal life, the names of her friends and enemies, and the chain of events with which she was connected, sometimes closely, sometimes obliquely. The lives of all men and women born in Russia between 1890 and 1900 were caught up in those events existentially and, more often than not, tragically. The age and the conditions it imposed on human lives are my book's two main protagonists. Even Moura's two husbands, who played only a marginal role in her story, were deeply affected by the Russian catastrophe. She herself belonged to a country, an era, and a class where no one was safe. Moura struggled, made compromises, and survived.

In 1938, as in 1958 and 1978, I knew I would write a book about her. Her youth, her life, her struggle, and the fact of her survival had to be documented. Apparently no other witnesses are left. In England she has been mentioned here and there in memoirs, diaries, and cor-

---

became a member of the new Russian court, and something of a favorite of Stalin's, who allowed her to leave the Soviet Union after Gorky's death (though he begged her to stay)" (Michael Korda, *Charmed Lives* [New York: Random House, 1979], 120). Or this: "Moura Budberg began translating in 1917.... She has received wide critical acclaim for her translations of Chekhov, Turgenev, André Maurois, and others" (dust-jacket blurb, *The Life of a Useless Man*, by Maxim Gorky, translated by Moura Budberg [New York: Doubleday, 1971]). Maurois's book on Proust was translated later and came out posthumously in 1975. Budberg never translated Chekhov or Turgenev.

respondence, and the London *Times* ran an obituary, but everything published relied on her own account of events. When I tried to verify her stories, I saw that she had been lying about herself all her life. No one who knew her "in my time" doubted the truth of her words—and she fooled us all.

Moura lived with Maxim Gorky for twelve years, but Soviet literary reference works provide no information about her: in the three or four cases where her name does appear, a footnote explains that Maria Ignatievna Budberg (her title of baroness is not mentioned), born Zakrevskaya, by her first husband Benckendorff, was for a time Gorky's secretary and translator—a half Russian, so to speak, who lived her entire life in London, where she died. Gorky dedicated his last (unfinished) novel to her, the four-volume *Life of Klim Samgin*, but the dedication is made without comment.

Moura is not mentioned in connection with Robert Bruce Lockhart (later Sir Robert), who can be found in the *Great Soviet Encyclopedia* in the article about the "Lockhart plot" of 1918, nor is she mentioned in connection with H. G. Wells, whose "unwedded wife" she was for thirteen years, following Gorky's return to Soviet Russia in 1933 and until Wells's death in 1946. Pavel Malkov, the Kremlin commandant who arrested Lockhart and Moura in September 1918, refers to her in his memoirs as "a certain Moura, his mistress," whom he discovered that night in Lockhart's bedroom.

The three men in Moura's life met different fates after their deaths. Lockhart, so vital, attractive, witty, and sympathetic, comes fully alive today in his memoirs and diaries. In old age he was famous and socially well connected, but Soviet writers and historians tried to slander him and destroy his reputation, portraying him as a venal fool and a vulgar spy, an imperialist agent who was both conceited and arrogant.[2]

---

2. That is how he was portrayed by the Soviet dramatist Nikolai Pogodin, Lenin Prize

H. G. Wells's long life has been described in numerous books and articles that discuss the hidden personal and sociopolitical problems that tormented him in his final years. Nowhere, though, can the details of his life with Moura be found, despite the fact that their long intimacy played a huge part in the writer's attitude toward Russia and in the disenchantment with the October Revolution that clouded his final years. His later works from the 1930s and 1940s have never been translated in the Soviet Union, and Soviet critics who do mention them say they were "full of satirical tendencies." The somber twilight of his life is depicted as the tranquil mood of resignation of a great man who has concluded that the Communist Party of Great Britain had "become his last hope."

As for Gorky, there is as yet no real biography—discounting, of course, the 123-page book about him written for schoolchildren. Excerpts from only some of his letters have been published, his photographs censored,[3] and his relations with his contemporaries distorted. The three volumes of the *Chronicle of Gorky's Life and Work* are full of mistakes and inconsistencies.[4]

I said that Moura fooled us all. She lied, but not, of course, like

---

winner, in his play about the "Lockhart plot" *Enemy Vortex* (*Vikhri vrazhdebnye*, 1953), which was made into a film in 1956. Pogodin also wrote *Kremlin Chimes* (1941), in which one of the characters is H. G. Wells, and *Missouri Waltz* (1949), a parody of President Truman and the United States. In 1967, Yury Krotkov, one of the first Soviet dissidents, published a confession entitled "Letter to Mr. Smith" in *Novy zhurnal* (vol. 86, New York). He writes: "Pogodin, before his death, returning home after a trip to America, admitted to his family and close friends that everything he had written about America [and England?] was *untrue*."

3. A photograph of Gorky taken by his son Maxim Peshkov in Saarow in 1923 appears in volume 15 of Gorky's complete works (Moscow, 1949). Gorky is sitting on a bench in the garden, and there is a blank space where I was standing.

4. *The Short Literary Encyclopedia* (1962–78) gives the date Gorky left Italy to return permanently to the Soviet Union as 1931, whereas the actual date was May 1933.

some mythomaniac or some silly girl making up stories. Her lies were clever and well calculated, and in London society she was considered one of the most intelligent women of her time (see the diaries of Harold Nicolson). Nothing had ever come her way of its own accord, effortlessly, through blind luck. To survive, she had had to be alert, adroit, and bold, and she had had to wrap herself in a legend from the very start.

Moura loved men—not only her three lovers but men in general. She made no attempt to hide this, even though she understood how it irked and aggravated women, and excited and troubled men. She used sex, she sought novelty and knew where to find it, and men knew that, sensed that in her, and took advantage of it, falling in love with her passionately and devotedly. Moral considerations, false modesty, mundane taboos did not affect her liaisons. Sex came naturally to her and in sex she had no need to be taught, to imitate, or to pretend. She never had need of its counterfeit in order to survive. She was free long before the "universal emancipation of women."

There was no place in Moura's life for a stable marriage and children (she had two, and only because, as she told me one day, "Everyone has children"), or for relatives and family relations; there was no place for a reliable tomorrow, money in the bank, or thoughts about life in the hereafter. In this respect she in no way differed from her contemporaries in postwar Europe and postrevolutionary Russia. In some ways, though, she was ahead of her time. If she needed anything, it was her own legend, the myth she had created about her life, which she cultivated, embellished, and reinforced as the years passed. The men around her were talented, clever, and independent, and gradually she became the brilliant, vital woman who gave them life, fully aware of what she was doing and prepared to answer for everything she undertook.

Before her death she burned her papers. Everything she had accumulated after World War II was in her London apartment. She had sent her prewar papers (1920–39) to Tallinn in Estonia years earlier.[5] They had burned (so she said) during the German retreat and the occupation of Tallinn by the Soviet army. Is this true? Or did she lie about that, too, when she told her daughter what had happened to her papers? Maybe. And maybe some day in the future they will turn up.[6]

My task has been to be precise, to respect the facts, and thus to maintain the objectivity a biographer probably should possess. I allotted myself the smallest role among the dramatis personae—not out of modesty but out of my wish to write a book about Moura rather than about my relationship with her or my feelings about her.[7]

I knew her in my early twenties and am writing about her fifty years later. But did I know her then? Yes, if "to know" means seeing and hearing someone over the course of three years, living together in the same house. But I didn't know her then as I know her today. I know her so much better after having thought about her for many years. I have learned the truth she concealed and distorted when she told us about herself. In those years she gave us the myth she was cultivating, not herself.

---

5. Revel began to be called Tallinn after 1919. Petersburg became Petrograd in 1914 and Leningrad in 1924.

6. Two witnesses (who asked not to be named) report going to see Moura on the eve of her departure from London to Italy a few months prior to her death. They saw a dozen large cardboard boxes filled with papers (not books) and tied up with strong rope. The boxes were shipped to Italy. Their subsequent fate was tragic: the house Moura settled in near Florence was too cramped to contain her "office," so a house trailer was bought and parked in the yard by the house. A desk and shelves were built in the trailer, and here Moura "worked." The electric wiring came through a cable strung from the house. One night a short circuit started a fire in the trailer and everything burned. This accident may have hastened Moura's death.

7. I knew most of the persons mentioned in this book. Of those I knew only slightly I would name F. E. Krimer, Alexander Tikhonov, Alexei Rykov, Flora Solomon, Fyodor Chaliapin, and Barrett Clark.

Nonetheless I neither renounce the myth nor wish to cover it up with reality and obscure it. I don't reject it because I need it, just as I need the reality. Together they constitute this book.

The unprecedented success of biography and autobiography over the past half century, especially in the United States, demonstrates that the interests of those who write biography and those who read it coincide ideally and with the same intensity as did the demand for the realistic novel a hundred or more years ago. There is nothing puzzling about this. It is a reaction to the modern crisis of the depersonalization of the individual and the resultant renewal of interest in personal history. We have learned so much about ourselves and others that we want to see myths from the inside out. The modern individual has been stripped naked, made complicated by a history that itself has become complex. With irresistible force and hunger we are drawn more and more to the unmasking of myths, to discovering their hidden essence, seeking identifications, answers, and structures. Order, harmony, law—the foundations of intellectual life—have become more necessary to us than anything else. They cannot give us the answers to the questions posed by our time and its increasingly complex history, but they can lead us in the right direction.

Literary biography has flourished in our day, but in two opposite directions. In one approach, the author frankly warns the reader that the book is a combination of history and fiction; neither a novel nor an academic work, it is rather a work of the imagination conceived as an entertainment. In the second method, everything is backed up, everything is documented in footnotes or endnotes or a detailed bibliography. A model of this latter type of work is the monumental biography of Henry James by Leon Edel, who has written:

> The only imagination allowed a biographer is the imagination of form. A biographer has a responsibility toward his facts; they must be interpreted. As Strachey put it, "Uninterpreted truth is

as useless as buried gold.".... I resolved to seek my truths in both an episodic structure and a psychological interpretation of [the] past.... To tell it in biographical form, as if it were a novel, and be loyal to all my materials was the delicate and amusing task I set myself.[8]

I have tried to follow Edel's method. The bibliography at the end of this book contains many of the sources I consulted. In addition, I have drawn on my memory of everything Moura told me, or said to Vladislav Khodasevich, or to the two of us together, or sometimes to all of us who lived congenially in Gorky's house in those years, in Saarow, Marienbad, and Sorrento.

There is no invented dialogue in the book, only words spoken at one time or another in my presence. Where there is direct speech, it is not an attempt on my part to add variety—all quotes are taken from witnesses or from published memoirs. For the most part, though, I have given direct quotes as reported speech.[9]

The original title of the book, *Iron Woman*, was a nickname given Moura in 1921 by Gorky. There is more to this than meets the eye. Gorky knew and was attracted to strong women his whole life. Moura was strong and modern, and, in addition to that, was thought to be a descendant of Agrafena Zakrevskaya, Pushkin's *bronze*

---

8. And further paraphrasing Lytton Strachey: "Biography has to be analytic, lively, human, and composed with becoming brevity.... The whole can be deduced from the parts.... A biographical subject is consistently ambiguous, irrational, inexplicable, self-contradicting; hence, it truly lends itself to irony and to delicacies of insight and sentiment" (Leon Edel, *Bloomsbury: A House of Lions* [New York, Lippincott, 1979], 13, 227, 229).

9. Two moments in the book require a comment: Moura's night with Wells in the apartment on Kronverk Prospect (in Petrograd), and the photographs Peters showed Moura. Both were described by her: the latter to me when she was pouring water from a pitcher over my head after washing my hair in Marienbad; and the former to Khodasevich on the train from Berlin to Marienbad.

Venus: therein lay the second meaning. The third meaning evolved gradually, as a hint at the "Iron Mask" and the mystery surrounding it. The identity of the man hidden beneath an iron mask permanently welded to his face who was brought to the fortress at Pignerol in 1679 and transferred in 1703 to the Bastille, where he died, remains a secret to this day.

Moura rapidly cleared the way for her own legend. The world she lived in before 1918 had been destroyed, and she had seemingly emerged from it unscathed, though perhaps not entirely. There was no one but her who could bear witness to her previous life. Her life in the world was easier to protect; after 1918 she had no roots, and Moura was in complete control. What happened to the legend after her death? It remained intact, as it had the last ten years of her life. This is not to say that Moura knew no fears, merely that the fears she knew were not the old fears our grandmothers knew but new ones, fears destined for their grandchildren: fear of prison, of hunger and cold, of being stateless without a passport, and probably the fear of secrets being uncovered. The joys were new, too: the joy of a free private life unhampered by a moral code of "what the neighbors might say"; the joy of surviving intact; the joy of knowing she had not been destroyed by those she loved.

NINA BERBEROVA
1978–1980

I

THE BEGINNINGS

What's past is prologue....
The Tempest, II, i, 253

IN THE 1920s and 1930s she was known as a graduate of Cambridge University and translator of some sixty volumes of Russian literature into English. She was called Countess Zakrevskaya, Countess Benckendorff, Baroness Budberg. Her father had been a senator and member of the State Council in St. Petersburg, though she herself had lived in London most of her life. Born Zakrevskaya, she was regarded as the great-granddaughter, or perhaps the great-great-granddaughter, of Agrafena Fyodorovna Zakrevskaya, the wife of a Moscow governor, to whom Pushkin and Vyazemsky had written poems. The poet Vladislav Khodasevich never doubted that Moura was a descendant of Pushkin's "Bronze Venus," and Sir Robert Bruce Lockhart in one of his later books refers to her as a Russian aristocrat.

In fact, though, this was a legend she had constructed, doubtless not all at once, but gradually, over many years, in stories about her past. She was actually the daughter of a Senate official, Ignaty Platonovich Zakrevsky, no relation to Count Arseny Andreevich Zakrevsky, Agrafena's husband. Moura's first husband, Ivan Alexandrovich

Benckendorff (born in the late 1880s), did not belong to the line of Benckendorffs who were counts and was only a distant relative of Count Alexander Konstantinovich Benckendorff, Nicholas II's ambassador to London and grandnephew of Nicholas I's chief of gendarmes. He belonged to a collateral line, that is, he had no title, though he was, like them, of the Baltic nobility. Cambridge University did not admit women before World War I, so Moura could not have studied there, though there were two women's schools in Cambridge: Girton, opened in 1869, and Newnham, opened in 1871. She was not a graduate of either of them but spent a winter at Newnham to improve her English, a language she had spoken from childhood. In 1911 her parents sent her to England, entrusting her to the care of her stepbrother, Platon Ignatievich Zakrevsky, a counselor at the Russian embassy in London. As for the sixty volumes of translations, that number was never realistic, though she did mention "thirty-six" to a close friend in 1924. Nonetheless, neither then nor in 1974, when she died, were there even that many. By the end of her life the total came to about twenty (over fifty years), and not all of those were from Russian.

What was true was that her second marriage entitled her to be called Baroness Budberg. She kept the name for the rest of her life (though few know it in the Soviet Union, where she is usually referred to as Zakrevskaya-Benckendorff: the dedication page of Gorky's four-volume novel *The Life of Klim Samgin* reads, "To Maria Ignatievna Zakrevskaya"). However, if the Budberg name and title were never discarded, the baron himself was, virtually the day after she married him.

I remember Khodasevich asking her once what she thought of her great-grandmother, whom Pushkin described in a letter to Pyotr Vyazemsky in September 1828:

> I've plunged into Society, having no other place of refuge. Were it not for your Bronze Venus, I would have died of ennui. But

she's amusing and nice, which is a consolation. I'm writing verses to her. And she has appointed me to be her pander (a job I was drawn to by my usual inclinations and by the present state of my own "Well-Intentioned," about which the same may be said as was said of the magazine of that name: heaven knows, the intention is good, but the result is bad).[1]

Moura had the ability, when she wanted to, of dodging direct questions. Her face—serious, intelligent, and sometimes beautiful—would suddenly take on a sly, sweet, feline look, and, with a half smile, as if such a question hardly needed an answer, she would retreat into silence.

Agrafena, Arseny Zakrevsky's wife, made Pushkin her "confidant." In 1828 he dedicated two poems to her in which one senses his admiration for her passionate nature, "stormy, mutinous, and wild." One of them is "Portrait" ("Portret"):

> With fire blazing in her soul,
> Her heart a storm of passion,
> She makes the partial universe whole
> Among our northern women of fashion;
> And heedless of Society's rules
> She races on till breath is sparse,
> The way a lawless comet hurls
> Across the stationary stars.

The other is "The Confidant" ("Napersnik"):

> I strain to capture every cry
> Of hard confession, tender pain:

---

1. Pushkin had gonorrhea at the time.

> Your language makes me wild again
> With passion's storm and mutiny.
> But hide your stories, hide them now,
> And hide your dreams from my inspection:
> I fear their feverish sweet infection,
> I fear the knowledge of what you know.

Agrafena appeared again as Nina Voronskaya in chapter 8, stanza XVI, of *Eugene Onegin*. In this passage (in the James Falen translation), Tatyana, now married to a general, is first seen in society by Onegin:

> She took a seat beside the chair
> Of brilliant Nina Voronskaya,
> That Cleopatra of the North;
> But even Nina, shining forth
> With all her marble beauty's fire—
> However dazzling to the sight—
> Could not eclipse her neighbour's light.

To his dying day, Khodasevich never knew that these poems had nothing to do with Moura. He sometimes quoted them to her saying, "You don't need to look for a model to live by, with a grandmother like that." And Moura would close her eyes a little and stretch sweetly —playing the kitten in such moments was, strange to say, somehow becoming to her despite her customary brave and resolute air.

Moura's father, Ignaty Platonovich, belonged to another branch of the Zakrevsky line. His ancestors were Ukrainian, Osip Lukyanovich and his son Andrei Osipovich (1742–1804), who at one time was director of the Academy of Fine Arts in Kiev. Ignaty, Andrei's great-grandson, was a landowner from the Chernigov district northeast of Kiev and a jurist who published articles about the law of inheritance, judicial reform in Bulgaria, the theories of the new school of criminal anthropology, and even social equality. When the family grew larger he moved to Petersburg and took a position in the Senate. He died in 1904 with the rank of procurator-general of the First Department of the Senate.

Moura, born in 1892, was the youngest of his four children. Her stepbrother, Platon Ignatievich, was Zakrevsky's son by his first marriage. His name appears on the roster of the Russian embassy in London (as a "junior gentleman of the bedchamber"), and later in Berlin, where he was an attaché. There were also twin girls, Anna and Alexandra (Alla), both of whom were later married—Anna to a man named Kochubei, and Alla to a Frenchman named Moulin.

The girls were educated at a boarding school for young ladies, but I never observed in Moura those typical "boarding school" traits which high-school girls in prerevolutionary Russia viewed with such contempt: a proneness to fainting spells and emotional hysterics, either sincere or forced; a kind of provincial aloofness from the realities of Russian life; semiliteracy in questions of art and literature; and a reverential admiration for every single member of the Romanov dynasty. Girls educated at high school, especially at a liberal one, who read Ibsen and Wilde, Gumilev and Blok, Marx and Darwin, knew that curtseying and embroidering and learning to pronounce *r* in the French manner were the lot of the unfortunate boarding-school girls, whom fate had forever banished from real life. To reach maturity without any training or guidance in understanding contemporary life—politics and society, art and science—seemed to my generation a sad anomaly.

But Moura was not of the embroidering and curtseying sort. She was clever and tough and fully aware of her uncommon abilities. She had a sense of responsibility, not just in feminine ways but in general. Knowing very well what her own capacities were, she learned to rely on her physical health and energy, and on her considerable charm as a woman. She knew how to be among people, how to live with them, how to choose them and get along with them. She was undoubtedly one of the exceptional women of her time—a time that showed no mercy or pity toward her or her generation. That generation, born between 1890 and 1900, was almost completely destroyed by war, revolution, emigration, the camps, and the terror of the 1930s.

After boarding school came England. Not France, where middle-class mothers took their daughters if they could afford it. France was cheaper than England, and French seemed a necessity then, while English was a luxury. And not Germany, where young Russian women went to study physics, chemistry, or medicine, rather than Parisian pronunciation. Platon was stationed in London in those years, and the ambassador there was his patron Benckendorff—a real count in this case, the descendant of the chief of gendarmes who had been Pushkin's enemy. At Count Benckendorff's house, on her trips down from Newnham, Moura met diplomats from the Foreign Office and the Continent. Among the guests was one of the first Englishmen "bitten by the charm of Russia," as he later put it. His name was Maurice Baring, and he was taking Russian lessons from the ambassador's eldest son, Konstantin, a tall, strong, good-looking man. Baring was a regular guest in the salon of Countess Benckendorff (née Shuvalova), who was as kind to him as a mother. He went on to become a translator of Russian poetry, the author of drawing-room comedies, and a friend of European writers; his collected works, which mostly consisted of now forgotten plays and late-Victorian novels, went through many editions.

Maurice Baring was a remarkable figure, of a type that could only have appeared in England and only in the stable world of the early twentieth century. He was on the best of terms with everyone; he went everywhere and everybody knew him. He adored the Benckendorff family, not only the count, Alexander Konstantinovich, steward of the Imperial Household and Knight of the White Eagle, and

Countess Sophia, and their sons Konstantin and Peter, but also the ambassador's brother, Count Pavel Konstantinovich, grand marshal of the Imperial Court and minister of the Crown Domains, who recalled later, in his memoirs about the Tsar's last days at Tsarskoye Selo, how he had himself poured the entire contents of the wine cellar—the wines went back one hundred years—into the Summer Palace toilet so that the revolutionary troops guarding the entrances and exits could not use it to get drunk.

Baring's affection for the Benckendorffs extended to all the members of the household, from the butler and chef (who was French, of course) to the various categories of hunting dogs, watchdogs, and house dogs. He always considered the summer he spent at Sosnovka, the Benckendorffs' estate in the province of Tambov, to have been the happiest time of his life. He felt completely at home with the count and his family and described those idyllic days in his memoirs, *The Puppet Show of Memory*. They went on a wolf shoot and played tennis and read Mark Twain aloud—in German—by the light of an old kerosene lamp; they played cards and rode in troikas and painted watercolors together. Baring learned to eat caviar and to speak Russian. The count read Pushkin with him, and Alexei Tolstoy, too, a favorite of everyone in the family. Until his death in 1945, Baring remained a warm friend of Russia. To those "accursed questions" which our century inherited from the last one—"Who is to blame?" and "What is to be done?"—he always answered: "No one is to blame" and "Nothing is to be done."

After Sosnovka, Baring had no desire to return to England and instead took a train to Manchuria, riding in a third-class coach "to get to know the people better" and to observe the Russo-Japanese War. He made the journey with the ambassador's son Konstantin, who was on his way to a naval assignment in the Far East. There Baring came under enemy fire, and when he returned to Moscow he became a war correspondent for the London *Morning Post*. He landed interviews with Stolypin, and later with Count Witte. In 1906 he moved to Petersburg. Six years later, after an assignment in Turkey, he made a trip around the world. During the Balkan wars he was a correspondent for the *London Times*. He spent a great deal of time in Petersburg during those years, writing plays and books about Russia. One of his last encounters with the Benckendorff family came when he translated the memoirs of the ambassador's brother in 1927. Baring used to say that he could never read the account of the wines being poured down the toilet without shedding real tears.

Won over by the grand style of Russian hospitality, he continued to make frequent visits to London, where he kept a house and where he took part in the social life entitled to him by birth and upbringing. His father had his own yacht, kennels, and racehorses; the family was invited to sit in the royal box at Covent Garden, and their house was known as one of the first to have electric lighting installed.

Through the Benckendorffs Baring met the Shuvalovs, the Volkonskys, and other aristocratic Russian families living in Europe. But his closest friends were the young men at the Russian embassy in London: Moura's half brother Platon, Ambassador Benckendorff's sons, and the young Ivan Benckendorff, their distant relative, who was, like them, a descendant of Ioann Benckendorff (1659–1727), burgomaster of Riga. The family had, at the time, four branches extending from the burgomaster's four grandsons: Ivan belonged to the fourth branch. Like Baring, all these young men were embarking on diplomatic careers and were called attachés, a term just then coming into common use.

It was at Maurice Baring's house that Moura, the youngest sister of Platon Zakrevsky, first met her future husband, as well as a good many other people from London society—diplomats, writers, financiers, lords, ladies, and celebrities, among them H. G. Wells, who noticed her.

There, too, on the eve of World War I, she was introduced to the young British diplomat Robert Hamilton Bruce Lockhart, then just beginning his career at the newly opened British consulate in Moscow. She met Wells and Lockhart several more times at parties at Baring's and at the Benckendorffs'. The year she spent in London played a decisive role in her life: in 1911 she married Ivan Benckendorff, who a year later was appointed secretary at the embassy in Berlin. A pleasant and carefree life seemed to be unfolding before them. At one of the court balls Moura was presented to the Kaiser, who struck her as "even funnier" than George V, his British kinsman. "Wilhelm had a sense of humor," she once said thoughtfully, recalling the ball at Potsdam Palace, where she danced with him two or three times.

Benckendorff had a family estate in Estonia, at that time still called Estland. He took his young wife to Petersburg, and then to Revel (later renamed Tallinn). The town was full of his relatives, with and without titles. In Berlin, the Russian ambassador was another Baltic nobleman, in this case the ancient Count N. D. von der Osten-Sacken. In less than two years, though, both the ambassador and his staff would have to leave Berlin: in August 1914 the young Benckendorff family returned to Russia, renting an apartment in Petersburg, now renamed Petrograd, where Moura's parents lived.

Their first child, a boy, was born in 1913, and when they moved Moura was expecting a second child. Their little girl was born in 1915. The three war years passed caring for the children; she nursed Pavel, then Tania. Moura also took an accelerated course as a "sister of charity" and began working in a military hospital where women of social rank and the wives of senior officials considered it their duty to work as nurses.

There she met the female half of official Petrograd; she remembered the admirers of Rasputin—silly, fat ladies who were the mothers of the girls who had been her classmates at boarding school. She never said so, but one sensed that she had nothing in common with these women, even though they belonged to the same set.

During the war, Ivan worked as a lieutenant in the Department of Military Censorship. When revolution broke out in February 1917, it became clear that there was little chance of getting a diplomatic assignment in the near future. That summer, he, Moura, and the two children and their governess left the capital for their country house in Estonia, intending to stay there until autumn. But when autumn came Benckendorff postponed his return to Petrograd, and in November many of their landowning neighbors began leaving for the south of Russia, or moving to Sweden (at great expense), or simply disguising themselves and going into hiding.

Moura was unwilling to stay in the countryside, and against the advice of her husband and his family, she returned to Petrograd alone, determined to save their apartment if she could and to see for herself whether she could continue living there with the children. She left despite the fact that the Germans had already landed 100 kilometers from Revel and were advancing; but she reached Petrograd, having considered turning back several times along the way. The apartment was subject to requisition, food was hard to buy, and she had to decide whether to stay alone in the city or try to return to the family in the country. She deliberated for about a month, and when she had finally decided to go back—which at heart was not what she wanted—she received news from Estonia that one night shortly before Christmas peasants from a neighboring village had come to the house, summoned her husband, savagely clubbed him to death, and then set fire to the house. The governess, Missy, had fled with the children and they were in hiding at a neighbor's.

Moura was very quickly evicted from her apartment. Travel to Revel had become virtually impossible since train service had stopped in October, and no one knew with any certainty where the front lines were, who was fighting on which side, or who was still loyal to the Provisional Government that had been in power up until the October Revolution.

Moura's account of these events, which I heard from her twice, was strictly factual, told with no emotion. She never discussed her feelings, past or present, at least not in the years I knew her, and no one would have ventured to ask her about them. She spoke of those times as matter-of-factly as she spoke of everything, with the exception of those occasions when she played the "kitten," preparing her interlocutor for an answer, which always turned out to be a non-answer, because it wasn't yes and it wasn't no.

Thanks to the careers of her brother and her husband, as well as to her sister Anna's marriage, Moura had belonged, before World War I, to the elite class of government officials in Petersburg society. After the October Revolution and her husband's murder, she belonged to a class doomed to destruction. By the winter of 1917–18 the shrewdest among them knew what they had lost: there was not a family without members who had vanished, fled to God only knew where, hoping to survive or wait it out; the old were dying of the deprivations and moral shocks they had faced. The Russian aristocracy—or, in other words, Russia's feudal class, which in the eighteenth and nineteenth centuries had produced significant men and women, educated as Europeans, energetic and sometimes genuinely humane—had arrived at the moment of its demise.

When the February Revolution began, the aristocracy was disorganized and unable to react in any constructive way to its own downfall. It was at a loss as to how to defend itself, or how to come to terms with that new reality by finding a new place within it. Less than a year later it had gone under, having failed to comprehend what was really happening, having failed to recognize the difference between a hunger strike and a social revolution. What is the peasant complaining about? Slavery? But serfdom has been abolished by law; he ought to be grateful! And let no man lay a hand on the Tsar: he is God's deputy, and rules by divine right. In the West, at such fateful moments in history, people join forces and act. In Russia, perhaps because compromise is a dirty word, people split into factions and fail to act.

In the winter of 1917–18, Petrograd was not yet the deserted and frightening city it would become by the end of the summer, but armed men were a common sight, as were people starving and old people in rags. Young men adopted leather jackets, in the Bolshevik style. Women wore kerchiefs and men wore caps, because hats, which had always been a symbol of aristocratic privilege and idle wealth, might make them an opportune target for a Mauser. The huge mansions on the islands and the old luxurious apartments on the left bank of the Neva had been expropriated or stood empty, littered with every sort of filth, waiting for such disposition as fate would decide. Moura could not find a single familiar face among the crowd on the streets. During those first days after the news of Benckendorff's death, there seemed to be only one place in the whole capital where she might find someone who still remembered and cared for her and could offer solace and affection: the British embassy.

Moura had neither money at her disposal nor anything valuable she could lay her hands on. Her sisters were in the south of Russia and her brother was abroad. She was turned out into the street by the Committee for the Needy, which had requisitioned her apartment. Her female friends were nowhere to be found. Nor could she locate any of her acquaintances from the hospital: the doctor had been shot and Rasputin's admirers had fled. She did find a colleague of her late husband's, a man named V. V. Ionin, who had been a secretary at the embassy in Berlin—tall and thin, Ionin had grown a beard to keep from being recognized. On Morskaya Street she bumped into Alexander Mosolov, a former lieutenant general at the Ministry of Crown Domains, who had always seemed to her cleverer than the rest, and she liked clever men. Somewhere outside Petrograd in Pavlovsk lived a relative of Kochubei's, her sister's husband, but Moura did not remember her address. None of these people was able to help her in any way.

There had been many changes at the British embassy, at 4 Palace Embankment, since December 1917: the staff had been completely reorganized and relations between the embassy and the country's new leaders altered radically. Secretaries had been shuffled around and two of the consuls had been sent back to England; the attachés sat at their desks with little to do, awaiting word of their fate. The Soviet government was on the verge of signing a peace treaty with Germany. The ambassador, Sir George Buchanan, who had been friendly with the ministers of the Provisional Government, was making final preparations to depart for London after the New Year with his wife and daughter.

From the beginning of the century the British embassy in Petersburg had employed in its secret service writers who were visiting Russia, younger writers usually. The Crimean War had made it clear that Queen Victoria's government knew woefully little about Russia and that intelligence activity there needed to be much more vigorous. During Buchanan's tenure in Petersburg clandestine work had been given to Compton Mackenzie, John Galsworthy, Arnold Bennett, H. G. Wells, and G. K. Chesterton (whose novel *The Man Who Was Thursday* was a favorite of two generations of Russian readers), all of whom passed through Petersburg before the 1914 war. Later Hugh Walpole went to Russia, where he became close to the artist Konstantin Somov. His friendship with Somov and the Russian Greek Mikhail Lykiardopoulos, translator of Oscar Wilde, enabled him to move easily in literary and artistic circles in 1914 and 1915; he knew Dmitry Merezhkovsky, Fyodor Sologub, Alexander Glazunov, and Alexander Scriabin; he spoke the language well and wrote novels on Russian themes, which were then fashionable in England. Accompanying him, often for short visits, was W. Somerset Maugham, young but already well known; and of course there was Maurice Baring, who lived in Petersburg more or less permanently. T. E. Lawrence made at least one visit, as did, much later, a very young Graham

Greene. But now none of them remained, except for Harold Williams, the London *Times* correspondent, who was married to the Russian journalist Ariadna Tyrkova. Exceptionally well informed on Russian affairs, Williams was still writing dispatches in 1918, though he was finding it increasingly difficult to get them to London.

That so many writers worked for British intelligence is astonishing, as is what those writers were sometimes asked to do. "Our professional intelligence experts in those days were recruited mainly from the ranks of the successful novelists," Maugham later told his nephew.

> With the money they'd given me—half of it was provided by America and half by England—I was supposed to help the Mensheviks buy arms and finance newspapers so as to keep Russia in the war and to prevent the Bolsheviks from seizing power. I told them I was the wrong man for the job, but they wouldn't believe me. They thought that my being a writer was a good cover for my activities. You see, on the surface of it I was visiting Russia to write articles on conditions there for the *Daily Telegraph*. I feel a deep sense of failure, complete and utter failure. My job was to stop the revolution. It was a huge responsibility. I can't imagine why they ever chose me. If they'd known me better they'd never have picked me, I'm sure of that. I'd no experience of that kind of thing at all. I didn't know where to begin.

When Robert Bruce Lockhart became a special British agent at the beginning of 1918, he was told "to do everything possible to prevent Russia from signing a separate peace with Germany."

Moura found neither Maugham nor Baring at the embassy that winter. She was greeted by Captain George Hill and Meriel Buchanan, Ambassador Buchanan's daughter, a friend from London. Moura promised to come by again and did in fact visit them often, but she never gave them her address because she had no real address;

she was staying at the flat of the Zakrevskys' old cook. At the embassy all were glad to see her. Christmas came, and then New Year's Day 1918. On the morning of January 7, a Monday, the Buchanans and eleven members of the embassy staff boarded a train that would take them on the first leg of their journey from Petrograd to London. General Sir Alfred Knox, who left with them, wrote that although most of the British colony and many others from the diplomatic corps accompanied them to the station, "only one Russian came, Madame B———." This may well have been Moura, and Knox may have withheld her name because Moura was still in Russia when he was writing his memoirs in 1920.

But who was Lockhart? He was born in 1887 and named after a legendary hero, the fourteenth-century Scottish king Robert the Bruce (1274–1329), founder of the Stuart dynasty. Son of a landowner, Lockhart spent a happy childhood in a family loyal to Scottish traditions. After school he went to Germany and Paris to study languages and, for a time, to Malaysia, wavering in his choice of career. In 1911 he suddenly decided to take examinations for the consular service. To the surprise of his parents, his friends, and himself, he scored at the top of the list of applicants. He was offered the recently created post of vice-consul in Moscow: the government recognized the need for more extensive contacts with a country that had been one of the signatories of the Triple Entente in 1907. The foreign secretary, Sir Edward Grey, considered it essential to open a consulate in Moscow as an affiliate of the embassy in Petersburg.

Lockhart knew next to nothing about the country. The Russians he knew in London (there were almost no Russians in Scotland) spoke English, even among themselves; he had never heard Russian spoken. He knew some Tchaikovsky romances, had read (and loved) *War and Peace*, had heard Fyodor Chaliapin in *Boris Godunov*. After Maurice Baring took him aside and described Sosnovka, Petersburg society, and Manchuria, he accepted Grey's offer. When he arrived in Russia in January 1912 he was twenty-five years old. It seemed a promising start to a diplomatic career. But did he want to be a diplomat? He was not yet sure himself.

Lockhart was sent on to Moscow almost immediately after his arrival in Petersburg. Buchanan and his staff at the embassy didn't really have time to take a proper look at him. The most remarkable thing about Lockhart was his easygoing directness. He was sociable, lively, and bright, not the least bit stuffy, a warm and sympathetic companion, with streaks of impetuosity and irony, and a quite open and natural ambition that no one found offensive.

His arrival in Moscow coincided with the visit of a parliamentary delegation of lords, admirals, generals, and bishops—an imposing body eighty strong. Their interpreter was "the inimitable and indispensable Maurice Baring," who was delighted to see him. Lockhart's association with Baring soon got him to all the grandest Moscow merchant houses. He went to late-night suppers at the Strelna, where he learned to drink champagne from a large glass filled to the brim, handed to him on a plate by a Gypsy singer, and to eat iced caviar on a warm bun. He went to the cinema and became a fan of the silent movie star Vera Kholodnaya. He discovered Chekhov, bought a beaver hat and a fur coat with a beaver collar, and rode in smart horse-drawn cabs that raced through the streets of Moscow.

During Lockhart's first year there, H. G. Wells visited Moscow, and the two men saw each other a number of times. The following year Lockhart was introduced to Maxim Gorky. By then Lockhart already knew Konstantin Stanislavsky and Nikita Baliev, owner of the Bat, a popular cabaret theater and favorite haunt of Moscow writers and artists. One of Lockhart's best friends was the "sturdy" Mikhail Chelnokov, mayor of Moscow. Lockhart was wined and dined and invited everywhere: society ladies taught him Russian and drove him out to their dachas, which were in some cases rather more like palaces than country cottages.

During that happy year of 1913, he took leave and went to England, where, in the hope of settling down to a respectable position in society, he married a young Australian named Jane Turner, with whom he returned to Moscow. Then he began to work in earnest, and was soon appointed consul general "for the duration of the war."

The following winter Jane nearly died in childbirth, and their baby did not live. Lockhart was devastated for a time, but war kept him up to his ears in work. By now he had a small but growing staff, and it was clear they would have to move the consulate to more suitable quarters. The Foreign Office allocated the necessary funds, recognizing that the Moscow consulate was becoming increasingly important as the war went on.

Lockhart was given to bursts of sustained hard work, followed by periods of indolence. The same was true in his private life: he could live ascetically for long stretches, and then he would plunge into nightlife for a week or two and surrender completely to his passions. These riotous periods usually coincided with the frosty, starry nights he so loved—Russian Christmas and the last week of Russian carnival.

When revolution broke out in Petrograd in February 1917, Moscow was suddenly engulfed in feverish activity. The embassy in Petrograd, the British correspondents, the Moscow consulate, and the consul general found themselves chasing down any scrap of news, rushing about the city, sitting by the telegraph or the telephone, and sending dispatches to Lloyd George in London. Finally, Lockhart set off for Petrograd on his own to meet the members of the Provisional Government—Alexander Kerensky, Pavel Miliukov, Boris Savinkov, Viktor Chernov, Vasily Maklakov, and Prince Lvov. Mayor Chelnokov had put him in touch with all of them.

The summer months of 1917 flew past. Lockhart traveled between his office in Moscow and the embassy in Petrograd, spending his nights on express trains. From spring until early autumn, the Allies sent numerous delegations to the new Russia. Lockhart functioned both as guide and interpreter for leaders of the British trade unions, French socialists ("the fiercest critic of the Bolsheviks was Marcel Cachin"), and members of the British Labour Party, including Arthur Henderson, who was a minister without portfolio in Lloyd George's cabinet. During this period of intense activity Lockhart met a beautiful young Jewess at a theater and began a liaison with her. The affair was soon public knowledge, as happens when people are on the lookout for news and something peripheral pops up which, though unrelated to the central events, is nevertheless also very important and interesting—so interesting that word reached Buchanan, who summoned Lockhart to Petrograd and took him out for a walk in the embassy garden. Buchanan told the young diplomat that it was time he took a leave and made a trip home: rumors had reached his wife that he had a mistress in Moscow. The ambassador's decision was not subject to discussion, and Lockhart left, scarcely managing, if he managed at all, to say goodbye to his mistress. He traveled through Sweden and Norway and across the North Sea, which had been mined by the Germans. Not until he reached England did he learn about General Kornilov's unsuccessful attempt to seize Petrograd and bring down the Provisional Government.

Lockhart passed a restful two weeks in Scotland before returning to London. There he was torn to shreds, but he defended himself from friends and relatives, from his grandmother (whom he somewhat feared), from his colleagues at the Foreign Office, and from the Russians he had known in the old days, and of course he spent very little time at home with his wife and small son. Members of the government asked him for reports, as did members of Parliament, who took him to lunch. Two months flew by. Then came the staggering news from Russia: all of the ministers of the Provisional Government whom Lockhart knew well had been driven out of the Winter Palace, and the country was now being run from an office at the Smolny Institute. Lockhart was shaken. Everyone was. On December 20, Lockhart was invited to the Foreign Office to share his thoughts on the events in Russia. In attendance were his old patron Lord Alfred Milner and several other cabinet members, including Jan Smuts, George Curzon, and Lord Robert Cecil. The next day he had a two-hour conversation with Lloyd George at Downing Street.

During those months Lockhart wrote extensively—and anonymously—for the newspapers, gave interviews on the Russian situation, and thought about seeking a new assignment at the Foreign Office. But by mid-December the possibility of sending him back to Russia was already being discussed. Lord Milner strongly advocated the idea: Lockhart missed the Kornilov uprising, and now he had missed the Bolshevik coup in October! He spent Christmas with his mother and father, awaiting the cabinet's decision.

Lloyd George approved the proposal to send Lockhart back, and no one objected. Lockhart was intelligent, he spoke Russian, he was observant, he knew how to cultivate contacts, he had wit and vigor and a great many friends everywhere. The mission the prime minister had in mind really required someone more senior, but he hoped Lockhart would be equal to the task: he was to "put a spoke in the wheels of the peace negotiations" to prevent Russia from signing a separate peace with Germany.

On January 14, 1918, Lockhart boarded a British cruiser sailing for Bergen. A month earlier, the Bolsheviks and Germans had signed a truce; on December 22 at Brest-Litovsk the first plenary session of a peace conference had begun. There was not a moment to lose.

Could Lockhart have imagined when he left Moscow that, after an absence of only four months, he would be returning to a different Moscow, a different Russia? October 1917 had overturned and scattered everything. Lockhart was now a "special agent": consuls and ambassadors in the old sense no longer existed. So he was a diplomatic agent, a spokesman, head of a special mission to establish unofficial contact with the Bolsheviks. The man who had taken his place as consul general in Moscow, Clive Bayley, had left. The embassy staff in Petrograd was preparing to depart for Vologda and from there they would proceed to Archangel to embark on the voyage home. Although the British government did not recognize the Soviet government, it was essential to both sides that they come to some sort of understanding, if only unofficially. In London, Maxim Litvinov, also a special agent, was already calling himself plenipotentiary of the Soviet government to Great Britain, although he, like Lockhart, was only an "unofficial channel for mutual contact."

Litvinov was the de facto Russian representative in England in January 1918 (France had no representative after Lev Kamenev was refused entry as a trade envoy). He had lived in London for many years before the revolution and was married to a most exceptional Englishwoman, Ivy Low, niece of the well-known journalist and historian Sir Sidney Low. Lockhart met Litvinov in London before returning to Russia. Rex Leeper arranged a lunch for them at Lyons' corner shop on the Strand; Leeper was a Russia expert at the Foreign Office, and Litvinov was his Russian teacher. The "Bolshevik commissar with unofficial diplomatic privileges" handed Lockhart a letter of introduction to Trotsky, which must have given Lockhart some reassurance that, having survived in the old Russia, he would somehow survive in the new Russia, too.

In Petrograd, neither Buchanan nor his replacement, Sir Francis Lindley, was to be seen. The staff had been cut to a tenth of its former size, and those left were mainly communications personnel and cipher clerks who were themselves about to flee. Sir George Buchanan, ambassador in Petersburg since 1910, an experienced senior diplomat and faithful friend of the Provisional Government, had returned to England, feeling that he was no longer needed after the Bolshevik coup. He was old and ill and had been eager to go home, and he did not anticipate returning. His post remained vacant. England apparently had no intention of recognizing the Bolsheviks in the near future: Russia, once her ally in the Triple Entente, was about to sign a peace treaty with the enemy. Now in the huge embassy palace on Neva Embankment there were new faces, and Lockhart had only a few weeks to familiarize himself with the new situation.

Lockhart was thirty-one when he arrived back in Petrograd. Moura had been stopping by the embassy after business hours for two weeks. She had three friends there whom she had known ever since she was married in London, when she used to run into them at parties at Baring's and Benckendorff's. She saw Lockhart on his third day in Petrograd and recognized him instantly, but he looked preoccupied: on January 30, the day he arrived, he was informed that the embassy staff was evacuating, that their baggage had already been sent to Vologda, and that he was to remain behind as the senior British representative in Russia. He learned from his colleagues that it was the same at other Allied embassies and legations: everyone was on pins and needles, there was no question of staying on, since a peace treaty might be signed any day at Brest-Litovsk.

Lockhart described those days, reconstructed from the diary he had kept since 1915, in his *Memoirs of a British Agent*:

> It was at this time that I first met Moura, who was an old friend of Hicks and Garstin and a frequent visitor to our flat. She was then twenty-six. A Russian of the Russians, she had a lofty disregard for all the pettiness of life and a courage which was proof against all cowardice. Her vitality, due perhaps to an iron constitution, was immense and invigorated everyone with whom she came in contact. Where she loved, there was her world, and her philosophy of life had made her mistress of all the consequences. She was an aristocrat. She could have been a Communist. She could never have been a bourgeoise.... During those first days of our meeting in St. Petersburg I was too busy, too pre-occupied with my own importance, to give her more than a

passing thought. I found her a woman of great attraction, whose conversation brightened my daily life.

Besides William Hicks and Dennis Garstin, there was a naval attaché at the embassy, Captain Francis Cromie, another of Moura's old friends from London. On Cromie's birthday Moura hosted a little luncheon for all of them. She could not invite them to her place, of course, so she arranged the party at their apartment. It was carnival week, and they ate innumerable blini with caviar, washing them down with vodka. Lockhart wrote humorous verses in honor of each of the guests, and Cromie made a witty speech. They laughed a great deal and drank toasts to Moura. It was their last carefree party in Russia: Cromie would be killed five months later defending the embassy in Petrograd from an assault by Red soldiers; Garstin would be killed by a Russian bullet near Archangel during the British intervention; and Hicks would die of tuberculosis in 1930. Lockhart was the only man among them who would live to an old age, dying in 1970.

Lockhart had immediately understood how alarming the situation was in the diplomatic community in Petrograd. The neutral powers were banding together and staying on, but the Allies, anticipating that a peace treaty between Russia and Germany would be signed, were preparing to leave and burning their papers. Their fate was still unclear. The government had decided to make Moscow their capital and would soon begin the move from Smolny to the Kremlin; naturally, the neutral diplomats would have to move there, too, but they had not yet agreed to do so. Meanwhile, the Allies were worried about getting out before German representatives—that is, enemy generals—appeared in Petrograd and Moscow. They were also alarmed by the German army's rapid advance all along the front, from Ukraine to the Baltic provinces and up into Finland, which they now partially occupied. Dvinsk had been taken, Pskov was threatened, and the fall of Petrograd, if not inevitable, was quite probable. Some diplomats—as well as some Soviet commissars—felt Moscow was vulnerable, too, and were considering Nizhniy Novgorod the Bolshevik government's next stage of evacuation.

On February 25, after protracted negotiations with Smolny and much consultation with home governments in London, Paris, Washington, Rome, and Tokyo, the decision was made to leave. The Americans left Petrograd the next day as did the Japanese, Chinese, Spaniards, and Brazilians; on February 28 the British, French, Greeks, Serbs, Belgians, Italians, and Portuguese left. Besides their staff, the English took with them about sixty members of the British colony in Petrograd and Moscow. The Soviet government provided them with a special train. They were to live on the train in Vologda until such time as they could be transferred to Archangel, where British cruisers were to pick them up.

The third secretary of the French embassy, Louis de Robien, described the farewell scene between the young Allied diplomats and their Russian friends. On the platform alongside the sleeping cars everyone was in tears: "Princess Urusova stood with Gentil, [Tamara] Karsavina with Benji Bruce, Countess [Moura] Benckendorff with Cunard, and Countess Nostitz with [Jacques de] Lalaingue." Bruce later returned to Petrograd for his ballerina (they had been married since 1915) and took her back to England. He also took with him Zhenya Shelepina, Trotsky's secretary, who subsequently married the writer Arthur Ransome, Oscar Wilde's biographer. And the niece of ex-mayor Chelnokov, Lyuba Malinina, was hastily married to Captain Hicks before his expulsion from Russia in September 1918.[2]

The British embassy in Petrograd was down to a skeleton staff. Francis Lindley, chargé d'affaires and Buchanan's unofficial replacement, was the last embassy official to depart for Vologda, leaving

---

2. The fourth such Anglo-Russian marriage was that of the ballerina Lydia Lopokova to English economist John Maynard Keynes, but that was later, in London, in 1925.

Lockhart as senior man in charge. Of the three men with him, he was closest to Captain Hicks, now acting as military attaché (though there was no longer an embassy to be attached to), and the two took an apartment on Neva Embankment, with tall windows that looked out on the river, the Peter-Paul Fortress, and the cloudy northern sky. In the mornings Lockhart could hardly take his eyes off the view, which he had imagined often in reveries back in London.

Before long, relations between Lockhart and Moura intensified. They fell deeply and passionately in love—in him she saw everything that life had stolen from her, and in her he saw the incarnation of the country he had come to love, the country in which he was making his career and to which he felt, now more than ever, profoundly tied. An unforeseen and, so to speak, illicit happiness grew between them at a time which for nearly everyone else was harsh, hungry, cold, and frightening. Each became the center of life for the other.

Around them, in addition to all their English, French, and American friends, were their Russian friends. In Moscow, there was the Ertel family: the widow of Alexander Ertel, writer and friend of Leo Tolstoy, and her daughters—Vera, who was Constance Garnett's friend and assistant, and Natalia (by marriage Natalie Duddington), who was a translator and author of a book on Konstantin Balmont, whose poems she translated into English. Mrs. Ertel had given Russian lessons to members of the British colony in Moscow, including Lockhart and Walpole; at one time her star pupil was Captain Archibald Wavell, later Field Marshal Lord Wavell, viceroy of India. There was Mikhail Lykiardopoulos, who worked at the Moscow Art Theater and knew everyone in the theatrical and literary world, and counted among his friends Valery Bryusov, Vyacheslav Ivanov, and Khodasevich. In Petrograd, the leaders of the February Revolution were now out, but Lockhart made new friends: Trotsky, Lev Karakhan (the deputy foreign commissar), and the foreign commissar Georgy Chicherin, "a Russian of good family and a man of great culture," as

Lockhart called him, disagreeing with Karl Radek, who thought Chicherin "an old hen" and Karakhan "an ass of classical beauty." He also met Yakov Peters, Felix Dzerzhinsky's right hand at the Cheka, and, later, Grigory Zinoviev.

The government's move to Moscow dragged on throughout that spring, during which time Lockhart shuffled back and forth between Smolny and the Kremlin. He had apartments in both cities. Trotsky treated Lockhart as the representative of His Majesty's government and on March 16 took him to the Kremlin on his personal train. Lockhart later wrote:

> In varying degrees of intimacy I got to know nearly all the leaders from Lenin and Trotsky to Dzerzhinsky and Peters, respectively President and Vice-President of the Cheka. I had a special pass into Smolny, the Bolshevik headquarters in Petrograd. More than once I attended a meeting of the Central Executive Committee in the main restaurant of the Metropole Hotel in Moscow, where in tsarist days I had taken part in entertainments of a very different kind, and on my journey from Petrograd to Moscow I travelled in Trotsky's troop train and dined with him.

At that time the German army, meeting no resistance, was slowly moving deeper into the south of Russia. Peace negotiations were dragging on. And Trotsky, according to Lockhart, was frank with him. One day Lockhart came upon the war commissar in a particularly excited state—there was alarming news from the Far East. "If Vladivostok is taken by the Japanese," said Trotsky, "Russia will be thrown into the arms of Germany."

"My daily work," Lockhart went on, "was mainly with Trotsky and with Chicherin, Karakhan, and Radek, who, after Trotsky's appointment as Commissar for War, formed the Triumvirate of the Soviet Commissariat for Foreign Affairs."

In February, Lockhart had received a pass for himself and his two colleagues signed by Trotsky:

SOVIET OF PEOPLE'S COMMISSARS.

Petrograd. February 27, 1918. No. 567.
I request all Organizations, Soviets and Commissars of Railway Stations to give every assistance to the members of the English Mission, Messrs. R. B. Lockhart, V. L. Hicks, and Dr. Garstin.

[signed]

L. Trotsky. Commissar for Foreign Affairs

P.S. Personal food stores not to be confiscated.

This document opened many doors for Lockhart. When peace was concluded on March 3 in Brest-Litovsk, he understood that his real place now was in Moscow. He immediately notified Hicks that he was needed in the new capital to help establish an office and consular residence. Without much difficulty they found quarters, hired a cook, and declared the "consulate" open. The old term, though, was no longer applicable. He had no office and the reception room bore no official name. As he wrote in *Memoirs of a British Agent*, there was one more consequence of the move to Moscow:

> Since saying goodbye to Moura in St. Petersburg at the beginning of March, I had missed her more than I cared to admit. We had written to each other regularly, and her letters had become a necessary part of my daily life. In April she came to stay with us in Moscow. She arrived at ten o'clock in the morning, and I was engaged with interviews until ten minutes to one. I went downstairs to the living-room, where we had our meals. She was standing by a table, and the spring sun was shining on her hair. As I walked forward to meet her, I scarcely dared to trust my voice. Into my life something had entered which was

stronger than any other tie, stronger than life itself. From then onwards she was never to leave us, until we were parted by the armed force of the Bolsheviks.

Thus Bruce Lockhart found himself in Bolshevik Russia, which England did not recognize, with a chancery in Moscow and a staff of four of his countrymen, a man without official status or diplomatic immunity but with extensive connections, thanks to his intelligence, personal charm, and ready sense of humor. A year earlier England had recognized the Provisional Government immediately after the Tsar's abdication, as had France, with even more enthusiasm, but after the October coup no similar action was taken nor could it be. But if in London Litvinov was calling himself ambassador, why couldn't Lockhart, too, insist on dignity in the interests of king and country? These moods, however, often gave way to their opposite. As early as April he felt that attitudes toward him were changing: he received fewer invitations, he dined less often in the Kremlin cafeteria (on a menu of horse meat and turnips), and he seemed to see fewer smiles on the faces around him.

The authorities were hinting that he enjoyed no special rights. Lockhart got the message and began to bombard London directly, bypassing Vologda, trying to persuade Lloyd George that Allied intervention on the side of the Whites against the Bolsheviks would be a failure and that the only thing to do was to intervene on the side of the Bolsheviks against the Germans. It is no surprise that Lloyd George and his cabinet and the general staff were quite taken aback by the British agent's appeal, which ran directly counter to their policy and their plans to overthrow the Bolsheviks.

Land Allied forces to assist the Bolsheviks? Yes, that was Lockhart's plan, and he thought it plausible: intervention could give the Bolsheviks the stability they needed to stand up to the Germans and thus assist the Allies, who had been through such enormous difficulties that year. Lockhart was convinced that such a plan would best serve the interests of his own country. The Bolsheviks should not be driven out only to be replaced by a junta of generals or a group of Socialists (among whom, as everyone knows, there are liable to be as many splinter groups as individuals). No, the Bolsheviks should be used, along with their new revolutionary army (which would give them a chance to order a general mobilization), to fight the war—not the old, tsarist war but a revolutionary war against that citadel of reaction, Germany. As a result, the Russians could also save their young revolutionary republic. Lockhart telegraphed London nearly every day about this plan, which he thought crucial to the future of both Europe and Russia.

Lockhart gradually realized that Lloyd George and his ministers, the general staff, and public opinion as well, thought this plan worthless. He complained to Hicks and Moura that in England, under the influence of the French, they were leaning toward wide-scale Allied intervention against the Bolsheviks, with support to come from the Czechs (now organizing in Siberia), from the Japanese in Vladivostok, and from the English themselves, who had occupied Baku in August. The latest news was that British cruisers were sailing to Murmansk. But did that make any sense? What could the Allies hope to achieve? In March and April of 1918, he had come to see that there was only one sensible goal for the Allies—to defeat the Germans, a goal that could not be achieved by joining forces with White generals or members of the Socialist Revolutionary Party. The prospect of victory over Germany energized him. The Russian people, led by the Bolsheviks, would sweep against the Germans, purge their country of the invader, save the new Russia, and thereby help save the Allies. The German army had occupied Picardy in March and started a bloody offensive on the Marne in May—the front now stretched from the Meuse to the sea. General Ludendorff was winning one victory after another, and it was no secret to anyone that his divisions were preparing for a new offensive, one meant to be decisive.

Without telling anyone Lockhart began to consider unknown factors: Boris Savinkov, General Alexeev, and the major industrialists (some of whom, like Alexei Putilov, were still hiding in Moscow, having sent their families to the Crimea). What kind of men were they? It was clear whom they opposed, but whom did they support? And, even more important, what backing did they have, what strength could they muster? Jacques Sadoul, a French "observer," maintained that no one supported the Socialist Revolutionaries, that only money was behind the industrialists, and that the generals were backed by Kaiser Wilhelm and the German general staff. That ruled out the generals, and as for the SRs, they had been in power once, in the Provisional Government, and lost it. A provisional liberal military dictatorship? Does such a thing exist? The Ukrainian hetman is a German puppet. Would it come to that? On the other hand, even Alexander Krivoshein, who was still in Moscow, was telling General de Chevilly, head of the French Bureau of Propaganda, that if the Allies did not assist the Russian counterrevolution, Russia would be forced to appeal to Germany for assistance, as Finland and Ukraine had already done.

Lockhart had one more idea: an Allied landing in, say, Archangel, without any declaration of intent, following Japan's example in Vladivostok. The Japanese were not advancing because President Wilson did not wish them to. The Allies could take up positions off the coast at Archangel, just as they had done at Murmansk, ready to move as the situation evolved.

Lockhart believed that he understood perfectly what was going on in the minds of the men running the Kremlin. "I am in contact with each of them here," he telegraphed London, and that was the truth. The proof of this is not only the document given him by Trotsky but letters like the one written by Foreign Commissar Chicherin on April 2, 1918, in connection with the arrival of Allied cruisers in Murmansk:

> Dear Mr Lockhart,
> In view of the alarming reports which are being spread on our northern coast and of the apprehensions regarding England's intentions as far as Archangel is concerned, we should be very much obliged to you for giving us some explanations about the situation in the above district, which would enable us to reassure our alarmed northern population and to dissipate its fears.
>
> Yours truly,
> Chicherin

Lockhart no doubt assured Chicherin that England, to the best of his knowledge, had no anti-Soviet intentions in the north of Russia.

Early in May Lockhart was beginning to have doubts, and by the middle of the month they had become quite serious. He was an envoy, an observer, his country's sole representative in Russia at a time of turmoil, but he lacked Buchanan's experience and prestige, and he did not have the support of other senior Allied diplomats. Given his ambiguous title of "British agent" and his youth, any thought that he might be treated as Buchanan's successor and carry that kind of weight was laughable. As for support from other Allied diplomats, everyone with rank, experience, and the know-how that goes with them had long been in Vologda.

But if Lockhart had no advisers more experienced and perspicacious than himself among those few remaining members of the diplomatic corps in Moscow, there nevertheless were other "observers" still in the capital. Carrying no more (and possibly less) weight and prestige than Lockhart, they had been left behind, like him, to maintain contact with the Kremlin. The two closest to him were Captain Sadoul and Raymond Robins. Sadoul was a Frenchman who later joined the French Communist party. Robins, a colonel in the American secret service, had been appointed representative of the American Red Cross by U.S. Ambassador Francis, and he remained in Moscow through the spring and early summer of 1918.

Sadoul, then thirty-seven, had been assigned to the French mission in Moscow after the departure of Ambassador Noulens, thanks to the patronage of the Socialist Albert Thomas, Clemenceau's minister of defense. Noulens (who succeeded Maurice Paléologue, French ambassador in St. Petersburg since 1914) had left Moscow, leaving behind several agents and a few correspondents for the Paris newspapers. Thomas had come to Russia when the Provisional Government was in power in order to pressure Kerensky and his government to continue the war against Germany, asking and then demanding that they not abandon their allies and go back on the oath they had given. Lockhart liked Thomas, describing him as a "jovial, bearded man, with a sense of humor and a healthy, bourgeois appetite." He may never have known that Thomas was a Freemason, just as Kerensky and his cabinet in 1917 were. Lockhart explains their refusal to conclude a separate peace by "the loyalty of Kerensky and others to the oath they had taken."

Thomas believed Captain Sadoul was able and energetic, and in September of 1917 he sent him to Russia. Besides his official designation of observer, Sadoul was accredited as a correspondent of the French press. Mainly, though, he was a correspondent for Thomas himself. Sadoul was not on good terms with General Lavergne, head of the French mission, nor with Consul General Grenard; however, Lavergne tried to tolerate him, realizing that losing Sadoul would mean losing his primary source of information. Not only did Sadoul have access to the Kremlin but, thanks to his acquaintance with Trotsky before the war, he was on the friendliest of terms with the Soviet war commissar. Sadoul's and Lavergne's divergent views of events in Russia did not prevent them from dining together often with General de Chevilly, head of French military propaganda and Lavergne's boss. When the French embassy was still operating normally in Petrograd, Sadoul had been an outsider who had exclusive ties with Smolny, but once the embassy was evacuated to Vologda, he began to represent France unofficially, since France, like Britain, did not recognize the Bolshevik regime. Grenard, who on top of his duties as consul general was also a French secret service agent, and René Marchand, correspondent for *Le Figaro*, were well aware that Sadoul had close personal ties with several members of the Central Committee of the Bolshevik Party and that he took advantage of this privileged position to keep his own government informed. Sadoul was not the only Frenchman in Moscow who sympathized ideologically with the Bolsheviks—a sympathy that was a far cry from the cautious and conservative views of Ambassador Noulens. Like Sadoul, Marchand was of the view that the Russian army, now that it was both "red" and a "people's" army, was eager to battle the Germans and that the Allies ought to assist them. This was the subject of Marchand's conversation with Ambassador Francis during a short visit to Vologda. He urged the United States to stop the Japanese occupation of Siberia and to cut off support to the Czechs and other counterrevolutionary forces there, explaining that Allied support for the new Russian government in the Kremlin was crucial if the gains won by the October Revolution were to be preserved

Sadoul's ideas were equally pro-Bolshevik. He envisioned a joint British, French, and American landing to help the Bolsheviks defeat Germany (the incarnation of world reaction) and consolidate their power. Support Lenin and the revolution—that was essentially his position; and he went so far in his dispatches as to speak of his "influence on Lenin and Trotsky," who were leading the world to change on a universal scale.

Sadoul's subsequent fate is curious. Having served on the western front before coming to Russia, once in Russia he started giving military training to Trotsky's troops, and in a few months became a Red Army instructor. He was dismissed from his post at the French military mission by order of General Lavergne in October 1918, and severed all ties with his French superiors. After the Allied embassies had left Vologda, Sadoul began carrying out special assignments for the Kremlin in Italy and Germany. In 1927 he was awarded the Order of the Red Banner. He was tried in France in absentia in 1919 and sentenced to death. In 1924, when France recognized Soviet Russia, Sadoul returned illegally to Paris, where he was arrested and put on trial, but in April 1925 he was acquitted of all charges. Trained originally as a lawyer, he returned to the practice of law. By 1932 he was French correspondent for *Izvestia* and a director of the Society for Franco-Soviet Friendship. The Germans arrested him during the Occupation (he was a Jew), but he was eventually freed. He was elected mayor of Saint-Maxime in the south of France, where he remained a dedicated Communist, and where he died famous and respected in 1956. In the 1930s his portly figure could be seen in cafés on the Boulevard Montparnasse, in the favorite haunts of Ilya Ehrenburg and Ovady Savich and their friends, where Sadoul held forth before delighted audiences with tales of his personal encounters with Lenin (but not Trotsky). His dispatches to Thomas were republished in 1971. As communiqués, they are short on facts but long on rhetoric, persistent and monotonous in their wordy propagation of ideas, expressed with sentimental feeling and an occasional tear.

Lockhart was closer to the second observer, Colonel Robins of the American Red Cross. Robins had brought his Red Cross mission to Russia in August 1917, across Siberia. Lockhart later wrote that he and Robins were in "daily and almost hourly contact," adding, "we exchanged information and shared our deepest secrets with each other."

Robins was well-to-do and educated, a man with a vivid imagination and "a great personality"; he was, in Lockhart's words, "a man of sterling character and iron determination." In the first weeks of Bolshevik power Robins saw Lenin frequently and dined with Trotsky, not so much to hear their views as to give them advice or argue—he could be straightforward and informal with them as only Americans know how to be. He thought big and had enormous energy and ambition. Like Sadoul and, later, Lockhart, he journeyed to Vologda to confer with his now exiled superiors. He spoke his mind there, too, and if he needed to know what Washington thought, he simply contacted the White House directly. Or if he wanted to know what was happening in Petrograd in his absence, he telegraphed Lenin:

> Vologda, February 28, 1918, 2:45 p.m.
> From Colonel Robins
> to President Council of People's Commissaires Lenin:
> What is the situation in Petrograd? What is the last news of German offensive? Was peace signed? Did the French and British Embassies leave? [They left March 1.] When and by which route? Tell about our arrival Lockhart, British Embassy.

To which Lenin replied:

> (Received February 28, 3:10 p.m.)
> Peace not signed. Situation without change. Rest will be answered by Petroff, Department of Foreign Affairs.
>
> [signed]
> Lenin

Lockhart wrote of Robins that, "like Lord Beaverbrook, he possessed in a remarkable degree the talent of extracting exactly what he wanted from everything he read, and dramatizing it afterwards in his conversation," noting that "his conversation, like Mr. Churchill's, was always a monologue, but it was never dull, and his gift of allegory was as remarkable as it was original." Back in 1912 Robins had run for the Senate from Illinois. "He was a worshipper of great men. Hitherto his two heroes had been Theodore Roosevelt and Cecil Rhodes. Now Lenin captured his imagination. Strangely enough, Lenin was amused by the hero worship, and of all foreigners Robins was the only man whom Lenin was always willing to see and who ever succeeded in imposing his own personality on the unemotional Bolshevik leader." Robins could not change Lenin's ideas or influence his decisions, needless to say, but he made an impression on Lenin just as he did on everyone around him.

Robins favored immediate U.S. recognition of the Bolsheviks, but Ambassador Francis had a somewhat different view. The mood in Vologda was dominated by the intransigence of the old senior diplomat Noulens, advocate of intervention and disciple of order and tradition, who was out for Lenin's blood. Neither Robins nor Sadoul was able to persuade anybody that "for Russia now there is no turning back." That argument may have carried weight in Moscow and Petrograd, among the handful of Americans, Englishmen, and Frenchmen still left, but in Vologda people were of a different sort altogether—professional diplomats, reporting back to their governments, who had been kept on pins and needles for weeks living in train cars supplied by the Council of People's Commissars, until they finally left for Archangel on May 14.

In Paris's Russian émigré community in the 1920s and 1930s, ex-members of the Socialist Revolutionary and Social Democratic parties used to maintain that only professional politicians have the right to engage in politics and to make judgments about political questions, that there is no room for amateurs in political life. They were laughed at (the memory of 1917 was too fresh), but no doubt they were right in a sense. Amateurs rarely take into account the ideology that underlies and guides politics, and therefore they fail to understand its role or the significance of its power over the masses. A political ideology, which is a kind of secular theology providing answers to every question of existence, from economics to man's place in the universe, seems less important than the immediate realities of political life. Robins ignored the Bolsheviks' ideology. He saw their aims quite clearly, both domestic and international; he understood their tactics and their overall strategy. But he never looked into the ideological foundation on which everything stood and from which everything stemmed. Wasn't this perhaps what happened later, in the 1930s, when the governments of Europe largely ignored Hitler's autobiography and paid little attention to his ideology? Did the leaders of Europe and America ever really grasp the fact that in a totalitarian state ideology always takes the place of ideas? Robins had understood the main thing, as he perceived it: the poor would be fed (not today, not tomorrow, but in the near future—and with the help of the American Red Cross); the greedy and the privileged would be rendered powerless; and, in this frozen land, flowers of real brotherhood would bloom. He was an American from the Midwest, a philanthropist and a humanitarian, an optimist who read the Bible every day, a man who was rich but whose sympathies were with the underdog.

Thanks to his Kremlin connections, Robins could ride through Moscow in his own car, flying an American flag. One day, while he was in the main post office, the car was stolen by "anarchists." The anarchists had taken over no less than twenty-six mansions in Moscow and were terrorizing the city day and night, committing murder, robbery, and arson. Early on the morning of April 12, 1918, heavily armed Cheka troops conducted a simultaneous raid on all eighteen anarchist headquarters, and in the melee more than a hundred were killed and five hundred arrested. Their headquarters were burned down, and bonfires were lit in the streets fueled by their literature. The planned raid was designed to destroy an entire "opposition party," one of whose demands was the execution of the Kremlin leaders as punishment for their betrayal of the revolution.

Even the optimistic Robins saw something ominous in that April raid. The following day, Yakov Peters, deputy head of the Cheka, took Robins and Lockhart on a tour of the mansions where the anarchists had been hiding out. The filth was indescribable. The dead lay where they had fallen; there was the stench of blood and open bellies; wine stains and human excrement blotched the Aubusson carpets. Peters explained that there had been no time to conduct a proper legal investigation and that instead of staging, as it were, some "comedy" of due process, the Bolsheviks had had to act. The German ambassador, the first since the peace treaty, was due to arrive in Moscow, and an order had been given to clean up the capital without delay. This was no time to indulge in the luxury of lawyers, witnesses, and juries; the Soviet government had too many enemies for that. The opposition had to be stopped then and there.

In May, when Robins was still in Moscow, he continued to "conduct himself with brash aplomb." Lockhart appreciated his eloquence, his self-confidence, his striking appearance ("an Indian chief with a Bible for a tomahawk"), his warm regard for Lockhart himself, and his cordial relations with everyone else. Sadoul, however, believed Robins and Lockhart were inveterate bourgeois, as he wrote to Albert Thomas on March 13:

The Americans recently sent Col. Robins to make contacts with Trotsky. He seems a clever and resourceful man and may be of use to us. Unfortunately, Trotsky has only limited confidence in him, first, because he belongs to the most imperialist and capitalist political party in the U.S., and second, because he seems too "cunning," too much the diplomat in his conversations with the War Commissar. British interests at Smolny recently have been ably represented by their consular agent Lockhart, who seems to most Bolsheviks to be more serious and more "lucid"

than Robins. Alas, Lockhart too, like Robins, is a good bourgeois. What we need here are left-wing socialists.

But in April and May, Sadoul was still learning things from
Robins, Robins from him, and Lockhart from them both. Lockhart
should have left for Vologda long ago, as Robins and Sadoul had, but
he feared leaving Moura alone and was reluctant to disturb their life
together, which was stable and happy. Nevertheless he decided he
would have to go. By that time the picture of Russia's encirclement
and its internal situation was as follows: On April 5 the Japanese
navy landed in Vladivostok. Large regular army units of the Czech
Legion in Siberia were operating from the Sea of Japan to Irkutsk and
threatening to cross the Urals. Savinkov, according to rumors, was
winning support in the upper Volga and preparing to open a route for
the Czechs into European Russia. There were reports that the British
were moving from Persia into the Caucasus. The Ukraine and Don
regions were occupied by the Germans, as was the Crimea. Germany
also occupied the Baltic provinces and was gradually taking control
of Finland. Allied warships off Murmansk had landed some 1,200
men (Soviet sources reported 12,000). A fleet commanded by Rear
Admiral Kemp had been there since March, with a land army under
the command of General Frederick Poole. An American warship was
expected any day.

Lockhart never forgot his last night in Moscow before he left for
Vologda on May 27. They all rode out one last time to the Strelna to
celebrate someone's birthday. By some miracle the place was still
open and the old Tatar waiters recognized their guests: "Your table is
always ready for you, Mr. Lokhar," said the waiters, waving white
napkins. A great deal was drunk, the Gypsy Maria Nikolaevna sang
to them as if for the last time, and at dawn Moura and Lockhart
drove to the Sparrow Hills and held each other for a long time, until
the sun rose over the Kremlin.

Three days later he was in Vologda. He conferred with both Noulens and Francis and spoke not of his doubts but of how he had become convinced in recent days that intervention was essential. Whether the goal of opposing Germany should include a secondary goal of opposing the Bolsheviks he was not yet quite sure, but he felt strongly that it would be risky to count on broad support for a counterrevolution, since nearly everyone was opposed to everyone else and no one would ever come to terms or agree to cooperate with anyone else.

Two considerations had effected this change in his thinking. One was purely external and had to do with his career: his recommendations had failed to win the support of anyone influential. Neither Asquith, nor Churchill, nor Balfour, nor Lloyd George, nor anyone in the war cabinet had been persuaded by his telegrams urging assistance to the Bolsheviks. Quite the contrary, General Knox had already vociferously demanded that Lockhart be recalled from Moscow and placed on trial for sympathizing with Lenin, Trotsky, and the rest of those bandits. The second consideration was personal, and its origins were harder to pin down. Whether as a result of greater political and personal maturity, or whether it was somehow connected with the deep emotional satisfaction he had found with Moura in Moscow, Lockhart had a new awareness of the appalling implications of a policy of "terror," however it might be justified. Since the day Lockhart had witnessed the aftermath of the raids on the anarchists, a different meaning could be discerned behind Lenin's phrases, Chicherin's smiles, and Dzerzhinsky's sanctimonious asceticism. It had been a bloody business, and it might very well happen again. He could not yet foresee, of course, the day the four grand dukes being held in the Peter-Paul Fortress would be lined up and shot in the courtyard, or the bloody scene in the basement of the Ipatiev house in Ekaterinburg and the copse of the Four Brothers, or the mine shaft down which his old acquaintance, the Tsar's brother

Grand Duke Mikhail Alexandrovich, would be thrown along with his cousins and his aunt.

So it was that Lockhart became an advocate of intervention. In March he had hoped that Lenin's government would ask the Allies to come to Russia's assistance; in April he began to see that there would be no invitation from the Kremlin and the best that could be hoped for was that the Kremlin would agree to intervention. Now, in May, he had concluded that even the Kremlin's tacit assent was not forthcoming but that intervention was critical nevertheless. It is not easy to account fully for such a complete turnabout in his thinking. If we assume that the threat Germany posed was actually as great as he thought it to be, then his advice was correct. In particular, he was right, as events proved, to insist that any intervention should be done rapidly and on a massive scale.

Lockhart's change of views pleased rather than surprised Noulens and his colleagues. Francis was also undergoing a crisis in his thinking, though of course it was not as serious as Lockhart's. There was now nearly complete unanimity in Vologda, according to a book Noulens wrote several years later. Among other things, the former French ambassador wrote of Lockhart: "At once intelligent, energetic, and clever, Lockhart was one of those whom the English government employs, with rare felicity, for confidential missions, and whom it reserves, should the occasion arise, for disavowal."

Lockhart returned to Moscow on May 31. Martial law had been declared in the city: a counterrevolutionary plot had been discovered, five hundred people had been arrested, and there was a letter from Chicherin on Lockhart's desk demanding an explanation for the Czech Legion's conduct in Siberia and their march on Kazan. Lockhart replied that the Czechs must be given safe passage as they had been promised, so that they could either return to their own country or be sent on to France to fight the Germans on the western front. In fact, they were fighting the Bolsheviks under the command of French officers.

Karakhan was avoiding him, Krylenko, the chairman of the Supreme Tribunal, was shouting at him, and Chicherin kept putting off the meeting Lockhart had requested. When he tried to track down the war commissar, he was told, "Comrade Trotsky's whereabouts are at the moment unknown." His own chancery was sometimes deserted all day: the young "observers" were out on various errands, having a Russian lesson at some lady friend's, shopping for fresh food on the outskirts of town, or feasting on blini and Easter cake—not just on Easter but on any day when there were ingredients to be had from the American Red Cross. Robins was generous in distributing his largesse, making life easier for them all. They went boating one afternoon at Sokolniki Park and played football with the Danes and Swedes. The thought of Lindley coming (to replace him? to bring him into line?) put Lockhart in a bad mood, but he tried not to brood over it. He did his job, sensing, however, that the summer which had begun for him and Moura that dawn on the Sparrow Hills might lead to difficulties in the end for British interests in Russia—to say nothing of what lay ahead for Russia, or for himself.

Very soon he saw that he had been right to predict that June would turn out to be a month of fearful events. A vague sense of dread turned into the ominous news that civil war had broken out in Siberia. There was a general mobilization of the Red Army, Savinkov escaped from a Cheka prison, Moisei Volodarsky was assassinated by an SR on June 20, and the royal family was taken from Tobolsk to Ekaterinburg. Volodarsky's assassination led to a wave of terror in both Petrograd and Moscow. July came and promised nothing better, to judge by Dzerzhinsky's edicts, which were pasted up on street corners.

All the talk now was of getting out. If any serious trouble was brewing then clearly it was going to come not from the Germans but from the Russians, who, the moment the Allied Expeditionary Corps under General Poole moved south from Archangel, would take them all hostage. But Lockhart didn't want to leave. Leaving would be a sign of moral weakness, it would mean admitting that circumstances had defeated him, that he was unfit for the job he had been sent to do. But there was another reason, which he understood but was power-less to do anything about, attesting to the fact that he was being unreasonable, even mad: leaving meant parting with Moura for good. His pulse quickened as he looked on with delight and admiration when Benji Bruce came to Russia for one day to collect his bride, Tamara Karsavina, and take her back to England.

Love and happiness—and the threat to them both—were now with him night and day. Moura had moved into the apartment Lockhart and Hicks had taken near the Arbat, at 19 Khlebny Lane. Compared to the House of Soviets and the private mansion Lockhart had lived in briefly, the apartment was modest, but it was comfortable, and there was adequate space for the three of them. His reception room had somehow turned by degrees into a common sitting room. He had a large study with books, a desk, armchairs, and a fireplace. Hicks and Moura got along well. And they had an excellent cook who pre-pared delicious dinners for them with food from Colonel Robins's Red Cross supplies. They lived like a family, not like bohemians, and Lockhart liked that. Moura felt serene and gay. She had fewer of her own friends now, since more and more of the friends they had were friends in common. All Moura's life, even her closest friends did not always know where she was living or with whom, where she was traveling or why, what hotel she would be staying at when she got there, who was putting her up in London, when she would arrive, or what her address was in Estonia.

That summer, she told Lockhart she had to go to Revel to see her children. Because mail and train service to Estonia had been cut off she'd had no news of them since she'd left them in the fall of 1917. On July 14 she departed for Petrograd. Knowing the situation in the Baltic provinces, Lockhart cursed himself for letting her go. He realized her journey was an act of sheer madness at a mad time, that the main thing for him now was not politics, Balfour, or his career, but Moura, her life, their intimacy.

He spent ten days beside himself with worry, and for another four nights he couldn't sleep or eat. On the brink of utter despair he had fainting fits and found himself unable to speak. Finally the telephone rang: she was calling from Petrograd. He met her at the station in Moscow the next day.

Lockhart had evidently overlooked something important, though. Rail travel to Estonia was impossible because there were no trains; so his anxiety about whether her documents would pass inspection on the train was irrelevant. In books and encyclopedias, both scholarly and popular Soviet historians always refer to the occupation of Estonia by Soviet troops in 1944 as "the restoration of democracy in Estonia," the word "restoration" serving as a reminder that the country had been Soviet once before, from November 1917 to November 1918 when the armistice was signed (in 1920, the Treaty of Versailles declared Estonia an independent republic). But this is not true. It's an old story—the practice was not unknown in tsarist times either—recounting events in such a way as to glorify the past. The Baltic provinces were entirely under German control that summer. After the Russian army's withdrawal in 1916, the German army controlled the Baltic provinces as far as Riga, and after the October Revolution, German forces moved east into Russia, with a front on the Narva–Pskov–Smolensk line, and were threatening Petrograd on the Dvinsk–Pskov–Luga–Gatchina line. There was no border anymore, only a front.

Even if Moura did risk her life by leaving Moscow for Estonia to see her children, whom she had left of her own free will, and chose to do so at a time that was complicated and difficult for Lockhart, it seems highly unlikely that she would take that risk a second time by crossing back into Russia to return, as promised, exactly two weeks later, as if she had booked train tickets in advance. Could Lockhart have been unaware that train service to Revel had been terminated the year before? Quite clearly Lockhart knew all of this, but at the same time, trusting Moura, he might not have correlated these facts with her trip, perhaps unconsciously avoiding close scrutiny of her plan.

Moura could have had several reasons for leaving Moscow and remaining out of contact for two weeks. First, she may have gone to Petrograd not just with Lockhart's consent but at his request, on a mission for British intelligence—so that his anxiety had to do not with her "Estonian trip" but with the fact that she was on a dangerous assignment. Second, he may have sent her on a secret errand to Vologda. Third, she may have had personal business in Petrograd that she did not wish to discuss with Lockhart. Fourth, she could have stayed in Petrograd in complete seclusion on business unrelated to British intelligence or her own past. Fifth, she might have gone somewhere else entirely unknown to us, and for an unknown purpose. And sixth, she might have been in Moscow the whole time, incommunicado or perhaps detained in connection with some matter that has never been brought to light.

Four and six seem most likely but some seventh explanation might easily be the most plausible, were more facts known.

When he knew that Moura was returning, Lockhart was elated. In his memoirs he wrote: "Nothing now mattered. If only I could see Moura again, I felt that I could face any crisis, any unpleasantness the future might have in store for me."

Moura knew everyone who came to see Lockhart, whether for business or pleasure. She knew the secret agents who visited him from Petrograd and she knew his friend Captain Cromie and all his colleagues. She met the British visitors who came to Moscow by circuitous routes to visit Russia for a week, or a month, on "commercial" missions, or cultural missions, or simply on their own initiative. She knew the American agents, too, Robins among them, as well as agents of the French intelligence service. She was always at Lockhart's side—it was what he wanted, and what she wanted, too. He introduced her to visitors as his interpreter. Lockhart did not take her with him on official business, of course, but she accompanied him to the theater, to restaurants, or to see Russian friends. They took precautions, and he trusted the servants completely.

He shared much, but not everything, with Moura. She apparently did not know about the place he kept in Moscow where he could hold confidential meetings with Savinkov and Pyotr Struve, where disguised tsarist generals could see him before journeying south to join forces with the "White" volunteer army. Quite recently Lockhart had met Kerensky there and given him a passport in the name of a Serbian prisoner of war who was authorized to travel to Archangel, and a personal letter to General Poole. Kerensky had grown a beard and was in hiding in Moscow, until V. O. Fabrikant, the SR, brought him to Lockhart at the beginning of the summer. At first Lockhart hid Kerensky in a safe place; then, having secured the passport, he smuggled Kerensky out to Murmansk with a platoon of Serbian soldiers. They had become acquainted right after the February Revolution, when Lockhart acted as interpreter during lengthy talks between Kerensky and Buchanan; the next year all this would be resumed in London, over lunch at the Carlton Grill. Kerensky always addressed Lockhart as "Roman Romanovich."

Events, meanwhile, had picked up their pace. On the opening day of the Fifth Congress of Soviets at the Bolshoi Theater in Moscow, the Left SRs, who had been in coalition with the government, sensed that their hour of destiny had come, and delivered speeches denouncing Bolshevik agrarian policy, capital punishment, the shameful peace treaty with Germany, and especially their opposition to any kind of cooperation with Germany. Riots and an insurrection broke out. On July 6 the German ambassador, Count Mirbach, was murdered by the notorious Yakov Blyumkin, who was simultaneously a Left SR and a member of the Cheka. The insurrection led to mass arrests and immediate executions. On the second day of the congress, the session opened without the Bolshevik or SR leaders on the platform; the Bolshoi was surrounded by troops and Lockhart was released only by virtue of a special pass. That night there was street fighting as the Left SRs were rounded up. "There is no time for legal niceties," Peters explained, "executions will be carried out on the spot." The same day, in Yaroslavl, Savinkov organized an armed revolt. Lockhart roamed the streets and was swept up in the excitement. Ten days later Karakhan told him that the Tsar had been murdered with his family; that day Lockhart also learned that the Allied embassies' personnel, still living in the same train cars they had been in for five months, had reached Archangel at last. One week later, the Czechs surrounded Kazan.

Rumors of the expulsion of foreign "observers" and "diplomatic agents" began to be taken very seriously. There was a sense that the denouement was approaching. Knowing that one day soon they would have to separate, Lockhart and Moura did not allow themselves superfluous words, which could only add to the wretchedness they felt, and faced the future with self-control and outward calm. Lockhart later wrote about those July and August days and the deep sense of anxiety he felt for her and himself and for the whole country, whose destiny seemed to have about it a kind of tragic finality.[3] There were moments when it occurred to Lockhart that what he really wanted was to stay there forever, and he wondered whether he could, but then the moment would pass. He was under no illusions about his own limitations or the contradictions within himself. Now, though, fate seemed to be not merely toying with him but was beginning to

---

3. He had recently read the assertion of the philosopher Konstantin Leontiev that Russia stands not at the beginning of its historical path but at its end.

land real blows. One was an encounter with a man whose name he did not know but who knew a good deal about him.

One day in the waiting room of the People's Commissariat for Foreign Affairs, Lockhart saw a middle-aged man sitting in the opposite corner of the large room: it was a German diplomat. It was the first time since England and Germany had been at war that he found himself in the company of a German official. The man scrutinized Lockhart keenly, as if wishing to speak to him; Lockhart at first turned away and then, with a feeling of foreboding, walked out of the room. The next day a secretary from the Swedish mission met Lockhart on the street saying that the German embassy had asked him to inform Lockhart that, in the first place, the Bolshevik ciphers had long ago been obtained by the Germans, who were not opposed to sharing the results of this discovery with the British, if they wished to make use of it and thus accommodate their government. And second, they knew that the British cipher—that is, the code Lockhart had been using to send his telegrams to London—had been in the hands of the Bolsheviks for a good two months.

Two months. That meant Chicherin knew everything Lockhart had communicated to Balfour since returning from Vologda in May. Trotsky and, of course, Lenin and Dzerzhinsky at the Cheka were aware of the contents of his dispatches to his government in London. This cipher was kept in his desk under lock and key. There were never outsiders in the flat when he or Hicks or Moura were not at home. The servants were above suspicion. And the key to the flat was never given to anyone. It was a blow from which he felt he would not soon recover. He would have to think hard now about how to proceed.

2

LOVE AND PRISON

> ...for several virtues
> Have I lik'd several women...
> *The Tempest*, III, i, 42–43

BACK IN MAY a new figure appeared in Moscow, an impulsive, daring, unbalanced man, one of those adventurers so abundant in Russian life since the end of the last century, a man who would have a hand in shaping Lockhart's fate. He came down from Petrograd to see Lockhart, bringing a detailed plan for the overthrow of the Bolsheviks. Under the influence of this intrepid, ambitious, and of course doomed man, Lockhart became convinced that without Allied intervention the Bolsheviks could not be brought down, and so he plunged wholeheartedly into the work of doing what he could to hasten their downfall. He no longer doubted that the Bolshevik regime must go.

The man who had arrived from Petrograd and was admitted to Lockhart's office by Captain Cromie was Georgy Relinsky, an experienced secret agent, Russian by birth but by that time a British subject and better known by his alias, Sidney Reilly. Born near Odessa in 1874, he was the illegitimate son of a Polish mother and a Dr. Rosenblum, who abandoned mother and child, after which Reilly's mother soon married a Russian colonel. Reilly quit school to seek danger, fortune, and fame. By 1897, after numerous adventures and journeys, he was working for British intelligence, who sent him back to Russia. There he married a rich widow, evidently having given her a hand in hastening the demise of her spouse. In 1899 he had a brief affair with Ethel Boole (Ethel Voynich, author of *The Gadfly*), and after that he became a permanent agent in the intelligence service, where he changed his surname to Reilly. Thanks to his excellent knowledge of foreign languages he was able to pass as a native Englishman, Frenchman, or German. Before World War I, he lived primarily in Russia, where he knew a great many people and traveled everywhere. One of his friends was the well-known journalist Boris Suvorin, editor of the *Evening Times*, the son of Alexei Suvorin, publisher of *The New Times* and owner of a large publishing house in Petersburg. Reilly was active in banking and knew many wealthy Petersburg businessmen, such as the millionaire Sir Basil Zakharov, a Greek by birth, who contracted to build warships simultaneously for England and Germany. Reilly also had close connections with the Petersburg firm of Mendrokhovich and Lubensky, who were in the business of importing and exporting arms.[1]

The company also procured naval supplies and equipment for Russia, and before the war Reilly made several visits to the United States, where he received large commissions in connection with his purchases. The last and biggest commission he did not receive,

---

1. Mendrokhovich is sometimes spelled "Mandrokhovich" and sometimes also "Mandrakovich." His friends called him Mandro, but when he was Lubensky's partner, that is, until 1911, he went by von Mandro. That name appeared in Russian newspapers in those years and undoubtedly caught the eye of Andrei Bely, who later used it as the name of his hero, the spy and villain "von Mandro," in his novel *Moscow*. Many of Bely's readers, including Khodasevich and Mark Aldanov, were puzzled by the origin of the name, which sounded enigmatic but gave no clue to the hero's origin or nationality. Surnames in Bely's novels were never without hidden meaning. The Baltic prefix "von" sounded especially jarring with a name that seemed halfway between Romanian and Hungarian. The riddle of the name's origin can now be considered solved.

however, because of the February Revolution. Later, in 1923, he brought an unsuccessful suit against his American contractors.

Reilly did not believe in divorce, but he did marry three times. His last marriage was in 1916, to Pepita Bobadilla, a Spanish actress. At that time he was living in Germany but traveling often to the United States, Paris, Prague. His various passports enabled him to travel in both neutral and belligerent countries. In 1918, the British government sent him once again to Russia, where he was to work under the British intelligence operative Ernest Boyce, establishing contact with Captain Cromie; with the head of the French secret service, Henri Vertemont; and with *Le Figaro* correspondent René Marchand. These latter two were introduced to him at the U.S. consulate in Moscow by the French consul general, Colonel Grenard.

Reilly was tall, with black hair and dark eyes, somewhat heavy, with prominent features and a self-confident, rather haughty face. Not stopping with Vertemont and Cromie, he wasted no time getting in touch with representatives of the Allied and neutral powers still in Moscow and Petrograd, and soon he established a network of useful informers, both foreign and Russian. He contacted men like the Greek spy Xenophon Kalamatiano, who worked for American intelligence (Colonel Robins was out of bounds); the British intelligence agents Captain George Hill and Paul Dukes, who had worked in Moscow before the war; and, of course, Bruce Lockhart. All these men had connections with the various anti-Bolshevik groups that existed at the time at every level of Russian society—from officers to clergy, from merchants to actresses.

After three years of dashing frantically all over Europe, meeting with General Denikin in Paris and Kerensky in Prague, plotting almost single-handedly to "bring down the Bolos" and install Boris Savinkov in the Kremlin, Reilly was shot by Soviet border guards near Byeloostrov on the Russo-Finnish border in November 1925 (*Izvestia* gives the erroneous date of June 1927). Pepita later published a book about Reilly that contained, in addition to her own memoir of him, a short autobiography, quite possibly written with her help. The book is hardly worth the paper it's printed on, but some information about Reilly can be gleaned from his letters to Pepita, given in full in some cases, and even in facsimile. Nevertheless the book leaves the impression that Pepita was not only not very intelligent but also out of her depth on Russian matters, confusing Zinoviev with Litvinov and calling the counterrevolutionary terrorist Georgy Radkevich, who threw a bomb at the Cheka offices on Lubyanka Square, "Mr. Schultz" because he was married to the terrorist Maria Schultz. The book also suggests that Reilly, despite his superhuman self-confidence, was completely out of touch with the reality of Russia after the revolution, believing as he did that only weak-minded fools were engaged in counterrevolution when what was needed was action, by which he meant destroying the Cheka. No one would have disagreed, however, with his view that they were "beastly cruel."

In fact, there was a more or less concerted effort in the summer of 1918 on the part of British, French, American, and even Swedish agents to establish and maintain contacts with opponents of the Bolsheviks—generals of the future White Army on the one hand, and Socialist Revolutionaries on the other—while at the same keeping channels open with members of the Russian liberal bourgeoisie, in and out of Moscow.

Lockhart put his old doubts aside and yielded to Reilly's sway. By mid-June he was convinced that Reilly was just the man they had needed all along: efficient, decisive, with a ready plan and the confidence that the future lay in his hands. Konstantin Nabokov later wrote in his memoirs:

In the spring of 1918 a special representative of the British government was sent to Moscow, Mr. Lockhart, the former Consul-General. From what I know of the instructions he was given, they can only be compared with some insoluble mathematical problem like squaring the circle. For practical considerations, he had to be an "eye" in Moscow, to keep track of the activities of the Bolsheviks and the Germans, and, insofar as possible, to protect the interests of the British in Russia. In addition, without having official rank, he was supposed to engage in official negotiations with Trotsky. Such a task would be feasible only under conditions of the friendliest relations between the two governments. Lockhart apparently worked conscientiously at this insoluble task, and at the same time had close dealings with organizations working for the overthrow of Lenin and Trotsky.

There was no contact with London, and contact with the French in Moscow was growing more dangerous and difficult: on August 2, when most of the Allied diplomats left Vologda for Archangel to join the landing force, those who remained behind were cut off from their diplomatic channel. On August 3, eighteen members of the French mission in Moscow—almost its entire staff—were arrested. There was no one who could tell Lockhart the strength of the landing force in Dvina bay. Twelve thousand? Thirty thousand? Thirty-five thousand? How were they armed, and what was the operations plan of the British general staff? The only thing that did reach him then were heavy packages, impressively large, containing banknotes whose value was diminishing quickly. Lockhart secretly kept close track of how he allocated the money.

The details of Reilly's plan were all in place. He had loyal men, he said, soldiers, each of whom Lockhart would furnish with safe passage through British lines at Archangel, and a letter addressed to General Poole. In the letter, Lockhart would inform Poole that some Latvian units were prepared to defect to the Allies and that their officers would have no difficulty leading the Allied Expeditionary Force from Archangel to Moscow, where Lenin, Trotsky, and other Kremlin officials would be arrested. Lockhart told Reilly he would first have to see the officers and consult his colleagues before giving anyone anything. If he felt the officers were reliable, he was prepared to give them all the money they required (an enormous sum, of course). Reilly replied that he had already arranged such a meeting: two officers from the Latvian regiment considered most loyal to the Kremlin, which the Kremlin drew on for its security force, could be at Lockhart's at a date and hour of Lockhart's choosing.

A summary of the events that occurred between May and the end of August in what was once Russia would present a picture so appalling that one would be hard-pressed to find anything analogous in the country's history, even in the Time of Troubles. The Czech advance was so rapid that they were now in position to cross the Volga outside Saratov. Lockhart had reliable information that this force numbered 45,000. In his memoirs, he later cited a figure of 80,000, writing that London insisted that he secure Lenin's permission to transfer the Czechs from Russia to the western front. Lockhart was deeply committed to saving the Czechs and perhaps even secretly hoped to be the man to do it. Years later the strength of these feelings could still be seen in his warm affection for the people of Czechoslovakia and his friendships with their leaders.

In addition to the Czech threat, there was a two-week insurrection in Yaroslavl (July 6 to 21), which, despite harsh measures, had not been easy to suppress. Savinkov was also operating northeast of Moscow in the Union for the Defense of the Fatherland and Freedom, which he had organized. At this time, the commanding general of the Red Army in the Volga region, Mikhail Muravyov, went over to the counterrevolution and threatened to open a route to Moscow for the Czechs. Large numbers of White Finns were volunteering to join the Allies at Archangel, where equipment was being unloaded and military units had already begun advancing toward Moscow, encountering only light resistance. In the south, British forces from the Persian Gulf had a foothold in the Caucasus and had occupied Baku on August 4. The situation was further complicated by the July 30 assassination in Kiev of Field Marshal von Eichhorn, German commander in chief in Ukraine: on August 6, Karl Helfferich, Mirbach's successor as German ambassador, left Moscow for Berlin in protest.

Dzerzhinsky, head of the Cheka and member of the Revolutionary Military Council, responded to the assassination with the harshest terror, prompt and relentless. According to the most generous evidence, a thousand people were executed in Petrograd, while in Moscow the numbers were "somewhat fewer." Political detainees were summarily executed. During the last three months it had become clear that Germany would find a way to coexist with Bolshevik Russia. Despite the assassinations of Mirbach and Eichhorn, relations between the two countries were unbroken, and over the summer a rapprochement between Moscow and Berlin developed slowly but surely. This situation caught the Allies unprepared; few in London had realized that the main enemies of Lenin and Trotsky were now the English and French, not the Germans. Meanwhile, Japan continued to hold Vladivostok, awaiting the signal to move westward into Siberia. France began implementing a plan to occupy the south of Russia and to that end was preparing to send cruisers through the Dardanelles into the Black Sea. Still friendly to the former Provisional Government, France was anxious to ensure that Russian state bonds (which were not recognized by the Bolsheviks) retained their value, lest financial ruin visit the thousands of French small investors who had once responded so enthusiastically to appeals to purchase them. On the western front, the French army, exhausted by frightful losses after four years of trench warfare, was desperately attempting to resist Ludendorff, who had launched an offensive at the beginning of the summer.

Lockhart, who in April had assured Lloyd George that intervention would drive a wedge between the Bolsheviks and the Germans, had radically revised his thinking about what they were up against and now considered the greater evil to be not the Germans but the Bolsheviks themselves. His cipher had been compromised, and he knew that Dzerzhinsky would have given orders to keep him under close surveillance. Lockhart had to be especially careful. The conspirators working with Savinkov, and all those connected in any way with the Allied consulates, were being watched. This could mean that Reilly's arrival in Russia and his frequent trips to Moscow from Petrograd were well known to the Cheka, despite the fact that Reilly was a master of disguises who knew how to cover his tracks better than anyone.

Lockhart's relations with Reilly gradually entered a new phase. The two of them now acted in concert, while each continued to channel sums of money independently to those who needed them. "200,000 paid out yesterday," Lockhart wrote in code. "Today paying out half a million." There were days when he never left his office, receiving visitors, some of whom came and went by the rear door. At last, on August 15, the two Latvian officers Reilly had spoken of entered his office. Colonel Berzin and Second Lieutenant Schmidchen said they had a letter from Cromie, who had introduced them to Reilly in Petrograd and sent them to Moscow. They knew that Captain Cromie had been the British naval attaché in Petrograd before the October Revolution and had stayed there to observe the Russian fleet at Kronstadt, lest it fall into the hands of the Germans, who occupied the southern shore of the Gulf of Finland. The two Latvians had gone to Cromie in July, announcing themselves as members of a militant anti-Bolshevik organization. When Cromie introduced them to Reilly, it was decided that Berzin and Schmidchen would need to see Lockhart.

Berzin did most of the talking. Schmidchen, younger and very thin, said little. With the Allies preparing to move into the heart of Russia, they believed that if Lockhart would agree to give them a letter to General Poole, they could get to Archangel and inform the commander in chief that the Latvian regiments in Moscow and Petrograd were hostile to the Bolsheviks and would defect immediately if they had the assurance of Allied support. These Latvian troops assigned to defend Moscow (and Petrograd) would immediately open a front, establish contact with the Allied army, and lead it into the capital. The Latvians, they said, had but one ambition, to return home to Latvia. And since there was no direct route to the Baltic states, they were ready to do anything if only the Allies would take Moscow, remove the revolutionary leaders, and thereby free the Latvians to determine the fate of their own country. They were visibly worried that Latvia might go over to the Germans rather than be allowed to become independent. They did not immediately demand money; they only needed the letter to Poole, or perhaps multiple letters for security, but they did ask that for safekeeping the money be turned over to Reilly, who was then in Moscow.

Rather than give them an answer, Lockhart told them to return the following day. When they left he called a meeting: among those present were Lavergne and Grenard (some of the French were already living in train cars parked on a siding at one of the Moscow stations, so certain were they that it was only a matter of days before they would begin their homeward journey either through Siberia or to the north). Hicks was present, too, but not Paul Dukes, who had been assigned to Russia after the February Revolution and who was still there.[2] It was unanimously decided to give the Latvians letters of rec-

---

2. Paul Dukes (later Sir Paul Dukes) was assigned to the Secret Intelligence Service, whereas Lockhart and his staff came under the Operations Section of the Foreign Office. Dukes worked in Russia independently and reported directly to London. He had agents working for him in both the Red Army and the Red Navy. He was also involved later (November 1918 and again in 1919) in mining the entrance to the Gulf of Finland, and he even got onto the Kronstadt naval base. He had informants on ships' crews in the Baltic fleet and in the army of General Yudenich, who led an especially successful offensive on Petrograd in April 1919, pulling back at the end of June only to renew his threat in the autumn.

ommendation to Poole, which would describe the situation and assert the readiness of the Latvian regiments to come over to the side of the Allies. In addition, since Lockhart had had to destroy the cipher that could no longer protect him from the Cheka and had lost touch with the outside world as a result, a decision was made to begin preparations for an eventual departure from Moscow to the north. Lockhart was in no hurry to implement this second decision, since he still did not know what to do about Moura. She could not exit officially with diplomatic personnel because she could never acquire the necessary papers, either from the Cheka or the Commissariat of Foreign Affairs. To leave her to find her own way out, risking the possibility of arrest by local authorities, partisans, Germans, Reds, or Whites, would be pure madness.

The next day Berzin and Schmidchen, in the presence of Grenard and Reilly, were given the letters of recommendation and cash. Reilly was setting up a solid base of operations in Moscow to oversee the entire conspiracy.

However, after a few days Lockhart received information that only some 1,200 Marines had been brought to Archangel from Murmansk (Sadoul claimed the force was 35,000). Lockhart had confidence in his sources, though, and acted accordingly. He knew that a force of 1,200 men was utterly inadequate to march on Moscow, even with the help of the Latvian regiments. He saw quite clearly that the Allies could easily fall into a trap and that nothing at all might come from these alluring plans. He decided then and there to withdraw his support from the whole scheme.

Reilly did not give in so easily. He had a craving for action, and with his fierce energy, vanity, and determination, he immediately responded with a counterproposal: a palace coup. They would bring an end to Bolshevik power not with military action but through a mutiny of Latvian guards inside the Kremlin.

Reilly believed in nothing so much as bribery. The Latvian troops, bribed with the aid of Berzin and Schmidchen and placed under Reilly's command, would forcibly enter the Kremlin's inner apartments, arrest the government, and murder Lenin (which Reilly considered doing himself). Meanwhile, on Reilly's signal, Savinkov would march into Moscow with his men and declare a military dictatorship. Reilly said he would need two weeks to prepare. When Lockhart had heard him out, he categorically rejected the plan, and so did Lavergne, Grenard, and Hicks. But Reilly was unfazed and prepared to engineer the coup single-handedly. These days he felt himself to be the last of the Napoleonic line. Let them all turn and run! He would stay on in Russia alone! He dashed to Petrograd, hoping to find an ally in Captain Cromie.

As it turned out, Berzin and Schmidchen were not leaders of an anti-Bolshevik Latvian plot but provocateurs, picked by Dzerzhinsky, who rehearsed them carefully in what to do and how to do it. Dzerzhinsky had sent them to Petrograd to gain Cromie's confidence, which they did, and then to Moscow for further instructions. He told them to contact Lockhart and Lavergne in order to secure letters and money (which could, and doubtless were, used later as evidence). The letters to Poole would help Berzin and Schmidchen get to Archangel, where they were to inform the commander in chief that disloyal Bolshevik units were ready to come over to the Allies. The whole operation was meant to lure Poole into a trap.

They had two meetings with Lockhart, and then Reilly lost track of them. His usual informers could not locate them anywhere. At Cheka headquarters, meanwhile, tension reached such a high pitch at the end of August—and events, as we shall see, moved so rapidly to a crisis— that the chairman of the Cheka, who was handling the "Lockhart plot," as the Reilly plot was then (and subsequently) referred to in the Soviet Union, had to turn the entire matter over to one of his two assistants. Both were Latvians, one named Yakov Peters, the other Martyn Latsis. Dzerzhinsky gave the secret Khlebny Lane file to Peters.

But what became of the two "hero-provocateurs,"[3] Berzin and Schmidchen? Forty years would pass before their very different fates became known.

Colonel Eduard Platonovich Berzin, rewarded by Dzerzhinsky with 10,000 rubles, continued the fight against counterrevolution as a loyal servant of the state security apparatus right up to 1932, when he was sent to Kolyma as the director of Far East Development Projects (DALSTROY). In 1937 he was finally granted leave to go back to Moscow. He packed and was given a hero's send-off, with music and flags, by camp directors and grateful prisoners alike, but he never even got as far as Vladivostok. He was taken off the ship at Aleksandrovsk, arrested, and sent to a camp in the Far North where, when his turn came, he was shot.

Schmidchen, whom Reilly and several others knew by the name Buikis, lived in Moscow to an old age. He resided his whole life on the same street and in the same apartment Dzerzhinsky had given him in 1918 as a reward.

In 1965, Schmidchen, living incognito on his Moscow side street, was unofficially rehabilitated. A Soviet reporter came to see him and told Schmidchen that he was a national "hero-provocateur" and that it was time to tell his story to the younger generation of Soviet youth, who might profit by the example of his heroic act of patriotism. The interview did not proceed without damning references to Trotsky, who, as Schmidchen explained, "fawned over Lockhart" and used to have "gourmet dinners" prepared for him. The menu of these gourmet dinners consisted, in Schmidchen's words, of cabbage soup "swimming in fat," of veal chops with fried potatoes ("huge helpings of them"), and also of "an enormous torte"—a treat we shall encounter again.

The interview ends with Schmidchen's story about a much more recent "hero-provocateur." It turns out that Schmidchen had worked

3. This new term came into Russian only after World War II.

with Colonel Rudolf Abel, who was caught spying in the United States and sentenced to prison. In 1962 Abel was exchanged for Gary Francis Powers, whose U-2 was shot down over the Urals on May 1, 1960. Schmidchen claimed to have been on very friendly terms with Abel and helped him in every way he could. "We worked in the same section" is Schmidchen's modest conclusion to his story.

But to return to Dzerzhinsky, who, in the heat of investigating the Lockhart case, had to turn it over to Peters. He was so shaken, even traumatized, after the murder of Count Mirbach, that he submitted his resignation on July 8, considering himself unworthy to continue as chairman of the Cheka. He believed he had been negligent, not only in allowing the German ambassador to be assassinated in the first place but also because the assassin, Yakov Blyumkin, a Left SR, was employed in his own agency. It took Dzerzhinsky until August 22 to recover from his nervous breakdown. The Soviet of People's Commissars reinstated Dzerzhinsky in his former job, and gradually—there was a huge backlog of work—he resumed his duties. Peters, who replaced him during those six weeks, had managed to familiarize himself with the Reilly–Lockhart affair. He learned immediately about the two visits the Latvians had made to Lockhart, and the next day he uncovered Reilly's new plan, proving that he must have had an informer among the small circle of Lockhart's closest associates. Peters had not yet decided how to proceed when, on the morning of August 30, Leonid Kannegiesser shot and killed Mikhail Uritsky, head of the Petrograd Cheka, as he was entering his office. Kannegiesser was a student at Petersburg University, a poet who wrote verses about his hero, Kerensky, mounted on a white horse. That same evening, in Moscow, Dora Kaplan[4] shot Lenin, wounding him seriously. Dzerzhinsky went to Petrograd as soon as he heard that Uritsky had been shot. Late that night, armed Cheka troops entered

---

4. Later, Soviet historians began calling her Fanny Kaplan.

the British embassy on the Palace Embankment, and when Captain Cromie met them on the stairs with a revolver in his hand, he was shot dead.

Peters was in Moscow, acting as Dzerzhinsky's deputy. After the attempt on Lenin's life he moved against those involved in the Allied representatives' counterrevolutionary conspiracy. On September 1, at 3:30 a.m., he ordered the arrest of the Englishmen living on Khlebny Lane. A squad of agents commanded by Pavel Malkov, the Kremlin commandant, entered Lockhart's apartment. They conducted a thorough search of the rooms and then arrested Lockhart, Hicks, and Moura, taking them to Cheka headquarters on Lubyanka Square. They were not the only prisoners brought to the Lubyanka that night. The Lubyanka was one of three secure citadels in Moscow, the others being the Kremlin and the Hotel Metropole, where the Commissariat of Foreign Affairs had its offices and where the Central Committee met.

Peters was thirty-two years old at the time. Photographs of him show a lean, trim, dark-haired man, something of a dandy, with prominent cheekbones, a strong chin, and lively, intelligent, cruel eyes. High cheekbones were not unusual for a peasant like him, whether Latvian or Russian, but what was unusual was his stylish, even European, elegance. There are three surviving photographs of Peters. In the first, taken when he was arrested in London in 1909 (about which more below), he looks intense and frightening. In the second, which he signed and gave to Lockhart as a keepsake, he is almost handsome, his wavy hair longer than usual, and an attentive gaze below straight eyebrows. In the third, dating from 1930, he is laughing: his hair now has streaks of gray, there are lines under his eyes, and he has a slightly crooked smile that reveals bad teeth, rendering his face vaguely unpleasant, even a little repulsive. He is wearing a white shirt and soldier's tunic, a leather jacket, black riding breeches, and high, well-shined boots. A heavy Mauser is hanging at his waist, and another one is lying on his desk.

He had an extraordinary past. Like Litvinov, he was married to an Englishwoman. In Latvia, where he was born, he had belonged to the Bolshevik wing of the Socialist Democratic Workers Party. He was arrested in 1907 and imprisoned for a year and a half; when he was released, he fled to London, where he married and began working as a presser in a wholesale secondhand clothing business. He spoke English well. He lived in East London, in Whitechapel, where other poor Russians had recently settled. They were mainly from the western and Baltic provinces, refugees from the 1905 revolution and subsequent persecutions. A group of young Bolsheviks formed around him, all members of a London club of Latvian Socialist Democrats. In 1909 they plotted the expropriation of a large jewelry business in order to pay for the printing of revolutionary pamphlets advocating Latvian independence, which would be sent back to Riga. Armed "expropriations" of jewelry stores, banks, post offices, and so on were common in those years. Peters and a dozen of his comrades, including his cousin, his brother-in-law, and two or three women, had agreed to this bold plan of action.

His experience of revolutionary activity back in Riga was child's play compared to this. The operation, known as the "Siege of Sidney Street," made criminal history in England. Like the robbery in which Patricia Hearst took part with the Symbionese Liberation Army in the United States decades later, there was an armed attack, forced entry (in the Sidney Street case, holes were bored through the walls), and eventually a police raid on the hideout of the terrorists that reduced the building to smoking walls. In the case of the Latvian expropriation, however, the police raid occurred the same night as the crime. The gang was apprehended, but not before three police officers were killed, all with the same revolver. It was Peters who killed them, but in the dark no one had seen his face and he was never identified. The affair caused a stir. As usual in those days, the terrorists were all considered anarchists. In the end, the leaders (three of them had been killed during the raid) were acquitted.

In May 1917, Peters hurried back to Russia, leaving his wife and little girl in England. He sped through the ranks of the Bolshevik organization, and soon he was Dzerzhinsky's right-hand man. His adamant, cruel strength had a certain sentimentality about it that gave him an air of fanaticism. Lockhart was brought into Peters's office the morning after his arrest.

Years later, on a quiet evening in Sorrento, as a pink cloud and smoke hung over Vesuvius, Gorky, Moura, and Khodasevich were sitting in soft armchairs, smoking cigarettes in front of the olive-wood fire, talking in low voices about the past, then already so distant (seven years!):

"You knew Cromie? What was he like?"

Moura, tapping the ash from her cigarette into a jade ashtray (which later vanished, probably stolen by the cook), said in Russian with her English accent, "He was...nice."

Silence.

"And you knew Peters? What was he like?"

"He was...kind."

I was there, too, not saying anything, just listening and looking out at the pink cloud, the smoke.

"You knew Reilly? What was he like?"

She sank back deeply in her chair, smiling with her eyes, enjoying the game of being mysterious, and Gorky was obviously admiring her.

"He was...brave."

But that was 1925, in Sorrento. In Moscow, in the early-morning hours of September 1, 1918, as Lockhart was being led into Peters's office in the Lubyanka, he saw before him a face that was severe and rigid, with piercing eyes, pursed lips, and "hair long and waving as a poet's." One Soviet historian gives the following pale and inaccurate description of Lockhart's arrest:

> Lockhart had a mistress living with him at the time. He and Hicks were sequestered in the office. They talked in whispers until midnight. At 1 a.m, Lockhart tiptoed out, trying not to look at the door behind which his latest sweetheart slept, and crossed into his own room, where he fell into bed.
>
> While Lockhart was getting dressed, the Cheka agents woke up Hicks and Lockhart's mistress, Moura. She had arrived from Petrograd a few days earlier and was staying in the flat.
>
> In the dining room were bowls overflowing with fruit. In the middle of the table was a huge biscuit-torte. All this had been prepared in Moura's honor, but remained untouched. By 6 a.m. the search was finished. Lockhart, Hicks, and Moura were taken to the Lubyanka.

And here is another description of that same night, by Pavel Malkov, Kremlin commandant:

> It was about 2 a.m. We found the right staircase without difficulty, lighting our way with cigarette lighters—for of course it was pitch dark inside—and climbed the stairs to the fifth floor (19 Khlebny Lane). I stationed my assistants just out of sight of the door and knocked loudly (the doorbells in most Moscow apartments did not work). Two or three minutes passed after that first knock before the shuffling of footsteps could be heard behind the door. The key clicked, the chain rattled, and the door opened slightly. There was a light on inside, and through the crack in the door I made out the figure of a woman I knew to be Lockhart's secretary, having met her once on a trip from Petrograd to Moscow.

I tried to pull the door toward me, but it wouldn't open. Lockhart's secretary had taken the precaution of leaving the chain on. Then I stepped into the light as much as I could, to give her a chance to take a good look at me. I spoke to her very politely and said it was imperative that I see Mr. Lockhart. The secretary did not even raise an eyebrow. Pretending not to recognize me, she started questioning me in broken Russian, asking who I was and what I needed.

Moura's British accent when she spoke Russian struck a great many people. It really was very strong. It is hard to believe she had acquired it naturally in the year (or two) she had lived in England. More likely she deliberately cultivated it. One of her tricks of speech was to translate idioms literally into Russian from English or French, or sometimes German, à la Princess Betsy in *Anna Karenina* or Anna Pavlovna Sherer in *War and Peace*. Out would come such expressions as "I got on my high horse" or "she's beyond beautiful."

Malkov continues:

I wedged my foot in the crack of the door, and demanded to speak with Mr. Lockhart personally, adding that I would explain the purpose of such a late visit only to him.

His secretary, however, did not give in, showing no intention of opening the door. It is not clear what the outcome of this altercation might have been—it was beginning to try my patience—had Lockhart's assistant, Hicks, not appeared in the hall. Seeing me through the crack, he produced something resembling a smile on his colorless physiognomy and undid the chain.

"Mr. Mankov!" he exclaimed (as the English called me). "May I be of service?"

I shoved Hicks aside and entered with my companions.

Without further ado, I demanded that Hicks take me to Lockhart.

"I'm terribly sorry, but Mr. Lockhart is in bed asleep. I'll have to wake him."

"I'll do that myself," I declared, in such a decisive tone that Hicks at last seemed to get the point and stepped aside, pointing to the door that led to Lockhart's bedroom. All four of us—my assistants, Hicks, and I—entered the bedroom. We found ourselves in a small, narrow room, furnished with two comfortable overstuffed chairs, a wardrobe of Karelian birch, a dressing table of the same wood with fancy trinkets scattered on it, and a wide ottoman covered with a large red rug that reached to the floor. There was a thick oriental carpet on the floor. The room had no bed in it at all. Lockhart was sleeping on the ottoman, and sleeping so soundly that he did not wake up even when Hicks turned on the light. I shook his shoulder lightly. He opened his eyes.

"Oh—oh! Mister Mankov!?"

"Mister Lockhart, by order of the Cheka, you are under arrest. Please get dressed. You will have to come with me. Here is the order."

I must say Lockhart was not particularly surprised nor did he protest. He gave the order only a passing glance and never did read it thoroughly. It was obvious that his arrest was not unexpected.

To give Lockhart some privacy while he got dressed and so as not to waste time, I informed him that a search would have to be made of the entire apartment, and after giving the bedroom a quick once-over, my assistants and Hicks and I went into the next room, Lockhart's office.

The desk drawers were filled with papers of various kinds, as well as pistols and cartridges. In addition there was a considerable sum of tsarist and Soviet currency in large denominations, plus Kerensky banknotes. I found nothing in the wardrobe or in any of the other places I looked. Nor did anything turn up in the other rooms, though we had searched them thoroughly, squeezing cushions and the upholstery of the furniture, and tapping walls and floors in all the rooms. As Peters had delicately instructed us, we did not rip open a single mattress or any of the upholstered furniture.

The Kremlin commandant published those memoirs in 1967. It is interesting how, after almost fifty years, he remembered Lockhart in prison after the arrest:

Lockhart whined and grumbled constantly. When he wasn't complaining about the food (his dinners were brought from the same dining room the commissars ate in, and the meals were pretty poor, really, but they were the best the Kremlin had to offer at the time), he was asking to see his concubine ("Moura," a pure Moscow type) or he was insisting on his right to see someone from the diplomatic corps. I answered his requests by saying that I had nothing to do with those matters and that he should address such requests to Dzerzhinsky or Peters.

There is a third eyewitness account of that night—Lockhart's own, from his *Memoirs of a British Agent*:

On Friday, August 30, Uritsky, the head of the St. Petersburg Cheka, was murdered by a Russian Junker called Kannegiesser. The next evening a Socialist Revolutionary, a young Jewish girl called Dora Kaplan, fired two shots point-blank at Lenin as he was leaving Michelson's factory, where he had been speaking at a meeting. One bullet penetrated the lung above the heart. The other entered the neck close to the main artery....

I received the news within half an hour of the actual shooting. It could hardly fail to have serious consequences, and, with a premonition of our impending fate, Hicks and I sat up late, discussing in low whispers the events of the day and wondering how they would affect our own unenviable situation.

We went to bed at one o'clock, and, worn out by months of strain, I slept soundly. At three-thirty a.m. I was awakened by a rough voice ordering me to get up at once. As I opened my eyes, I looked up into the steely barrel of a revolver. Some ten armed men were in my room. One man, who was in charge, I knew. He was Mankoff, the former commandant of Smolny. I asked him what this outrage meant. "No questions," he answered gruffly. "Get dressed at once. You are to go to Lubyanka No. 11." (Lubyanka No. 11 was the headquarters of the Moscow Cheka.) A similar group of Cheka agents was dealing with Hicks, and, while we dressed, the main body of the invaders began to ransack the flat for compromising documents. As soon as we were ready, Hicks and I were bundled into a car and, with a gunman on each side of us, were driven off to the Cheka headquarters.

Lockhart and Hicks were held overnight in an empty room at the Lubyanka. Moura had been taken elsewhere. At nine o'clock Peters entered. Lockhart nodded to him as one does to an old acquaintance: Peters, Lockhart, and Robins had spent such an interesting day together four and a half months ago, when Peters was assigned by Dzerzhinsky to give them a personally guided tour of the "anarchist nests" liquidated the night before. The mansions had still been smoldering ruins and the blood had not yet been washed off the sidewalks. The operation, which had been carried out on Trotsky's orders, had seemed to Lockhart to be both brilliant and ominous in its ruthlessness. Now Lockhart and Peters had new roles: the prisoner and his jailer.

Peters told Lockhart and Hicks that they were free to go. (They later learned that Peters had telephoned Chicherin for instructions.) They went home. Moura was not there. The maid had also been taken and was still not back.

Even though it was Sunday, Lockhart went to the Dutch legation to see W. J. Oudendijk, head of the Dutch mission, who officially represented British interests. Lockhart presumed that he would be deported along with Hicks and the French. He was afraid to think about the possibility of being separated from Moura. Oudendijk told him what had happened in Petrograd the night before: Cromie had been shot at the embassy and all British officials there were under arrest. With a sinking feeling Lockhart went to find Major Allen Wardwell, Robins's successor at the American Red Cross mission. Wardwell promised to do his best to see Chicherin, and that assurance alone helped Lockhart regain his self-control.

The newspapers were filled with bulletins about Lenin's condition. Two bullets had been removed. "Red Terror" was being hailed as the only reliable way to deal with the enemies of the October Revolution. It would start any day, and on an unprecedented scale.

Lockhart returned home. The streets were deserted, and armed soldiers stood on every corner. The apartment was deserted as well. Unable to sleep that night, he decided the next morning to go to the Commissariat of Foreign Affairs to see Karakhan. He was received at once and got straight to the point. Did the Cheka have any charges to bring against Moura? Karakhan promised to inquire and to do what he could to help. It was Lockhart's birthday. He spent it alone with Hicks, who prepared a dinner of coffee, black bread, and sardines.

On Tuesday, September 3, the papers were full of the "Lockhart plot." He was charged with blowing up bridges, plotting to murder

Lenin, and other crimes. Cromie's death was also described in detail. The article said he had fired first. The "Anglo-French bandits" and their leader Reilly (who had disappeared and was the target of a massive manhunt) had been declared enemies of the people subject to execution.

On September 3, 1918, an official statement appeared in *Izvestia*:

Conspiracy of Allied Imperialists Against Soviet Russia

On this date, 2 September, a conspiracy organized by Anglo-French diplomats, at the head of which was the chief of the British Mission, Lockhart, the French Consul General Grenard, the French General Lavergne, and others, was liquidated. The purpose of the conspiracy was to arrange the capture of the Council of People's Commissars and the proclamation of a military dictatorship in Moscow; this was to be done by bribing Soviet troops.

The entire organization, which was built on a strictly conspiratorial basis, and which made use of forged documents and bribery, has been disclosed.

Among other things, instructions were found that in the event of a successful revolt, forged secret correspondence between the Russian and German governments was to be published, and forged treaties were to be manufactured to create a suitable atmosphere for reviving the war with Germany.

The conspirators acted under cover of diplomatic immunity and with certificates issued over the personal signature of the chief of the British Mission in Moscow, Mr. Lockhart. A number of these certificates are at present in the hands of the Special Investigating Commission (Cheka).

It has been established that 1,200,000 rubles were spent on bribery by one of Lockhart's agents alone, a British lieutenant,

Reilly, during the last week and a half. The conspiracy was disclosed thanks to the loyalty of the commanders of those Soviet detachments which the conspirators offered to bribe.

At the headquarters of the conspirators an Englishman was arrested who, after being brought before the Special Investigating Commission, said that he was the British diplomatic representative, Lockhart. After the identity of the arrested Lockhart had been established, he was immediately released.

The investigation is being energetically pursued.

That morning Lockhart resumed wandering through Moscow on foot. He learned that some forty Englishmen had been arrested in Petrograd. His first stop was the American consulate. The Americans were inclined to regard Reilly as a provocateur, working for the Cheka. Lockhart knew that was not the case. Not wanting to go home, he went again to see Karakhan. It seemed to him that this time the deputy foreign commissar was less reassuring about Moura. Lockhart then decided on a desperate course of action: he resolved to go to the Lubyanka and ask Peters himself what had happened to Moura.

When he walked in and asked to see Peters, a guard with a Mauser gave him a strange look. Lockhart was led into Peters's office, where he began by saying that there was no conspiracy, that the whole story was a fabrication, but that even if there were a grain of truth in it, Moura knew nothing about it. He asked Peters to release her at once. Peters stood and patiently heard him out. He promised that he would take into account everything that had just been said, and then, looking directly at Lockhart, he declared, with a certain delight in his eyes, "You have saved me some trouble. My men have been looking for you. I have a warrant for your arrest. Your French and English colleagues are already under lock and key."

Lockhart was led away to an interrogation room.

Moura was somewhere nearby, maybe in that same wing of the Lubyanka, but Lockhart did not know exactly where and there was no one to ask. He heard and saw much those first days. People were dragged out of their cells to be shot or beaten. In the corridor the very first night he saw a young woman he recognized: Dora Kaplan. She was being led somewhere. He knew that his friends in the Dutch and Norwegian legations were thinking about him and taking all possible steps to help him, but what might they be?

After a few days, Peters entered Lockhart's cell and gave him two books to read, a Russian translation of H. G. Wells's latest novel, *Mr. Britling Sees It Through*, and Lenin's *State and Revolution*. He did not sit down on the stool or the cot but stood by the window and said that the Frenchmen and Lockhart's other "colleagues" were in a common cell in the Butyrki prison, while only he was in solitary confinement here. Peters moved on, as he liked to do, to his favorite subjects —England, his daughter, his duty to the Party, capitalism, which was rotting away, and how his heart sank a little whenever he had to sign the order for an execution. Then, after a moment's silence, he mentioned Lockhart's love affair with Moura. That was also a favorite subject with him, as subsequent events would show.

They were both standing by the window when Red Army troops formed two close ranks in the courtyard below. Between them walked three figures—old men, fat, bald, and obviously ill. Lockhart recognized Ivan Shcheglovitov, Alexei Khvostov, and Stepan Beletsky, former tsarist ministers. The blood of Lenin, shed by Kaplan, demanded vengeance.

"Where are they going?" asked Lockhart.

"To the next world," Peters answered.

The official figures for the first months of the Red Terror (August and September 1918) are known. A total of 31,489 persons were subject to punitive measures on Russian territory: 6,185 shot, 14,829 jailed, 6,407 sent to camps, and 4,068 taken hostage. Such was the Cheka's response to the shots Dora fired.

On September 8, Peters had Lockhart brought into his office. "We're transferring you to the Kremlin," he said, "to Beletsky's apartment." This did not bode well: the Lubyanka was considered safer. The transfer was made that night. The apartment was small, clean, and comfortable, in the old Cavalier House (now destroyed). The apartment had once been assigned to the empress's ladies-in-waiting. To Lockhart's horror and disgust, Schmidchen was put in with him the next day. He was not prepared for that. Schmidchen tried to engage him in conversation but Lockhart did not utter a single word. Thoughts of Moura gave him no peace of mind. The Cheka took hostages. Was she one of them? What was she accused of? How and where was she being questioned? And by whom? Was she being tortured? Lockhart finally asked for pen and paper and wrote a letter requesting the release of Moura and his Russian maid. It could do no harm. The letter went off to Peters.

A day later Schmidchen was taken out and Peters visited Lockhart again. He appeared satisfied, even happy. Lockhart would later learn from Karakhan what Peters had just heard: that René Marchand, correspondent of *Le Figaro*, had betrayed them all. Marchand's testimony had compelled Peters to carry out widespread arrests that same day among subjects of the Allied powers.

Three days later Peters came to inform Lockhart that his case was to be heard by a revolutionary tribunal; Nikolai Krylenko, the public prosecutor, would bring charges of sedition against him. He added that he had decided to accede to Lockhart's request to free Moura. She would receive permission to bring him packages of food and books, tobacco and linen, despite the fact that *Izvestia* editor Yury Steklov was publicly advocating that Lockhart and Lavergne be shot. Peters even offered to take a note to Moura, provided it was written in Russian. He was in a calm, magnanimous mood, hinting that Marchand was "completely our man." He promised to instruct the Kremlin commandant to get Lockhart two hours' daily exercise in the open air on the Kremlin grounds.

And all of it was true—the walks, the clean linen, the right to have books brought to him. There was even a long letter from Moura, which came stamped with the official seal of the Cheka, and an inscription in bold handwriting: "Deliver letter sealed. Read by me. Peters." When ten years later Lockhart wrote about this episode, he called Peters "this strange man, determined to show me that a Bolshevik could be as chivalrous in small matters as any bourgeois."

Lockhart hadn't washed or shaved or changed his clothes in six days. He felt almost human again, despite his looming trial. When he had washed and changed into clean clothes, he played a game of solitaire with a deck of cards Moura had sent him. She had thought of everything. There was a fountain pen, a notepad, even handkerchiefs. He was particularly touched by the books she chose to send him, and indeed her selection says a good deal about her tastes and interests at the time: Thucydides, Ranke's *History of the Popes*, Schiller's *Wallenstein*, Stevenson's *Travels with a Donkey*, Rostand's *L'Aiglon*, *The Life and Letters of Lord Macaulay*, Kipling's *Captains Courageous*, Carlyle's *French Revolution*, and Lenin and Zinoviev's *Against the Current*.

When Karakhan came to see him after his first week in the Kremlin, Lockhart told him outright that he knew who had implicated him and that the testimony against him was false; he knew Marchand had betrayed them in an open letter to President Poincaré and given a copy of it to the Soviet authorities, but the whole thing was a preposterous invention. Karakhan, who usually adopted a joking, ironic tone in conversation with Lockhart, looked mockingly, almost cunningly into Lockhart's eyes: "He gave us his report with a list of names of those present at the secret meeting at the American consul-general's." Lockhart burst out laughing: "I wasn't there!" "Yes," Karakhan replied in his usual half-serious, unhurried manner, "fortunately for you, you do not seem to have been present."[5] He gave Lockhart news of the outside world, and it was excellent: the English were making no progress in the north, and the Bolsheviks were beating the Czechs in Siberia and driving them east. On the western front, the Allies were driving the Germans back. Austria and Bulgaria were on the verge of collapse.

Yes, that really was good news, and now that Moura was free, and the war with Germany was coming to a favorable end for his country, all that remained for Lockhart was to hope that the outcome of his own predicament might not be a disaster either.

That was a help to Lockhart during those days, threatened as he was by a double catastrophe, personal and political: indefinite if not permanent separation from Moura, and an end to his career as a diplomat who had made a series of blunders for which he had only himself to blame. Even if his life were saved, it would be irrevocably altered.

A woman was coming down the hall outside his room—no, it was not Moura. It was Maria Spiridonova, the leader of the Left Socialist Revolutionaries, who was imprisoned on his same corridor. When they saw each other they exchanged a solemn, wordless greeting. She was ill and nervous with dark shadows under her eyes and she looked much older than her years. Another prisoner whom he sometimes met on his walks was General Brusilov, once commander in chief under the Tsar. He walked with difficulty and used a cane. Later he was freed and rehabilitated.

On September 22, Peters strode into Lockhart's Kremlin apartment, smiling and leading Moura by the hand. It was Peters's birthday, and he had decided to treat Lockhart to a surprise. Better even than

---

5. Marchand's denunciation was published in Izvestia on September 28, 1918, and in Petrograd Pravda the next day.

receiving a present, he said, was giving one. He sat down, and Moura stood behind his chair. Three weeks earlier, when she had been arrested and placed in confinement, *he* had succeeded in winning freedom for *her*. Now *she* had come to free *him*—he sensed it, but couldn't yet explain it. What was most extraordinary was the myth they would later create—was it a silent understanding, or did they discuss it?—that it was *he* who in the end had rescued *her*. That sounded more natural, easier to believe, since he was a diplomat, with diplomatic immunity. But the truth was that he did not have diplomatic immunity, being only an unofficial "agent" during a revolution in a country whose government his own government did not recognize. She, born a countess and widow of a rich Baltic count, wasn't shot, or exiled to Solovki, or locked up for ten years in the cellars of Butyrki prison; rather, she was freed from custody a week after her arrest and walked out of her Cheka cell unharmed, with Peters leading her by the hand. None of their friends ever questioned the myth that she was imprisoned by the Bolsheviks and threatened with a death sentence, or the myth of Lockhart's diplomatic immunity. Nor have these myths ever been subjected to scrutiny. They arose naturally out of certain facts: the young Russian aristocrat, twice a countess, was a friend of the "British agent," who used his position to rescue her, when in fact it was Gorky who rescued her, as she would say when she had grown older, failing to mention that the incident she was referring to happened three years later and in Petrograd, not in Moscow in 1918. Lockhart was hardly in a position to rescue anyone. He was to be tried before a revolutionary tribunal for the "Lockhart plot," with the authorities demanding that he be shot immediately. And later he actually was sentenced to death in absentia, when he was back in England. Lockhart knew that he had been freed thanks to Moura, and, as their subsequent relations show, he was grateful to her. But this is jumping ahead to a still distant future, under other skies, amid circumstances unforeseen by either of them.

Peters was sitting; she was standing behind him. He was talking about his revolutionary past and his duty to the Party, reminiscing about the heroic Sidney Street days and recalling the horrors of tsarist times. She was looking over his head, past his dark shock of hair, directly into Lockhart's eyes, and, with Peters rambling on obliviously, she opened one of the books she had brought Lockhart and placed a note in it. Lockhart watched her, terrified, calculating the angle of a mirror in which, with a slight turn of his head, Peters would see everything. But he noticed nothing and kept regaling them with stories of his heroic exploits from age fifteen on behalf of the Socialist cause. When Peters and Moura left the room, Lockhart rushed over to grab the book, Carlyle's *French Revolution*. The note inside was brief: "Say nothing. All will be well." That night Lockhart could not sleep. He wandered through the rooms of the Kremlin apartment, imagining where his road would lead him. What he now knew for certain was that it would at least lead him out of Cavalier House, out of the Kremlin, and back into the world of responsibilities, conflicts, and changes. He would not finish his days here but would return to England after all.

There is a story I once heard Gorky tell over tea one evening, in Saarow, in 1923. It is not in Gorky's collected works, probably because it was never written down, or if it was, it must have been destroyed, because it is not among his fragments or unfinished drafts either.

The story was to be called "The Countess." It was about a man who worked for the Cheka, a ruthless and dedicated member of the Party whose job was arresting people and having them shot. But that did not satisfy him. He wanted to get his hands on a countess, a real countess, the kind he had only read and heard about. But he didn't have one. Though he had some wives of high officials, even a governor's wife, he kept waiting, knowing that eventually he would have her, his countess would be brought to him. One day when the Red Terror was in full swing he was sitting in his office signing execution orders, smoking, and thinking about the historical grandeur of the moment. Suddenly the door opened and in walked his assistant, cartridge belts draped over his shoulders and a Mauser on his belt. Wiping the sweat from his brow, and with his cap cocked to one side, he said, "Come and get her! She's here, the one you've been waiting for."

When Khodasevich and I were alone later that night, we agreed that Gorky would never write that story, or if he did, that he would never publish it. Khodasevich even thought he might "not allow it to remain among his papers." I agreed, and only a little while later, when the conversation was trailing off, did I realize that we had different things in mind. I thought what made the story so compromising was that Gorky was himself now living with a "countess" who was in every sense but the legal one his wife and the mistress of his house. But Khodasevich was not thinking of Moura at all: he was thinking about Peters.

Two weeks would pass before Lockhart returned to his own country. Everything was different now, though. Moura came every day, bringing him (from that inexhaustible source, the American Red Cross) sardines, wine, butter, and biscuits, and she ate all these delicacies with him, or pretended to. There was a severe food shortage in Moscow. Even in the cafeteria where Chicherin and Karakhan took German, Scandinavian, and Persian diplomats to lunch, the menu was often limited to thin soup, wheat porridge, and heavy unbuttered bread made with straw and coarsely ground oats.

Moura could visit Lockhart only for an hour or two, and while she was there they were left alone. They hardly ever spoke about the future, that is, about when he would be released; both of them understood that this would bring their relations to an end because he would not be allowed more than a week free in Moscow before he left. They spoke about the past. And he tried to learn the details of her current life, what she ate and where she went. Twice he made her describe her recent imprisonment with the widow of the former war minister

Vladimir Sukhomlinov, a strong woman who supported those around her and went to her death without fear. Moura told him about how she had found herself outside on the street after her release and how she started walking, as in a dream, in the wrong direction. She walked for a long time before she realized she was going the wrong way. There was one thing she did not tell him: the first time she was questioned, when she denied their affair, five photographs were taken out of a fat file lying on the desk. They showed her on Lockhart's lap, Lockhart embracing her, and both of them in bed. She had fainted for the first time in her life. When she came to, she had to ask for a towel or simply a cloth: they had doused her with a carafe of water. Peters was standing over her.

Now on her visits to the Kremlin she wore what few beautiful items she had left, clothes made before the revolution by exclusive dressmakers. What was still wearable needed attention, but she had never been taught how to sew; nor could anything be laundered, for there was no hot water or soap. Cool autumn nights were beginning. The leaves were mostly gone on the trees around Arbat Square and in the courtyards on Khlebny Lane, where she continued to live in Lockhart's apartment. The bare trees seemed frightening that autumn, ominous precursors of a winter that promised to be disastrous. It would be the first—and maybe not the last—deadly winter.

Vertemont was in hiding, having taken refuge at the Swedish embassy; Reilly had gone underground, still threatening to single-handedly turn the Kremlin upside down, if not the whole of Moscow and all of Russia, to give Siberia to the Japanese and the Caucasus to England. Every corner of Moscow and the suburbs was being combed by the police, but he eluded them easily. The French and English hostages who had been released from Butyrki prison were expecting Lockhart's release soon, at which time they would go home via Archangel and Sweden. The Russians implicated in Reilly's activities were being rounded up and shot. Moura brought news of the disappearance of a great many people he knew in Moscow, news of Allied victories on the western front and the inevitable defeat of Germany, the possibility of an early peace, and the civil war being fought in the south and in Siberia, where the Red Army had sent units but the Czechs were resisting.

Most of all, though, they talked about themselves and their love. Moura wondered privately at times what was in store for her, and with whom, and where. The day the British had learned of Lockhart's arrest they had taken Litvinov into custody in London, and now there were rumors of an exchange, to be followed by a severing of even unofficial relations between the two governments. Lockhart would be deported and Moura would remain behind. Of the two of them he was by far the one more inclined to believe the reassuring Anglo-Saxon illusion that "everything will work out." By contrast, she was extremely sober, serious, clever, and astute. She had done everything she could to win his release; she would do everything she could to ease his departure. What more could she do for him, and anyway, what more did he need from her? And what more could she do for herself? Nothing. She could not leave; she would have to stay here, despite the cold and hunger, despite typhus and the Spanish flu epidemic, with nothing to throw over her shoulders but rags—rags of pure silk, to be sure—and with an awkward surname, a liability under the circumstances, bequeathed her by her murdered husband. She would not even have a roof over her head once the Khlebny Lane apartment was confiscated.

The day after he visited Lockhart with Moura, Peters returned with the Swedish consul general. He wanted to show the Swede that Lockhart was alive and well, receiving the same food as Peters himself was, and that he was not being tortured in the dungeons of the Cheka, as had been alleged in the Western press. On the following day *Izvestia* published Marchand's letter. Though Lockhart's name did not appear in it, and though Lockhart was now certain that he would not be shot, he was still worried that he might be held in solitary confinement for ten or fifteen years or more.

On September 26 the door of his Kremlin apartment opened and Karakhan walked in. He wanted to know Lockhart's views on the likelihood of an early truce between the Allies and the Bolsheviks. He also said that they did not intend to put Lockhart on trial: he would be released soon. When Karakhan left, Lockhart, to collect his thoughts, opened a volume of Schiller and began translating into English Wilhelm Tell's monologue, beginning, "Through this deserted valley must he pass."

On Saturday at 6 p.m. Peters arrived again with Moura. He was dressed in a leather jacket and khaki trousers, and a Mauser was strapped around his waist; there was a broad grin on his face. He declared that on Tuesday Lockhart would be released. Peters was in good spirits—there was something mischievous in his eyes. He promised to give Lockhart two days to settle his affairs, which meant Lockhart would be leaving Moscow on Thursday. In no way embarrassed by Moura's presence, Peters began talking about the conspiracy. In his opinion the Americans were in just as deep as the English and French (a hint at the role played by Kalamatiano, who was later sentenced to death). Then he asked Lockhart whether he wanted to stay in Russia for good, become a Soviet citizen, work for the revolution. The future, he said, would be wonderful; in ten or twenty years Russia would be the happiest and freest country in the world. "We will give you work. We will make use of you. Capitalism is finished, after all, right?"

"He evidently could not understand," Lockhart wrote twelve years later in his memoirs, "how I could leave Moura." When Peters left, Lockhart and Moura laughed and cried, hugged and interrupted each other. Moura told him that the French who had been held hostage since the beginning of September were still locked up in Butyrki prison and that every day Wardwell sent them all, Moura included, a share of his American provisions. He had enough to go around, and no one was refused. She also said that there had been a frightful scene between the Danish ambassador and Chicherin, when the ambassador suddenly became convinced that the Cheka was going to shoot Lockhart and informed London by telegraph. The British government replied with a menacing note to Commissar Chicherin. And she told him how everyone had held their breath and almost given up hope while Lenin hovered between life and death. Supposedly when Lenin finally regained consciousness, his first words were, "Stop the terror!" Now it was settled. Lockhart and all the others would be released and allowed to leave the country. He was indeed being exchanged for Litvinov, who had been held at Brixton prison since September 2. Litvinov would leave London at the same time as Lockhart left Moscow; when Litvinov and his party reached Bergen, Lockhart and his party would be allowed to cross the Russian frontier into Finland. Moura had vast quantities of news. Hicks, Grenard, and Vertemont had been hiding in the former American consulate, but the Cheka had flushed them out. And Hicks didn't know whether he and Lyuba Malinina would have time, between their release from prison and their departure by train, for a wedding ceremony.

Moura left late that night. Lockhart pondered the utter bleakness of a future in which he could never return to this city, this country, this woman. He felt he lacked the strength to leave. He thought about Peters's offer: stay in Russia, be with Moura, remain together forever. He knew there were some, like Sadoul and the young Pierre Pascal, who had decided to stay.[6] But he also knew that he could never

---

6. Pierre Pascal, who sympathized with the Bolsheviks in 1918, had been sent to Russia in 1916 as a member of the French military mission in Petrograd. He did not return to France until 1933, barely escaping being arrested and shot as a spy. He became a Slavic scholar and well-known translator whose books included a study of Archpriest Avvakum. He held the Russian chair at the École des Langues Orientales from 1950 to 1960, and later at the Sorbonne.

become a Bolshevik. He had his own country, and he had a duty to it and to those who had sent him here eight months before; he owed them an account of what had happened and an explanation of his conduct.

Moura had grown ill, and was weak with fever and headache, but she kept up her visits. What had once been unthinkable was now inevitable—separation, probably permanent. She was with him from morning until evening, though she was so weak she could hardly stand. Sunday and Monday were their last days together; no one bothered them. At noon on Tuesday, October 1, Karakhan came to say farewell. At three Lockhart was taken under guard to his apartment on Khlebny Lane. They were to leave the next evening.

At the last minute Peters gave Lockhart a signed photograph of himself. Then, rather sheepishly, he handed Lockhart a letter to his wife and asked him to deliver it to her in England. They said goodbye.

To finish the story of Peters, this far from ordinary Chekist agent: Lockhart delivered the letter as requested to Peters's wife. She and their daughter, May, after a lengthy application procedure, received permission from the Soviet government to join Peters in Moscow in the 1920s. He turned out to be married to another woman, though he had never divorced his British wife. She found work as a maid (or, on other evidence, as a cook) for the well-known American communist Anna Louise Strong, editor of the *Moscow News*, an English-language Communist paper. Peters's daughter studied in a ballet school in 1933 and went on to become a telephone operator at the British embassy in Moscow (relations between the two countries had normalized). May was legally a Soviet citizen, even though she was a British subject born in Britain. In the late 1930s, OGPU agents seized her on the street. After twelve years in prison, she was sentenced in 1952 to ten years in a concentration camp. In 1955 she was still alive. Despite attempts by the British government to contact her and secure her release, she was never able to return to England.

As to Peters himself: on October 19, 1930, he wrote an angry and strident article in *Izvestia* for the thirteenth anniversary of the Cheka-OGPU. A panegyric to Dzerzhinsky (who died in 1926) fills most of a page and is followed by Peters's article about the criminals who might have destroyed Bolshevik Russia in its youth, but for the vigilance of the Cheka, Dzerzhinsky, and Peters himself. Together they saved Russia from the restoration of the monarchy and the capitalist system. He names those wicked enemies—Churchill, Poincaré, Reilly, and Lockhart—who plotted the ruin of the revolution and the partition of Russia, who bought off the dregs of Russian society, who planned uprisings and the demolition of bridges and railroads, and who were prepared to take the extreme measure of cutting off Moscow and Petrograd from their food supplies and starving their inhabitants to death. Only René Marchand's heroic letter and the Cheka's vigilance had saved the country. (Exactly one year after writing his letter, Marchand resigned from the French Communist Party.)

Seven years later, Peters—along with Latsis and other ex-lieutenants of Dzerzhinsky, and hundreds of other officials of the Cheka-OGPU-NKVD—was shot, on Stalin's orders, by the men who had replaced them. Those men were themselves later liquidated. Trotsky mentions Peters's disappearance in 1938 in his *Bulletin of the Opposition*, in an article about the first elections to be held in the Soviet Union since the Stalin Constitution:

> In the final minutes before counting the ballots, it turned out that 54 party candidates had disappeared. Among them were the deputy chairman of the Soviet of People's Commissars Valery Mezhlauk, six members of the government, Alksnis, commanding general of the Air Force, seven other generals, and also Latsis and Peters, who had served in the Cheka since the day it came into being.

The apartment on Khlebny Lane was in disarray. Troops guarding it had stayed there for a time after Lockhart's arrest. His money and a valuable pair of pearl cuff links were gone. The wallpaper had been ripped and the overstuffed armchairs slashed. Lockhart was not allowed to leave, but he could receive visitors both Tuesday and Wednesday. After a night alone with Moura came the final day. Peters had taken care of every detail. Lockhart began packing his suitcases.

At nine p.m. the Swedish consul picked him up and drove him to the station, where he saw the French and English hostages arriving from prison. There were some forty Englishmen in the group and at least as many Frenchmen. They walked together along the tracks to a siding beyond the station, where their train was waiting. It was a warm evening, almost like summer. Everyone carried his own baggage; their escorts—there were not many—took up the rear of the procession. Hicks, who had managed earlier that day to marry Lyuba Malinina, the niece of former Mayor Chelnokov, was taking his bride home with him. Lockhart walked silently with Moura. She was faint with fever, and she stumbled in her French high heels; her long coat was too warm and heavy, but it was the only coat she had. Latvian Red Army troops were guarding the train, which was dimly lit from within. Wardwell, who had come to see his friends off, and Lyuba Malinina's Russian relatives huddled together while everyone boarded the train. Moura and Lockhart stood beside the huge railroad car without speaking to each other. An agonizing hour passed; the train was delayed. The soldiers' presence made them uncomfortable, and it seemed to Lockhart that everyone was trying not to think about what was happening. The same thoughts kept swarming through his head: the border, Stockholm, Bergen, Litvinov, the North Sea crossing. Should he stay a few days at his uncle's in Scotland before reporting to Downing Street? No, he would go straight to London. What if at the last minute the train was not allowed to leave?

Expecting the signal at any moment, they both started to talk about trifles, the weather, ordinary and boring things they had never discussed with each other before. She was standing next to him, and he kept recalling a quarrel they'd had a few days earlier over something minor, how she had said angrily that he was "a little clever, but not clever enough, a little strong, but not strong enough, a little weak, but not weak enough," which had made him lose his temper. She had said it because he had hurt her, and he understood there was some truth to that.

He finally noticed that Moura could hardly stay on her feet. The train showed no sign of leaving. He walked along the cars, found Wardwell, and asked him to take Moura home. She did not insist on staying. Wardwell took her by the arm and the two of them walked back along the tracks. Lockhart watched her disappear into the darkness of a train station at night. He stepped into his dim compartment alone. It was two in the morning when the train finally pulled out.

3

THE STRUGGLE

O tiger's heart wrapt in a woman's hide!
King Henry VI, Part III, I, iv, 137

WHERE WAS SHE to go now? Where was her home? Did she or didn't she have a choice? Major Wardwell, head of the American Red Cross mission in Russia, while not quite an official envoy, was still in essence a political figure, as had been his predecessor Colonel Robins. Originally quartered at the American consulate, he had taken all his food stores and moved into a separate building on the grounds of the Norwegian mission nearly a month before. Back in the spring the Norwegians had moved into the compound itself—with its spacious courtyard, garden, and outbuilding—when it still belonged to the Americans. After diplomatic relations between the United States and Russia were severed and Ambassador Francis had left Moscow for Vologda with his entire staff, the Norwegians leased the building. Wardwell was staying on in familiar lodgings as a guest of sorts. He certainly did not dare to bring Moura home with him that night. He was an expansive and hospitable man, and he shared his condensed milk, cocoa, canned beans, and other bounty generously with everyone—those under arrest and those still free, allies and neutrals alike, representatives of powers great and small. Nonetheless, he had to exercise caution, for he had seen in recent months that the Bolshevik government was making little distinction between England and France on the one hand, and the United States on the other. President Wilson continued to reject any interference in Russia's internal affairs and stood firmly against intervention. (Poincaré and Lloyd George were naturally of the opposite opinion.) Washington had ordered Wardwell to observe strict neutrality in everything that concerned White House policy toward Moscow, and that ruled out taking Moura to his quarters at the Norwegian legation. Nor could he take her to any of their mutual "neutral" friends: her relations with many of them had been compromised over the past month, and now contact with Moura could only complicate matters for the Swedes and Danes, for whom matters were already complicated enough. The English and French nationals outside the diplomatic community (if indeed any remained in Moscow) were also out of the question. They were under threat of arrest, if they hadn't been arrested or deported already, and were now leaving Moscow with their families with all deliberate speed.

That left her Russian acquaintances. But who were they? In the years before the revolution, neither Moura nor her family nor the Benckendorffs had had anything to do with Moscow. She and Lockhart might have discussed her options when she visited him in prison in the Kremlin, and together they may have discussed where she could go, where she might find sanctuary. The Soviet newspapers had never mentioned her among the dozen or so names from Lockhart to Kalamatiano and from Colonel Friede to Vertemont. Lockhart's maid had a sister who lived somewhere in Moscow beyond Taganka; there was Maria Nikolaevna, the old Gypsy singer who once told their fortunes in Sokolniki. Or might she find one of her girlfriends from school, living now by selling what remained of her jewelry at the Smolensky Market on "aristocrat's row"? Moura did have funds: Peters had returned some of the money crammed into Lockhart's desk drawers and stolen by the police. But Lockhart could not leave her very much because if a large sum were found in her possession she could be suspected of counterrevolutionary activities. No one was safe from being searched now, least of all her. He left her only enough to live on for a few weeks. But where would that be?

The night of Lockhart's departure, sick and worn out, she ended up back at Khlebny Lane. She still had the key. She never spoke about the subsequent days and weeks in Moscow. She knew only one thing, that she was not being followed: no tails were assigned to her. But that was not enough to put her mind at ease, much less make her happy—happiness was out of the question. Ill with a fairly mild case of Spanish flu, utterly alone in an essentially alien city, she realized something had to be done. She would have to summon all her strength and take steps to get past this despair, which was a thousand times more frightening than what she had felt a year ago when on a Petrograd street corner she first learned of Benckendorff's murder from a stranger. That was in a city she belonged to, with foreign embassies, shops where you could buy a loaf of bread, friendly faces everywhere. Here there was Red Terror, the Lubyanka, and separation from the man she loved, her first love—she had never known love until then—now broken off forever.

December was cold and snowy. She budgeted her money carefully. When it was gone, she went to the Smolensky Market and sold her diamond engagement earrings, the last of her possessions. Though half the money she got for them was immediately stolen, there was enough to buy a ticket for the overnight train to Petrograd. This was a sure step: she belonged there; Moscow had nothing to offer her. She left after Christmas. She stood in the corridor of a third-class railway car for a time, and passed the evening sitting on her suitcase on the platform at the end of the car. There were people hanging on the steps all night long.

Nothing is known about Moura's last days in Moscow. Did she say goodbye to anyone? Was there anyone to say goodbye to? Did she find any of the people who had been in prison all autumn for the "Lockhart plot" and now, in December, were free? Who were they, and did she seek any of them out? Did she say goodbye to Peters? Or did he know without her telling him where and when she was going?

November and December were full of major events. On November 11 the Allies and Germany signed the armistice; Europe, the United States, and Japan had emerged from the war victorious. From November 28 to December 3 the "Lockhart plot" was tried before the Revolutionary Tribunal of the Central Committee. None of the principal defendants—Lockhart, Vertemont, Lavergne, Grenard, Reilly—was present. The tribunal sentenced all of them to death by firing squad and declared them outlaws. Two others, who were present, were also sentenced to death: Colonel A. V. Friede, a tsarist officer, and Xenophon Kalamatiano, who worked for American counterintelligence. Eight received sentences of five years at hard labor, and one more, a certain Pshenichko, was sentenced to prison "until the cessation of Czechoslovakian military operations against Soviet Russia." Moura read all this in newspapers pasted up on a wall at the corner of Povarskaya Street and Nikitsky Boulevard in Moscow. Small groups of people would cluster there silently, always silently, and stone-faced. They would read about who was to be shot and for what, who had been assigned to bring their shovels to snow removal detail the next day (government shovels were not provided), and who was eligible to receive a ration of herring, or wheat, or oats mixed with straw. Moura did not have a ration card and was living there without a permit.

Civil war was raging in the south in the first months of 1919. In the east, Bolshevik troops were fighting Czech-SR forces on one front and Japanese-backed Cossack units on another. In the west, General Yudenich had begun an offensive that was advancing with such success that the fall of Petrograd seemed inevitable. But at least in Petrograd, Moura had a roof over her head—she was staying with former Lieutenant General Alexander Mosolov, who had been head of the chancellery at the Ministry of Crown Domains before the revolution. She had known him during the war when she was volunteering at the military hospital where Mosolov was a director.

In that dying city (for the first time in her life) Moura had to think about a job, a real job that paid money. Never before in her life had she had occasion to think about finding useful employment in order to earn a living. The idea seemed almost ludicrous at first, but soon it ceased being merely funny, and she gradually became serious, committed, and finally resolved. She would work. But how, and where?

Mosolov was living in his huge high-ceilinged prewar apartment with a view of the Neva, crowded now with strangers who had been assigned living space there. Moura still lacked a ration card and residence permit. She moved into a room behind the kitchen, where once a servant had lived. On her third day in Petrograd she was arrested on the Troitsky Bridge: she had in her possession two ration cards, obtained in exchange for a sable muff. The cards turned out to be counterfeit.

She spent about a month in the Cheka prison on Gorokhovaya Street. Not until a week after her arrest did she decide to tell them to telephone Peters in Moscow. The request was met with incredulity: Wouldn't she prefer to talk to Lenin himself? She said nothing and began waiting. Two more weeks passed. She was kept in the basement, in a common cell that held not political prisoners but petty criminals accused of theft, prostitution, or trading on the black market. The occupants changed every few days; she alone was not released. Finally, she was called in for interrogation. Again she told them to telephone the Lubyanka. This time her request was received with some surprise but without sarcastic comments. Four days later she was released.

The year 1919 was frightful. For many the very symmetry of the two nines remained forever an ominous symbol of death by starvation, typhus, Spanish flu, subzero temperatures in houses that were falling apart and being dismantled (the parquet floors were burned as fuel), and death by decree of the all-powerful Cheka. Dead horses lay where they had fallen, their frozen legs jutting out of the snow into air that was twenty degrees below zero. Unoccupied buildings stood bare of window frames, doors; everything had been stripped for firewood. In the snowdrifts, blizzards, and black nights, Petrograd was unrecognizable. People fled if they could because soon the city was surrounded on three sides by civil war and it became impossible to leave. There was no bread, lard, soap, or paper. In the halls and kitchens of occupied apartments, where water pipes had burst, there were skating ponds right up until early April. May was as still and peaceful as a forest meadow: patches of grass sprouted up in streets once paved with wooden paving blocks, while the gaping potholes in Nevsky Prospect were being filled with tar by workers registered for fifth-class rations—that is, by those who had no steady job. Most of those assigned to street clearing and repair could hardly stand up, much less lift a shovel. Alexander Benois, wrapped in a shawl like a peasant woman, walked across Winter Palace Square to and from his offices in the Hermitage, and Professor Shileiko's approach could be heard from a distance, his wooden heels clomping the pavement, his swollen feet in socks full of holes and bound with rags. And in Maxim Gorky's apartment on Kronverk Prospect, where no less than seven or eight people lived that winter (not counting visitors and occasional overnight guests), there was a steady flow of scholars, writers, actors, artists, and even circus clowns, who came to see Gorky with requests for his signature on a requisition for galoshes, or aspirin, or a ticket to Moscow, or a pair of spectacles, or a letter attesting to the reliability of the bearer.

Gorky's apartment was near the zoo, which was now deserted. The lions and tigers had died of starvation long ago, and the deer and camels had been eaten. Only Professor Pavlov, who had recently discovered the conditioned reflex, managed (thanks to Lenin's special order) to get enough food to feed his laboratory dogs. Dr. Voronov's monkeys survived, too, until the doctor fled (his specialty was rejuvenation) to Switzerland. The monkeys were dead within two days. Gorky readily signed whatever was set before him, but his name usually carried little weight. The seat of power in Petrograd was occupied by the supreme authority in Russia's north, Grigory Zinoviev, chairman of the Soviet of Commissars of the Northern Communes and chairman of the Petrograd Soviet of Workers and Soldiers Deputies—Zinoviev was Lenin's right hand, and he held unlimited power in the former capital after the government was transferred to Moscow. It was at Zinoviev's insistence that Lenin issued the July 1918 order shutting down Gorky's newspaper, *New Life*.

This had been a heavy blow for Gorky—it is no exaggeration to say that it took him five years to recover. Not long before the paper was shut down, in the spring of 1918, Gorky was asked in the press to state where he got the money to start a newspaper. *New Life* had been launched on May 1, 1917, before the October Revolution. Zinoviev, who had come from Switzerland with Lenin in April, apparently suspected that Gorky was being subsidized by the same foreign source that had enabled Lenin and other Bolsheviks to return to Russia. Gorky resented this implication, taking it as a personal insult. He answered that the money had been given him by Ernst Grubbe, a liberal banker and old acquaintance of Gorky's who had gone abroad. (Grubbe was one of the two owners of the banking firm Grubbe and Nebo, whose sign was still hanging on Nevsky Prospect.) Grubbe had donated money to other public causes, including the Free Society for the Development and Propagation of the Exact Sciences, which had been founded at his initiative after the February Revolution. Gorky wrote that Grubbe had given him 270,000 rubles to start his newspaper and that he, Gorky, had come up with the rest out of his personal funds—money he had earned when his complete works were published by A. F. Marx as a supplement to Marx's journal *Niva*.

Gorky's account was not strictly accurate, however, and his story does not jibe with that of one of his creditors. Grubbe was not the only contributor. Lacking the necessary funds in February 1916, when he had decided to start a liberal-radical newspaper, Gorky looked for backing and found three sponsors who each gave him 150,000 rubles: Ivan Sytin, the well-known publisher; Boris Gordon, editor and publisher of the largest daily in Rostov-on-the-Don; and Grubbe. The venture fell through, however, and Gorky used the money in April of the following year to start *New Life*. When Gordon saw the first issue in May 1917, he felt it was too "communist" and demanded his money back. An arbitration court decided the matter in Gordon's favor and Gorky was ordered to pay him back. Neither Sytin nor Grubbe asked for their money back. In August 1917 Gorky wrote a note to Gordon thanking him for the 150,000 rubles and stating that he was returning the entire sum. Here is the text, from the Boris I. Nicolaevsky Collection at the Hoover Institution in Stanford, California:

> Esteemed Boris Abramovich!
> I am gratefully returning the 150,000 rubles that you loaned me in March of the current year.
> Please accept my warm gratitude for your help.
>
> M. Gorky
> 8.VIII.17.

When Gordon got the note, however, there was no money in the envelope. On May 8, 1949, at the request of Mark Aldanov and Boris Nicolaevsky, who had emigrated, Gordon gave Gorky's note to them, and included a detailed account of his own version of events. Gorky would hardly have written such a note of thanks without enclosing the money, as the court had ordered him to do. The money may have been taken by the person entrusted to deliver the envelope, or Gorky may simply have forgotten to enclose the money. Gordon insisted, however, that it was not in the envelope and that he never received the money Gorky owed him.

The Soviet press continued to accuse Gorky of selling out to the bankers. He responded that Lenin himself had at one time accepted money from the merchant Savva Morozov for his newspaper *The Spark*, but that was to no avail. Until the very day *New Life* was shut down, neither Gorky nor his closest associates on the paper—Alexander Tikhonov, Vasily Desnitsky, and Nikolai Sukhanov, the Social Democrat and historian of the Russian Revolution—could believe that it would actually be suppressed.

New Life opposed the Bolshevik coup of October 25 (November 7, New Style) on the grounds that it was premature. Gorky viewed the immediate aftermath with some fear and trepidation. On November 23 he wrote: "The nation's affairs are in the hands of blind fanatics and unscrupulous adventurers, conspirators and anarchists in the Nechaev mold." Not to be outdone, the Soviet press in December called him a "sniveling bourgeois." These exchanges continued. The suppression of other newspapers and the beginning of the Red Terror enraged Gorky, who wrote: "In these days of madness, horror, the triumph of stupidity and vulgarity..."

Zinoviev was nominally on the editorial staff of *Petrograd Pravda* but in fact had absolute authority over the paper. He was in close contact with *Pravda* in Moscow, and the attacks on *New Life* were clearly coordinated. An anonymous front-page article in *Pravda*, in all likelihood written by Zinoviev or one of his surrogates, asserted that Gorky's paper had "sold out to the imperialists, industrialists, landlords, and bankers" and that its editors were "on the payroll" of the bankers.

To retire to the countryside and relax, as his highly placed friends kept recommending, was something Gorky neither could nor would do. There was work to be done. He was appalled at the prospect of the advancing winter of 1918, by the daily deaths and deprivations, which threatened to wipe off the face of the earth not only middle-aged and older scholars and scientists of world renown but the entire intelligentsia as a class. The only ones with some hope of survival were those who could claim a proletarian background and those who by some miracle had been hired by the Soviets to work in a bureau or supply depot.

Gorky had an idée fixe that went back to his youth and that eventually, in the final years of his life, assumed maniacal force. Culture, he believed, could be popularized, propagated on a mass scale, by means of an encyclopedic series of great books containing the achievements of all nations and all ages, in every branch of science and art. All those great works of the past, from Homer to modern times, would be published in alphabetical order and would "enable the world proletariat to free itself from the chains of world capitalism, and enable the intelligentsia to form a correct understanding of world culture in its entirety." If the original works contained complexities beyond the grasp of the ordinary working-class reader, then experienced translators or specially trained cadres of editors were to simplify and rewrite them. Gorky himself, in February or March of 1908, had actually been planning to rewrite Goethe's *Faust* from scratch. Maria Andreeva, Gorky's wife at the time, wrote to their friend Nikolai Burenin, that it would "be something amazing."

Translations with commentaries, or the classics rewritten, published for the audience he had in mind, would, in Gorky's opinion, facilitate the coming of the world revolution, provided that anything pernicious or superfluous in them was expurgated once and for all. The originals would never be republished, and in time would rot away in library basements and private collections. In print runs of millions, sounding a clarion call, uplifting the spirit and dispelling religious superstition and every kind of morbid decadence, this colossal series of books in all the languages of man would educate the youth of the world and open the eyes of workers and peasants to the greatness of such names as Newton and Pavlov, Hippocrates and Yablochkov, Shakespeare and Saltykov-Shchedrin, Sechenov and Jack London—and thousands more. It was, of course, a project for the future and one that would require a minimum of 10,000 ideal translators, but a more modest project could be undertaken in the meantime: first, a series of translations of progressive works of Western and Oriental literature; and second, a series of popular books about the scientific achievements of the greatest minds of the human race. In 1909 Gorky wrote his friend and publisher Ivan Ladyzhnikov (he was privy to all Gorky's personal and financial affairs) from Capri advising him to approach the well-known conductor Serge Koussevitzky, who had just married a wealthy woman from Moscow, about financial backing for their "encyclopedia," as Gorky then called the series of popular scientific books he planned to publish: "Point out to him that our Encyclopedia will be strictly scientific in nature and broadly democratic."

The idea ripened in Gorky's mind for the next fifteen years, and in September 1918 Gorky decided to organize a publishing house, to be called Universal Literature, under the auspices of the Commissariat of Enlightenment. Its purpose would be to realize the first phase of his old project: a mass edition of new (and in some cases old) translations of mainly nineteenth-century European and American works. Gorky's ostensible goal was educating the uneducated reader, but there was another alongside it, which Gorky thought was equally if not more important: to give the scholars and writers participating in the project top-priority ration cards and thus enable them to avoid death by starvation. His plan would make them eligible to receive not only herring and flour but a pair of galoshes as well.

Universal Literature issued its first catalog in early 1919. Tikhonov, who later wrote memoirs about Gorky, was the managing editor. There were two separate series of books from the outset: a "standard" series and a "national" series. Standard authors included Oriental and medieval works. Contracts were signed and, thanks to Gorky's efforts, ration cards were issued. He wanted to become the "director of culture," and he did, so effectively that by winter his associates in Universal Literature even received an allotment of firewood.

The first three volumes came out in July 1919, though as early as February Gorky had begun to complain of delays in the printing schedule due to the lack of paper, printer's ink, glue and thread for binding, and decent presses; and in June he threatened to halt operations, despite the fact that "all available literary manpower [that is, translators] has been mobilized, and several hundred books are now under way." It was then that the idea of going abroad first began to take hold of him. It was then, too, that Lenin started urging him to take a trip to Europe "to restore your health." By 1920, however, the situation at Universal Literature had gradually improved. In little more than three years they had managed to publish some two hundred titles—no mean achievement given the difficulty of obtaining materials at the time.

Moura never said how she survived those cold and hungry months in Mosolov's apartment at the beginning of 1919. That year her mother died in the south of Russia. Her sisters were in the south, too, or had possibly fled to France: the Kochubei family later lived in Paris, as did Alla Moulin, who divorced her French husband in the early 1920s and committed suicide a few years later. Moura once said of Mosolov that he was handsome and clever and had a "heart of gold." In his memoirs, *At the Court of the Last Tsar*, he admires the "nobility, kindness, meekness, and perspicacity" of the last tsar and shows his adoration for the entire family. Mosolov, who was sixty-five in 1919, did not hesitate to take Moura in, although he was probably quite unaware of her recent Moscow exploits. Rather suddenly one day, Moura went to Universal Literature because someone had told her about Kornei Chukovsky, who worked like an ox but nonetheless was living on the edge of starvation in Petrograd with his wife, Maria Borisovna, and their three children, of whom the eldest, Nikolai, was fourteen, and the middle child, Lida, was eleven. Moura knew Chukovsky less as a translator of English and American literature than as an organizer of the soirées at the Anglo-Russian Society that had flourished during the war. After Moura had returned to the capital from Berlin with her husband, she frequented those soirées, and she had met Chukovsky at one of them. She didn't know exactly what he had translated, nor had she heard anything about him as critic and author of several books, but she remembered him well enough—his large ungainly figure, hands down to his knees, great shocks of black hair falling over his forehead, and a huge Cyrano nose. She had been told that he needed someone to translate Galsworthy's novels and Oscar Wilde's fairy tales for a new publishing venture of Gorky's. She decided to find him and ask for work.

She had never translated into Russian. Later she did translate from Russian (and French) into English, but her Russian was inadequate. In fact, she seemed to enjoy showing off her imperfect knowledge of the idiomatic nuances of the language, and relished her slightly mannered pronunciation of certain Russian words. Chukovsky went out of his way to be nice to her. He did not assign her anything to translate but he did find work for her at the office. She was very thin at the time, with large eyes and prominent cheekbones; her teeth needed attention, but there was neither money, nor anything to clean them with, nor any dentists, owing to the complete absence of instruments and medicine. She worked for Chukovsky for several weeks. He managed to get a third-class ration card for her, and she registered properly in the city under her maiden name, receiving her identity card, which in those days served as a passport. Early that summer Chukovsky took her to meet Gorky.

They arrived late in the afternoon for tea. There was a samovar on the table. The tea was thin and weak, but it was real, not carrot tea. The large dining room had a sideboard and dining table; all the other rooms were used as bedrooms. There were many rooms and many people in the apartment, especially since it wasn't clear who lived there and who was only staying temporarily, who was spending the night and who would get up and leave after being there all day. Or who was about to go to Moscow and who had just returned from Moscow that morning.

The original apartment at 23 Kronverk Prospect (now Gorky Prospect) had been on the fifth floor, number 10, but Gorky's wife, Andreeva, had found it too small and they had all moved downstairs to number 5—really two apartments combined.

At various times different women presided over Gorky's dinner table as mistress of the house. A rift with Andreeva had begun as early as 1912, but she and Gorky continued not only to see each other but to live under the same roof. Andreeva was living now in the large drawing room on Kronverk but was frequently away on business, and by this time Gorky was living with Varvara Tikhonova—Shaikevich by her first marriage. She had later married Alexander Tikhonov, Gorky's managing editor at Universal Literature. Living with Tikhonova on Kronverk were her fifteen-year-old son, Andryusha, from her first marriage, and a daughter, Ninochka, born after her marriage to Tikhonov. Nina became a well-known ballerina in France, a pupil of Olga Preobrazhenskaya and a member of the same generation of dancers as Tamara Tumanova, Irina Baronova, and Tatiana Riabouch-inska. The striking resemblance between Nina and Gorky puzzled those few who did not know about his affair with Varvara. Nina was born around 1914, and those features which in Gorky were crude and common were transformed in her, thanks to the astonishing grace and charm of her mother, into an endearingly upturned nose, light blond braids, and a delicate, supple figure. I cannot say whether Tikhonov lived in the apartment on Kronverk at this time, but I think not. Another permanent resident there from 1919 to 1921 was a young woman named Maria Heintse, nicknamed "Molecule," who was the daughter of an old acquaintance of Gorky's from Nizhniy Novgorod, a pharmacist killed by the Black Hundred during the 1905 revolution. She had been adopted by Gorky, who liked adopting orphans. Everyone knew of his adopted son Zinovy, the brother of Yakov Sverdlov. Zinovy even bore Gorky's real surname (Peshkov), and were it not for Gorky's first wife, Ekaterina Pavlovna Peshkova, and for Andreeva, Gorky would no doubt have adopted a good many more.

Also living in Gorky's apartment on Kronverk were the artist Ivan Rakitsky, who was a kind of adopted son himself; Andrei Diederichs and his wife, the artist Valentina Khodasevich, niece of the poet; and, in 1920, Andreeva's secretary, Pyotr Kryuchkov, a lawyer who lived with her intimately despite being twenty-one years younger, moved into the room adjoining hers.

Andreeva was then at the height of her third career. The first had begun before she knew Gorky, in Stanislavsky's theater. When she met Gorky she interrupted her acting career and accompanied him to the United States and then to Capri. She made a comeback in 1913, when she realized that she and Gorky would inevitably break up, and joined K. N. Nezlobin's theater. Now Lenin had appointed her commissar of the Petrograd theaters, and she was devoting all her time to reorganizing the Bolshoi Dramatic Theater, formerly the Suvorin. She mostly ignored Varvara Tikhonova and her children, though Gorky's affair with Tikhonova, who had once visited them on Capri with her husband, had at first been difficult for her to bear. Tikhonova had left her first husband and married Tikhonov in 1909. At the time we are concerned with here, Tikhonova was considered the mistress of Gorky's household.

Andreeva's first husband had been a privy councillor by the name of Andrei Zhelyabuzhsky; they had had two children, a daughter Ekaterina, and a son Yury, who became a film director. In 1904 Andreeva joined the Bolshevik Party and became a personal friend of Lenin's. She was devoted to the party. When the famous Moscow millionaire Savva Morozov shot himself, he left her (not in his will, but through a third party) 100,000 rubles, of which she kept 40,000 for herself and donated the rest to the Bolshevik wing of the Communist Party. In the autumn of 1919, the Gorky household was preparing for a second terrible winter. The Tikhonovs left, and Andreeva's son and daughter-in-law moved in for a while. Gorky's son by his first wife, Maxim Peshkov, a member of the Bolshevik Party since 1917, also came for a visit from Moscow. Maxim was on good terms with Dzerzhinsky and Peters, having worked for them in the Cheka first as an instructor in the literacy campaign and then as a courier with an automobile assigned to him. It was during his visit that Andreeva played Desdemona at the Bolshoi Dramatic Theater for the last time; she was fifty-two then and looked thirty-five. Soon after that, Maxim went abroad, where he became a diplomatic courier in Berlin, traveling to Italy and those European countries which were gradually establishing diplomatic relations with the Kremlin.

The house was always full. Almost daily, visitors who had stayed until midnight and were afraid of being attacked if they left would sleep over. A bed would be made up for them on the ottoman in the dining room. Khodasevich stayed over whenever he came to Petrograd from Moscow. His niece Valentina was only eight years younger, and he was very fond of her. Once in a while old friends of Gorky's or friends of his friends, would come all the way from Nizhniy Novgorod to see him. A place was found for everyone.

No one ever complained of overcrowding. There was always plenty of room. It was not uncommon for fifteen people to be present at tea, which could last from five to midnight. Dinner was at midday. There was enough food, but of course there could be no thought of anything fancy. There were rumors in Europe at that time that Gorky was living like a millionaire, but that wasn't true. His associates from Universal Literature came for tea, as did two administrators from the House of Scholars (another one of the institutions inspired or even created by Gorky), Anatoly Rodé and M. P. Christie, and writers from the recently opened House of the Arts. The most frequent guests were Zinovy Grzhebin, future owner of a big Berlin publishing house; F. E. Krimer, soon after appointed director of Arcos Ltd., the Anglo-Soviet trade organization in London; Artemy Khalatov, chairman of the State Publishing House (Gosizdat) and head of the Commission for Improving Living Conditions of Academics (KUBU); the Orientalist Sergei Oldenburg; Albert Pinkevich; Vasily Desnitsky; Kornei Chukovsky; Evgeny Zamyatin; Fyodor Chaliapin; Boris Pilnyak; Larisa Reisner and her husband Fyodor Raskolnikov, who was commissar of the Baltic fleet; the artist Mstislav Dobuzhinsky; the director Sergei Radlov; and also, when they happened to be in Petrograd, Leonid Krasin, Anatoly Lunacharsky, Alexandra Kollontai, Lenin, and other members of the government.

The prevailing mood in the house was unconventional. Almost everyone had a nickname, and the jests, practical jokes, anecdotes, and miscellaneous amusements, sometimes silly, sometimes incomprehensible except to those in the "inner circle," never let up. Naturally, Theater Commissar Andreeva did not take part in such foolishness. But Rakitsky, Valentina (later head designer at the Kirov Theater), Molecule, and Maxim, when he was visiting, all had a keen sense of humor. They invented charades, composed comic verses and fantastic tales about things that supposedly happened only yesterday but in reality never happened at all. They entertained Gorky with such amusements at the tea table, providing him with his only chance to laugh in a day filled with worry, disappointment, anxiety, intrigues to be disentangled in the institutions he oversaw, and efforts to parry the machinations of Zinoviev, his personal enemy.

Today it is hard to imagine the unparalleled power Zinoviev had held since the October Revolution, standing third in line after Lenin and Trotsky ahead of Kamenev, Lunacharsky, Chicherin, and Dzerzhinsky. Every morning in *Petrograd Pravda* Zinoviev would write "I announce," "I order," "I forbid," "I will punish mercilessly," "I will not allow." Backing up his words was a monstrous apparatus of incredible power that he held in his hands and controlled, giving neither himself nor anyone else a moment's peace. Everything he did received the Kremlin's approbation, post facto of course, and he knew it. He had lived with Lenin in Switzerland. He had taken the train with Lenin through Germany to Petrograd. And now he was for all intents and purposes the dictator of the Russian north, basing his rule on Uritsky's brainchild, the powerful apparatus of the Cheka.

Rakitsky was called "Nightingale"; Andrei Diederichs, "Didi"; Valentina Khodasevich, "Kupchikha" (Merchant's Wife); Pyotr Kryuchkov, "Peppycrew"; and Gorky himself, "Duke." When Moura arrived with Chukovsky and told them she was born in Chernigov Province, she was immediately pronounced Ukrainian and dubbed "Titka" (Auntie). They all liked her very much. Chukovsky did not press Gorky to hire her as a translator, but they asked her to come again, which she did, and she began visiting more and more often. A month later, when the days grew colder and the nights longer, they offered her a room at Kronverk.

There was nothing strange in that. A year earlier, Rakitsky—the Diederichs' old friend from Munich, where all three had studied painting and breathed the air of the Blue Rider—had arrived at Kronverk half dead, barefoot, and unshaven. They let him wash up, fed him, and dressed him in Didi's jacket and Gorky's pants—and he never left. He stayed until 1942, in fact, when he died in Tashkent, having been evacuated with Maxim's widow and her two daughters. Molecule also stayed on for quite a while, until she married the artist Vladimir Tatlin, and when Khodasevich arrived sick from Moscow they tried to talk him into staying, but he declined. Titka moved in little by little, alternating between Kronverk Prospect and Mosolov's. Mosolov's apartment was scheduled to be requisitioned for some new scheme of Zinoviev's, and soon the day came when Titka stayed with Gorky for good. A month later she was typing his letters on an old broken-down Underwood they found in some storeroom, its owner unknown, and she was translating into English, French, and German his appeals to the West for aid for starving Russian scholars. One in ten of those letters made it through by some miracle. Herbert Hoover, director of the American Relief Administration, was the first to respond to them in 1920, organizing a shipment of ARA packages for Russia's perishing intellectuals. And since neither Molecule, who was studying at the university, nor Valentina, who was painting portraits, had any interest in organized housekeeping, it gradually fell to Moura to take over supervision of the two old servants (the Diederichs' cook and maid) and of household affairs in general. "We've got ourselves a house boss," said Maxim when he came from Moscow and saw the happy change on Kronverk. "Our boss-free days are over."

Andreeva gradually and tactfully extricated herself from the center of that family picture, and Moura gradually and tactfully established the very best relations with her.

Gorky's room was next to Moura's. Beyond Gorky's bedroom was a small office filled with books and papers, which opened onto the dining room. Next to Moura on the other side was Molecule's room, and next to that an empty guest room, which was rarely unoccupied. Continuing in that direction were Andreeva's and Peppycrew's rooms and Andreeva's office, a sunny, elegantly furnished room with windows facing the street. In the other direction was the Diederichs' suite, where Rakitsky lived as well.

Within a week after moving in Moura had made herself indispensable. In the morning she read through the letters Gorky had received,
filed his manuscripts, organized what had been sent to him to read,
prepared everything for the day's work, picked up pages discarded
the previous day, typed, and translated foreign texts as Gorky needed.
She knew how to listen attentively and silently, seated on the couch
while he sat at his desk, looking at him with her intelligent, thoughtful eyes. If he asked what she thought about this or that—Issay
Dobrowen's music, Gumilev's translations, Blok's poetry, the wrongs
Zinoviev was inflicting on him—she knew how to answer. She suspected she was the cause of Zinoviev's mounting hatred for Gorky,
that Zinoviev knew all about her, and that Gorky did, too.

Khodasevich wrote:

> When, why, and how Gorky and Zinoviev became enemies, I do
> not know. Possibly there were old scores dating back to before
> the revolution; possibly the enmity arose in 1917 or 1918, when
> Gorky was publishing *New Life*, a newspaper partly in opposi-
> tion to the Leninist line that the Soviet government shut down
> at the same time as the rest of the opposition press. In any case,
> by the autumn of 1920, when I moved from Moscow to Peters-
> burg, matters had not progressed so far as all-out war, but
> Zinoviev was trying to harm Gorky wherever and however he
> could. People under arrest whom Gorky tried to help would
> sometimes find themselves in greater jeopardy than they had
> been before he had interceded on their behalf. Provisions, fuel,
> and clothing that Gorky worked hard to obtain for scholars,
> writers, and artists would be commandeered on Zinoviev's
> orders and distributed to some other unidentified agency. Seek-
> ing Lenin's protection, Gorky telephoned him time and again,
> wrote him letters, and even traveled to Moscow to make a per-
> sonal appeal. No one could deny that Lenin tried to help, but he

never went so far as to rein Zinoviev in, because although he valued Gorky as a writer, Zinoviev was a tested Bolshevik whom he needed even more. In a recent magazine article, a scholar reminisced with naïve emotion about the time he and Gorky were at one of Lenin's receptions and Lenin warmly urged Gorky to go abroad for rest and treatment. I remember very well how that advice disappointed and annoyed Gorky, who thought Lenin just wanted to get rid of someone who was persistently interceding for "enemies" and lodging complaints against Zinoviev. For his part, Zinoviev never relented. The minor victories Gorky achieved from time to time may have even fueled his energy. His audacity reached the point that his agents would open and inspect Gorky's correspondence, including letters from Lenin himself. Lenin sometimes sent these letters in envelopes that were sewn around the edges with thread and sealed together at the ends with wax. And yet Zinoviev still somehow managed to read them. Gorky himself told me so. Shortly before my arrival, Zinoviev subjected Gorky's apartment and its colorful inhabitants to a general search. At the same time reports reached Gorky to the effect that Zinoviev was threatening to arrest certain people close to him. Whom did he have in mind? Doubtless Grzhebin and Tikhonov, but all too likely he was contemplating one more blow—right at Gorky's heart, you might say.

Here Khodasevich is alluding to Moura.

She regarded her future coolly and soberly, with the same equanimity she had felt when she had appraised herself and her circumstances, knowing she was strong enough to struggle, even with those in power. In this way, too, she delighted Gorky and became dearer to him by the day. Where did she get such strength, he wondered, at the same time despising his own weakness, knowing he could do nothing, or almost nothing, to help her. A world-famous name? But could a name really save anyone in Russia now? Powerful friends? But such men would renounce all friendship in their ironclad commitment to the realization of their idea. Gorky knew something about Moura, but not a lot: he knew about Lockhart, about Peters, about her friendship with Mosolov (who had been picked up on the street and had vanished, his apartment looted). She did not tell Gorky everything, of course, and he thought the murder of Benckendorff and her separation from her children was the most significant fact of her life. He asked her to tell him more about her children, whom she hadn't seen in more that two years, an unacceptable state of affairs. She needed to get out of Russia. She needed to get back to them.

Gorky loved to listen to her stories. He always liked hearing about the lives of people whose existence and way of life were so different from his own and from those in his immediate circle, the old revolutionary underground, the current party with its intrigues and alarms. She had had a brief, idle, and elegant youth, which had collapsed at the first blow of the punishing ax. He had had two marriages, arrests, deportation, world fame. And now there was his declining health, the long-neglected tuberculosis that even the air of Capri couldn't help, and the persistent cough of the inveterate smoker.

There were iron men and iron women, but he was not one of them. He was spitting blood, and his teeth were falling out. He was only fifty-two, but, as he was told, he was a man of the last century, when old age set in at fifty. And it was the previous century speaking in him when he sized her up, this woman of iron: That's how she is, afraid of nothing, going her own way day after day, and she can't be broken by Zinoviev, or the Cheka, or the fact that her husband was beaten to death and her children are God only knows where. A woman. She should be in lace looking at him with rapt eyes, waiting for him to decide her fate, but she was not waiting for him to give her anything at all, nor was she asking for anything. Not that he had anything to offer.

Sometimes she would take a cigarette and, inhaling deeply, gaze into a dark corner of the room and listen to the sounds in the house: Andreeva leaving for the theater with Kryuchkov, the Diederichs with a visitor, the clattering of dishes, Molecule humming to herself while reading a book. It was warm and cozy and homey there. She hadn't known that feeling before—not as a child, not in London, not in Berlin, not in Revel, not even in Moscow. With Lockhart in Moscow her own nonchalance had frightened her at times. *His* nonchalance, on the other hand, had made her happy. It was only while listening to the Gypsies, when the singer began in her low wail to sing about love and suffering, that thoughts of all this coming to an end, that suspicions about the future, had crossed her mind. His hand had rested in her hand, his light eyes had looked into her dark eyes, they were drinking wine and talking, talking, talking about their love. Robert Bruce. To her, Bruce. At home in England, Bob. Now he was home, with his wife and son. And she was here. But she knew that life at Gorky's, though comfortable, was false; comfort had never really helped anyone. She would leave, she knew that. She would leave to be with him.

"What are you thinking about?" the man with the glasses and the droopy red mustache sitting at his desk would ask. They always used the formal "you" and addressed each other by name and patronymic. And she would answer pensively: "My children."

But these cozy intervals (minutes, not hours) were rare. Usually there was a crowd in the dining room in lively conversation for hours around the samovar, or Dobrowen playing the piano, or Chaliapin singing, or Gorky either reading or secluded in his office with Grzhebin, or Christie, or Kryuchkov. Gorky was often sick during the years 1918 through 1921, and he aged a great deal. He coughed up blood but had grown used to it, and attached no special significance to it. He smoked constantly and drank quite a lot, though no one ever saw him drunk. He drank when there was something to drink, and when everyone else was drinking. No one thought that harmful anymore than they thought of smoking as harmful.

The closing of *New Life* had been a blow to Gorky's personal relationship with Lenin, and their friendship of so many years' standing had hit its lowest point. Only Kaplan's attempt on Lenin's life made Gorky go back and reevaluate Lenin. When Lenin recovered from his wounds, relations between them became friendly again, although they never regained their former level of mutual trust. But with Zinoviev there was no rapprochement. Gorky had no reason to forgive him for anything, and clearly Zinoviev's hostility toward Gorky would never abate, for two reasons. First, as the person closest to Lenin, Zinoviev could not bear the thought that Gorky might take his place in the great man's heart. The second reason was Moura, about whom he knew everything. He felt sure she was working for British intelligence, and that became the pretext for searching the house on Kronverk, which was humiliating for Gorky and dangerous for everyone living there.

Nothing was taken. As a formality they opened the Diederichs' and Rakitsky's bookcases and chests of drawers. They spent a short time in Molecule's room, where drawings by Malevich and Tatlin hung on the wall. The rooms of Andreeva and Kryuchkov, who were out of the house that day, were left untouched. But they spent two hours rifling through Moura's linens and papers, dresses and books, while she, very pale and afraid of losing her fortitude and dropping the thread she had been clinging to all these months, leaned against the door jamb and smoked herself into a stupor, now and then pushing back with icy hands the dark locks of hair that fell over her forehead and ears, watching herself the whole time, and feeling a certain joy that her hands weren't trembling.

No one was more disturbed, upset, and outraged by the search than Gorky himself. He left for Moscow immediately to demand an end to Zinoviev's persecution and harassment.

Gorky had come to feel that his wholly friendly and constructive criticism of the Bolsheviks, coming as it did from one of their own (he had been with them since 1903, which anyone who wasn't blind could see), was being unfairly perceived as a hostile attack. The Terror horrified him, because it was reality, and, as he was fond of saying, he did not like reality; he liked pretty dreams and illusions that brought tears to his eyes and a lump to his throat. It is strange, given his rejection of mysticism, that he thought that if you believe wholeheartedly in an illusion it can cease to be an illusion and become real: man is God and there is no limit to what he can achieve, because he possesses reason. And reason—in this he was adamant—is all-powerful, it has only to be developed, elevated, cultivated. But how could this collective and therefore immortal reason be reconciled with facts like the dissolving of the Constituent Assembly? The executions in the Peter-Paul Fortress? The summary liquidation of thousands of hostages after the murder of Uritsky? Gorky may have had a tendency to blind fanaticism in his youth, and there is no question that he became fanatical in his old age after 1930, but during the early years of Soviet power Gorky was not a fanatic.

He had always been a fanatic about one subject: enlightenment, the dissemination of knowledge. And not just scientific knowledge but art, literature, and poetry—activities in which the human spirit seeks not profit but beauty, not practical utility but the creativity of genius, not knowledge for its own sake but for the joyful awareness of one's own freedom and one's own powers, and the wonderful possibility of self-expression.

He held the firm conviction, instilled in him by reading Chernyshevsky and Dobrolyubov, that a writer (and he decided he would become a writer) has a pedagogical mission and that a work of art has a conscious purpose, existing to serve progress, to improve the world on all three levels of human existence: mental development, moral perfection, and economic well-being. These three levels covered all of mankind's needs and gave every person the right to be called a Man. Baudelaire's poetry, Shakespeare's tragedies, Beethoven's sonatas, Rembrandt's paintings, right up to Flaubert's novels and Chekhov's stories—all these were the direct result of a conscious intention to serve a useful purpose. He drew no distinction between art and its utilitarian counterfeit, nor could he have: he couldn't imagine a work of art not designed to improve one of the three levels of human existence. All his life he preferred Semyon Podyachev to Vyacheslav Ivanov and Nikolai Yaroshenko to Cézanne. For a while, in the 1920s, his inclinations embarrassed him, and for the first time he began to think about artistic questions. He listened to what the people around him—poets and every kind of artist in the visual and performing arts—were talking and arguing about. It seems incredible nowadays, but with his questions he was actually seeking artistic advice about what he should do and what he should think. By the 1930s he had stopped learning and was no longer embarrassed about anything, nor was he interested in revising his ideas. He wrote thirty volumes but he never understood that literature offers only an indirect answer to life, that art involves play and mystery, that there is a riddle in art that has nothing to do with flaying an opponent, humorless glorification, righteous living, or radical convictions. That riddle is as impossible to explain to someone who has not experienced it as it would be to explain a rainbow to someone blind from birth or an orgasm to a virgin. Or the Sermon on the Mount to an orangutan or the power of the First Amendment to the U.S. Constitution to someone who mourned the death of Stalin.

Intellectual life in Petrograd revived in 1920. Not only were the House of Scholars and the House of Arts opened, but so were the House of Letters and the Zubov Institute of Art History. Books of poetry appeared with covers designed by Mstislav Dobuzhinsky, painstakingly produced and set in the Elizabethan typeface. Poems. At Universal Literature Moura got to know some of the poets writing them: men in patched pants and secondhand sweaters and army shirts, women in capes and velvet hats with feathers. It was as if they had borrowed costumes from the wardrobe of the Alexandrinsky Theater.

Alexander Blok stopped by and sat down in the editorial office next to Moura's typewriter. "I walked over here from Pryazhka," he explained, as if he had to justify his presence, "to give you this. This is for you. I'm finding it hard to write now, but this was something that had to be written. Of course it's nothing special. But there is something to it."

It was Blok's *Gray Morning*, just published. She opened the slim volume in its yellow cover. On the first page a poem had been written out on a blank sheet in a firm, round hand:

> You were not meant for me, it seems.
> Why did you come into my dreams?
> It happened in a dream one night:
> Thus of his Lady dreams a Knight,
> A fallen soldier sees his foe,
> A man in exile—home fire's glow,
> A captain sees the ocean waves,
> A maiden—morning's rosy haze. . . .
> But my dream was incomparable,
> Inexplicable, unrepeatable,
> And should it come again and start,
> The blood would not regain my heart. . . .
> And I myself do not know why
> I'm telling you this dream of mine,
> And why these useless words and lines,
> Aren't to oblivion consigned.

She kept that little book. Later she took it with her to Estonia, were she left it, just as she left all her papers, all her letters from

Sorrento, London, Prague, Tallinn, Zagreb, Paris, addressed to her wherever she had lived during twenty years of wandering from country to country. And everything burned at the end of World War II, when the Soviet army occupied the cities and countryside! Whether the fires were started by Soviet bombs or by the retreating German army was not always clear, but either way, all her papers went up in flames.

Gorky returned from Moscow empty-handed, with no reassurance that the searches would stop or that he would ever be allowed to have a newspaper again. He was coughing badly at night, and he ran a temperature every day. Dr. Manukhin, who was once a member of the Bolshevik party and who treated him for many years, had recently made a medical breakthrough in the treatment of tuberculosis and was subjecting his spleen to high doses of X-rays. Most doctors in Russia considered that quackery, but Manukhin had saved his life many times, Gorky said, adding that in 1914 he had even defended Dr. Manukhin in print. In the 1930s, when Manukhin was an émigré, he continued giving X-ray treatments, but the French doctors shut down his practice. In Paris he was known as a frequent visitor at the Russian Orthodox cathedral on the rue Daru.

Gorky returned to Petrograd and began talking about women, the new women. He had always spoken tenderly of women, but now he was saying that iron coursed through their veins and that they were in some ways far ahead of men. He had always spoken about the courageous Ekaterina Peshkova, his first wife and Maxim's mother, whom he had divorced in 1904, as if she were something fragile and precious, although Peshkova was nothing of the kind. She accepted their divorce "without hysterics," she was a "progressive" woman and a member of the Socialist Revolutionary Party, but he, too, after all, was no outdated reactionary, bound by the patriarchal past! He had left Peshkova with two children (their daughter died in 1906), but she did not cry; she was "hard." He had left her because he had met

Andreeva, a woman who, to the horror of Petersburg society, had left
her family, her husband and children, and the Stanislavsky Theater to
join Lenin's party, and then, for Gorky, she left the stage as well. If
anything she seemed even harder. The outlook he had inherited was a
thousand, no, a hundred thousand years old: a woman should be obedient, submissive, the reflection of a man. But the women around
him—Molecule, Valentina, Moura—had no wish to be a reflection of
anyone. They knew what they wanted—to survive on their own
terms—and they made Gorky feel weak and lost. His ancestors had
reached for the switch, the knout, the poker. His grandfather had
beaten his grandmother; his father had raised his hand against his
mother. But he couldn't even raise his voice when Moura told Gorky
she would leave without him, that she would not wait for him and
would go alone if necessary. The last thing in the world he could say
to her was, "I will not let you go." Words like "I'll protect you and
keep you safe, I won't let anyone harm you" sounded unreal: if he
was unable to get what he wanted in Moscow, then he was in no position to protect her. What was even stranger, Moura seemed not to
expect anything from him; she was not asking him to protect her,
keep her safe, shield her. She looked away whenever he asked, "So
what have you decided?" She would not answer. A well-wound mech-
anism was at work inside her that he did not understand very well
and never would. He gave Moura a penetrating look and, unaware
that Vyazemsky's "Bronze Venus" was not her great-grandmother,
said:

"You're not bronze, you're iron. Nothing in the world is stronger
than iron."

"We're all iron now," she replied. "Would you like us to be lace?"

The house was thrown into turmoil when a telegram arrived for
Gorky from Herbert Wells. The famous English writer wired to say
that he was "coming to have a look at Russia." He had welcomed the
February Revolution, and the October Revolution, too; he had

declared to all the world his enthusiasm, both in print and in personal correspondence, for the signing of the peace treaty at Brest-Litovsk. Russia had proved smarter than all the rest: she was the first to escape that slaughterhouse. Now he was writing his "old friend Maxim Gorky," expressing his admiration for the new Russia, which was showing the world the way and serving as an example for everyone: overthrow the tsars and don't make war! In England he was free to say what he wanted. Russia had the wisdom to put an end to a senseless war. His last book, *Mr. Britling Sees It Through*, had come out in translation and been enormously successful among Russian readers; his earlier books, too, were read by all literate Russians in the early twentieth century. It is worth noting the three men who came together in the publication of *Mr. Britling* in Russia: Wells wrote it, Gorky printed it in his journal *Chronicle*, and the translator was Lockhart's close friend Mikhail Lykiardopoulos. From 1912 to 1917 "Lyki," as Lockhart and his friends called him, worked for intelligence and, posing as a Greek merchant in 1915 and 1916, traveled to Germany. Evidently he was involved not only with Russian military espionage but also the British Secret Service (he knew six languages well); in 1918 he turned up in England, where he lived and worked the rest of his life without having any further contact with his former Russian friends who were émigrés.

Gorky met Wells for the first time in 1906 in the United States, at a banquet given for Gorky by Gaylord Wilshire, the editor and publisher of *Wilshire's Magazine*. They had read each others' work in translation; their correspondence, especially after their second meeting in London in 1907 (Gorky was there for the Fifth Congress of the Communist Party and the two of them were guests at the same society party), was friendly and steady, if not terribly frequent. When Gorky received the telegram he explained to Wells that there were no hotels in Petrograd—that is, the buildings were still standing, but they were empty, the hotel staff had been mobilized and was finishing off General Yudenich, and there was no electric lighting or bed linen. There was nothing to eat; nor were there any restaurants. It would be better if Wells stayed in some private home, with him, for example, on Kronverk. Wells gladly consented, writing that he would come with his son, spend two or three days, and then make a trip to Moscow to speak with Lenin, whom he'd long wanted to meet.

So Wells came, accompanied by his oldest son, Gip. Wells was ruddy-faced, portly and wore a tweed jacket. Petrograd, which he called Petersburg and had once visited in 1914, entranced him. He was happy to see Gorky and Andreeva, whom he remembered from America and whom he called "Madame Andereyevna." The House of Arts organized a dinner in his honor at the Eliseev mansion (on the corner of Nevsky and Morskaya); the food was meager, but the Eliseev servants and the Eliseev silver and crockery saved the day. Wells immediately won everyone over with his intellect, jolly conversation, quick gestures, and readiness to accept absolutely everything with unconcealed enthusiasm. If there was any grumbling that evening, it was only from a few malcontents who managed to get invited despite attempts to exclude them; they maliciously showed up intending to protest to Wells about how they had been treated and the desperate straits in which they found themselves. They even tried to undress (not in front of the ladies) to show Wells the state of their underclothing and, while they were at it, the skin stretched tight over their ribs from lack of food. But if they tried to say something in their perfect English, French, or German—or Italian, in Akim Volynsky's case—they were quickly and firmly ejected. It was explained to Wells that due to a misunderstanding some relics from the accursed past had crashed the party, but he should pay them no mind.

Moura interpreted from Russian to English and English to Russian for days on end. This was especially hard for her at the meetings of the Petrograd Soviet to which Wells had been invited. Somewhat surprising is the fact that she was officially assigned to him by the Kremlin, as Wells later wrote. Gip, who was not quite twenty, had studied Russian and knew the language: Wells had persuaded an English school in Oundle to offer Russian classes for the first time in England, and he had sent Gip there. Before their departure Gip had also taken private lessons from S. S. Koteliansky, the translator and friend of Virginia and Leonard Woolf.

Gip tried to give Moura what help he could, but Nightingale and Valentina immediately hooked him up with a young crowd, and he was away from Kronverk from morning to night. He was interested in everything. Wells sat with Gorky in his office during the day, Moura perched between them, and their conversations—about the future education of the uneducated, the brotherhood of nations, the uses of technology to conquer nature, and world peace—went on for hours. In the evening the conversation continued at the tea table. In Gorky's dining room Wells met Pavlov, Zamyatin, Chukovsky, and Chaliapin. The two or three days he'd intended to be there stretched into two weeks. Wells went to the Hermitage, to Smolny, to *Othello* at the Bolshoi Dramatic Theater, to the harbor—in short, everywhere—and made repeated trips to Nevsky Prospect to view the boarded-up stores. He took a walk on Vasilievsky Island, where rows of wooden houses had been razed and chopped up for fuel. He took an interest in what was being written about in the newspaper *The Life of Art*. He asked to be taken to number 2 Gorokhovaya to have a look at how that famous institution, the Cheka, worked.

But that was one place Moura did not take him.

Gorky and Wells's two previous meetings in New York and London had allowed them to become acquainted but they had never had a long, undisturbed conversation. They held each other's books and politics in high esteem: they had a common desire to remake the world and improve man and the conditions of his life; they shared a belief in reason and the march toward progress, by force if necessary. In 1908 Gorky was planning to rewrite *Faust*, and during World War I,

Wells was planning to rewrite world history, to give it a new interpretation—from creation to the modern age, which was bringing the world to an end and culture to its demise. The two writers agreed that their role was to try to prevent that from happening. Both of them had always believed that only knowledge and universal enlightenment could halt the decline of civilization and rescue mankind and that they were the ones to lead mankind down that path. The idea of a universal encyclopedia seemed a panacea for all evils not only to Gorky but also to Wells.

Wells remembered going to a session of the State Duma at the Tauride Palace in 1914 with the ever faithful Maurice Baring. Wells had been shocked and angered by the huge portrait of Nicholas II hanging in the Russian parliament. He couldn't believe his eyes: The Tsar in the parliament? Why was he there? What did he and a parliament have in common? He saw Russia as the "last outpost of humanity," a nation of "frozen savagery," and his esteem for Gorky rose even more. He formed a high opinion of Gorky's *In the World*, the second volume of his autobiographical trilogy, when it came out in English translation in 1917, and Gorky, who was reading *Mr. Britling Sees It Through* at approximately the same time, wrote Wells an ecstatic letter:

> [Late December 1916–early January 1917],
> Parus Publishers
> 18 Monetnaya, Petrograd.

To H. G. Wells
Dear Friend!

I have just finished reading the proofs of the Russian translation of your latest book, *Mr. Britling*, and want to express my admiration, what a fine book you have written! It is beyond doubt the best, boldest, most just and humane book written in Europe during this accursed war! I am sure that after this is over, when we become more humane again, England will be proud that the first voice of protest against the brutalities of war, and such an energetic protest at that, rang out in England, and all honest and intelligent people will utter your name with gratitude. It is a book which will live for many years to come. You are a great and fine person, Wells, and I am so happy to have seen you, to be able to recall your face, your splendid eyes. Perhaps I'm expressing all this rather primitively, but I simply want to tell you that in this time of universal barbarism and brutality your book stands out as a great and truly humane work.

You have written a fine book, Wells, and I cordially shake your hand and love you very much for it....

Devotedly yours,
Maxim Gorky

By the end of his second week in Petrograd, Wells suddenly felt depressed, not so much from the conversations and meetings as from the city itself. He talked about it with Moura. He vaguely remembered her from before the war in London, before she left for Berlin with Benckendorff. They had met a few times at parties given by their mutual friend Maurice Baring, but for some reason he could not remember Benckendorff at all. He remembered her before her marriage, too. They had been introduced at a ball at the home of the Russian ambassador in London, Count Alexander Benckendorff, by the ambassador's regal wife. That was nine years ago. She was twenty then. Now he confided in her, describing the strange moments of depression which he hadn't known before and which, when he was alone, seeped or insinuated themselves into his memories of the old Petersburg, insignificant memories, but dear to him and which his first few days here had revived. He was glad to be able to talk to her about those increasingly frequent "dark spots" in his mood. He could not talk about such things with his "old friend"—how horribly sad he felt looking at the buildings and monuments, the bridges and churches. Did this make any sense? After all, everything could easily be painted and spruced up, and most assuredly they would do just that. Yet it all seemed irreparably spoiled to him, all the beauty of the city he had so admired before that damned world catastrophe of 1914. And the enthusiasm, the uplift, the feeling of celebration when the revolution was victorious had somehow faded.

But she, being iron, did not join him in mourning the Russian past, nor did she share his joy when he spoke to her about the bright future that awaited mankind with Russia leading the way. Moura had an innate ability to make everything hard easier and everything terrible not as bad as it seemed, not so much for herself or other women but for men, who, she knew, liked her. She took Wells on walks, flashing her sly, gentle smile, along the embankment of the Neva, and to Saint Isaac's Cathedral, which was already being turned into a museum of atheism, and to the Summer Garden. There the leaves were falling with a light rustle, gold and red, on overgrown paths that were now deserted.

He thought about staying on, but when he reached Moscow on October 12, he saw that there was no point remaining there for long. In Moscow there was no one to sit with quietly and carry on long, witty, utopian conversations of the kind he was accustomed to having in his London club over a bottle of vintage port, where everyone, starting with G. K. Chesterton, was a marvelous and diverting companion. His attempt to have such a conversation with Lenin was quite futile. Wells had been given a pass to the Kremlin and an appointment had been made. Before that he visited museums and took a look around the city. Immediately after his meeting with Lenin on October 15, Wells took a train back to Petrograd. In *Russia in the Shadows*, Wells called Lenin "the Kremlin dreamer," while Lenin told Trotsky that Wells was a "petit bourgeois." Attempts were made to entertain the English visitor, but in vain, and Wells left disappointed by the Russians' inability to carry on a conversation.

Wells slept well in Kronverk that night, and woke up refreshed the next day. He roamed through the city again, stopping by KUBU, the Commission for Improving Living Conditions for Academics, which in those years was housed in the Marble Palace, on Millionnaya Street. He heard there that Russian academics were in desperate need of lard and flour, without which they would not survive the coming winter. Every day he learned something new—he was avid for the new and loved to learn. Moura translated strange phrases for him which meant nothing to him even in English. What was the "consolidation of living space for intellectual workers," or the significance of the kerosene petition being sent to Zinoviev's office? And why all the heated discussion of snow removal duties and confiscation of ration cards for university professors who did not report with a shovel on their assigned day? These were boring details of Soviet daily life whose significance he failed to grasp.

On the eve of his and Gip's departure, their hosts gave a farewell supper at Kronverk, and, through a connection at a food depot, some bottles of wine were found to throw a proper send-off for their renowned guest. Everyone in the household was there except Molecule, who was visiting relatives. Moura, who had moved into Molecule's room on the day Wells arrived and had been sleeping on the ottoman, now had the room and bed to herself. They dispersed late after the supper, in a merry mood. It was about one in the morning when Moura went to bed. The wine, the conversation, the unusual food (they managed to find five tins of sardines, they made potato salad, and their connection had supplied excellent cheese and three big jars of stuffed peppers), and Wells's promise to stop in Tallinn on his way to London to see her children and write to her about them (by diplomatic pouch)—all this kept her from falling asleep right away. She was thinking about how he was free to go wherever he wished, to come here and return home as he liked, while she was stuck waiting, though no one else knew it, for the day the

Gulf of Finland would freeze over (probably early in December) so that she could escape to the West over the ice. She finally fell asleep around two.

She awoke with a start. Someone was definitely in the room. She reached out and turned the switch at the head of her bed. The light went on and the dining-room clock chimed simultaneously—it was constantly chiming, it was an antique clock, but in her half sleep the absurd thought flashed through her mind that the chiming of the clock was somehow connected with turning on the light, and she immediately switched it off to stop the chiming. But she managed to catch a glimpse of Wells standing at the foot of her bed.

In the gossipy atmosphere of Gorky's house, where everything was subject to collective discussion, and where both the witticisms and the jokes—sometimes even at the expense of the master of the house himself—touched not only on the ordinary mundane details of household life but also on the personal lives of all who lived there, what happened that night inspired fantastic variations for many years to come: Tortured by insomnia, Wells paced through the apartment for hours and finally decided to look in on Moura to have a farewell chat with her. Or: consumed with passion, Wells tore off Moura's blanket, she gave him a swift kick and sent him flying out into the hall, and he wove his way back to his room, to his cold bed, with a bump on his forehead as a result of slamming into the door jamb. Or: she invited him in to sit on the couch; they smoked and talked a little, and, when he saw that Moura had fallen asleep, Wells tiptoed back to his room. There was a fourth variation... or was there? Probably not. Everyone knew that Moura had not chased him away and that he had sat cozily on her couch in his pajamas (which had just come into fashion then in England; Gip had brought a pair for Maxim). The story inspired endless jokes and witty comments, but an invisible line was drawn that could not be crossed.

Life resumed its normal course. Moura was working both at

Universal Literature and at home, running the household and accommodating the guests. Arrangements were being made for Gorky to take a trip abroad the next year, in 1921. His health was not good, and it was clear to everyone that if he stayed in Russia he would only get worse. Lenin was telling him the same thing, and advised him to go. Andreeva and Peshkova, who came from Moscow, agreed. Both of them spoke with Gorky about how it might be a good idea for everyone to spend some time abroad. It was decided that Maxim would become a diplomatic courier, which would allow him to spend time in Germany and Italy.

But Moura was not willing to wait. The Neva had already frozen over, and in three weeks or so the gulf would freeze as well. Everyone was walking around the apartment with blankets thrown over their shoulders, and in the evening they sat by the stove. She sat there, too, and thought about leaving.

Despite the fact that officially Moura went by her married name of Benckendorff (she was Zakrevskaya only to Gorky and Universal Literature), which presumably might have helped her prove Estonian citizenship (Estonia received its independence after the Versailles conference and was no longer connected in any way with Russia), leaving legally was no longer an option. The government deadline for declaring an intention to leave the country after forfeiting Russian citizenship had already passed. Those with the right of option—French, Greeks, Poles, Balts—had long since been repatriated. These were people who not only had lived most of their lives in Russia but in many cases had even been born there; nevertheless, they had all left for their "homeland," and Moura had missed her opportunity.

She left in December, and of course everyone knew where she was going. How she was caught and ended up at Cheka headquarters in Petrograd she never did say. "It was slippery and cold. It was dark." Even, "It was frightening." On that moonless night, the group of five she was with, led by Estonians to the Estonian shore, not far from the mouth of the Narova River, could not have gotten lost. But a Soviet border guard happened to look down from a high bank when he should have been looking elsewhere. When the call came from Gorokhovaya, Gorky went straight to the Petrograd Cheka. The officer in charge was Uritsky's deputy, Gleb Boky. A telegram was sent to Moscow, addressed to Comrade Dzerzhinsky. Gorky's first wife, Peshkova, an old friend and great admirer of Dzerzhinsky's (it was through her that Maxim got his job in the Cheka), interceded. "Thanks to Gorky's efforts, Moura was released," as Khodasevich put it succinctly. Dzerzhinsky gave her permission to leave the country.

The details of her journey in January 1921 are not known. At the time people were still leaving Petrograd by way of Finland. During those months the situation in the Baltic was different than it had been in the summer of 1918, when Moura told Lockhart she was going to see her children, but there still were no passenger trains running from Petrograd when Moura left Kronverk. Only in Estonia itself, fifty kilometers from the Russian border, was she able to board a train that would take her to Tallinn.

Over the first few months of 1921 the rest of the Kronverk household gradually realized that soon they all might end up in Europe. Lenin was writing Gorky from Moscow, telling him, "Leave!" and adding with ambiguous humor: "Or else we'll exile you."

Everyone knew he would leave, but they were unsure—as he doubtless was himself—whether Moura would wait for him in Estonia in the hope of meeting him nearby. It was anyone's guess. Had the night with Wells given them grounds to doubt her feelings for Duke? Gorky prepared for his departure. Andreeva had been appointed to the Berlin Trade Office and was to move there in the spring with Kryuchkov. Maxim, who was about to get married, was expecting notification of his assignment any day. It was decided that Nightingale would go to Germany with Andreeva and Peppycrew, and work in the Trade Office with them as an expert in antiques and art. The certainty that Nightingale would look after his son gave Gorky some peace of mind. Maxim's immaturity, or rather what seemed to be his prolonged adolescence, had started to worry Gorky in earnest. He hoped Nightingale and Maxim's bride would take him in hand. Maxim had married the daughter of a Moscow University professor, Alexei Vvedensky, a school friend of Chaliapin's daughter Lydia, in whose home she and Maxim had met.

Gorky had plenty of other things to worry about: business affairs at Universal Literature and the other institutions he had created (if only Zinoviev wouldn't shut them down after his departure!); the New Economic Policy that Lenin was planning to introduce; the Futurists; the starving population on the Volga, where there were reports of cannibalism; the poverty in the cities; the dying out of the intelligentsia in the capital; and his own financial circumstances. What would he live on in Europe? Would his royalties be enough? Would he be able to sit down right away and start writing? What was the significance of the fluctuations in the currencies of the various European countries, both victorious and vanquished? And, ignore them as he might, there were his own health problems: he was getting thin, his heart was weakening, he was coughing up blood, and he had trouble sleeping. Gloomy thoughts crept into his mind: another year or two without paper, grain, meat, milk, soles for shoes, and electric lights, and Russian culture would perish—just as it was beginning to blossom, it would surely perish. There would be nothing left.

Moura got off the train at Tallinn (as the old Revel was now called), the capital of Estonia (not Estland, as it was known before the revolution), at the end of January. It was a clear day, and ahead of her lay the meeting with her children and Missy: she had learned from Wells's October letter that they were alive. The city seemed gay to her, elegant, European somehow, filled with white bread and fragrant toilet soap, people, shops, and newspapers. She glanced around, casting her eyes over the town square as she walked off the last step of the station porch, followed by a porter carrying her old prewar suitcase. She hailed a cab, but then two men in black uniforms took her by both arms from either side. "You're under arrest," a voice said in perfect Russian, and she was pushed into a carriage with its hood raised. Her suitcase was placed at her feet. One policeman sat next to her, and the other jumped onto the box. He grasped her elbow firmly in his hand. She couldn't find the words, at least not right away, to ask "Why?" or "What for?" She said, "Everything is in order."

"What is in order exactly?" the policeman asked derisively, and she responded: "My documents, my visa, my ticket, my letter of permission, the money I took out legally." She tried not to hurry and to separate her words with commas.

He said there would be an interrogation, that she had violated the law and therefore was under arrest. And that now she should keep quiet.

She did. At the police station she was put in a clean cell that smelled of disinfectant. A woman came and searched her, frisking her all over. Then she demanded the key to her suitcase, opened it, and shook everything out. But what was there? Two nightgowns, her last holey stockings, shoes with pointed toes like those worn in 1913, a piece of English soap Gip had given her as a present just before his departure, a few trifles. Then she was left alone in her worn fur coat and the hat Valentina had made her out of a scrap of old beaver fur. She sat like that until three o'clock, when they brought her food: meat soup with a dollop of fat, a piece of white bread, and a boiled potato, buttered and sprinkled with dill. All of it seemed very tasty to her and for a while she decided the future wasn't so frightening after all.

Then she was led in for interrogation. She learned a good deal about herself: she had worked for Peters at the Cheka; she had lived with Peters; she had lived with the Bolshevik Gorky; she had been sent to Estonia as a Soviet spy. (In Estonia she was accused of being a Soviet spy; in Lockhart's entourage she was assumed to be working

for British intelligence; after emigrating in the 1930s she was said to
be a German spy, just as Peters had written about her in 1924.)[1] She
also learned that when news had reached Tallinn a week earlier of her
plans to come to Estonia, the brother and sister of her late husband,
Ivan Benckendorff, supported by other Benckendorff relatives (the
Shillings, Shellings, and von Shullers), had appealed to the Estonian
Supreme Court that she be deported immediately to Petrograd and
forbidden to see the children. Trembling, Moura told the investigator
that she wanted a lawyer.

The investigator did not object. In silence he drew a sheet of paper
from his desk drawer and handed it to her. It was a list of attorneys in
Tallinn typed in the old orthography, clearly from the prerevolutionary period. Some of the names had been crossed out with purple ink.
She ran her fingers over the names, mouthing them silently as she read
them slowly to herself.

The names were Russian, German, and Jewish. She was afraid
of the Russians; they could be friends and associates of General Yudenich, men who despised Gorky and would likely be prejudiced

---

1. To my knowledge, Moura's name appeared in the Soviet press—as a German secret agent
and a woman with a generally "shady" past—only once in sixty years: in the journal *Proletarian Revolution* (no. 10, 1924: 28–29). In "Memoirs of Cheka Work During the First Year
of the Revolution," chapter four of *The Lockhart Affair*, Peters writes:

> I have already said that Lockhart was immediately released after his first arrest, but
> arrested along with him was Baroness [!] Benckendorff, his lover. A few days after
> Lockhart's release he turned up at the office of the deputy people's commissar for for-
> eign affairs, Comrade Karakhan, informing him that he wished to speak with me not
> in my official capacity but man to man. I gave my consent, and Lockhart came to see
> me at the Cheka. Walking into my office, he was quite embarrassed. He told me that
> he was on intimate terms with Baroness Benckendorff and would like to request her
> release. I did not recount this story at the trial because it could have been extremely
> dangerous for Lockhart's career—Baroness Benckendorff, according to the confes-
> sion of another detainee and to documents found with Prince P., had been a German
> spy during the imperialist war.

against her. It was too terrible a time, even lawyers could not remain dispassionate. She knew the German names, few in number and every one of them a member of the Livonian nobility, the Teutonic Order, crusaders who had sat on their lands on the shores of the Baltic Sea since the thirteenth century. There were very few of them because the Teutonic Order had not entered the free professions but had served in the guards, the ministries, and the State Council. They all seemed to be related to the Benckendorffs by blood or marriage. That left the Jews. The names didn't mean anything to her. Before the revolution she hadn't known any Jews, not one, and there were no Jewish girls at her boarding school. Nor had she met any Jews at the Russian embassies in London or Berlin. At Gorky's she had met Zinovy Grzhebin, and someone had told her that Chukovsky was a Jew. Rodé was Romanian; Christie, a Greek. She found herself thinking that all was lost, that no lawyer could save her now. And then there were no more names. There was a grayish strip and she pointed to it cautiously.

"Which one? Rabinovich? Rubenstein?"

She was taken back to her cell and she fell asleep without undressing. That night she took a drink of water from the tap and rejoiced that her watch was still on her wrist. Yes, the ticking of the watch made things easier to bear. But not much.

Toward evening the next day she was taken to a different room. A guard was sitting in the corner, armed to the teeth, his sullen face young and pimply. The lawyer walked in, threw open his fur coat, and unwound a long, elegant silk scarf.

After that it was as if an empty train car had come detached and suddenly started rolling down the tracks on its own. The injunction against seeing her children was lifted on the third day, and so was the threat of deportation back to Russia. They accepted her written promise not to leave Estonia and let her go. The lawyer who had posted bail for her arrived at the last minute to give her some important information.

"First, you will be followed. You will be tailed from morning to night and then at night, too," he said quickly and softly. "Second, they are willing to give you permission to be here for three months, but then you'll have to leave because it's doubtful they will grant an extension. Third, none of your friends will invite you to their homes and none will come to yours. And they will not acknowledge you on the street. A boycott. They will ignore you. Absolutely. It would be good to change your name and get out of town, go to the country. Or try to get a visa for somewhere in Czechoslovakia. No, not Czechoslovakia. Switzerland. No, they won't let you in there either." Suddenly he broke off in confusion and grew thoughtful. "Maybe the best thing you could do would be to get married."

Something flashed across his face—sympathy, pity, or momentary melancholy? Then he left. She collected her things and walked out to the street where a carriage was waiting for her. She stepped in, and they set out over deserted cobblestone streets, wheels clattering, for the address where she knew Missy was living with the children. It was the old Benckendorff mansion, which had been partly damaged by fire but later restored.

Her little girl was not quite six years old; the little boy was seven and a half. The girl didn't remember her, but the boy said he did. No emotions were shown: Missy was raising them as she had been raised nearly half a century ago in England and as she herself had raised Moura and her two older sisters twenty years ago in Chernigov Province and later in Petersburg, in the home of their father. She taught them to speak when they were spoken to, never to initiate a conversation themselves, and not to ask questions or show their feelings. When they used the potty they should ask in a whisper for permission to wash their hands. They were not to make noise or touch anything until it was given to them. The children were healthy; they had grown up on fresh butter, chicken cutlets, and white buns. Moura spent two weeks with them without ever leaving the house.

The three months granted her by the visa passed without her seeing any of the people she knew. Was there anyone left in the city who might once have known her and would at least want to shake her hand, if not rejoice at the sight of her? She doubted such a person was to be found. She took powders for insomnia. The tail assigned to her had absolutely nothing to do. There he stood, on the corner. The winter sun played on his brass buttons. Missy took the children out—one of them to school, the other to kindergarten. They had been told long ago that they were the children of a hero who died at the hands of the Bolsheviks while defending their Estonian homeland. The estate had been mortgaged and the property sold off, leaving only the house. The money from the sale was in the bank (their financial affairs were in perfect order), earning interest, and Missy explained that she felt nothing but gratitude for the Benckendorffs, young and old.

Not long before Moura's visa expired in April, her lawyer, R., came to tell her that he had done what he could and had managed to get her an extension. He also said that since she was not only visiting the children but had moved in with them (Benckendorff's heirs were disputing this, asserting that the house did not belong to Moura), the brother and sister of her late husband were cutting off all financial support to the children and henceforth would pay no more bills, even doctors' bills. "But they are not about to take the matter to court," said R., "because word would reach the newspapers, and the Benckendorff name would be bandied about in the press." After a short pause he added, "There's already been some talk."

She asked him indignantly why they thought it was their decision whether to go to court or not, when it was she, not they, who should be suing. He looked at her as if she were a madwoman who had lost all powers of comprehension, and said pensively, "You wouldn't stand a chance."

She did not ask why. She didn't want to know. A vague idea suddenly occurred to her to seek the protection of the Soviet representative (though she didn't know whether the Soviets had a diplomatic mission here or just a commercial one). But doing so would mean, of course, only one thing: going back.

Early in June, the lawyer returned, but he was not alone. He introduced her to a very tall, slender young man with blond hair, who clicked his heels and had the manners of a dandy from the military. "My friend and assistant," he said. The three of them sat for an hour and talked about the weather. Assistant for what? she wondered. He had graduated from the Corps of Pages but had no legal education. What was her lawyer getting at? That night, though, unable to fall asleep, she came to understand why they had called on her. He was throwing her a lifeline: she could marry Baron Nikolai Budberg, idle and of no great account but quite unattached, a young man who saw himself stuck in Estonia when his real métier was to inhabit some different world altogether, where he would dine with beautiful women in Montmartre, or float down the Grand Canal in a gondola, reclining on velvet pillows.

When she saw the lawyer again it was July, everyone had gone to the seashore, and the city—peaceful, carefree, and well fed—was emptying out. He told her that he respected her and respected Gorky, whom he had once seen on a Moscow street called Blacksmith Bridge, although there is no bridge of any kind there. Gorky had been standing at the entrance of the Moscow Art Theater with a beautiful lady. The lawyer had removed his hat and bowed to the writer, the voice of the Russian land, and the writer had returned his bow. He finished the story and told Moura that he had managed to get her visa extended one last time, but that there would be no third time in October.

Not in the least embarrassed by the delicacy of the matter, he calmly laid out his cards: the young man he had introduced her to a month ago was from the well-known Budberg family. His father had cut him out of his inheritance, and his mother had turned him out of the house, all because he was living beyond his means. In sum, he was poor. Like Moura herself, but for utterly different reasons, he could not remain here; besides, he had already shot himself once out of boredom. But (and here the lawyer took a deep breath, letting his words sink in) he was an Estonian citizen, he could get visas to Berlin, Paris, London. If he married, his wife would be Baroness Budberg and an Estonian citizen, and all doors would open for her, too. "I do all this," said R., "for my favorite writer. For the world-renowned author of *The Lower Depths* and *Chelkash*."

Moura couldn't remember whether she had ever read *Chelkash*. She said she would think it over. She understood his speech on three levels: political, financial, and practical. And he understood that she understood him.

In the thirteenth century Nikolai Budberg's ancestor Beninhausen-Budberg had left Westphalia for the Baltic coast, which at the time was in the possession of the Teutonic Order, under Swedish control. Four hundred years later, the King of Sweden granted a Budberg descendant the title of baron, which the Russian government recognized two hundred years later. After the War of 1812, the Budbergs became known in Russia as high-ranking military men and statesmen. They included the Russian minister of foreign affairs and State Council member Andrei Budberg (1750–1812), and the governor of Estlandia under Nicholas I, Bogdan Budberg.

The writer Nikolai Leskov had very little love for the "Livonian nobility," and, indeed, what was there to like about them? They were not especially respected in Russia. These Baltic barons did not enter the free professions, or if they did so, only very rarely. They made careers in the military and the tsarist bureaucracy. In a very real sense, they were pillars of the autocracy, often occupying high posts in the Baltic region itself, where they had their ancestral lands. Nikolai Budberg received the same schooling as his ancestors: an elite military academy followed by entry into the Guards. He was twenty-two in 1917, a few years younger than Moura. He had not fought with

Kolchak or Denikin, and he had bungled his chances for a career with Yudenich. There was absolutely nothing for him to do in Estonia. His family had renounced him, not so much for gambling at the club as for his conduct, which was considered unworthy of his ancestors. He had no profession or prospects whatsoever. Tallinn, finally liberated from tsarist control and plunged into a new era by the Treaty of Versailles, was full of hardworking, conscientious, upright people, among whom there was no place for hedonists, parasites, or mere descendants of Livonian knights.

After his first conversation with the discreet lawyer, Lai (as he was called by those who still associated with him) recognized that Moura could provide a means of escape from his miserable existence in this provincial "hole." Summer was now ending, and in September he went to see her. Somewhat embarrassed, he told her about himself, concealing certain indiscretions. She understood immediately that he had to leave and (for a start) had to have something to live on in Berlin. She was his salvation from this backwater, where he had absolutely nothing to do. Precisely what he did intend to do with his life she didn't ask. After that second visit she understood that he was her lifeline as well—not only would a new name and title rehabilitate her but an Estonian passport would enable her to travel to any country she liked. This was more than she could have hoped for.

During those months what little news reached her from Petrograd came only by a circuitous route. The mails were not working, of course, but Andreeva and Peppycrew passed through Helsinki on the way to Berlin in April, and in May Moura heard from Peppycrew. He wrote her that Duke was seriously ill. He had finally decided to go to Europe for treatment and would be leaving very soon. Gorky was now in contact through the Soviet Trade Office with both Peppycrew and Ivan Ladyzhnikov, the director of Kniga Publishers in Berlin. Peppycrew wrote that Gorky was worried about her, worried by rumors that she had been brought to trial for their friendship. He had instructed Kryuchkov to send her a decent sum of money, which would be easy to do, since as Gorky's agent Ladyzhnikov had been accumulating royalties from foreign translations, mainly *Childhood* and *The Lower Depths*. Kryuchkov also wrote that Universal Literature seemed to be moribund, but that new plans, also universal in scope, were being made thanks to a surge in energy among the intelligentsia as a result of the New Economic Policy and the fact that people now had butter to eat. He informed her that Duke was not writing anything new in the way of literature because he was completely tied up writing letters to the great men of this world about the starving population of Russia. Every day letters went out to Romain Rolland, Upton Sinclair, John Galsworthy, Herbert Hoover, and others, as Kryuchkov well knew, since the entire correspondence passed through his hands.

Reading Kryuchkov's letters, Moura realized as early as July that she couldn't put off the matter of marriage any longer and would have to act. When the day came for Gorky to leave Petrograd and travel to Berlin, she had to be ready to meet him. Reading between the lines of Kryuchkov's letters Moura guessed that Varvara Tikhonova had moved back to Kronverk (she was right), but she was hoping that Gorky and Tikhonova would not go abroad together, that it wouldn't come to that. Anyway, Tikhonov would not allow it. (Moura was right about that also.) But Moura still had to hurry with the papers and the wedding because, in essence, her decision had been made. After all, Tikhonov could very well get an assignment to travel to the Berlin Trade Office, and then Varvara Tikhonova would end up in Europe with Gorky.

As we now know, in the second week of July, Gorky sent telegrams to Gerhart Hauptmann, H. G. Wells, Anatole France, John Galsworthy, Upton Sinclair, Thomas Masaryk, Vincente Blasco-Ibañez, and other writers in Europe and America enlisting their support for the starving people of Russia. On July 18 an appeal was published in

Vossische Zeitung, having been passed along by Hauptmann. On July 23 the Communist paper *Rote Fahne* reprinted it and added that Gorky would be leaving for Finland in a few days. This seriously alarmed Moura, and although she didn't believe it entirely (she did not think Gorky would leave Russia before the autumn), she began to consider what she might do if he actually did leave for Helsinki before she got her new Estonian documents. Early in August, Kryuchkov forwarded a letter to her (dated July 13) from Gorky himself. He wrote that he would be in Europe shortly. The London newspapers ran the text of Gorky's appeal for famine relief and announced that Gorky was already on his way to Helsinki. Some newspapers asserted that from there he would go to Berlin via Tallinn; others thought he would go to Sweden and Norway. Moura realized, of course, that he would go through neither Sweden, Norway, nor Tallinn. From Helsinki he would proceed to Berlin by ship via Stettin, meaning she had to see him in Finland. Having no other choice, she hurried over to the Soviet representative's office, where she knew she would find Georgy Solomon, a Soviet diplomat and friend of Krasin's who had recently arrived in Estonia to head the Soviet diplomatic mission.

Solomon, who left Tallinn in 1922 to work for Arcos in London, was friendly not only with Krasin but also with Arcos director F. E. Krimer, whom Moura knew quite well from Petrograd: both Krimer and his wife had been frequent guests at the apartment on Kronverk. Solomon broke with Moscow in 1923, and in 1930 his memoirs, *Among the Red Autocrats*, came out in Paris (they were later translated into English, French, and German). He thus became one of the first "defectors," or, as they later came to be called, dissidents. He published a second book in 1931, *Lenin and His Family*, and died in 1934. Solomon was among those who had accepted the October Revolution and had a diplomatic career for a few years but then resigned, leaving Russia to thrive as citizens of England, France, or the United States, sometimes breaking with Moscow scandalously, their pictures

splashed across the front page of the newspapers (like Grigory Besedovsky in Paris), and sometimes fleeing incognito (like Yakov Ganetsky's son Lev in Rome), changing their names and disappearing
without a trace.

Solomon came from an educated, intellectual Petersburg family.
He had lived abroad, knew many languages, and his elegant speech
and appearance made him stand out from the mass of awkward, uneducated Soviet diplomats (especially from those who came later),
with their wooden faces and pseudo-intellectual speech. He immediately issued a permit for Moura to travel to Helsinki, and the next day
she left by ship to meet Gorky. The passage was dangerous because
the English had mined the entrance to the Gulf of Finland in 1917 and
1918 to defend Kronstadt from the Germans.

Moura had no choice but to believe the newspaper reports that
Gorky was on his way to Finland. She certainly wanted to believe
them. There was the letter dated July 13 that Gorky had mailed her
through the Berlin Trade Office (Maxim, who started working that
summer as a diplomatic courier between Moscow, Berlin, and Rome,
may have carried it there) in which he confirmed that he was trying to
leave as soon as possible, for two reasons: to raise money for famine
relief, and to seek treatment for his heart and lungs.

But Gorky could not leave in August, and the telegrams in the London newspapers proved premature, though through no fault of their
own. Gorky actually did leave Petrograd for the Finnish border, spent
three days (August 20 to 23) in Byeloostrov, and then went back. The
trip had been made with one goal—mental and physical rest. In the
last few weeks he had lost a lot of blood. His temperature hovered
above 39° C, and Gumilev's arrest on August 3 and Blok's death on
August 7 had left him particularly depressed.

Moura spent two days looking for Gorky all over Helsinki. On
the third day she left without having found him. In Berlin, Maxim,
with whom she also corresponded, as she did with Kryuchkov and

Ladyzhnikov, received the desperate letter she had written upon her return to Tallinn and wrote to his father to say what had happened: "Titka went to Helsinki to meet you. Her family affairs are in a bad way. We've summoned her to Berlin. She's coming in two weeks. This is what I thought: let's get a group of us together [that is, Maxim and his wife, Nightingale, and Moura] and go to Italy, to the sea." This was evidently how the newly married Maxim pictured his honeymoon.

Two weeks later Moura received notification from the Estonian State Bank that the Dresden Bank had transferred a thousand dollars to her account. She divided the sum equally among Missy, Lai, and herself.

That summer not only were Andreeva and Kryuchkov in Berlin (in an apartment rented for them by Ladyzhnikov near the Kurfürstendamm), but so were Nightingale and Maxim and his wife, Nadya. By that time everyone called her Timosha—only Gorky ever really called her Nadya, and then only while he was getting to know her. The three of them all lived in an apartment Nightingale had found before the newlyweds' arrival from Moscow, a five-minute walk from Andreeva and Kryuchkov. In the same neighborhood, on the Fasanenstrasse, Ladyzhnikov lived in an apartment with his wife and daughter, and ran his publishing house, Kniga. Ladyzhnikov was one of Gorky's closest friends, and acted as his agent in all his business dealings, primarily his financial affairs. Though not a member of the Bolshevik Party, in his youth he had been an ally of Lenin's, whose ideas he shared. With Lenin's blessing and a budget approved by the Commissariat of Enlightenment, Ladyzhnikov was now continuing his publishing business, which was devoted almost wholly to the publication of Gorky's works. Although taciturn and morose, Ladyzhnikov was a calm, energetic man, with an excellent grasp of business affairs and who remained devoted to Gorky to the end of his life. Gorky loved and trusted him.

Ladyzhnikov had been in the book business since long before World War I, when he had worked for a publishing house called Demos in Switzerland. It was moved to Berlin and renamed Kniga when Gorky was still living on Capri. Kniga Publishers, with which both Grzhebin and Tikhonov (who were still in Russia) were connected, had been created primarily to maintain copyright on its foreign-language editions, since at that time no international agreement between Russia and the Western world existed to protect those rights. But there was also a second goal: to publish books abroad that Russia could import (with the permission of Glavlit, the Soviet censorship agency), there being no paper in Russia.

Ladyzhnikov began corresponding with Moura in the spring, undoubtedly at Gorky's request. Acting as Gorky's agents, Ladyzhnikov and Kryuchkov had been forwarding his letters to Moura since early July, when a diplomatic pouch had been established to send personal and business correspondence through the Soviet Trade Office in Tallinn. The Trade Office was also involved with Kniga Publishers and was a party to the agreement for the publication of Gorky's collected works.

Moura wrote Ladyzhnikov at least once a month to keep him apprised of her situation in Estonia. When she received the money, she wrote to Berlin that she had gone to Helsinki to meet Duke, but Duke was not there. Confident in Ladyzhnikov's discretion, she also informed him of her decision to marry.

When he heard from Ladyzhnikov, Gorky wrote back: "What exactly did Maria Ignatievna write to you and *when*? That lady is behaving mysteriously and foolishly. Lord help her!" In this "Lord help her!" and also the words "foolishly" and "that lady" his poorly concealed irritation comes through. But this was all part of Moura's plan. Everything she admitted to Kryuchkov, Ladyzhnikov, and Maxim, and everything she eventually wrote to Gorky directly, was always carefully weighed.

Moura liked to write letters and took them seriously. In August of that year she wrote an especially great number: to Berlin and Petrograd, to her sisters in Paris, to London. But the letters to London went unanswered.

Lai was coming to see her two or three times a week now. In town, within their circle of von Shullers, Shillings, and Shellings, gossip was circulating, which Lai gladly shared when he came to call: the more gossip there was, the more he was amused. The whole Baltic coast, it turned out, was talking about the upcoming wedding of "the Chekist" and "the good-for-nothing." People argued over whether she was in service to England or Germany, because rumor had it that Moura had had an affair with Kaiser Wilhelm when Benckendorff was serving as secretary at the Russian embassy in Berlin on the eve of the war. Moura, however, was not amused. She was not in a mood to be. Her money was running out, and the life her sisters led in Paris seemed like hell to her: Anna and her family were impoverished, and no one knew where Alla was or with whom.

All of September and the first half of October 1921 were spent putting her documents in order. Such formalities delayed the wedding, though there may also have been some reluctance on both sides. The following facts are known: On October 16 Gorky left Petrograd for Helsinki, accompanied by Grzhebin and his wife, Maria, and their three daughters. Between the 17th and the 29th he stayed in Helsinki; he was so weak they were afraid to let him travel. Moura had acquired a second visa from Solomon that enabled her to leave Estonia, and she met Gorky in Helsinki around the 20th. One month later, Gorky wrote to Valentina Khodasevich from Berlin:

> In Finland I saw Maria Ignatievna, who was wearing sturdy boots and a warm fur coat. She has grown thin and has become somehow even sweeter. As ever, she knows everything and is interested in everything. A superlative person! She wants to

marry some baron, but we're protesting vociferously. Let the baron pick himself another fantasy! This one is ours! Right?

On October 29, Gorky left Helsinki for Berlin via Stockholm. Maxim, Timosha, and Nightingale met him at the station. He proposed staying with them for a few days, but that turned into a week, which turned into two weeks. He ended up staying more than a month. The reasons for the delay were many: there were meetings and correspondence with his American and European admirers who had been drawn into the cause of famine relief; there were the Berlin doctors he had to see; there were financial complications arising from finalizing plans for his collected works; and then there was something else, something that he could discuss only later with Ladyzhnikov. Finally, on December 2, on the recommendations of his doctors, he left for a sanatorium in the little town of St. Blasien in the Black Forest. Maxim, Timosha, and Nightingale delivered him there barely alive. After they left, first Kryuchkov, then Ladyzhnikov, and then Ekaterina Peshkova took turns visiting him. Peshkova, too, had come from Moscow to rest and to see her close friend Mikhail Nikolaev, Kniga's deputy director.

With them at St. Blasien was a man with an unusual destiny who led the sort of remarkable life rarely seen in the world: Gorky's adopted son, Zinovy Peshkov. Zinovy was the younger brother of Yakov Sverdlov, comrade-in-arms of Lenin, who called Sverdlov a "professional Bolshevik." After the October Revolution, Sverdlov held the post of president of the Russian Republic and chairman of the Central Committee and played a role in the murder of the Tsar's family (in his honor Ekaterinburg was renamed Sverdlovsk); he died in 1919. Zinovy was a fifteen-year-old orphan in 1899 when Gorky, who was then living with Peshkova and two-year-old Maxim, decided to adopt the younger brother of his old comrade from the Social Democratic Party. Gorky gave the boy his name (Peshkov), raised him, and gave him an education. In 1914, while spending the summer with Peshkova and Maxim in Italy, Zinovy signed up with the French Foreign Legion. He was deployed on the first day of the war, and on May 9, 1915, leading his platoon on a heroic charge, was wounded in the arm, which had to be amputated at the shoulder. In 1916 he returned to the Legion, fought in several battles, and after receiving various medals and getting promoted to the rank of colonel was sent with the French mission to China, Japan, and Manchuria.

He traveled all over the world. He was in the United States several times and in Africa, where he commanded the Legion in the colonial war between France and Abd al-Karim. World War II found him serving in the French army with the rank of general. In 1941 he went to London and put himself at the disposal of General de Gaulle, who sent him to General MacArthur as liaison officer.

Peshkov retired in 1950, but in 1964 (at age eighty) he was asked by de Gaulle, whose government had just recognized the People's Republic of China, to help ease any resulting tension between France and Taiwan. General Peshkov went on to head the French mission in Japan. When he retired from public affairs, he settled in Paris, where he died on November 28, 1966, in the American Hospital at Neuilly. He was buried in the Russian émigré cemetery at Sainte-Geneviève-des-Bois, in a spot set aside for Russian veterans of the two world wars. It may sound strange, but this proves without a doubt his membership in one of the many White émigré military organizations.

Peshkov maintained the friendliest of relations with Gorky until 1928, when Gorky first left Italy for Russia. He had a daughter (he was twice divorced) who came with him to visit Gorky. Gorky called him Zina, loved him very much, and trusted him completely. In 1921, the moment Zinovy learned that Gorky was in Germany, he went to St. Blasien and spent about two weeks there. He later visited Gorky in

Sorrento, in 1925, and saw Moura, too, in both Paris and London, after 1924.

By the fall and winter of 1921, Gorky and Moura were able to correspond using normal mail and no one, except perhaps mail inspectors in Estonia and Germany, was reading their letters. She finally sent him a full account of her marriage to Budberg, and Gorky's reaction was much less harsh: "I received a letter from Maria Ignatievna," he wrote to Ladyzhnikov on December 28. "She actually is married [she was not married until early January 1922] and has fallen ill with tuberculosis. Tell Peter Petrovich [Kryuchkov] I don't have her address[!], she didn't indicate it, but the letter is from Estonia."

Soon after that Moura received another check from the Dresden Bank.

She spent Christmas with her children and Missy. The wedding date was set at last. Lai was impatient to get out of Tallinn and married Moura with a ticket for Berlin in his pocket. He had no interest in the Christmas holidays, which only delayed his departure. Finally everything was ready. Moura telephoned her lawyer, took Missy with her, and the four of them—the bride, the groom, and the two witnesses—walked into a nice, clean, bright office where their future obligations to one another were read to them in two languages. That evening Lai boarded a train, seating himself where he could see "the lights of the Kurfürstendamm," as he put it. Moura waited a few days before going to St. Blasien. She wanted to write one last letter to London, not to Lockhart or Wells but to Maurice Baring. He would certainly answer; he had no reason not to.

But why did those other two fail to answer? She had written them each twice. The post office had not returned the letters. Did that mean the letters had been received? The possibility of censorship did not worry her very much, but she wrote with obvious caution, reminding them that if they wanted to write her they should not forget for a moment that the letter would be read by persons hostile to her before she received it. But all that turned out to be beside the point: neither Wells nor Lockhart replied.[2]

Moura's letter to Baring was lively and gay but also circumspect. She asked how he had spent the past years, whether he had written and published many books. Was he homesick for Russia? How were all their friends, so dear to her heart—Walpole? Ransome? Hicks? Lyuba Malinina and Zhenya Shelepina? And, by the way, where was Bruce? Where was H. G.? Has something sensational come from the pen of their old friend Somerset Maugham?

A reply came very quickly. Baring wrote her with a timidity and wariness that was unfamiliar to her. He congratulated her on her return "home" to the old Europe, which belonged to her and to which she had always belonged, and always would. He wrote that he was sorry, infinitely sorry, that he couldn't send her H. G.'s address; he was traveling from college to college in the United States giving lectures on the future of the world and how to improve it. He was enjoying enormous and deserved success. The same went for Bruce's address; he was either in the Balkans or Hungary, either the director of an international bank or possibly connected with the Foreign Office, and recently, so people were saying, had decided to try his hand at journalism.

Why she didn't go to St. Blasien to see Gorky after reading this letter we don't know. Not only did she not go but, without telling anyone, she went to London the next month without even stopping on

---

2. Two years ago I was asked to authenticate more than forty letters from Moura to Lockhart spanning the years 1919 to 1921. I concluded that they were unquestionably genuine. She began sending them from Petrograd through the Swedish embassy, where she certainly had acquaintances, and she continued to send letters from Estonia. She had not received an answer to any of the letters, to judge by their contents: alternating sweet words and complaints. What is most striking about these letters, though, is that basically they are all the same letter written more than forty times! [Author's note added in 1987.]

her way through Berlin. She saw some people in London, we do not know whom, but in any case neither Wells nor Lockhart was there. She spent a week there before returning directly to Tallinn. Later she mentioned the trip in passing to Khodasevich: "I had to go, I had to see London. No one was there? I did see some people. But the main thing was the city. I couldn't wait any longer."

Now she had not only "sturdy boots" and "a warm fur coat" but also a black pleated silk skirt, light stockings, kid gloves, a white angora beret worn low over her forehead and covering one ear according to the latest fashion, and a white angora scarf to match. In London she went to a hairdresser, the very best, with a sign outside reading "Gaston de Paris." When she got back to Tallinn she discarded the frayed velvet cape that reached down to her ankles, the big black hat with the feather, the French-heeled shoes with the pointed toes, and her old worn sable tippet like so much trash.

She did not stop in Berlin on the way back because she had decided to keep this trip a secret. That evening she simply transferred at the Friedrichstrasse station to another train which sped her eastward. The conductor in the international car took her brand-new passport that still smelled of glue and told her she would not be woken at the border or troubled with document or baggage inspections, and that in the morning he would bring her coffee. He clicked his heels respectfully and wished her a good night, calling her "Frau Baronin."

She was playing a game that she could not afford to lose. She knew she must not forget even for one minute what her goal was, the same goal she had set herself three years ago: to survive no matter what.

On December 25, 1921, Gorky wrote to Lenin from St. Blasien:

> They work splendidly, these Germans! Just think: on December 20 the total number of unemployed in the whole country was 47,000! It's hard to believe, but it appears to be true. At the sanatorium where I'm staying, construction of a huge new

building is under way. They're dynamiting a mountain, putting up walls, and making gravel for concrete—and how intelligently, efficiently, solidly it's all being done!...Journalists are pounding on the door, but I don't want to talk to them. They distort everything in an intolerable and malicious way.

"They've started collecting food and money," he informed Lenin, "for the starving." But the work, in his opinion, had not been properly coordinated. "They don't know where to send the money or what to do with it." He felt "agents" should be appointed to oversee the relief operation, "people who would know where to send everything and what to buy and in general would speed up the whole business of getting grain and food products into Russia," and, since he no longer doubted that Moura would come back to him, he strongly urged to Lenin that this assignment be given "to Maria Fyodorovna Andreeva and Maria Ignatievna Benckendorff, a most energetic and well-educated woman—she speaks five languages." Gorky wasn't calling her Zakrevskaya now, but he had decided henceforth to ignore her new name.

Wells, Gorky, and Moura in Petrograd, 1920.
Photograph by M. S. Nappelbaum.

PHOTOGRAPH OF BEARER.

Certified Photograph and signature of Robert H B Loc

SIGNATURE OF BEARER.

Robert Bruce Lockhart's passport, 1916.

Actress Kay Francis as Moura in the film *British Agent*, 1934.

Gorky and Wells in Gorky's study on Kronverk, 1920.
Photograph by M. S. Nappelbaum.

A view of Kronverk Prospect. Gorky's residence was on the fourth floor of number 23 (large building in center of photograph).

Valentina Khodasevich's room in the Kronverk Prospect apartment. Her portrait of Gorky appears on the left.

Rakitsky, Gorky, and
Valentina Khodasevich
in fancy dress at the Kronverk apartment, c. 1920.

Gorky in his office in
Petrograd during the period
of *The New Life*, c. 1917.

Moura (second from right) at the wedding of Alexander (far left) and Alexa (far right) Korda, 1950.

Wells and Moura on vacation, 1935.

At a dacha outside Moscow, 1961.
Standing: Ludmila Tolstaya, wife of A. N. Tolstoy;
seated from left to right: Moura, Pyotr and Anna
Kapitsa, Valentina Khodasevich.

Moura at home in London, 1970. This photograph
by Cecil Beaton accompanied the Kathleen Tynan
profile of Moura that appeared in *Vogue*.

4

ITALIAN INTERMEZZO

> I'll note you in my book of memory.
> *King Henry VI, Part I*, II. iv, 101

THE DRESDEN BANK was one of five large German banks, all beginning with the letter D, that had offices in the major cities of Germany. Vladimir Korolenko's letters to Gorky were placed in the Berlin office of the Dresden Bank along with other letters Gorky had brought with him to Berlin that autumn. Gorky himself never went to the bank, however; Ladyzhnikov had complete authority over all of Gorky's transactions and held a joint account with him.

Gorky's faith in Ladyzhnikov was such that Gorky entrusted him with his literary affairs as well. In one letter written from St. Blasien Gorky directs Ladyzhnikov to go to the Dresden Bank, find the Korolenko letters, and give them to Grzhebin, who will make copies for their publication. Curiously, when Gorky left Petrograd for the West, he took the originals of letters he had received from various people, including Lenin, with him and deposited *copies* in the Petrograd Public Library for safekeeping.

Ladyzhnikov wholly merited Gorky's trust. He survived the 1930s, Maxim's death, the death of Gorky himself, the liquidation of Kryuchkov, and, later, the death of Andreeva, to whom fifty years of friendship bound him. He buried both his wife and his daughter and died at an old age, in 1945. Up until the very last day he was working on Gorky's archives at the literary institute in Moscow named in the writer's honor, trying to sort out the unimaginable chaos, which he eventually did, identifying all the letters and manuscripts.

In 1902 Gorky finished *The Lower Depths*, which was staged by the Moscow Art Theater. On May 10, 1903, the German translator August-Karl Scholtz wrote the author about the success the play was enjoying in Germany—in Dresden, Munich, and Berlin (where it had a 600-performance run), as well as in Vienna, Prague, and Budapest. It was produced by Richard Valentin at Max Reinhardt's theater.[1] Quite a large sum of money was accumulating abroad, not only from these productions but from the publication of Gorky's works in German and from the matinees where Gorky gave public readings. What money he received, however, went directly to the Bolsheviks for the purchase of weapons (as Litvinov revealed in a memoir). He was afraid that any day now he might find himself either outside the law or in exile, and with Ladyzhnikov's approval, Gorky decided to entrust the collection of money due him in Germany, as well as its safekeeping, to a third person who would act as his agent. Twenty percent would go to the agent, forty percent to a Bolshevik account (about which Gorky informed Lenin in good time), and forty percent would be deposited in a bank in Gorky's name. But who could do such a job? Only a brother, a member of the Bolshevik faction, of course, someone who had permanent residence in Europe and knew the ins and outs of collecting fees from European theaters.

Gorky finally settled on Alexander Parvus, who subsequently, in 1917, would help Lenin get to Petrograd from Switzerland. Gorky was living in the Crimea in 1903 when Parvus came to see him and

---

1. Regardless of what Soviet sources say, Reinhardt did not produce the play, but Reinhardt played the role of Luke when it was performed in his theater.

receive his proxy. He came illegally (in his youth he was involved with the terrorist group the People's Will), on a fake passport, and spent two days in Sevastopol. Gorky met him at the train station, where the contract was signed. They had known one another before. Konstantin Pyatnitsky, the publisher of the Znanie group and a close friend of Gorky's, served as witness. Parvus returned to Germany with the signed document in his pocket.

Parvus was a member of both the Russian and the German Social Democratic parties and had prominent acquaintances among German Socialists. He knew Max Reinhardt and was friendly with many famous people in Central Europe. Born in 1867, he had begun his adventurous career—political and criminal—at an early age.

His real name was Helphand. He had left Russia when he was barely nineteen and gone to Switzerland to study in Basel and Berne. In Zurich he met Georgy Plekhanov, Pavel Axelrod, and Vera Zasulich, whom he won over with his youthful enthusiasm and hatred for tsarist Russia. Like everyone who knew him in his younger years, they were amazed at his intellect, energy, and fanaticism, which, however, did not impede either the clarity of his thought or his capacity for theoretical reflection. In Germany he joined the German Social Democratic Party and a year later was already quite at home in Rosa Luxemburg's house, where he met August Bebel and Karl Kautsky (to whom he later introduced Trotsky), argued with Eduard Bernstein, became editor of the Socialist *Arbeiterzeitung*, and began writing for Lenin's *Spark*.

His basic idea was that of "permanent revolution," which Trotsky adopted and elaborated on after meeting Parvus and getting to know him better.[2] Permanent revolution was supposed to begin with a general strike on political grounds. The economy of the country had to be

---

2. Some Social Democrat historians claim that Trotsky took his idea of permanent revolution entirely from Parvus (see *Sotsialisticheskii vestnik* 11 [1940]: 172).

dealt a mortal blow. The bourgeoisie had to be fatally split and would then crumble. Russia, the most reactionary country, would become the first "victim" of the general strike and destruction of the state, and other countries would follow her example. Parvus believed the general strike was the best means of bringing about revolution— stronger than terror, propaganda, barricades, or civil war, and certainly stronger than a constitution. The general strike was supposed to be the first step toward the decisive and irrevocable liberation of Europe and Russia from capitalism.

In the years before World War I, Parvus wrote some fifty articles in two languages (Russian and German) and published a dozen books on political and economic questions in Europe and the economic collapse that world revolution would bring about. His theory that world war was the first step toward revolution was far from universally accepted, but he saw the Russo-Japanese War as the prologue to revolution, and in 1904 he published an article in *The Spark* entitled "War and Revolution" in which he predicted what would happen in 1905. His relations with Lenin were uneven, however, and for a while—when he became close with Trotsky—Parvus went over to the Mensheviks.

Trotsky was twenty-six years old when they met. He was immediately enthusiastic about Parvus's ideas, and very soon "permanent revolution" acquired its final form. In his pamphlet *Before the 9th of January*, published with a foreword by Parvus, Trotsky came down wholly on the side of those who considered the general strike a more powerful means than either terror or the barricades. Acknowledging the role Parvus played in his life, Trotsky would later write in his autobiography: "Parvus was without a doubt one of the chief Marxists at the turn of the century."

By 1904 they had become so close that Trotsky and his wife lived with Parvus for a while in Munich. In 1905, Trotsky and Parvus made their way to Petersburg on fake passports. The real general strike (the first in Russia's history) came in May and October, that is, after the 9th of January, and the revolution of 1905 followed, confirming the prognoses of Parvus and Trotsky. Trotsky became chairman of the First Soviet of Workers Deputies, and after his arrest Parvus assumed the position (in the now underground Soviet) until he, too, was arrested. When they were still at liberty they jointly published a newspaper, whose circulation jumped from 30,000 copies in its first few days to 100,000 copies daily, vastly exceeding the distribution of the Bolsheviks' *New Life*.

They had achieved their immediate aim, but they had to keep their ultimate goal in mind. Both were tried and exiled to Siberia, from which they escaped separately. Soon thereafter they found themselves again in Germany.

Parvus's description of their joint actions is curious: "We were strings of the same harp played by the storm of revolution." By the summer of 1907, they were living together again in Munich. They were much more interesting and necessary to one another than were any of the other Social Democrats, Russian or German, including Lenin, who at the time doubted that Russia could skip the stage of bourgeois revolution (without the experience of Europe of 1848 behind her) and go directly to Socialist revolution and the dictatorship of the proletariat.

The 130,000 gold German marks that Parvus collected from Reinhardt's theater came into his hands at a very opportune moment, as did the money for the strike committee of the Petersburg Soviet, which Parvus pocketed. Neither Gorky nor the Bolshevik faction ever saw any of it. The German Social Democrats reacted variously. Philipp Scheidemann and Friedrich Ebert maintained the best of relations with Parvus, but the majority of Party members turned their backs on him. Rosa Luxemburg wrote her husband Leon Jogiches, clearly sympathizing with Parvus and not Gorky (later, however, when Parvus wanted to see her, she wouldn't receive him). Luxemburg wrote:

> Yesterday I saw Karl [Kautsky] and his wife, who told me the most awful news about what people are saying here about Parvus. They might have been talking about an idler and swindler. And Gorky is doing this systematically through his agents! On Sunday we're going to have a small conference on the subject at Karl's at which Gorky's agent is supposed to show me documentary proof of Parvus's swindling.

During those years Gorky had visited America and settled in Italy. His fees had grown many times over; in the United States, where his visits had made him famous, he was paid $5,000 for a single pamphlet, and the seventeenth edition of *Foma Gordeyev* in America enabled him to settle on Capri. Generally speaking, by 1903 or 1904, the money was rolling in, but he parted with it just as easily. In 1904 he sent 700 rubles through Alexander Bogdanov to Lenin in Geneva for his newspaper *Onward*; when he got the money, Lenin wrote Bogdanov: "See if you can squeeze a little more out of Gorky."

Gorky's money and the strike committee money put Parvus on his feet. At first Parvus's behavior didn't disturb Gorky; he decided to resort to an arbitration tribunal. In 1905 we find Ladyzhnikov in Berlin negotiating with Lenin and Krasin (whose conspiratorial name was Nikitich), a future commissar and the first Soviet ambassador to France, to start a publishing house for the Bolsheviks in Berlin for the purpose of importing illegal literature into Russia. To fund it Ladyzhnikov now had to demand that Parvus pay the money he had taken from Gorky. Parvus did not give it to him, however, and though the arbitration tribunal ruined Parvus's Socialist reputation, the affair did not impede his future success in the slightest. He was expelled from the German Social Democratic Party, and the Russian Social Democrats ostracized him, but he took it better than might be supposed. He had 130,000 gold marks in his pocket, and he had nothing against starting a new life. Trotsky was one of the last to turn his back on Parvus, around 1908, by which time the pupil had long ceased to need the teacher. Making one shady deal after another, Parvus was finally deported from Germany in 1910 and went to Turkey, where it took him five years to become a very rich dealer in the military procurement business—chiefly with Germany. In 1915 Trotsky publicly disassociated himself from Parvus in *Our Word*, dismissing him as a still-living but for Trotsky purely historical figure.

But nothing helped Gorky recover this money: not his official complaint to the Central Committees of the Russian and German Social Democratic parties; not the Russian-German SD "party commission" appointed to try Parvus; not the intervention of Kautsky or Bebel; not the fact that Ilyich (Lenin) and Nikitich (Krasin) took Gorky's side in the arbitration tribunal. Gorky had a second task on top of getting the money back from Parvus: "not to give a trump card to the bourgeoisie." This one was much more easily accomplished than the first, and both sides managed, albeit with great difficulty, to keep the matter out of the public eye. In fact it wasn't until 1930 that Gorky finally broke his silence, and in his revised essay on Lenin he gave a brief, though not entirely accurate account of what had happened twenty-seven years earlier. But Gorky had a reason by then for revealing this old secret: in 1930 he decided to return to Russia for good. After two trips there he had realized that travel was getting too hard for him and that he would have to move back permanently. In 1933 he finally took the fateful step that influenced not only the rest of his life but the lives of all those closest to him. His lines about the Parvus affair were his farewell to his long European past:

> My business with the German Party was of a rather delicate nature. A prominent Party member, afterward the notorious Parvus, had received from Znanie Publishers authority to collect author's fees from the theaters for my play *The Lower Depths*. He received this authorization in 1902 in Sevastopol, at

the train station, where he had come illegally. The money he collected was to be divided up in the following way: 20 percent of the total sum to him, and of the rest, I was to receive one quarter, while three quarters went to the funds of the Social Democratic Party. Parvus knew these conditions, of course, and was even delighted by them. The play ran for four years in all the theaters in Germany. In Berlin alone it was performed more than five hundred times, and Parvus must have collected a 100,000 marks. But instead of money, he sent a letter to K. P. Pyatnitsky at Znanie, in which he good-humoredly informed him that he had spent all the money on a trip to Italy with a young lady. As I was concerned personally with this doubtless very pleasant trip only to the extent of a quarter of the money, I considered myself justified in writing to the Central Committee of the German Party about the remaining three quarters. I communicated with them through I. P. Ladyzhnikov. The Central Committee remained quite unmoved by Parvus's trip. Later on I learned that he had been demoted by the Party; frankly speaking, I would have preferred to see his ears boxed. When I was in Paris some time later, an extremely pretty young woman was identified to me as Parvus's companion on his Italian trip.

Parvus became friendly with the Young Turks and got a job as representative for the Krupp works in the Ottoman Empire. He also quickly established contact with one of the wealthiest men in Europe, the Greek Basil Zakharov, like Krupp an unscrupulous purveyor of weapons to any state that wanted them. It was right before the war, in the spring of 1914, that Parvus felt steady on his feet, having banked his first million. Beginning that winter, he started to bring in major orders for Germany: grain, coal, weapons. For him Germany's victory meant Russia's defeat. Russia's defeat meant revolution and an end to the capitalist world.

In 1915 Parvus started to receive money from the imperial German government, a portion of which he distributed to his disciples, associates, and confederates.[3]

Parvus was already on easy terms with many German diplomats in Constantinople. He had met the German foreign minister Gottlieb von Jagow and had revealed his plans to him. Parvus asked that financial aid be given to the so-called Russian defeatists, who were Russian exiles on the extreme left, living predominantly in Switzerland, and to some of the militant nationalists struggling for their own independence. Jagow promised him backing. Parvus considered the first task to be severing Ukraine from Russia. His plan was to create a united anti-Russian front with German money. The German government discussed his plan, with which they sympathized, feeling that Germany might thereby bring pressure to bear on the Russian tsar and so hasten separate peace talks. By the end of 1915 Parvus had been made chief adviser to the German general staff on the revolutionary movement in Russia. He received a million gold marks for his work in Zurich, Bucharest, and Copenhagen. He went to Berlin, Vienna, Copenhagen, and Switzerland. He amazed everyone with his energy, health, and physical strength (he weighed more than 300 pounds). But the Social Democrats no longer considered him one of their own, calling him a "speculator" and a "Turkish agent." Rosa Luxemburg knew of Parvus's adventures and broke off relations with him, and Trotsky refused to meet with him. Lenin did what he could to avoid him. Only Scheidemann and Ebert remained loyal to the end. For his own prestige, and partly to camouflage his activities, Parvus opened the Scientific Research Institute for the Study of the Consequences of War in Copenhagen, but this functioned mainly to gather the international political and economic intelligence he needed. He

---

3. In the Nicolaevsky Collection of the Hoover Institution in Stanford, California, there is a receipt signed by Parvus for one million gold marks (1915) paid by the German government.

brought Russian émigrés across Germany to Denmark and took them in to work at the institute. The old and quite ill leader of the Menshevik Social Democrats, Yury Martov, who lived in Switzerland, felt that Parvus's behavior was "indiscreet."

In Copenhagen Parvus arranged for comfortable apartments for his associates, paid them respectable salaries, and hired his relative Jacob Fürstenberg-Hanecki to be one of his closest assistants and his link to Lenin and the other Bolsheviks in Zurich and Geneva. Some historians think that Hanecki was planted in Parvus's office by Lenin (if true, Parvus had no inkling) in order to learn what was going on in the Copenhagen institute and to keep an eye on Parvus, for whom Lenin had no sympathy whatsoever. Possibly this explains Hanecki's later successful career in the People's Commissariat for Foreign Affairs, where he served as deputy foreign minister.

In March 1917 Parvus decided that the Provisional Government would sign a separate peace with the Germans, the peasants would divide the land, and the soldiers would throw down their weapons. It was then that he sent a telegram to Petrograd: "Your victory is our victory!" He received no reply.

Evidently without Lenin's consent (but without any expression of protest either, that is, with Lenin's tacit approval), Parvus helped arrange the transport of several groups of Bolsheviks from Switzerland to Russia in April 1917. This did not soften the hostility of Lenin and Zinoviev to Parvus, though they took advantage of the opportunity to travel by sealed train to Petrograd in April 1917. Lenin did not give Parvus a visa to enter Russia, and he let him know that if he showed up without a visa he would be sent back immediately. Parvus continued to repatriate Russian Socialist émigrés until the end of the summer of 1917, according to Soviet historian M. N. Pokrovsky, citing information from British intelligence.

By this time Parvus was suffering from megalomania, to which he had always been susceptible. He wanted to open two hundred daily newspapers at once, in Russia, China, Afghanistan, and Japan, in a deal estimated at 200 million. Certain scandals came to light involving Scheidemann and Ebert, who had backed him longer than anyone else. Despite having become quite rich, he saw that his reputation had been badly tarnished. His dream of a German victory was shattered by the 1918 Allied offensive in France. He left hastily for Switzerland, bought a castle outside Zurich, installed women, old friends whom he wined and dined, and all sorts of riffraff. The Swiss authorities deported him to Germany for having "orgies." In 1920 he bought another castle, or rather, palace, outside Berlin, on Wannsee Island. There he lived on a grand scale, receiving throngs of friends, among them former ministers, diplomats, German Social Democrats, and members of the government. He was surrounded by liveried butlers, secretaries, a majordomo, and a chef. He prescribed his own etiquette. The riffraff were now gone. The women were high-class coquettes, actresses, beauties. It was here that he predicted World War II and quarreled in print with President Wilson, Clemenceau, and Lloyd George about the Treaty of Versailles. It was here, too, in the summer of 1921, that a visitor came from Berlin to see him: the deliberate, portly, unsmiling Ivan Ladyzhnikov, a man he had known as "Gorky's agent" back at the turn of the century, a Bolshevik who was not a member of the Party but was sympathetic to that faction of Social Democrats which was now in power in Russia.

Ladyzhnikov came straight to the point. He demanded the money that belonged to Gorky and that Parvus had squandered "on a blonde": 130,000 gold German marks—$35,000 at the going rate of exchange—plus 3.5 percent interest over seventeen years. In his unhurried monotone bass, Ladyzhnikov explained that he was not speaking about an arbitration tribunal this time, but a state trial. If earlier Gorky had feared the damage litigation could do to his reputation, he now had nothing to worry about. Ladyzhnikov was going to court—a real civil court. A German court.

When Ladyzhnikov left Petrograd for Berlin in February 1921, knowing that Gorky would be leaving before long, too, provided he didn't "give up his soul to God" (Ladyzhnikov loved the old Russian expressions, as well as Slavonic words, but he was also a realist who did not put much stock in Dr. Manukhin's spleen X-rays), he obtained Gorky's power of attorney to initiate proceedings against Parvus to recover the old debt. Ladyzhnikov knew Gorky's projected and actual earnings a year in advance, down to the last kopek. They were not inconsiderable compared with the income of other Russian writers, who by that time were severely impoverished in Paris, Prague, and Belgrade, to say nothing of those remaining in Russia. But for Gorky the money was insufficient. The yellow press before the revolution, and the White émigrés after, published the story that Gorky was a millionaire living in luxury and owned numerous villas, but it was all just a fabrication. It was after he divorced his first wife, Ekaterina Peshkova, that he began to complain in letters about his lack of money and difficulty paying bills.

There were many reasons for his constant fretting: though Andreeva never went against Gorky's wishes, she pressured him into donating significant sums to the Bolshevik Party to fund various revolutionary publications that he sometimes contributed to, or refusing his fee for an article or even a book so the money could be sent to the Party. He was living in the public eye in Russia and Europe, and at his villa on Capri (rented, not owned) there were always four to six guests, sometimes even more. There was a cook and a servant. Peshkova was in Russia with their son Maxim, and Gorky regularly sent her money: "Ekaterina Pavlovna must also get a little money. Please! Just borrow it somewhere on interest, all right?" She had an apartment and a maid in Moscow, Maxim was in school, and in the summers they went to the Italian Riviera. There were at least seven people who lived for many years entirely on what Gorky sent them, including two old friends from Nizhniy Novgorod, the wife of the writer Ivan Volny, and an Italian woman who was often a guest in Sorrento with her son. Gorky also supported his adopted son Zinovy Peshkov before World War I.

Ladyzhnikov realized that Gorky was going to need a lot more money. No matter how many sensational articles were written about him in the European and American papers, the print runs for his works would undoubtedly decline in postwar Europe. It was an open question whether Gorky would be able to write screenplays, regardless of his desire to do so. Ladyzhnikov had the feeling that Gorky wouldn't be able to, and time proved him right. The "family," which was supposed to settle in Germany, or Italy, or somewhere else very soon, would be much bigger than his prewar Capri family, and in a recent letter Gorky had to ask Ladyzhnikov, "Can you give me twenty-five thousand?" There would be Moura, who would have to support a governess and two children in Estonia; Maxim, his wife, and, probably, their children; there would be Nightingale, who had never earned a penny and would always be a homebody, a hypochondriac, and just plain lazy, even though everyone agreed he was a nice, homey fellow and quite charming in his way (Ladyzhnikov called him a "scarce item"); then there was Peshkova in Moscow, who was now advising Dzerzhinsky on cases involving the liquidated Socialist Revolutionary Party. She had been an SR and was considered a specialist on matters relating to it, but she worked without pay, out of principle, though principles were of no use to members of the SR Party who were repressed. Andreeva and Kryuchkov were still on the staff of the Berlin Trade Office, so there was no need to worry about them. But very soon the serious question of publishing an edition of Gorky's works in Russia would come up. If, owing to the lack of paper in Russia, Ladyzhnikov were given permission to open a publishing house in Berlin to publish Gorky and perhaps with time even other Soviet writers, then could he at last schedule the publication of the collected works he and Gorky had been planning? Wouldn't all print media ultimately end up in the hands of Gosizdat, the state publishing house? It must be said that his misgivings on this score were not unfounded: in 1924 Gosizdat became Gorky's sole publisher.

It was a little early, however, to consider this eventuality an imminent danger. The fluctuations in European currency disturbed Ladyzhnikov much more. The Austrian schilling was now worthless; the German mark had started its decline, though the catastrophe was still a year off. Meanwhile the date for Gorky's arrival in Berlin was approaching: at first it was set for August, then September. Ladyzhnikov knew that Gorky would arrive without any money, that the old prewar contracts had lost their force, and that extracting something out of European publishers for anything published after 1916 would not be easy. He was right again, and when Gorky arrived in Europe in October, his entreaties about money resumed. He had brought his collection of jade with him from Russia in order to sell it. He also tried to get word to Lenin through Peshkova that he was in Berlin and impoverished. Lenin wrote to Molotov in December 1921 that it was essential Gorky be "added to the list of people being supported abroad at the expense of the Soviet state." Insofar as is known, however, nothing ever came of that. But by the beginning of 1922, Ladyzhnikov had a surprise for Gorky: Parvus's first payment on his old debt.

That Parvus reluctantly agreed to return the money is not really surprising. With all his expenses, with three houses in Copenhagen, a castle in Switzerland, and millions in a Geneva bank, with his mistresses and Wannsee palace (later used by the Gestapo and now open to the public), and with all his other wealth, $35,000, even with the customary 3.5 percent yearly interest, was not a large sum for him. What is amazing, though, is how determinedly those who knew about it kept it a secret, through the 1920s. Andreeva, Maxim, Moura, Kryuchkov, and perhaps Peshkova knew. I myself was present in Gorky's office in Saarow when Gorky told Khodasevich about it, but at that time I was totally deaf to monetary discussions. Not only did I keep mum, I retained only a very vague memory of the conversation. Had Khodasevich not reminded me of it later I would never have remembered Gorky's admission at all. Khodasevich also reminded me that when Gorky first complained to him about Zinoviev, it had to do with Zinoviev's insinuation in the press that the money Gorky had received to start *New Life* had come as a subsidy from Parvus. Khodasevich not only never told anyone "Gorky's secret" but he never even made a note of it for himself and never alluded to it in his memoirs, *Necropolis*, or in the afterword to his reminiscences of Gorky, which I published after his death in *Sovremennye zapiski* (vol. 70, 1940). Nor did I reveal it in my autobiography (*The Italics Are Mine*) when I described the scene of our departure from Sorrento in April 1925. I wrote that when the Italian driver's carriage rolled out onto the road toward Castellammare, Khodasevich said, "He won't get the Nobel prize, Zinoviev will be purged, and he'll go back to Russia."

What Khodasevich actually said was: "He won't get the Nobel prize, Zinoviev will be purged, Parvus's payments will cease, and he'll go back to Russia."

Parvus had just died, three months before that happened.

Evidently even Parvus wanted the matter kept secret. His secretaries and lawyers knew how to hold their tongues. But why was Gorky so afraid of disclosure? After all, he had been the victim, and now money was being returned, which by rights belonged to him. What was there in this that demanded confidentiality? The truth was that he didn't want to be a victim, he was ashamed of being a victim, ashamed that he, an intelligent man, had been fooled, that his comrade Social Democrat had deceived him. Parvus's whole career between 1903 and 1922 was such that it was shameful to have had anything to do with him at all—especially for a Russian writer, a Bolshevik, a friend of Lenin's, even if he wasn't a Party member. Gorky was a late Victorian by character and habit, and for late Victorians shame was a cloud constantly hanging over them, even more threatening than it had been for the early Victorians.

Their shame was always connected with some secret—whether it be personal, family, group, social, or even national: a grandfather's "social disease" caught in his youth, or the suicide of a nephew, or the illegitimate child of a sister, or the insanity of an aunt, or a scandal in the card club involving a man who had been a member for so many years, or a comrade's betrayal of the Party. If your country lost a war, or suffered a "national disgrace" (in the vernacular: got itself into a mess on an international scale), the only way to erase it from memory was not to talk, listen, or think about it. To forget it.

Shame for someone else and shame for himself somehow converged in Gorky, and it was just as awkward for him to be robbed as it was to rob someone else. Seeing a statue without a fig leaf in a Naples museum while standing next to a woman caused him such inner torment that he would turn dark red and hide. Seeing a woman with bare breasts onstage was unbearable torture for him. He was embarrassed by the wet diapers of a peasant baby, by obscene words muttered by a passing stranger, and he was especially embarrassed by his own suspenders, forgotten and left hanging on a nail in the lavatory in the morning; embarrassed, too, for a stranger's shamelessness, for anything that violated the last century's code of behavior: a lamp left on when two people were in each other's arms, when the code said it was supposed to be dark; the unbuttoned pants of the housepainter loudly singing an Italian song about the sun, love, and Sorrento; the little pile the fox terrier left in the garden in the morning.

Parvus made payments four times a year beginning in January 1922. Ladyzhnikov would deposit each $2,000 payment in the Dresden Bank. Kryuchkov forwarded the sum first to Saarow, then to Marienbad, and later, starting in the spring of 1924, to Sorrento.

Gorky received $26,000 in all. There were delays throughout 1924. In January 1925 the money didn't come until February. Then Ladyzhnikov wrote Gorky that Parvus had died suddenly in December 1924 and that the payments would stop. A will had not been found, heirs—children from four common-law marriages—were turning up every day, and sorting out who was a lawyer, who a business partner, and who a plain and simple crook had so far proven impossible. As for capital assets, there were none that he could see.

Ladyzhnikov and Kryuchkov soon found out that a son had turned up in Berlin—Parvus's son by his first wife, a man of about twenty-five who was devoted to Soviet power and worked in the People's Commissariat for Foreign Affairs in Moscow. Evgeny Gnedin went to Berlin with permission from the central authorities in Moscow to see to his father's millions—not to claim them for himself but to turn them over to the Soviet authorities.

It was 1927 before Gnedin received his share of his father's estate, 100,000 Reich marks, which he immediately transferred to the Trade Office—"for the struggle against capitalism"—as he had promised. His subsequent fate was no different from that of thousands of other Soviet officials. In 1939 he was serving as first secretary at the Soviet embassy in Berlin when he was arrested—having apparently been denounced by Mikhail Koltsov. Lavrenty Beria tortured Gnedin with the help of an assistant, after which he was sent to a concentration camp for twenty years. Sixteen years later, after Stalin's death, he was brought back and rehabilitated. Like the rest of the staff at the People's Commissariat for Foreign Affairs, he suffered when Molotov replaced Litvinov as part of Stalin's pro-German policy in the months leading up to the Hitler–Stalin pact.

Reflecting on this period in Gorky's life, I have to say that the years from 1921 to 1927 (his first trip to the Soviet Union was in 1928) were happy ones, although he never had any doubts about whether to return to Russia or not.[4] His best work was written during this time, and despite illness and financial worries, he still had Italy. They were happy years for his son, his daughter-in-law, and even Moura. In the summer of 1922, when I saw her for the first time, it was clear that she and Gorky had come to some arrangement, they had settled on the kind of life they wanted to have together, and it was going smoothly. But it was not that way from the start: for a whole year, between 1921—when Moura was shuttling between Tallinn and Helsinki, Tallinn and London, putting off going to St. Blasien, and June 1922, when I met her, she evidently did not know what conditions to set or what concessions to make. In the fall of 1921 she wrote to Gorky that she had married, when in fact she didn't get married until January 1922. In December she informed him that she was on her way to see him, but she never arrived. When he left St. Blasien in April to move in with Maxim, Timosha, and Rakitsky in an apartment in Berlin that Andreeva had rented for him at 203 Kurfürstendamm, Moura was in Estonia. It's difficult to imagine her taking until June—more than six months after their short rendezvous in Helsinki—

---

4. After financial worries the most pressing problem was getting permission to distribute his journal *Beseda* in Russia, and after that the SR trials that were going on in Russia in 1922. Witness Gorky's letter to Rykov, cited here in full:

Alexei Ivanovich!

If the trial of the Socialist Revolutionaries ends in murder it will be premeditated murder, murder most foul.

I beg you to tell L. D. Trotsky and others what my opinion is. I hope it will not surprise you, for throughout the revolution I pointed out to the Soviet authorities a thousand times the senselessness and criminality of wiping out the intelligentsia in our illiterate and backward country.

Today I am convinced that if the SRs are murdered, this crime will incite a moral blockade against Russia on the part of socialist Europe.

M. Gorky. June 1, 1922

(Letter from the Hoover Institution, Stanford, California)

to decide to go live in his house at long last. Did they disagree about the conditions of her freedom, or did some extraneous circumstance prevent her from coming? Might Lai have demanded that she stay with him, threatening her? Or was Tikhonova reluctant to agree to break up with Gorky? Whether money or political considerations were also part of the mix remains unknown.

When Gorky moved to Heringsdorf for the summer with all his people on May 30, 1922, Moura finally made her decision to join him. Three months later, when the whole family came to live in Saarow, their life together had clearly stabilized.

Her face radiating peace and calm, and her large, wide-set eyes sparkling with life—maybe it wasn't quite true, or more likely it wasn't the whole truth, but her bright, quick mind, her profound ability to understand her interlocutor after hearing only half a word, and her reply, which would flash across her face before she spoke, and her sudden pensiveness, and her odd accent, and the fact that everyone who spoke to her or even sat next to her was somehow convinced that he or she alone was more important to Moura at that moment than anyone else in the world—gave her an aura of warmth and rarity. She did not cut her hair, as was the fashion, but wore it in a knot low at the nape of her neck, looking as if it had been pinned up in haste, with one or two locks falling from that wave of hair onto her forehead and cheek. Her lightly penciled eyes were always eloquent, saying exactly what people wanted to hear: something serious or funny, sad or smart, soft and cozy. Her body was straight and strong; her figure was elegant even in simple dresses. Evidently she was already bringing well-cut, well-made suits from England and had learned to go around without a hat (something new at the time) and to buy herself expensive comfortable shoes. She did not wear jewelry, but a man's watch on a wide band was strapped snugly around her wrist. Her fingers were always ink-stained, giving her the look of a schoolgirl.

There was something cruel in her face, which was a little too broad, with her high cheekbones and wide-set eyes, but she had an unbelievably endearing, feline smile. Were it not for that sweetness, Moura would have come across as mannish and dry. Now, slender and strong, she had learned to conceal her animal or feline way when she wanted to; only her health spoke to her staying power. I remember her sick in bed only one time. I came into her room at night. Dawn was barely breaking out the window. I heard her moans. She was tossing and turning under the sheet. I tried to cover her with a blanket, when suddenly she asked for a basin. I flew to the washroom and held her head in my arms while she vomited up something green. By morning she was striding about the room and collecting her hairpins.

In Germany and Czechoslovakia she was responsible for everything having to do with the pension or hotel where we were all staying, and later, in Italy, she managed the house, which she had rented, and the cook, whom she had hired. When I arrived with Khodasevich at the German seaside town of Heringsdorf, and saw for the first time that spacious dacha, the Villa Irmgard, on the Baltic coast, Moura was in Estonia with her children. When she returned, we came out to Heringsdorf a second time. I was introduced to her, and we learned that they were moving to Saarow for the winter, an hour and a half from Berlin. Gorky wanted us to move there with them.

Gorky was coughing and chain-smoking. The Black Forest, where he had spent the winter, had not really helped him. As soon as he left he felt worse, and in Berlin all the progress he had made in St. Blasien was lost. Dr. Kraus (or Maus), who was treating him, found he was suffering from a heart condition and nervous exhaustion, but he ruled out even thinking about treating his heart until his lungs healed and the tubercular process was stopped. Gorky wrote Lenin from St. Blasien: "I'm undergoing treatment. Two hours a day I lie in the open air in all weather. They don't spoil us here: rain or snow, out we go. And we lie there meekly! There are 263 of us here, each more tubercular than the next. Living is very costly."

She was with him now in Heringsdorf. The house was large, and the "young people" didn't bother him. On Kronverk they had spent little time alone; here they were together day and night. The same guests came to visit: Ladyzhnikov, Grzhebin, Chaliapin, Alexei Tolstoy, Zinovy Peshkov, Kryuchkov. Kryuchkov was now not only Andreeva's secretary but a senior official in the Berlin Trade Office and attorney for both Andreeva and Gorky. A strange intuitive understanding formed between Kryuchkov and Moura that had no need of words, an understanding of what could and could not be accomplished, what was and what wasn't necessary.

When Gorky began to feel better, they would go for afternoon walks by the sea. In Saarow, then in Marienbad, and later still in Sorrento, he (and whoever was with him) walked slowly; he had a long, yellowing, drooping mustache, his hair was in a crew cut, and he wore a broad-brimmed black hat pushed back on his head. In the morning he would wear big wire-rimmed glasses to read the newspapers and write his letters.

In truth, he had been sick all his life and long ago had reconciled himself to that fact. He had somehow grown accustomed to his tuberculosis, which was probably what sent him to his grave in the end. He never felt particularly different in the Black Forest, or Berlin, or the house in the pine forest in Saarow where he was taken in the fall. It was called a sanatorium but that only meant a doctor lived there who was at the service of guests around the clock. We went to Saarow, too, but we lived more modestly, in the Bahnhof Hotel, and walked to the sanatorium almost every day after dinner. He liked having people around him.

During the winter, the off-season in a small place that livened up only in the summer, there were very few people and it was quiet. Gorky and his entourage lived in spacious comfort. Downstairs were the "children's rooms," that is, those for Maxim, Timosha, and Nightingale, and a room for Valentina Khodasevich when she came to visit. On the second floor were Gorky's room and a large, cold, sparsely furnished room used by Moura. A new period in her life had begun by then: a typewriter had been purchased, a daily routine established, and order created. Even so, right up to January 1923, no one could have said how permanent this state of affairs was. Or whether Gorky meekly accepted her frequent travels and her annual three-month absences. She invariably went to see her children three times a year—a custom which, once adopted, nothing could change—disappearing every summer, Christmas, and Easter, stopping in Berlin on her way to Estonia and back.

Moura was becoming increasingly preoccupied by something that threatened to spoil all her plans and undermine her future. This was the problem of her legal husband, Baron Nikolai Budberg, who, as she told Khodasevich, could wind up in jail at any moment. For what? For unsavory card debts, writing checks that bounced, disputes with women over unpaid alimony, and what he felt to be perfectly harmless romantic blackmail. He could easily ruin Moura's reputation, too, especially since he was starting to get involved in pseudo-political adventures as a member of some Russo-German union that was apparently illegal. She had wanted a good name but got just the opposite, and all her money was being spent on him.

Khodasevich was one of those people who knows how to listen and likes doing so. He never interrogated her, it was always Moura who started talking. He was especially good at listening to women, with whom he generally felt closer and more at ease than he did with men. They were drawn to him by the undivided attention he gave them, by the seriousness and force of his interest. It would never occur to him—and they knew it—to instruct them, or patronize them by speaking paternally or giving unwanted advice. He listened with complete attention and reacted only when he knew they expected and wanted him to. When he did respond, it was in his own way—not like a father, or a brother, or a teacher, or a lover, but like an old and devoted friend. At such times he was sincere, it couldn't have been anything else, and never struck a single false note. Only later, after the encounter, did any criticism, irony, or judgment creep into his thinking. But he never expressed his doubts, not even to me. They could only be guessed at obliquely.

She told him a lot, far from everything, of course, and not only because I was often in his long narrow room, sitting in a corner by the window reading a book. She talked to Khodasevich because she had become friends with him, as many women did before and after her. She didn't ask him for advice; she knew perfectly well what needed to be done. I would half listen to what they were talking about. She was nine years older than me and treated me like an adolescent. My presence did not inhibit her. It seemed to me that she had no one else in the world to talk to.

One evening, when we were alone, he remarked offhandedly: "She's planning to ship him to Argentina."

I knew that he was talking about Budberg. The next spring, Gorky felt worse again and was preparing to leave Saarow, and Dr. Kraus (or Maus) was talking again about the Black Forest. One night Khodasevich went for a walk with Moura after dinner, and when he came back late I was lying in bed reading another book: "She's shipping him to Argentina."

"What if he comes back?" I asked.

"From there it's not so easy, you know."

At that time Moura was of course more interesting to me than all the others, Gorky included, but I knew we could never be close, primarily because we were not equals. At Christmas, when Bely, Viktor Shklovsky, Grzhebin, Ladyzhnikov, the actor Konstantin Miklashevsky (an admirer of Valentina's and the author of *The Hypertrophy of Art*), and of course Andreeva and Kryuchkov all came to Saarow for Christmas, Moura was in Estonia. I missed her. I missed her intelligence, her vitality, her mystery, the mystery surrounding her, which was not like a veil thrown on at will or an artificially constructed system but a mystery that was inseparable from her and that radiated a special, unvarying aura. Between Christmas and the New Year I had to go to Berlin for a day or two, and one evening at the Zoo Bahnhof, I spotted her in the crowd, walking arm in arm with a tall blond (possibly Budberg). Dressed completely differently from the way she dressed at home in Saarow, she looked elegant and gay. The day before a letter had arrived from her from Tallinn saying that she was busy with Christmas parties for the children and might be held up as much as a week. My first thought when I saw her was to try to keep her from seeing me. And she didn't notice me, she walked right past without looking to either side. When I told Khodasevich I had seen her that evening but she, beautiful and animated, thankfully hadn't seen me, Khodasevich said that anything was possible when it came to Moura, that somewhere out there beyond the walls of the Saarow "sanatorium" she led a complicated, restless, and not always happy life, and that she told us things that hadn't happened and was silent about things that had. So it continued twenty years later, long after Saarow, when she kept to herself her meetings with Harold Nicolson and her breakfasts with Somerset Maugham, her friendship with Vita Sackville-West, and the receptions she attended at the French embassy in London.

The "sanatorium" was just an ordinary pension in the middle of a pine forest. The doctor in residence looked after Gorky and tried unsuccessfully to enforce a diet. There were no other patients in the pension at the time, so a very Russian life was led on both floors. There was a constant stream of guests. Gorky got up at eight, drank coffee, and worked through the mornings. The train from Berlin delivered visitors by noon. After a noisy Christmas, when Gorky's guests filled the entire house and even our Bahnhof Hotel, things quieted down, but there continued to be some regular visitors: Andreeva—in Moura's absence—came every Sunday with Kryuchkov;

and also Grzhebin and Ladyzhnikov, who still owned their publishing house, although Gosizdat was threatening to take them over. From time to time foreign journalists would show up, but usually they were not allowed to see Gorky, especially in Moura's absence, since she was now considered his official interpreter. Valentina was there, too, having come from Petrograd to stay for the spring. She told us in strict confidence that "the feeling back home is that Duke is overrated" and that Vladimir Mayakovsky, Vladimir Tatlin, and the avant-garde in general, who were all Valentina's personal friends, were saying, "It's time to throw Gorky overboard." They felt his writing was out of date. "Who needs it?" (Valentina's favorite expression when she didn't like something.)

Andrei Bely stayed at the Bahnhof Hotel for a time, as did the publisher Solomon Kaplun, who had a case of unrequited love for the talented young pianist Tamara Miklashevskaya, who threw him over for Leonid Krasin, ambassador-in-waiting to France when France decided to recognize Soviet Russia in 1924. In February or March I met Boris Nicolaevsky, a deeply knowledgeable Menshevik historian who kept in touch with the European Social Democrats and collected books and documents on the history of the Russian Revolution. He had asked his brother-in-law, Alexei Rykov, to take him along the next time he went to see Gorky, which he did. Nicolaevsky was planning to propose to Gorky that they jointly edit a historical journal, *Chronicle of the Revolution*, to be printed in Berlin and sold in Russia, in which they would publish documents pertaining to the February and October revolutions. He was thirty-six years old at the time. He was tall and heavy, taciturn and alert, with intelligent eyes, curly hair, and a high-pitched voice.

On one of his subsequent visits, when he came without Rykov to discuss the future journal in earnest (it never got off the ground; Soviet Russia would never allow the importation of such a publication), he walked in on our *pelmeni* party. The idea of feasting on these handmade favorites, Siberian dumplings the size of ravioli, had had everyone in the house talking excitedly for days. We had studied a cookbook and, with Nightingale's help, talked the sanatorium cook into turning the kitchen over to us for a day. After we had gone downstairs and taken our posts (Nightingale immediately stretched out on three chairs: his favorite position was lying on his side with his head propped up in his hand, either on his bed or on a sofa, or, barring that, on three lined-up chairs), Gorky came down wearing an enormous apron—a sheet tied at the waist—and, rolling up his sleeves, began making *pelmeni* with us. What Timosha, Valentina, and I did was hit-or-miss, but what Gorky did was high art. A total of 1,500 were made. He had learned the art working for a baker in his youth. The meal made Nicolaevsky, who possessed a splendid appetite, enormously happy. Many years later, when he and I were having lunch at the Russian Tea Room in New York and eating *pelmeni* (he ordered three portions for himself, one right after another), I reminded him of our Saarow *pelmeni*. He said he'd never forgotten them.

Of the few foreign correspondents Gorky did receive, only one became a regular visitor for a while, first in Saarow and then in Günterstal, where Gorky's doctors sent him in the summer. He was a young American, Barrett Clark, who later described his visits in a memoir entitled *Intimate Portraits*. Clark had written a letter in English requesting an interview, and it was his great good luck that Moura read it and replied with a day and hour when Gorky would be happy to see him. Clark supposed he was going to see an "old lion on his death bed." It would be the first time Moura played her part of mistress of the house, secretary, interpreter, and literary agent in the presence of an outsider. She played it brilliantly, and Clark was utterly enchanted. He writes that she was "charming, original, and knew her business magnificently," that she possessed a mixture of "attention, tact, and tranquility." After a few visits he began coming to Saarow without ceremony and was sad to see that "Gorky lives in poverty thanks to the paltry fees he collects from the editions of his stories and articles." Gorky wondered whether his play *The Judge*, then running in Moscow (it had opened in February 1919), could be translated and produced in the United States. Clark jumped at the idea, and the two of them simultaneously suggested that Moura should translate it. She immediately consented. Gorky gave her the manuscript and promised to think about the possibility of further translations.

In the spring of 1923 Saarow was abandoned in favor of the Black Forest. For one thing, the summer season at Saarow would start in a month, which threatened to transform the quiet life of the sanatorium. For another, Gorky's tuberculosis had worsened again, and he was coughing up blood. Instead of going back to St. Blasien, however, he went to Günterstal, which was closer to Freiburg im Breisgau.

Khodasevich and I went back to Berlin for a while, but everyone else remained in Saarow briefly (Moura was again in Estonia) before moving on. At the end of the summer Clark came to Günterstal to pick up Moura's translation of the play. This time it was Maxim and Timosha who enchanted him. Maxim, the "tennis clubber," spent entire days on the tennis court (Clark notes that in Russia he had a "post in Lenin's government"). Timosha was temporarily in charge of the house. Moura wrote him that she was not running the house at the moment because she was so busy with a new translation project—Chekhov's letters to Olga Knipper. But disappointment was in store for her: when she finished the work, which had posed insurmountable difficulties for her, she discovered that the letters were being published simultaneously in England and the United States in a translation by Constance Garnett.

Clark was unhappy with Moura's translation of *The Judge*. It was "crudely" done and not "finished"; it was "more like a pony than a translation"; he would have to rework it totally. The only consolation was Moura's promise of a new preface by the author himself: "I have talked Gorky into writing a foreword to my translation of the play especially for you."

Clark admired the pride Moura took in being "the least Russian of all Russians," and, as a young journalist just starting out on his career, he was particularly grateful for the fact that she had helped him gain access to the "great writer" and obtain the rights to publish and produce Gorky's play. So he sat down to rework her "pony," trying to lend it "some shape, which is essential for publication."

The play was never produced, but it was published in an "authorized translation by Marie Zakrevsky and Barrett H. Clark" in 1924 in the Modern Drama series. Clark's last visit to Günterstal was not a success. A German neighbor had killed Maxim's cat, and Maxim had got into a fight with him and nearly killed him. After that it was unthinkable for Gorky to stay on; he would have to go to Berlin and wait there for an Italian visa. He had news from the Soviet ambassador in Rome that Mussolini "has no objection to Gorky's coming to Italy to take up permanent residence on the coast of the Gulf of Naples." There were, however, two conditions: he could not engage in political propaganda, and he could not live on Capri. Gorky readily agreed.

Moura spent the summer of 1923 "with the children" as usual, but she also spent part of it in Berlin, perhaps because she was bored in Günterstal: no one, or almost no one, ever visited. Moura came to see us six times in two months when we were living in the Krampe pension on Viktoria-Luise-Platz. During that time she was getting Budberg ready for Argentina. On September 14 she finally left for Günterstal along with Khodasevich. I saw them off at the train station in Berlin.

I remember standing on the platform, watching the train pull out and thinking about her. Her energy, her vitality, her desperate instinct for survival were all things I could feel and understand. Moreover, "survival," as I understood it, didn't simply mean not dying from starvation, cold, poverty, and disease, that is, the "death on a bench on a boulevard in a strange city" that Beckett wrote about later. Survival meant not sinking to the bottom, not being content with the absence of books, music, clean linen, and warm clothing, or the lack of knowing, capable, vital people around you. Survival meant not reconciling oneself to the fate of a refugee thrown helter-skelter out of the grim reality of Russian life and into the postwar Europe of the Roaring Twenties and jazz music, but seeking out those who had picked themselves up after the revolution, the civil war, the Red Terror, those who had finished their studies and mended their broken bones, those who were drowning but had scrambled onto dry land. I already knew then what women of Moura's circle were up against in Berlin, Paris, and Prague, former mother's darlings, delicate and easily frightened, girls from finishing schools who had no education, wives of White officers and officials in tsarist embassies who had never worked a day in their lives, whose teeth were now falling out, their palms calloused from cleaning other people's apartments, their brains petrified from the experiences they had been through, experiences they could neither surmount nor comprehend. Wash other people's floors? Embroider in cross-stitch? Make hats? Be a powder-room attendant in a nightclub? Or take a nursing course and earn the right (as a foreigner without a work permit) to seek work as an aide in the municipal hospitals of Laënnec and Val-de-Grace, emptying bedpans? No one would give her a stipend, or a new dress, or an apartment with an elevator. She did it on her own, climbing up like an acrobat on a high wire to hear Dobrowen play the piano, seduce Blok, talk to Bely about Rudolf Steiner, or Viktor Shklovsky about Laurence Sterne, and ride now in a wagon-lit with Khodasevich, the cleverest of men, a conversationalist she would remember all her life. In her energy, independence, and freedom, in her break with her grandmothers and great-grandmothers, both real and invented, bronze Venuses and butterflies in silk and lace, I saw my own energy, my own ability to survive, and my own break with the past.

Only one thing bothered me: her enigma, her mystery, and her lies had in them a streak of something dark and devious I could never quite understand. Shouldn't I try to overcome that? How fine it would be if there were no ambiguity behind the masks. But I told myself I was reasoning like Ant No. 987 654 321 carrying a twig on my head three times my own weight (and glad to be carrying it, the fool!), whereas she was not an ant and never would be. She was a hawk. A leopard. And I had met her not so that I could emulate her but so that, by watching her, I could survive in my own way, a different way, becoming neither a hawk nor a leopard.

But there was one thing I could take from her, I thought. She knows what *savoir vivre* means—and it's not just the opposite of *savoir crever*, which Khodasevich understood long before Beckett did, that is, knowing how to croak as opposed to knowing how to live. *Savoir vivre* is the ability to resist succumbing to the suicidal impulse—the desire to cease to be. Even more, though, Moura's *savoir vivre* was the irrational desire to live at a level which her generation had never experienced or even been promised, but which she had promised to herself.

The patronizing way she patted my round cheeks and carefully curled hair did not offend me. In our own way, we had each decided never to return to a caveman's existence, and we had both experienced moments of responsibility and choice. We saw our actions not as a series of female whims, not as the universal sins of our time or the result of an imperfect environment, but as emerging from a part of ourselves for which we personally had to answer.

It was a difficult time for her. She had obtained the necessary papers to put Budberg on a ship to South America, and she had given him her word that she would send him a specified sum every month, but he got off the boat in Antwerp or Cherbourg and came back having decided that her spoken promise was not enough and demanding a notarized letter. They never saw each other again. She also had to save her sister Alla, or rather come to her aid. Alla was living alone in Paris and over the years had become addicted to narcotics. The intense dramas that accompanied her numerous affairs had finally destroyed her. Now she was taking money from anyone who would give it to her and had fallen into a serious depression, which would lead to her suicide.

Khodasevich returned a week later. He had gone to see Gorky regarding *Beseda* (*Colloquy*). This journal, edited by Gorky, Bely, Khodasevich, and with Professors Bruno Adler and Friedrich Braun as science editors, had been started in the fall of 1922. It was to be bimonthly and unaffiliated, in the tradition of the Russian "fat" journals, printed in Berlin. There would be an equal number of foreign and native contributors. But Gorky had to ask permission from the authorities in Moscow to distribute the journal in Russia. Like Gorky himself, Kaplun, the publisher of *Beseda*, decided not to wait for the Kremlin's formal permission, and the first issue came out in May 1923. Gorky attracted some high-profile European writers to the journal, including Romain Rolland, Galsworthy, Wells, Bernhard Kellermann, Stefan Zweig, and Franz Hellens. But if permission were not eventually secured, the journal couldn't exist. Every month Gorky heard rumors either directly from the Kremlin, or through Peshkova, or in letters from his correspondents, that *Beseda* had been given or was about to be given permission. Despite the uncertainty, Gorky continued inviting contributors from both inside and outside Russia and wrote a series of stories for the journal. He was always discussing the plans he had for its future.

The problem was far from being resolved by the winter of 1923. Nor had the Italian visas been approved. The situation in Germany, both political and economic, was becoming more and more difficult. Those who had somewhere to go, did. We didn't, so we went to

Prague on a hunch. That was on November 16, and on the 26th Gorky followed us with the whole household to "wait for Mussolini to deign to send me a visa."

Moura insisted on remaining in Czechoslovakia. What was the point of settling in ravaged, impoverished Austria, where life was even more "abnormal" than in Germany? It was impossible to get a Swiss visa at that time, and everyone felt that in a month or two the Italian visas would come (they came in April 1924). On December 6, we all moved from Prague to Marienbad, which was boarded up for the winter and dusted with snow. It was like being in Saarow: Gorky liked to stay in places during the off-season. Moura went immediately to Estonia and returned on January 13. We were staying in the Hotel Maxhof, where Czech reporters were rarely admitted and then only briefly. This time we were all living on one floor, in seven or eight rooms that opened onto a wide hallway.

An industrious, quiet life began. Gorky spent the morning writing and then would go out for a short walk down the snowy lanes. We had no guests except Kryuchkov, who came twice on business. Everything in town was closed: the stores, the theater, the health spa. Before dinner Gorky wrote letters, and in the evening, over tea, there were long conversations. He would share the day's news with us: they were still promising the visas; they were still not letting *Beseda* into Russia; the first and second issues were lying in the basement of Epokha publishers, and the third was being printed but there was no place to store it. He had begun to lose patience noticeably, and he informed Kryuchkov and Ladyzhnikov (who was now connected with Gosizdat) that he would not publish anything in Russian journals and would have nothing to do with Russian publishers until permission was granted to distribute *Beseda* in Russia.

"You could write to Ilyich about *Beseda*," Maxim told him, but there was no point in writing Lenin: Lenin had had another stroke. He was paralyzed and could not speak. Everyone knew it, not only from the papers but from Peshkova's letters. When Lenin died on January 21, 1924, Peshkova sent them a telegram. Moura did not let Gorky shed any tears. She felt that the best therapy was work. As Khodasevich later wrote:

> The next day Moura sat him down to write his reminiscences of Lenin. There was every reason to believe they would be translated into many languages. He had barely finished when, as if by coincidence, Kryuchkov arrived from Berlin. He was now the director of Mezhdunarodnaya Kniga, the Soviet publishing agency for books to be sold outside the Soviet Union. He argued compellingly to Gorky that as the "stormy petrel of the revolution" he was obligated to speak up about the great leader of the revolution. In other words, in this instance he had to break his pledge and allow his memoir of Lenin to be printed in Russia. Kryuchkov took the manuscript away with him. In the Soviet Union it underwent the most drastic censorship cuts and changes.

But these cuts and changes were nothing compared to the changes Gorky himself subsequently made under pressure from Lenin's widow, Krupskaya.

Lenin's death alarmed Gorky, but it also fundamentally changed Gorky's attitude toward him. He had felt Lenin's greatness fully for the first time when Lenin was wounded by Dora Kaplan, on August 30, 1918. The moment Gorky learned of the assassination attempt, all his resentment of Zinoviev vanished, and he recognized that Lenin had been right about everything and that he, Gorky, in all his petty quarrels with the chairman of the Petrograd Commune, had been wrong. Now he was once again filled with remorse. This man of "greatness," of "genius," had died, and Gorky felt orphaned and frightened by a premonition of his own future obscurity. He gave his article on Lenin to Kryuchkov, who immediately took it with him to Berlin. Before Kryuchkov's departure, he and Moura had a long conversation about business matters. They had to give some thought to future finances: the projected income from editions of Gorky's works in Europe and the United States was not reassuring. Did they have a hunch that Parvus's payments might be cut off? Each time Ladyzhnikov informed them of the receipt of another payment at the Dresden Bank, a sigh of relief passed through the house.

Moura had an important conversation with Khodasevich, too. One evening after everyone else had gone off to their own rooms, they were left sitting alone at the empty table in the room at the end of the hall that had no name and was used in the morning for breakfast (dinner was served downstairs, in the hotel's huge empty dining room), and in the daytime by Maxim and Timosha for their art projects. Here Nightingale would sometimes stretch out on three chairs, and it was here that Timosha and I curled each other's hair for family holidays.

I awoke in the middle of the night. The light was burning in the room. Khodasevich's bed was untouched. The clock said half past two. Surprised, I threw on a robe and walked out of my room. The door at the far end of the hallway was open, and I could hear people speaking softly. I walked up to the door. A solitary light was burning overhead. They were sitting opposite each other, and there was tension in their muffled voices.

Unnoticed, I cautiously went back and lay down, but something was troubling me, and I couldn't fall asleep. About half an hour passed and Khodasevich, pale and tired, walked into the room. "What happened?" I asked. He replied: "She intends to do everything in her power to get him to go back to Russia."

It had always seemed to me that this was what Maxim wanted his father to do, too, though neither Timosha nor Nightingale were sympathetic to the idea. It seemed strange coming from Moura. But when

Khodasevich explained her reasoning it seemed sound. The print runs of his foreign-language editions were falling catastrophically despite Galsworthy's and Rolland's assurances that he was, as ever, the greatest of them all. Much was happening in Europe that neither Gorky nor anyone around him knew anything about. Virginia Woolf had written an article recently on Arnold Bennett that would have been unthinkable ten years earlier. Claude Farrère, the author of *L'Homme qui assassina*, was forgotten even in France, although he was still alive. In the United States, there were new writers now, some of them even more remarkable than Mark Twain, Upton Sinclair, and Jack London. Gorky had been forced to abandon his work on a screenplay about the seventeenth-century Cossack leader Stenka Razin, which a French studio had asked him to write: it was turned down in Paris before he ever finished. He made a vow to have nothing more to do with "film illusions." It was becoming clear that he must forget once and for all the high fees he had earned before the war, when America paid him 2,000 gold rubles for a printer's sheet of two dozen pages!

Much that had been coming out of Russia in the last year irritated and even embittered Gorky. When he learned that Krupskaya was compiling a list of banned books to be removed from the libraries, a list that included the Bible, the Koran, Dante, Schopenhauer, and another hundred authors, he decided he would have to renounce his Soviet citizenship and declare it publicly in a letter to the London *Times*. He would give "them" an ultimatum: either let *Beseda* into Russia or he would start publishing in émigré journals. That in particular frightened Moura: "What will we live on then?" The question was of no small importance. Khodasevich wrote about this later:

> I don't know to what degree Gorky took the possibility of contributing to an émigré journal seriously. I think he pictured it as a tempting but inadmissible act, something like giving up his Soviet citizenship, which he attempted from time to time, writing a

letter to the Party's Central Executive Committee which, moved to tears, he knew in advance he would never send.

One evening when everyone else had gone to bed, Moura called me into her room saying, "Let's have a chat." I have to do justice to her intelligence. Speaking directly and without the slightest insistence, without ever wavering from the tone of a friendly conversation conducted in bedroom slippers, she conveyed with perfect clarity and tact that her monarchist sympathies were known to me, that she had proven well enough her hatred for the Bolsheviks, but Maxim (Gorky's son), you know yourself what he is, he knows only how to squander money, and Alexei Maximovich [Gorky] has to support him and so many other people. "We need no less than ten thousand dollars a year; foreign publishers alone can't give us that much, and if Alexei Maximovich should lose his position as the premier writer of the Soviet republic then they won't pay him anything at all. And Alexei Maximovich himself would be unhappy if some incautious act should spoil his biography.

"[...]For the good of Alexei Maximovich and the whole family he has to stay on good terms with the Bolsheviks. In fact, he has to do everything in his power to improve relations. This," she added significantly, "is essential to us all." After that conversation I began to notice that Alexei Maximovich's moods were making everyone around him uneasy and that I was suspected of being a bad influence.

Of course he may have been a bad influence, but he played no role of any sort in what happened next: pressure from Moura, Maxim, Kryuchkov, Andreeva (a Party worker), and Peshkova (a bona fide associate of Dzerzhinsky's) couldn't help but be a hundred times stronger than Khodasevich's influence. That year Moura did not stay with us long: on February 6, having just returned to Marienbad from her annual Christmas, she was already leaving again, not "to visit the children" but to go to Berlin on business. On the 12th she wrote to Gorky that Gosizdat was demanding that Ladyzhnikov merge his publishing house, Kniga, with theirs, and furthermore that a Gosizdat representative had turned up in Berlin and was offering Gorky a contract for his complete works and promising a print run of 40,000 copies.

These negotiations kept Moura in Germany longer than usual. At the end of March she returned just long enough to help Gorky and his family move from Marienbad to Italy: the visas had finally arrived. On May 5 she was in Berlin again, and Gorky, not without some irritation, was asking Kryuchkov in a letter from Sorrento: "Where is Maria Ignatievna?"

Our visas had come about three weeks before theirs did, and on March 13 we had left for Italy on our own. We finally joined them in Sorrento on October 9, 1924.

The house in Sorrento, the Villa Massa, was big. In the garden there were palm trees, agaves, orange trees, and lemon trees, but the villa was uncomfortable and expensive, and the town felt too close. After passing the summer and the beginning of the fall there, Moura started looking for more suitable lodgings. I went with her to look at the available houses.

Maxim had bought a motorcycle that could carry three passengers, two in the sidecar and one on the "saddle" behind him. Timosha and Nightingale would usually sit in the sidecar and I would sit on the saddle (the thought of Nightingale sitting on the saddle was inconceivable). When Valentina came to visit, Maxim put us in the sidecar, driving us up hill and down dale, to Ravello and Amalfi. Gorky never used the motorcycle: going fast frightened him.

I remember a day in November when the three "children" took a trip south to see Paestum, and Moura and I went to Capo di Sorrento to look at Il Sorito, the villa belonging to Duke Serra di Capriola, which was for rent. It stood on a promontory to the west of Sorrento, a marvelous spot: to the south there were hills; between them, the cypress trees of a cemetery where the Russian artist Sylvester Shchedrin, who had lived and died here, was buried. To the north shimmered the entire panorama of the Gulf of Naples. Beyond the shoreline, jutting out to the west, you could faintly make out the island where Gorky had been forbidden to show himself and where he had spent six years of his life. But old friends came from Capri to see him, fishermen who had known him since 1907, including his old cook, Signor Cataldo, whom Moura promised to hire if they took Il Sorito. In 1926, he had to be let go: not only did he turn out to be a thief who also padded the books but he was in the service of the Fascist police and was spying on Gorky, Moura, and their guests.

I loved Il Sorito immediately and started badgering Moura about renting it. One thing was stopping her: the owners insisted on keeping one-quarter of the house (with a separate entrance) for themselves.

I had been amazed before at Moura's art in dealing with maids, servants, postal officials, salesmen, and owners of pensions and hotels. All you heard was "Frau Baronin" or "la Signora Baronessa," and she would go from room to room, opening and shutting windows, testing faucets, turning lights on and off—nothing escaped her attention. And everyone yielded to her.

Duke Serra di Capriola lived in Naples, where his two grown sons had houses, but his two daughters, who were unmarried and no longer young (or so it seemed to me at the time, when I was younger than everyone), would stay on to live at Il Sorito.[5] Their quarters consisted of two rooms and a balcony located directly under Khodasevich's and my rooms. The older daughter, Matilda, who was dark-haired, quiet, and about thirty years old, taught Timosha and

---

5. One of the duke's ancestors was ambassador to Russia under Paul and Alexander I and had married Princess Vyazemsky.

me to fox-trot; the younger, Elena, who was mannish and independent, spent all day driving through the surrounding countryside in her open car. In time we would all become friends.

Back at the Villa Massa, Gorky and Khodasevich were sitting in the garden. Moura said: Nina wants that villa of the duke's. Let's do something nice for Nina. What do you think? The bathtub there is small though, and to get to the toilet you have to cross the balcony. At the word "toilet" Gorky flushed red and began to tap his fingers nervously on the table and hum something. The next day it was decided we would take the villa.

Around that time I heard some astonishing news from Khodasevich. He told me that Moura had seen Lockhart. Where? When? In Prague, in August. She had finally found him, although finding him wasn't terribly hard, he was prominent enough. She just had to make up her mind to meet him, and she had.

What was surprising was that their paths had crossed three times in the last year, and they could easily have met by accident, the way heroes meet in old-fashioned novels, somewhere unexpected, thereby making it easier for the author to settle their fates. Lockhart had been in Freiburg in the summer of 1923 when Moura was in Günterstal; then he was in Prague; in 1924 he was in Marienbad. But they never came across one another. She knew nothing about him except that he was somewhere in Central Europe. She did not correspond with Baring and saw him rarely when she was in London. Just when she was there and how often—en route to "see the children"—can never be known, but she was. Her Estonian passport allowed her to stay in London for short periods, and beginning in 1924 she even saw Wells there from time to time. Only at the end of the previous summer, after she had gotten Gorky settled in the Villa Massa, did she go to Tallinn via Austria and Czechoslovakia and, stopping on her way in Vienna, picked up Lockhart's trail. Her old friend William Hicks, nicknamed Hickie, was working at the office of the Cunard Line in Vienna. This was the same Hicks who had been arrested at the Lubyanka and released with Lockhart a month later, thirty-six hours before his forced deportation to England. That day he had arranged to marry Lyuba Malinina and bring her with him. It had taken them sixteen days to sail to Aberdeen.

The rest is known from Lockhart's diaries and from his book *Retreat from Glory*. After a telephone conversation with Moura, Hickie called Lockhart in Prague. Lockhart had been living there since 1920, serving in the English mission as a commercial attaché and, since 1922, as a director of the Anglo-Austrian Bank. Its central office was in Prague, but Lockhart was in charge of other branches in Budapest, Vienna, Belgrade, and Sofia. He was given a choice to live in either Belgrade or Prague, and he chose Prague because he had long known that there was marvelous fishing to be had around Prague, and none in Belgrade.

It was Moura. Her voice sounded as if it came from another world. It was slow and musical and very controlled. She had escaped from Russia. She was in Vienna, staying with the "Hickies." For four years she had heard no word from me, almost no news from the outside world. The receiver shook in my hands, as I asked a few idiotic questions: "How are you, my dear?" and "Are you all right?" Geduldiger [a bank official] was in the room. His presence unnerved me. I have always hated the telephone. Yet, in that moment I remembered like a flash how during those days of crisis in July 1918, when she had gone to Estonia and it seemed unlikely that we should ever meet again, I had rung up her flat in St. Petersburg from Moscow seven or eight times every day to ask if there was any news of her. She had come back at great risk to herself, walking across the frontier in the night. She had joined me in Moscow and had remained with me to the end through my imprisonment by the

Bolsheviks until that last farewell at the railway station when I was sent out of Russia under a Bolshevik escort. Now after a separation of six years I was speaking to her again—and on an accursed telephone. "Let me speak to Hickie," I stammered at last. Quickly I shot my questions at him. "May I come for the weekend? Can you put me up?"

When everything was arranged I walked out of the bank and went home in a stupor of uncertainty. Entirely owing to my selfishness and self-indulgence my married life had not been exactly a success. My job in the bank was unpleasant and precarious. I was heavily in debt, and for a moment I clutched rather desperately at the idea of cutting myself loose from England and making a new start. It had been done before. It might be done again. But there were several buts. I was six years older and much nearer forty than thirty. My prospects of earning a living for myself were far from bright, and there were my wife and my boy, a postwar child, to consider. Finally, I had just become a Catholic, and divorce would mean a complete break with my new resolutions.

The next night I left for Vienna, my mind still not made up. I arrived at 6:30 and went straight to mass at St. Stephen's. After mass I walked to my hotel. I was to meet Hickie at his office at eleven. I did not know if Moura was to be there or not. We were to go out to Hickie's villa in the country for the weekend. I sat in the hotel, drank my morning coffee, smoked a chain of cigarettes, and tried to read a newspaper. At half-past ten, I began to walk slowly down the Karntnerstrasse. The sky was cloudless, and the sun beat down fiercely on the pavement, turning the asphalt into a soft putty. I looked into the shop windows to pass the time. Then, as the clock struck eleven, I turned into the Graben, where above a large bookshop the Cunard Company had its office on the first floor.

Moura was standing at the foot of the steps. She was alone. She looked older. Her face was more serious and she had a few gray hairs. She was not dressed as in the old days, but she had not changed. The change was in me—and not for the better. In that moment I admired her above all other women. Her mind, her genius, her control were wonderful. But the old feelings were gone.

We walked up the stairs to the office where Hickie and his wife were waiting for us. "Well," said Moura, "here we are." It was just like old times.

We collected our suitcases and took the little electric railway out to Hinterbrühl.... We all talked at once, and laughed at every word. Yet it was rather a nervous laughter. Hickie, good, gentle, and very English, was, I knew, a little uneasy. As we were leaving the office, he had mumbled something about being careful, and I knew exactly what he had meant.

Lyuba Hicks led the conversation, talked very quickly, and jumped from subject to subject, recalling episodes from the revolution and picnics in the country and games of rounders at the Yusupoffs' country house at Archangelskoe. Moura was the only person who seemed completely self-possessed. For myself I was tongue-tied with that dread of anticipation, which is so much worse than the actual ordeal. I knew—we all knew—that this thing had to be talked out, and after luncheon Lyuba and Hickie left us alone, and Moura and I walked out to the hills behind the villa.... For a few minutes we sat in silence. Then I began to ask her about her life since our separation, and in a calm, matter-of-fact way she filled in the gaps. She had been in prison and had tried to escape. She had been released and had tried to flee from Russia across the ice of the Gulf of Finland. Then she had met Gorky, and he had befriended her, given her literary work to do, and made her in some sort his secretary and literary agent. Finally, she had obtained a foreign passport and she had gone back to her old home in Estonia. The land had been confiscated, but the house remained. It was a home for her two children whom she had to educate. She was paying for her own and her children's keep by translating Russian books into English. She had translated six books a year for six years and does 3,000–4,000 words a day. She had translated most of Gorky. She is making £800 to £900 per annum. Her energy was quite marvellous; her translations extraordinarily good.

When it was Lockhart's turn to speak, he "stumbled miserably," not knowing what to say.

When I looked back on those six years in Prague and Vienna, they seemed to stand out starkly sterile in the barrenness of their achievement. I had lost even my old impudent self-reliance. She had heard that after the war a son had been born to me. She did not know, until I told her, that I had become a Catholic. Clumsily, stammeringly, like a schoolboy pleading guilty to his housemaster, I blundered through the record of my debts and my follies. "Oh God!" she whispered softly.

She despises me for not throwing over everything and taking my courage in both hands, but the truth is that even if everything were favourable and there were no obstacles and no obligations I should not want to do it. There was a mist before my eyes and my temples throbbed violently.

She told him it would be a mistake to return to the past. "Yes, it would be a mistake," she said, and began walking down the path to the villa. That night the four of them sat up very late telling old stories. Lockhart told them about the time in the summer of 1918 when he helped Kerensky escape from Russia through Archangel, having given him Serbian papers, and about the time they saw each other in London in 1919. Reilly had run into Kerensky in 1921, in Prague. "In those days," Kerensky told Lockhart, referring to 1917, "only the Socialists could count on the support of the people. But the Socialists were absolutely incapable of organizing and leading the army, which was so necessary right then." They talked about the future, and about the inevitability of revolution. Lockhart wrote: "Moura predicted that the economic system of the world would alter so rapidly that within twenty years it would be closer to Leninism than to the old prewar capitalism....If the capitalists were wise enough, it would come about without revolution."

Lockhart was supposed to return to Prague on the evening train the next day. Moura decided to go with him. There were no sleepers on the train, and they sat up all night in a crowded first-class carriage. Some bitterness showed in Moura's face. They recalled Trotsky's temper tantrums, Radek's wit, Kollontai's love affairs, Peters's English wife, and Chicherin's sexual quirks. Lockhart told her about Reilly's subsequent fate, how he had met him in London later, and about his wild schemes, megalomania, and audacity—and about the complete lack of understanding of Russian reality both past and present which had been his ruin.

He told her about Wells, who had come to Prague the year before. Together they had gone to see the touring Moscow Art Theater, and Wells was wildly enthusiastic about their performances. He talked about fishing, golf, and tennis, and the Gypsy orchestras in the Prague restaurants. Karsavina was in Prague. They reminisced about Petrograd, and the horrors didn't seem all that horrible anymore.

But now he was getting old and putting on weight, and he had days when he was so depressed that he didn't know what to do. He dreamed of becoming a writer. He told her about Thomas Masaryk and Eduard Beneš and about Masaryk's son Jan, his close friend. He had never had a close friend before. And about his financial affairs, which, like everything else in his life, were in great disarray, even though he was on the board of several Central European banks and industrial firms and was on familiar terms with the finance ministers of at least ten countries.

Early the next morning they said goodbye at the Prague train station. He had to be at his bank, and she said she was going to Berlin and Tallinn but that she would come back to Prague again. "As I drove home," Lockhart writes, "I felt nervous and ill at ease. Was my indecision due to lack of courage, or had the flame of our romance burnt itself out?"

He described this meeting with Moura twice: once briefly in his diary and a second time in his memoirs in 1934. These entries make it clear that he did not tell her he had separated from his wife after his son's birth, after she and the child had visited him in Prague in 1921, or that he had had an affair with a young actress from the Moscow Art Theater while the troupe was on its European tour in 1923. Most important, he hid from Moura the fact that he had met Lady Rosslyn half a year before. She was a young society beauty, the third wife of Lord Rosslyn, and Lockhart had linked his fate with hers: they had been in Austria together the previous summer, and recently she had come to see him in Prague. She was Catholic, and had converted him to her faith.

About all that he said nothing. But what about Moura's confessions? How could there have been six translations of Gorky's works every year, when between 1921 and 1924 she translated only one play (with the help of Barrett Clark) and a collection of Gorky's stories (*Fragments from My Diary*), which had just come out?

Beginning in August 1924, on her way to and from Tallinn, she would stop off in Berlin and Prague. Sometimes it was Zagreb, or Belgrade, or Vienna—Lockhart let her know where he was going to be and when. It was only in England that she did not see him during those years: Lady Rosslyn lived there, and his relations with her, although no longer a secret within his small circle of society friends, were only just becoming known to the rest of London society. His wife and son lived there. But was Moura actually ever in London then? There is only indirect evidence that she was.

The final year of Parvus's payments began with Lenin's death in January 1924 and ended with our leaving Sorrento in March 1925. On the surface things remained unchanged. Gorky was working in the mornings, reading newspapers, journals, books, and other people's manuscripts. He was taking walks with his fox terrier and admiring the Italian sky, people, climate, music, and the view from his balcony. Moura was still leaving three times a year to "see the children," and Maxim was gluing stamps into an album (he had a fine collection) and riding around on his motorcycle, a heavy, solid Harley-Davidson, with whoever wanted to go with him. When guests came they stayed at the Hotel Minerva across from Il Sorito on the same winding road that led from Sorrento through Capo di Sorrento to the marvelous, then still-desolate spots that lay opposite Capri looking west toward the slowly setting sun. Valentina came to visit in January, staying with us in the house as usual. She painted portraits (Gorky's and mine) and taught us to dance the Charleston, which she had recently learned from Mayakovsky. This year served as a divide between the two periods that defined Gorky's life abroad. He began having serious thoughts about returning to Russia, especially after Parvus's payments ended and before Gosizdat's first advance.

Gosizdat had an easy time convincing Gorky (through Kryuchkov and Ladyzhnikov) to sign a contract for his complete collected works. Moura, Maxim, and the others, including Peshkova, who happened to be in Sorrento, encouraged him as well. The "complete" collected works meant not only the twenty-five or thirty volumes of his works now in the hands of Kniga, but also everything he would write in the future, and all the other odds and ends that would be printed in separate collections. At first Gorky did not understand this, and he even attempted to prove that he had already "promised" to let Grzhebin or Kaplun publish some things he had written. Ladyzhnikov explained to Gorky that he couldn't do that, though, and that Ladyzhnikov himself was going to work for Gosizdat in its Berlin office. If Grzhebin and Kaplun wanted to go to court, then let them. There was no reason for Gorky to get mixed up in such matters.

Grzhebin and Kaplun were by this time on the brink of ruin. *Beseda* was falling more and more behind schedule. In fact, it was barely breathing, despite the persistent rumors that it would soon be let into Russia, which Moura gaily reported in one of her letters to Khodasevich. At the beginning of 1925, a double issue, numbers 6–7, came out: it was the final issue. The journal was prohibited in Soviet Russia. Through the Berlin Trade Office, Gosizdat signaled that the time for reconciliation between writers "there" and "here" had passed, and if a distinct boundary between émigré and Soviet writers did not form of itself, then they would draw one once and for all.

Thus a complex business arrangement was devised that eventually led Gorky—slowly and tortuously—to his decision to go back. Parvus's death and the cessation of payments; the refusal to let *Beseda* into Russia; the shrinking number of his readers—especially young readers—in Germany, England, and the United States, and the resulting reductions in printings of his works by foreign publishers; the difficulty of obtaining money from those foreign publishers; the feeling that the decline of interest in his work was irreversible and could only worsen, and, as a result, the constant lack of money—all this forced him to turn his attention in the other direction. Gosizdat was pressuring him to come back, trying to execute all the points of the new contract; it was the rare letter from Russia that did not ask the dogged question of when he was coming home, where he was loved and appreciated. Maxim would soon be thirty, and it was time to put an end to his games and his idleness. There was Timosha's pregnancy, and then there was even Moura's attitude and behavior toward him, which was not entirely the way he had imagined it would be when she had finally come to see him that time in Heringsdorf. The decision was made gradually, perhaps as early as 1926, but it was not until 1928 that it was carried out.

At a family council in February, it was decided to sell Gorky's collection of jade figurines at Sotheby's in London. Gosizdat's delay in sending money (this was the first delay, but later there were quite a few) and Ladyzhnikov's resulting frustration at not knowing how to respond to Gorky's requests for payment, had brought things to such a pass.

Gorky's enemies had long claimed that he had nabbed the jade collection for himself from the Hermitage in 1918, in the name of "rescuing artistic treasures." That was slander. Other rumors had it that a tsarist general who was in Liaoyang in 1904 on matters that were as much commercial as they were political had admired the collection and asked the Chinese whether they would give it to him, which they gladly did. In October 1917 it was confiscated from the general (by a commission that many of Gorky's friends served on at the time, including Valentina's husband, Andrei Diederichs) and given to the Hermitage, which presented it to Gorky soon after. Still others thought that the collection had never belonged to the Hermitage at all, that there was another collection of jade in the Hermitage, and that Gorky's was given to him for safekeeping by Ernst Grubbe, the director of a private Petersburg commercial bank, who had given Gorky money for *New Life* before leaving Russia after October. Four years later, when Gorky took the collection abroad with him, Grubbe refused it and gave it to Gorky. However it was acquired, the wooden box with its little hooks and lock was dragged out from under Nightingale's bed one day so the collection could be photographed. When the photographer came from Naples, Maxim called me in and told me to set the twenty-three figurines on a red velvet cloth on the dining table. They ranged in height from four or five inches to eight inches and taller.

The photographer arrived carrying a very big, antique camera that looked like a small trunk. He covered it with a black cloth and then began to adjust his lens. Maxim asked that I not absent myself for even a moment. He himself had decided to stay by the photographer the whole time, to keep his eye on him, and my role consisted in being close by, either in the room or next door, in case Maxim should suddenly need assistance. Gorky glanced in the doorway once, but Maxim shooed him away. The photographer took a long time to get set up, then they gave him something to eat, and then he went back. Maxim was standing by the figurines, and I was pacing from the dining room to the foyer and back again. Moura came out of her room to admire the collection, rearranged the figurines to suit her own taste, smiled at the photographer, and left. Finally, all the figurines had been photographed, the black cloth neatly folded up, and the camera put away in its mahogany case. Maxim went out to his motorcycle to take the photographer back to town, and I shouted to him that there were only twenty-two figurines. He looked at the bill that the photographer had given him. He had photographed twenty-two figurines. I realized immediately that Maxim must have miscounted, but he did not agree. He went to Moura's room and said: "Titka, give the jade back."

She walked out, not understanding what he wanted. Maxim thought that she was teasing him, but that was not her intention. A heavy awkwardness hung in the air. The two of us collected the figurines in silence and put them away in their box. I told him: there were twenty-two figurines all along, not twenty-three. It was perfectly clear. Maxim argued with me: he couldn't have made a mistake like that. And the photographer couldn't have stolen them. He never took his eyes off him. Yes, I said, yet anyone can miscount. It's nothing to get worked up about.

With this the story of Gorky's famous jade collection ended. It was sent to London, where it was sold. Moura seemed perpetually worried that first Italian winter, and indeed she had many reasons to be— her sister Alla in Paris, Budberg in Argentina, and her children in Tallinn. Money could only partly assuage her constant concern. "What will happen? How will it all work out? Or will it?" There was also Gorky's health: he was sick in January while she was away, and Timosha and I had taken turns watching over him day and night. He wouldn't go to a hospital. This upset the doctor, who assured us that only a hospital could save him. When Moura came back, he could barely stand. Her attempts to make a career as a translator had been disconcerting failures. Parvus's death placed a question mark over their living arrangements, which turned out to be much more tenuous than everyone had imagined. Gosizdat? That might turn out to be the straw at which the drowning man grasps. Or it could prove a granite rock to stand on. It all depended on how the drowning man behaved. Moscow could give an ultimatum: come back or we'll cut off payments. In this Maxim was Moscow's ally, but he was hopeless when it came to getting anything done. Andreeva could help and did, and so could Peshkova in Moscow.

In her first book of memoirs, Nadezhda Mandelstam wrote about Peshkova as head of the Political Red Cross in the 1920s and 1930s— she was a kind of intermediary between political criminals and the Cheka, the NKVD, or the GPU.[6] It came about because of her friendship with Dzerzhinsky, whom she esteemed for his "moral qualities." She had got Maxim a job with him, and he, too, admired Dzerzhinsky

---

6. The Political Red Cross was originally called the Polish Red Cross. It was established soon after the October Revolution for the purpose of repatriating Poles to their homeland when, after the Versailles conference, Poland became independent. When all the Poles had been returned to Poland, repatriation came to an end, and Peshkova, with the permission of the Cheka's head, began working to bring relief to political prisoners. She undoubtedly helped ease the fate of a dozen (out of dozens of thousands) of those arrested during the Red Terror.

and sometimes even dreamed about returning to Russia and working for him again. As head of the Political Red Cross, Peshkova appealed to the head of the Cheka on behalf of imprisoned Socialist Revolutionaries (she herself had belonged to the SR party in her youth). They were being shot and exiled despite her efforts, but nevertheless, SRs who lived in exile in Paris believed in her and every year collected money for packages for prisoners, which they sent to her. Nadezhda Mandelstam writes:

> Prisoners' wives beat a path to, the "Political Red Cross" and Peshkova. They would go there, in essence, simply to be able to talk to someone and ease their souls. It gave them the illusion of activity so essential in periods of prolonged waiting. The "Red Cross" had no influence whatsoever. Through it one could occasionally send a package to a camp or find out about a sentence already passed or an execution already carried out. In 1937 they liquidated this odd organization, thus breaking the last link between prison and the outside world.

If the Political Red Cross never really helped the prisoners and their families, it unquestionably did help the woman who led it. Thanks to her work with Dzerzhinsky, Peshkova became a "Kremlin lady": she traveled abroad twice a year and stayed away for long periods of time. She even paid visits to her old friends, now émigré Socialists, who had played a role in Russian politics before the October Revolution. So far as I know, she continued seeing Ekaterina Kuskova and Lidia Dan right up to 1935. There was no way she could help their friends and associates (who at one time had also been her party comrades), but she had an aura of indisputable propriety, if not perspicacity. In Europe she felt just as sure of herself as she did at home in Moscow; when Maxim was growing up she had spent many years with her son on the Italian Riviera and in Paris. There was something in her of the old radical revolutionary Russian women: firm principles, sternness, and, as happened all too often, Victorianism and Puritanism. She didn't understand Maxim's humor and did not share his enthusiasm for soccer, the latest airplanes, stamps, or polar expeditions. But in Sorrento she felt good and found everything satisfactory. She took a daily four-hour sunbath on the balcony of the dining room wearing a bathing suit in the January sun. In the stories she told she placed particular emphasis on Dzerzhinsky's energy, the purity of Lenin's ideas, and the fact that they were all waiting for Gorky's return to Russia, since without him there was and would be no literature. If he didn't come back soon, he might be displaced in readers' hearts by someone a little flashier, a little younger, and, most important, a little louder. And what kind of future did their only son have in Europe? Maxim was not developing here at all. Khodasevich writes:

> From the first day of her arrival there were long conversations in Gorky's office, after which he would walk around practically on tiptoe and try to open his mouth as little as possible. Ekaterina Pavlovna had the look of a mother who has come home to find that in her absence her little boy has got himself into mischief, learned to smoke, and is mixed up with bad little boys— and, like it or not, a sound thrashing was in order. At times their conversations would take on the tone of a family council, to which Maxim would be invited.

The summer after our departure in 1925, Moura didn't go to "see the children"; instead they came to see her. Missy brought them both to spend two months in Sorrento. Pavel was twelve and Tania ten. Valentina (who soon returned to Russia for good) painted Tania's portrait, and Pavel sat in the garden reading a book. When he was asked what he was reading, he would say: "I'm reading Gorky's *Mama*." Gorky wrote me about Tania in a letter: "Tatiana Benckendorff is a young lady who speaks in a bass voice and sings the Estonian national anthem excellently. A remarkable little girl...Valentina is painting her portrait with bows."

That summer there was an especially large number of guests, and the Hotel Minerva was always full. Those who visited included Vsevolod Meyerhold and Zinaida Raikh; Nicola Benois, the chief designer at La Scala in Milan; the singer Zoya Lodi; and Vyacheslav Ivanov. To entertain the guests, and especially the children, a motorboat was rented on the eve of their departure and an excursion organized around the Gulf of Naples—Capri, Ischia, Posillipo, Naples, and Castellammare. But Gorky's nerves, as Valentina wrote in her memoirs, "were bad for a number of reasons." She recounts how, when everyone had finally left, Timosha went into labor. Maxim went out for ice (it was an exceptionally hot day), placed it in the shade under the stairs, and put beer in it to cool. Everyone was very excited. Nothing was ready, and they had great difficulty finding a doctor.

Peshkova arrived on September 12, missing her daughter-in-law's delivery, but five days after her arrival she was witness to an event that in all likelihood hastened Gorky's decision to return to Russia. On September 17 the Italian police conducted a search at Il Sorito, or rather, a search was made (like the one in Petrograd six years earlier) of Moura's room (she had left with the children and was not yet back), and partly of Gorky's room. They did not look downstairs at all. Officers of Mussolini's police force examined books and newspapers, and they confiscated some manuscripts and correspondence. Armed to the teeth, the young Fascist guards strolled through the remaining rooms very slowly, looking at everything with unconcealed curiosity. For several days after that the house was under surveillance night and day.

Gorky immediately got in touch with Platon Kerzhentsev, the Soviet ambassador in Rome. He threatened to leave Italy immediately and move to France, where he was "already sending M. I. Zakrevskaya to find and set up a residence either outside Paris or in the south of the country." Gorky undoubtedly understood what going to France would mean for him: France was the very center of the Russian political emigration, and he not only would be unable to work on his novel there but would find it hard just to live. He despised the émigré community and it repaid him in kind, but he could not ignore them altogether. He read the Paris Russian newspapers and journals carefully and paid attention to rumors and sometimes even silly gossip that reached him in a roundabout way from Paris. If he were to settle in France, he would not have a moment's peace.

Kerzhentsev, who by that time had already been a welcome guest at Sorrento and was on the friendliest of terms with Gorky, immediately filed a protest with Mussolini in person. Apologies were duly made, and the whole incident was labeled a misunderstanding. The papers and manuscripts were returned in proper order. The ambassador, who conveyed to Gorky Mussolini's personal apologies, was sure that Gorky and Zakrevskaya would soon visit Russia. Gorky, although seriously distressed by the search, decided in the end to stay on in Italy and leave Sorrento only for limited periods.

Taking this into account, Duke Serro di Capriola decided to make some capital improvements on Il Sorito and suggested that Gorky and his family spend some time in Posillipo, west of Naples. They agreed. A villa was rented in that elegant Italian town full of foreign tourists. On November 20 Moura moved Gorky, Maxim, Timosha, Nightingale, and Gorky's first granddaughter, Marfa, to the Villa Galotti, where they stayed until May of the following year. During these months Gorky managed to write the first chapters of his new (four-volume) novel, *The Life of Klim Samgin*, which he considered the most important undertaking of his career. The novel was dedicated to M. I. Zakrevskaya. It was during these weeks that the decision was finally made to return to Russia as soon as the novel was completed. Until that time, Gorky intended to remain in Italy.

He realized, as did Moura, that completion of the novel was now bound up with their parting. Neither of them had any doubt that she would never return to Russia with him.

She herself had a most unpleasant experience as a result of the search at Il Sorito. On her next trip to Estonia she was arrested at Brenner, on the Italian–Austrian border. She was led off from the train under guard and her luggage was taken away to be searched; she was held in the station for a few hours, where a body search was also conducted. When they let her go, many of her papers were not returned to her. She told no one at Sorrento about this but Gorky and Valentina. Gorky was enraged and immediately had a call put through to Kerzhentsev in Rome, but this time no apologies were offered and no explanations given. Nor did the ambassador take any action when Gorky complained to him.

In Moscow Moura had once been considered a secret agent of England; in Estonia, a Soviet spy. In France the Russian émigrés thought she was working for Germany, and later, when she lived in England, it was thought she was an agent of Moscow. Peters, who changed his mind about her, wrote in 1924 that she was a German spy who had worked for the Cheka. What Mussolini's government suspected we don't know. In any event, Moura had no choice but to fire Cataldo, the cook from Capri who had worked for Gorky before the war. A nanny was brought from Switzerland to care for Marfa, and a female cook was hired to take the man's place.

5

THE DEAL

How beauteous mankind is! O brave new world,
That has such people in't!
The Tempest, V, i, 183–84

MOURA'S FACE BEGAN to change markedly during these years, gradually losing its feline look. Careworn and serious, at moments it would turn somber. She took painstaking care of herself, as if trying to preserve that rare and treasured quality that Lockhart had once loved and had found again a year before, and which Gorky had written about in 1921 after seeing her in Helsinki—her interest in everything, her attentiveness to everyone, her ability to know everything, see and hear everything, and judge everything. Lockhart later wrote that during the 1920s she gave him "extensive information," which was invaluable to his work in Eastern Europe and among the Russian emigration. Until 1928, when he moved back to London and became a highly visible journalist on Lord Beaverbrook's *Evening Standard*, his work at the bank brought him into close contact with Czechoslovakia, Hungary, and the Balkans. He was always looking for and finding informants right up to his retirement from the Foreign Office in 1948, before, during, and after the war, whether he was working at the bank, writing for newspapers, or assigned to the Political Intelligence

Department or the Political Warfare Executive at the Foreign Office. With Moura's help, but also working on his own, he reestablished his contacts within Russian émigré communities. She, and through her Gorky, served as his "channel" to what was going on behind the scenes in literary, theatrical, and to some extent political life inside the Soviet Union. Before long he was considered, more than ever before, one of the foremost experts on Russian affairs, and there were some who thought of him as the leading authority on Russia old and new.

An uncommonly capable man, Lockhart could write interesting articles for any magazine based not just on his own experience but also on the comprehensive information that reached him about current affairs. His writing was never banal or conventional but always lively, interesting, and original. He could write about the latest player to emerge on the Kremlin scene or provide fascinating details about the most recent to fall from favor and be ousted. He could effectively deploy anecdotes to make his points. One of those winters, Karakhan came to Prague with his wife, the ballerina Marina Semyonova, and Lockhart, knowing Karakhan's tastes, took him around to the best restaurants with Gypsy choruses and Romanian orchestras. He had last seen Karakhan the day of his release after a month's imprisonment in the Kremlin. Now the two of them were dining on venison in sour cream, listening to Gypsy songs, and carousing until dawn. Lockhart knew how to cultivate as well as widen his circle of acquaintances, sensing how he might benefit in the future no matter what his career: international banking, the Foreign Office, or journalism.

Seeing Moura regularly somehow fit snugly into that future. She too liked to expand her circle of acquaintants and did so easily, from Soviet VIPs and world-famous writers to the Russian émigré "depths" in Paris, from bureaucrats in the Berlin Trade Office to aristocratic Baltic in-laws who were struggling to stay afloat. Had the two of them already reached some agreement? Had they set an agenda for their business meetings, meetings that doubled as an opportunity to spend time together as old friends, which were so enjoyable for him and so essential and at the same time so incomplete for her? Or was an agreement reached much later, between 1930 and 1938, when she was perfectly free to carry out his instructions and contacts had been put in place at both ends—until those contacts disintegrated in the late 1930s through no fault of her own. They would meet every three or four months in some capital of Central or Eastern Europe (sometimes in Zagreb). In each they had a favorite restaurant and regular hotel and familiar train station and reliable telegraph office.

A turning point for Lockhart was 1928. His occasional articles in the *Edinburgh Review*, the *New Statesman*, the *Fortnightly*, and other magazines, and his later work in the *Evening Standard* on such topics as Eastern European finance, Russia, world politics, the Balkans, and the Czech president Masaryk were popular with readers. Lockhart's friends regularly told him he could become a prominent and influential journalist. His friend, Jan Masaryk, young son of the president, felt that Lockhart was wasting his time working for a bank. Harold Nicolson, who was the son of the former English ambassador to St. Petersburg and was beginning his own brilliant career during those years, said people were noticing Lockhart's articles and asking about him.

For a short time in 1925 he had left the board of directors of the Anglo-International Bank (as it was then called) in Prague and accepted a post as manager of the Intelligence Department of the Anglo-Austrian Bank, but he soon found himself combining the two positions, feeling the old pull toward undercover political service. "My life in London was pleasant enough," he later wrote. "My duties were to keep my directors posted about economic and political developments in Central Europe. I supplied them with a daily news bulletin.... I maintained a close contact with the Central European legations in London. The range of countries was extended to include Germany and Italy [which I visited] at regular intervals on the bank's business." That is how Lockhart described the situation in 1934 in memoirs entitled, significantly, *Retreat from Glory*; thirteen years later, in 1947, there would be a sequel called *Comes the Reckoning*. These trips to Germany and Italy made it easier for him and Moura to meet in those two countries.

The *Evening Standard* was considered the gutter press, but it had an enormous circulation. Beaverbrook also owned the *Daily Express* and *Sunday Express*. Popular papers "made the weather in England," and Lockhart was put into circulation right away. No sooner had he returned from interviewing Kaiser Wilhelm in Doorn than Beaverbrook told him he was expecting not only columns and articles from him but books as well, books about his assignments in Russia. It was no secret to anyone that his stay there had been one long chain of adventures. He must tell how he became friendly with Trotsky, how he had conspired with the counterrevolution, and how he had landed in prison. And describe the person who had freed him. Lockhart was embarrassed. "She didn't free me," he said, "I freed her. Thanks to my diplomatic immunity." It is inconceivable that Beaverbrook, who in 1918 had been the minister of information in Lloyd George's cabinet, did not know that Lockhart had been sent to Lenin's Russia as a simple observer and had never enjoyed the kind of status that would have given him immunity. Lockhart, however, was not about to let the legend established so long ago fall to pieces. He steered the conversation on another tack. Beaverbrook appreciated his discretion: in Lockhart he had found a true gentleman.

Discussions about making a movie based on his memoirs began before Lockhart had even started writing the book. While dining at Beaverbrook's one evening Lockhart was asked by Samuel Goldwyn, the Hollywood movie magnate sitting next to him, "When will your book be finished?" "If they give me a leave before tying me up with newspaper work, then two years," Lockhart replied. Beaverbrook agreed to give him a leave to write the book. So Lockhart, happy and free, set out in 1929 to travel across Europe—he called it his "European tour in the grand manner"—on the model of the great Englishmen of the past. He was now quite at ease with moneylenders and with their help was paying off a portion of the debt he had accumulated since he was in Prague. He traveled to Paris, Germany, Switzerland: "I wanted to see my boy who was in school in Switzerland. Moura was returning to Berlin, after having acted for a long time as secretary and translator to Gorky at Sorrento. Jenia, too, was there and wished to consult me about the possibilities of a film contract in England."[1]

Lockhart was held up for a week in Berlin, where he saw Moura. Which European capital she cited as her primary residence we do not know, but her son, Pavel, was also attending school in Switzerland (as she told Lockhart), and she was on her way to see him. They dined at Foerster's, a well-known Russian restaurant in Berlin. "I asked her about Gorky. He has definitely left the Western world in order to devote the remainder of his life to the education and development of a new Russia. Since his return to the Bolshevik fold he has sold over 3,000,000 copies of his works in Russia alone. By the Russian people he is worshipped like a god." Despite his respect for Gorky, however, Lockhart was disturbed that a writer who had struggled against tyranny all his life would at age sixty-two persuade himself that tyranny, violence, and the suppression of individual liberties were justified if they led to a higher goal.

When he submitted *Memoirs of a British Agent* for publication, he wrote Moura about it. Given her relationship with Lockhart and the

---

1. At this same time, when Lockhart's affair with Lady Rosslyn was at its most intense, Harold Nicolson wrote him a friendly letter: "To support you in Max's affections [Beaverbrook had remarked to Nicolson that Lockhart was wasting his substance on drink and lechery] I told him that not at all, you were merely bothered by your friendships with several different women at the same time." In 1927 Lockhart was conducting an affair with Jenia, a young Russian émigré actress he had met in Prague and later helped break into German theater, where she became one of the best-known actresses in Germany.

role she had played in saving his life, he wanted to show her what he had written and ask for her approval. He could not possibly have expected the answer he received from her. In his diary on June 18, 1932, he wrote:

> This morning I had a shock—a letter from Moura in which she requests me to alter the part in my book referring to her. She wants it made more formal. She wants to be called Mme. Benckendorff all through. She is as conventional as a Victorian spinster. And why? Because I said that fourteen years ago she had waving hair—whereas it is "flat as a Ukrainian's"! Therefore, my description is shallow, false, etc., and this is obviously all that the episode meant to me! Therefore either the full love story or nothing. This will be very difficult. The book, however, will have to be altered. She is the only person who has the right to demand an alteration.

Nevertheless, the book did get published and was enormously successful in England and the United States. It brought him money and fame and was translated into several languages. Two years later the film *British Agent* was released in England. It remains one of the finest historical-adventure movies of the time, not only because of its content—Russia, revolution, conspiracy, prison, the vicissitudes of a love affair between an Englishman and a Russian—but also because the part based on Lockhart (Stephen Locke) was played by Leslie Howard, and the part based on Moura (Elena) by Kay Francis, a beautiful black-haired, big-eyed actress with a soft gentle face and slender waist. It was directed by Michael Curtiz, who went on to make *Casablanca*. The review in *The New York Times* was enthusiastic:

> A situation richly veined with striking dramatic values has been utilized with considerable vitality in *British Agent*, which was

presented at the Strand yesterday. Against the lurid backdrop of the Russian upheaval and collapse during the war, the Brothers Warner dramatize an episode from R. H. Bruce Lockhart's autobiographical chronicle of last year. As Britain's unofficial emissary to the revolutionary government, Leslie Howard is enormously helpful to the drama, while the momentous and delicate climaxes which crowd the story come to life on the screen in vigorous melodramatic style.

However, the critic did have some reservations:

Although the love of the young Briton and the fascinating Russian spy has been described with the proper tenderness and urbanity, it still fails to escape a rather furiously unimportant appearance alongside of the really great events with which the new film is concerned.... In addition, it is the misfortune of *British Agent* to contain in its dialogue a line in which Kay Francis boldly announces to her lover that she is a woman first and a Cheka spy second, or words to that effect.

Lockhart was invited to the screening and he took Moura with him. They arrived to find that the screening had been arranged for him alone: no one else had been invited. The two of them sat in the middle of a small theater, whose emptiness made it seem enormous. In that emptiness, that darkness and silence, Moura relived the past, not daring to touch Lockhart's hand, doubtless afraid that if she did she would lose him forever. It is possible that he regretted having invited her, suspecting how hard it was for her. A good film had been made of his good book, flattering his vanity, and he was happy and proud. When it was over, she hid her face from him, and once they were out on the street they went their separate ways.

At the *Evening Standard* Lockhart wrote gossip columns as well as serious articles on politics, political philosophy, and, above all, topical themes in foreign policy. His writing style had the same vivacity as his conversation. At the time he could not have foreseen that he would stay at the paper until 1938, when he would be recruited once again for military-political work. For now he was enthusiastically learning journalism, a quick study as usual, mastering what he needed and discarding what he didn't. Those who once had given their blessing to his diplomatic career felt that he was squandering his talents on the pages of a scandal sheet. Moura let her views be known about his work at the newspaper. In June 1931 she wrote "exhorting me to pull myself together and saying that I can do something better than act as a lackey to Max [Beaverbrook]."

Lockhart was not offended. He needed Moura. Because of her he had maintained his contacts with Russian circles and Russian life. He was gradually becoming Beaverbrook's right-hand man and he enjoyed Beaverbrook's complete trust. Lockhart was neither a Tory nor a Liberal but rather a conservative—a conservative, however, without any tinge of the feudal—who was always at home in the company of London's aristocrats. He hated and despised the petty bourgeoisie, but he was also a long way from worshiping traditional monarchism and regarded the dynasty as one of England's essential state institutions. He had a high opinion of Russia's transformation, although by that time he knew about the intensifying repression there. He still respected Lenin as an important figure of our time, counting him among the prophets of his youth, who also included Walter Scott and Napoleon.

Lockhart made good use of his many contacts. His meetings with Moura were essential. She knew people at all levels of London (and even international) society, as he noted: "Her circle of acquaintances was extraordinarily varied and ranged from ministers and literary giants to obscure but intelligent foreigners" (such as Georgy Solomon and the lawyer who had once helped her in Tallinn). He never talked to her about British politics or about England, only about Central Europe, Eastern Europe, the Baltic states, and Russia. She was still making trips to Estonia on business known only to the two of them. She told him stories about André Gide's trip to the Soviet Union and Alexei Tolstoy's visit to London. Despite her cool reaction to his memoirs and especially to the film, they continued to meet, linked now by professional ties. Lockhart took notes:

> Saturday, 4 October 1930
>
> Lunched with Moura at the Savoy. She leaves today for Genoa and then Berlin....Discussed Arnold Bennett's new book *The Imperial Palace*. H. G. Wells agrees with Max [Beaverbrook] that it is rotten. Moura says Arnold Bennett is bored with Dorothy Cheston, his actress-wife...and has lost his inspiration since she made him give up wearing shirts with myosotis flowers on them!
>
> Discussed Gorky: now...poor, has given all his money away, makes about £300 a year, cannot get foreign currency from Russia now, sells 2,700,000 copies a year...Gorky is too emotional to be a critic.

> Tuesday, 6 January 1931
>
> Letter from Moura...She writes cheerfully and kindly. She is a big-minded and big-hearted woman.

> Friday, 6 March 1931
>
> In the afternoon met Moura at the Wellington. Sat there till 8:30 drinking sherry. Then went on to the Hungarian restaurant where we remained till two a.m. I felt very ill after drinking so much. She—as usual—never turned a hair. Naturally, we discussed Russia the whole evening. Moura thinks we are all wrong about the Russians. She thinks, like Wells, that the capitalist-

finance system has broken down and that Russia will succeed with her Five-Year Plan—not necessarily in five years, but in the sense that she will make rapid progress towards becoming an industrial nation like the U.S.A. She saw Gorky a few weeks ago. He is now ultra-Bolshevik, has returned to his own class, believes implicitly in Stalin, and justifies the terror from which formerly he shrank. He and Moura both believe in the danger of foreign intervention. Moura assures me that the recent trials in Moscow were by no means "faked."

Friday, 29 January 1932

Lunched with Moura. She showed me a letter from Gorky. He asks her to get all the English books on the history of English caricature. He signs himself: "Yours sorely grieved, Maxim Gorky—author—over forty, tawny-haired, bad-tempered and overwhelmingly famous."

He has a great love for animals. When Wells was staying with him in 1919, he had a Great Dane. It went everywhere with Gorky. It was called Diane. It even went for walks with Wells. One day it went for a walk by itself and never came back. It had been eaten by a starving populace.

Tuesday, 21 June 1932

... dined with Moura at the Eiffel Tower [a restaurant in London].

Monday, 27 June 1932

Went to Test match [England vs. India] for an hour with Moura—it was very slow and uninspiring cricket.

Friday, 2 September 1932

Lunched with Moura, who has returned [from Germany]. Gorky has been very ill in Berlin—lung trouble again. Attended by Prof. Kraus. Had to have oxygen. Age 64. Was not allowed to go to Holland to attend the antiwar congress. Bolshevik trade union delegation wanted him to go on to Paris. Moura would not let him go [on account of his health].

Wednesday, 14 September 1932

Lunched with Moura. H. G. Wells has returned to England from Grasse to spend a month here and to see his friends. He is taking Moura to Shaw's *Too True to Be Good* on Friday night. H. G. will be 66 on Thursday the 22nd. Except for his women he has no real men friends. He takes little interest in the young men and unlike Gorky does not put himself out to encourage them. He has his two legitimate sons whom he likes, but does not allow to interfere with his life. His two sons, by Rebecca West and Amber Reeves he looks after generously.[2] Anthony, the West boy, he used to like. Then H. G. just slipped away. He is an adept at slipping away and never seeing people again.

Saturday, 8 October 1932

Lunched with Moura at the Berkeley Grill and had coffee with H. G. Wells, who was lunching with a rather "sexy" American girl. At 66 H. G. looks marvellously young. He has the skin of a man twenty years younger. He is writing his novel on the world a hundred years hence [*The Shape of Things to Come*]. . . . Moura squabbles violently with him about Russia and foreign politics.

Thursday, 20 October 1932

My luncheon to H. G. was rather tedious. I was quarter of an hour late. Tommy and Harry [Lady and Lord Rosslyn] turned up at Boulestin's to see Moura. My other guests were [Count]

---

2. Lockhart was mistaken. Wells had a daughter by Amber Reeves.

Bernstorff and Randolph [Churchill]. H. G. rather "crotchety" because Moura talked to Bernstorff and was very anxious to command the conversation.... Moura left for Paris. H. G. went to station with her.

Thursday, 17 November 1932
Saw Moura at 6.30. She says Harold [Nicolson] is jealous of my success. She is going with H. G. to Paris and then goes to Sorrento to Gorky.... She showed me a correspondence card. On it H. G. had written in very small neat handwriting: *Dear Moura! Sweet Moura!* He sends her lots. Gives her presents.

Saturday, 13 May 1933
Lunched with Moura at the Perroquet. She is going with H. G. to Salzburg on June 2nd. She has just returned from Berlin.... Moura's stories are always amusing.

Wednesday, 21 June 1933
Moura is back again.

Wednesday, 6 September 1933
Lunched with Moura... Moura tells me that this year Gorky is not coming to Italy but is going to the Crimea.... Gorky also told Moura that at the opening of the White Sea Canal, Nekrasov, the former Kerensky Minister of Railways and an engineer, wept tears of emotion at the completion of so great an achievement by Russians! He was employed on the construction.

Thursday, 6 June 1935
Lunched with Moura. She attacked me violently for not breaking away from Beaverbrook and for my self-indulgence and lack

of courage. Said it was a scandal for me to prostitute my talents in this way. Not only were people saying that I was superficial and without principle but that I already *was* superficial, and without principle. True—*que de souvenirs! que de regrets!*

It goes without saying that Wells never went to see Gorky in Sorrento, with or without Moura, but she liked stoking the legend about the intimacy Wells and Gorky shared. She would recount the long conversations the two of them had in America back in 1906 and others they had when they met again in London. But the portrait was not true: in the United States, Gorky and Wells saw each other only once, at a reception at Gaylord Wilshire's, and in 1907 in London they met only briefly, exchanging just a few words. Later Moura published five letters from Wells to Gorky with a somewhat coquettish foreword that did not explain the paltry number. But then she also liked to bolster the legend of the friendship between Wells and Lockhart, who met occasionally at the Carlton Grill early on and then rather more frequently during World War II, until the Carlton Grill was destroyed by a bomb.

There can be no doubt that Moura made several trips to London from the mid-1920s on, but it is impossible to say exactly when she first went there for reasons having nothing to do with seeing Maurice Baring. It might have been in 1925: she was away from Gorky's villa when it was searched in September, and she was gone again in December. Or it may have been in 1926. One thing is clear from information scattered through the various biographies of Wells: by 1927 their acquaintance had resumed, they had started up an irregular correspondence, and Moura had once again begun to play a part in Wells's life.

In the mid-1920s, after he broke up with Rebecca West, H. G. was living with a woman who would gradually become his enemy both in private and in public. Meanwhile, since he loved the French Riviera more than any other spot in the world, he began building a house of his own design in the hills of Grasse, marvelously situated twenty kilometers from the coast.

Wells adored that house from the day he laid the first stone right up to the moment he had to leave it. All his life he had dreamed of having a house set in the heavenly climate of the Mediterranean coast. Everything had to be comfortable and beautiful: comfortable so that he could write his books about remaking the world, educating mankind, and urging the human race down the path to progress (by force if necessary); and beautiful so that every morning he would find himself delighted and happy, and he could invite eminent, important, influential, clever men, and well-born, elegant, clever women, who would also find it utterly delightful. But when the house was finished he felt that the woman with whom he had been planning to spend the rest of his life (he was sixty, she was thirty-eight) had in fact turned out to be jealous, cynical, indiscreet, demanding, vain, and unbearably capricious.

Odette Keun launched her career in the 1920s determined to conquer the world, to take it by storm, and to bite and scratch anyone who might try to get in her way. She behaved like many women of her generation who had finally been freed from Victorian morals and had learned to converse in a new way. Write books? Certainly. She had already published one, an account of her travels in Soviet Russia (written in French, it was called *Sous Lénine*—Wells wrote a flattering review, which was what led to their being introduced). Draw landscapes? Marvelously, if you asked her. No one understood music as well as she did, and she had (in her view) the most brilliant and original opinions on ballet and international politics.

For Wells a night with Moura was no mere trifle and was not easily forgotten: when he returned from Russia he told Rebecca West that he had "slept with Gorky's secretary." He disdained euphemism and called excessive delicacy hypocrisy. Although West considered herself a progressive woman and had taken her pseudonym, as is well known, from Ibsen's *Rosmersholm*, she had a good long cry. But five years later when he told Odette Keun the same thing, Odette went into a rage, forbade him to travel to Paris or London, and threatened to break some very beautiful and valuable object standing on his mantel. Whenever he went away on a trip, she now wrote him every day that she had absolutely nothing to do in the house on the Riviera and that she would kill herself if he didn't come back right away. But that did not work, and by the late 1920s, as his biographers inform us, he went from being an irregular correspondent of Moura's to being a regular companion.

In 1928 Wells realized that Moura's life with Gorky was coming to an end. Gorky had decided to go to Russia the next spring[3] to see for himself the new achievements and transformations, and to try living there for a while to determine whether his health would allow him to live there permanently, if not in Moscow then in the Crimea. His royalties from Gosizdat were getting harder to collect due to new restrictions on transferring money out of the Soviet Union. Lockhart knew from Moura that for all those years she had been conducting Gorky's correspondence in three languages (he wrote in Russian himself and always in longhand). Moura said he was doing the right thing, that she had always known this would happen and was ready for it. But she also knew that Gorky would arrive at this decision slowly: several years might pass (and several trips be made) before he would take the final step.

Wells was being seen in London less frequently now. He had too many obligations, intentions, plans, promises right and left, public

---

3. In their splendid biography of Wells, Norman and Jeanne MacKenzie provide incorrect dates for Gorky's trips to the Soviet Union. His first trip back after he left in 1921 was in the spring of 1928 (not 1927); this was followed by visits in 1929, 1931, and 1932. He returned permanently to the Soviet Union in 1933. Gorky spent the whole of 1930 in Sorrento due to illness.

appearances, not to mention his habit of putting out a book a year, or at least trying to. His novels alternated during these years with political books, which many called philosophical: how to reshape the world, how to make everyone happy, how to lead mankind toward progress. And this new stage for Wells, firmly in place in the late 1920s, with its insoluble problems which had to be solved but for which there was no solution, led to something even more insoluble: What if mankind did not want progress? Would it be necessary (and possible?) to hit them over the head with a stick so they went where they ought to be going?

First he sent greetings to the peace conference, then he cursed it. He passionately believed in the League of Nations as a panacea for all evil, before he later became disenchanted. His aphorism, "The correlative of a New Republic is a new education," inspired him to write a book on biology, another on economics, and a third on the natural sciences. He felt his mission was to prepare the human mind for a new system of education (to be accessed from a world knowledge bank, "a world brain: no less") and for the creation of a world government. People would tell him jokingly—over cigars and port—that half of his pupils would consist of semiliterates. He would reply that *he himself* would start by teaching them to read.

He was constantly irritated not only with others but with himself, and this state was aggravated by moving back and forth from London to Grasse and Grasse to London. In October 1930, Moura was again in London (Gorky was in Sorrento). A year earlier she had brought her children and Missy to London from Estonia. She had decided to establish herself in England once and for all after Gorky returned from his first trip to Russia in 1928 and began talking about living there permanently. When the Il Sorito era came to an end, Missy and the children were installed in permanent quarters in London, and she decided to stay elsewhere.

Starting in 1931, Moura began to be mentioned here and there as

Wells's "companion" and "friend." When they were apart their correspondence was becoming more and more regular, while relations
between H. G. and Odette deteriorated so much that he had to admit
that their separation could come at any time (and that meant losing
the house, too, which was so dear to him). By the spring of 1933, it
was all up to him. He arranged to meet Moura in Dubrovnik, where
a session of the International PEN Club was to be held. They were
inseparable all through the congress, and when it ended they spent
two happy weeks together in Austria. On May 14, Moura left Wells
and managed to get to Istanbul just in time to say goodbye to Gorky
before his final departure for Russia. He was sailing from Naples to
Odessa with Maxim and Timosha, Rakitsky, and two Soviet writers—Samuil Marshak and Lev Nikulin.

That spring Wells finally left his house in the south of France for
good. He took an apartment in London and moved there permanently. Odette, however, would not leave him in peace. That would
not have been consistent with her character. In 1934 she published
something like a reminiscence of her life with him in the British
weekly *Time and Tide*. It portrayed a great man who was prostrated
by each one of his failures (and there were many) until something new
came along to dispel his insecurities—a man who had decided to have
a good time with her and then had left her flat. The sketch was malicious and indiscreet, and it afforded Wells some very unpleasant
weeks if only because her description loosened the tongues not only
of his enemies but also of old friends who had known him since his
youth, such as Somerset Maugham, who remarked, "Who could have
thought that our hedonist has fits of rage!"[4] Odette had called Wells a
"parvenu," a man who imagined himself a Lord God of Sabaoth to
whom all was permitted, when in fact he was only amusing himself

---

4. Maugham once asked Moura "what she saw in the paunchy, played out writer." Moura
answered, "He smells of honey" (Ted Morgan, *Maugham*, 382).

with people, playing with them in order to dispel his own boredom. Having written thirty books about thirty ways to redeem the sins of the world, he was inventing idols for himself and then demolishing them, like a child breaking every dish within reach. She felt he was more dangerous to his friends than to his enemies, that he was coarse, vulgar, and petty, though he imagined himself a titan. His autobiography, in which he poses as a "thinker," was written to vindicate himself.

Wells could not help but take revenge, and four years later he answered Odette with his novel *Apropos of Dolores*, in which he caustically, deftly, and very cruelly settles the score with his former lover. Wells could not abide the "new women." A former Socialist and Fabian, he mourned the old "beauty in life—a flat in Chelsea and a little cottage in South Cornwall." He cursed the emancipation of the new generation. "Under contemporary conditions," he wrote, marriage is "a resentful unproductive partnership," with the parties caught up in "that subtle and tortuous conflict of individualities to which all who belong to the new world are doomed." The hero of the novel kills his intolerable lover and tells himself: "I find myself emerging today into a state of contentment with Brittany, myself and the universe." At the very end of the book a woman appears who brings peace and freedom to the author-hero. It is not hard to recognize Moura.

In those years there was every imaginable kind of radical congress in Amsterdam, Paris, and other capitals of Europe. Wells sent welcoming telegrams protesting Fascism, Nazism, rearmament, and the inaction of the League of Nations. He became president of the International PEN Club and tried to influence writers, poets, and critics, constantly raising his already high-pitched voice, trying to persuade them of the utility of progress and the futility of aesthetics and fuming at those listening and talking to him, the majority of whom were indifferent to those issues.

In this frame of mind he decided in 1934 to go talk things over with Roosevelt in the United States and Stalin in the Soviet Union.

The White House made a strong impression on him with its "Brain Trust," which he met there. His conversation with Stalin did not go any better than his conversation with Lenin had fourteen years earlier. He had planned on lecturing Stalin on the state of the world, but Stalin barely listened to him (through an interpreter) and was obviously bored. When Wells asked what Stalin would have him tell Roosevelt, Stalin had nothing to say. Wells had wanted to be a "*postillon d'amour* between the two giants," but it did not come to pass.

However, the biggest disappointment was his meeting with Gorky, who had returned to Russia for good one year earlier. Gorky, in Wells's opinion, had turned into "an unqualified Stalinite." As president of the International PEN Club, Wells spoke about the necessity of "championing freedom of expression in art and literature," while Gorky looked "sidelong at me with that Tartar face of his, devising shrewd questions to reveal the spidery 'capitalist' entanglement he suspected me of spinning."

Gorky's admiration for Wells had started to wane in the early 1920s. In a letter to Kryuchkov on November 17, 1924, he wrote: "Don't send me any more books by Wells, I'm tired of them. His writing is getting worse and worse. At present in Europe the number one writer is Knut Hamsun." Wells wrote that Gorky "produced excuses for [the official control of] thought and expression," maintaining that Russia "could not tolerate opposition," and, even worse, Gorky was rejecting other liberties and human rights, including birth control and the right of women not to have children!

Moura was waiting for Wells in Estonia. She wanted to show him the country where there was so much tied up with her own destiny. He arrived from Moscow irritated and disenchanted, saying that the Russians had betrayed him. As he wrote in the concluding pages of his *Experiment in Autobiography: Discoveries and Conclusions of a Very Ordinary Brain (Since 1866)*: "I went by the train called the 'Red Arrow,' the Soviet echo of the *Flèche d'Or*, from Moscow to

Leningrad and thence I flew to Tallin. I am finishing this autobiography in a friendly and restful house beside a little lake in Esthonia." Those were happy days.

It was summer. Two weeks passed in perfect isolation—no people, no letters, no telephones, no newspapers even. They returned to London together, and she moved into an apartment two steps away from him. She promised to stay with him as long as he wanted, but said she would never marry him.

Many people close to Wells were stunned: his old friends Beatrice and Sidney Webb, Socialists who had known him since his youth, Wells's sons and their wives, George Bernard Shaw, all of whom had been to his house in France and knew about his break with Odette Keun. The talk took a long time to die down and always came to the same conclusion: it won't last. Beatrice wrote in her diary that Shaw had told her that H. G. was "ill and worried...he has fallen to the charm of 'Moura,'...'She will stay with me, eat with me, sleep with me,' whined the lovesick H. G. to G. B. S. 'But she will not marry me.' H. G. aware of old age, wants to buy a 'sexual annuity' by marriage: 'Moura,' looking back at his past adventures, refuses to give her independence and her title away. And no wonder!"

Some of Wells's preconceptions in his later years were congruent with Gorky's. Gorky was taking to grotesque lengths what Wells was preaching in a more moderate form. Whereas Wells was carried away by the idea of a universal encyclopedia that once and for all would give to the literate, semiliterate, and illiterate a true understanding of the world, the human race, democracy, civilization, and the brotherhood of nations, Gorky was obsessed with an idea of his own that dated to 1905, the idea of "culture for everyone." An encyclopedia was only the first step toward realizing this vision; there also needed to be biographies of the great people of the past, written by the best contemporary authors, in simple language accessible to all; and, finally, there would be editions of the foremost classics of all nations, in new translations specially written for universal comprehension by a team of talented translators. He himself would choose the authors and the people to translate them; the translators would then rewrite and translate Homer, Shakespeare, Dante, Goethe, and Pushkin into all existing languages. In 1933, when he moved to Moscow, Gorky began to notice that prominent Soviet writers had started to avoid him. He did not associate this with his project, which would become a mandatory assignment for everyone capable of holding a pen, without exception. In fact, however, those who were worried that they might be conscripted for this work, which did not at first seem like the folly of a sick man but only a passing whim, were trying not to catch his eye. In 1924 Zamyatin wrote gently about when the first steps for Universal Literature were being discussed in 1919:

> It was hard enough to repair a water pipe or build a house but very easy to build a Tower of Babel: "Let's publish a pantheon of Russian literature, from Fonvizin to the present. A hundred volumes!" Smiling ever so slightly, we believed, or wanted to believe.... A whole section was organized devoted to "history in pictures": show all of world history, no more, no less. This was Gorky's idea.

Between 1928 and 1929, Gorky had become the editor or a member of the editorial board of a dozen periodicals. He spent entire days and nights editing manuscripts sent to him from the provinces, from factories and collective farms, adding commas and correcting the grammar. Then he would write long letters to the author explaining why he should study and ruminate on one or another of Gorky's works. After that he would send the piece to one of the journals he oversaw, where it was either printed or tossed in the wastebasket for lack of space.

There were countless tasks before him. In 1917 he thought he had a duty to "explain to village women [by means of lectures, pamphlets, and so on] what equal rights for women means." In 1934 he asked Professor Prigozhin and the academician Nikolai Marr to work on a multivolume project, *The History of Women*, stretching from preclassical society to the Soviet era. Professor Prigozhin was highly critical of Gorky's plan, and nothing ever came of it. Other "histories" were luckier. Nine of them were proposed and accepted: the history of taverns, famine and crop failure, disease and epidemics, monasteries, the police, farming, the revolutionary movement, the history of the Russian soldier, and the history of squandered talents. After that Gorky turned to poetry: "We need hundreds of poets capable of igniting passion and the will to act," he wrote. The ranks of poets around him thinned.

A writer named Vladimir Zazubrin complained in a letter to Gorky that he couldn't get material from well-known writers for *Kolkhoznik* (*Collective Farmer*) magazine. They all say: "What the hell do I care about your *Kolkhoznik*?" Recently he had brought together some writers he hoped to recruit, among them D. P. Mirsky. At the end of the meeting Mirsky said, "That's not something I know how to do. I can only write about an author and his works. There's nothing I can do for you. I refuse."

In 1932, Gorky came to the conclusion that "fiction is the most valuable material to illustrate and document history" and that "literary scholars must be required to report on their trips through the provinces." Excited by one of J. B. S. Haldane's books (Moura had recommended it to him), he insisted that Samuil Marshak ought to get it into shape for *Kolkhoznik*, that is, translate it into "very simple language." He was correcting books as well as manuscripts now, simplifying them: "This will come in handy in the future." Meanwhile he was confusing Jean Giraudoux and Jean Giono, and Moura wasn't there to explain the difference to him. When Viktor Shklovsky wrote *The Successes and Failures of Maxim Gorky*, he had to publish it in Tiflis with Zakavkazskaya Kniga because Gosizdat in Moscow wouldn't take it. Shklovsky wrote: "Gorky's prose is like frozen meat that can be printed in chunks in all magazines and newspapers at once." The futurist Nikolai Chuzhak wrote: "There's nothing to learn from Gorky: he teaches life after the fact, which testifies to his impoverishment." The Central Committee subsequently prohibited any disrespectful criticism of Gorky on December 25, 1929.

In his letters to Kryuchkov, who was later executed, Gorky sometimes let fall phrases that make one wonder whether he was in his right mind during the last years of his life. Was his long-standing tuberculosis the cause of some kind of brain damage? "It is possible," he writes in connection with his proposal to translate world literature, "that some books will need to be newly rewritten or even augmented, and some cut."

For a while his vision of collective writing overrode everything else. He was handing out topics on which several writers were supposed to write novels: a series of books on friendship, on the revolutionaries of the 1860s ("show that to Alexei Tolstoy and Nikolai Tikhonov"). All this came to nothing, and he managed only to lose old friends and alienate those who had been close to him since 1917: Vsevolod Ivanov, Mikhail Bulgakov, Sergei Sergeev-Tsensky, Vyacheslav Shishkov, Alexander Afinogenov.

Some of these writers made an attempt to get through to Gorky by bringing up things that were bothering them. Aleksei Chapygin wrote to him about the grim fate of Klyuev, at which point the correspondence broke off. When Ivanov complained to him about the abnormal relations between authors and editors, Gorky did not answer. Gorky himself had noted in 1931 that "in Moscow, all meetings are cheerful, only writers' meetings are sad," but that did not give him pause.

What he demanded of movies and the visual arts in those years was no different from what he demanded of literature. The cinema must be useful; it must teach something. The primary function of painting was to illustrate history since 1917. To his favorite artist Pavel Korin he assigned the theme "Russia Departing": the picture was supposed to depict "all classes and all professions."

As for literature, the linchpin of socialism, Gorky said that poets must struggle against bohemianism and develop the genre of choral singing for the new collective farms: "I insist that poems be topical and have concrete historical content." He had changed his attitude toward the peasantry long ago; old prejudices had kept him from accepting Bolshevism during the early years of the revolution. Now he was promising writers a new magazine: *The Kolkhoz Countryside.* At one meeting in his house, in the presence of sixty people, he ordered a major poem about farming from Alexander Tvardovsky, whereupon Tvardovsky wrote "Land of Muravia" and said that Gorky had taught him how to write poetry.

Meanwhile Gorky was reevaluating the books he had once loved, saying that *Robinson Crusoe* was an imperialist novel and that Dostoyevsky's *House of the Dead* should be printed only in excerpts, and even then with annotations. In the last year of Gorky's life the only contemporary writer in the West with whom he had not broken was Romain Rolland; even Upton Sinclair and George Bernard Shaw were rejected. He scolded Stefan Zweig for knowing "nothing about Russia." He thought D. H. Lawrence was "in the service of decadence," and he was looking for a Soviet writer who could write an "anti-Freudian novel."

He had come to the conclusion that what critics needed to do was pick out several stories on a single theme and "discuss five or six authors as one," on the principle that criticism ought to teach rather than assign praise and blame. Criticism had to be coordinated or else "everything would go at cross-purposes: some would be swearing at Chekhov and others praising him."

Between the time Gorky first traveled to Moscow and finally settled there, Moura lived very little in Sorrento. When she did come it was chiefly in the winter. She was now living in London, but she was constantly taking trips. In Gorky's letters to Ladyzhnikov and others we come across brief messages about her: "M. I. has gone to Estonia," or "M. I. left for London." Sometimes in his letters one finds the phrase: "Got a letter from London." Usually this is followed by some scrap of information or something banal that someone had said or done (a Russian émigré he had once known personally), or about the decay of Europe. She was trying to cheer him up. Not only did Moura keep him current on all the gossip and rumors but she was also managing, or trying to manage, his literary affairs with foreign publishers. She had a little luck, but not much. A great deal was now being translated right in Moscow. As far as the movies were concerned, Gorky had no prospects, despite the fact that Moura, with Wells's help, had started working for the renowned director Alexander Korda and for J. Arthur Rank, whom Lockhart knew. Korda was just then starting work on a film based on Wells's *The Shape of Things to Come.*

Movies with Russian subjects had become fashionable, and Moura, who was getting to know the people around Korda and Rank, started working as a consultant on Russian matters. She was assisted by a man named Sasha Halferson, who worked for Korda and followed her around obediently, trying to be useful. She took him where he could not go, and he introduced her to the people she hadn't met. He was crazy about her, and through him she was able to get steady work as a collaborator or adviser to Korda at a time when producers and directors were interested in making films like *The Last Days of the Tsar*, *Tovaritch*, and *Mysteries of the Winter Palace*. Still acting as Gorky's literary agent, she shifted her efforts from trying to get his books published to trying to get his plays performed, and in doing so she found herself an ally—the theatrical agent B. N. Rubenstein. Rubenstein sold Gorky's play *Somov and Others*, which was having a successful run that year in Russia, but negotiations with the theater fell apart at the last moment: Moura sent a telegram saying Gorky intended "to rewrite the play" and in the meanwhile she would submit another, recently completed play *Egor Bulychev and Others*. This second play did not work out either, but Moura's work as a literary and theatrical agent and Korda's colleague gave her the opportunity to meet people, to be seen, and to have a wide circle of acquaintances. She became acquainted with people from the émigré circles of "high society," which were much more democratic in Paris, but were quite insular in London, where she met the three Benenson sisters from St. Petersburg. The eldest was Flora Solomon, a friend of Alexander Kerensky's; her sister, the Countess Fira Ilinskaya, wife of the Polish ambassador in London; and the youngest, the artist Manya Harari, who twenty-five years later would become the English translator of *Doctor Zhivago*. In their home Moura met some interesting people, including Kerensky himself a couple of times. Lockhart often lunched with Kerensky at the Carlton Grill, where he had once invited him along with Lloyd George. Lockhart had acted as interpreter, as he had when he brought Kerensky to lunch with Sir George Buchanan, the former English ambassador to Petersburg, who in 1917 had been of considerable help to the Provisional Government and Kerensky personally. In Lockhart's diary entry of June 17, 1931, we find an interesting description of one of these luncheons:

> Gave lunch to Kerensky in the Carlton Grill. Max, to my surprise, turned up and took quite an interest in Kerensky. Kerensky, who is forty-nine, looks marvellously well. He had his right kidney out for tuberculosis just before the revolution, and has never had a day's illness since. He has two sons: both in England and both engineers. One is building the new Thames bridge; the other is with a roadmaking firm in Rugby. Kerensky, Lenin and Protopopov [tsarist minister of the interior] all came from Simbirsk. Kerensky's father was a state official and was Lenin's

guardian or trustee. His ancestors were priests. Kerensky never knew either Lenin or Trotsky and had only seen them once or twice at a distance. Max asked Kerensky why he did not shoot Trotsky in 1917. Kerensky replied that Trotsky took no part in the July rebellion of 1917. He also asked him whether he was the best orator in Russia. Kerensky replied that he could not say, but that in 1917 there was no meeting, however hostile or Bolshevik, which he could not dominate and finally turn by his oratory....

What was the reason of his collapse? Kerensky replied that the Germans forced on the Bolshevik rising, because Austria, Bulgaria, and Turkey were on the eve of making a separate peace with Russia. The Austrians had decided to ask for a separate peace less than a fortnight before the Revolution.

Max: "Would you have mastered the Bolsheviks if you had made a separate peace yourselves?"

Kerensky: "Of course. We should be in Moscow now."

Max: "Why didn't you do it then?"

Kerensky: "We were too naive."

Kerensky, who after the October revolution was in hiding for nearly eight months, fled to peasants in the Pskov government to start with. In spite of the price on his head no one ever betrayed him. Last year he came to Oxford to lecture and attacked the Bolsheviks. They obviously complained, for the next time Kerensky went to our Passport Control Office in Paris he was refused a visa unless he gave an undertaking not to talk about Russia. [Ramsay] MacDonald and [Arthur] Henderson pointed out that England, the great home of liberty, had reached a funny stage when it demanded that Kerensky, when asked his opinion about Russia, should say: "I have one, but the British Labour Government do not allow me to express it."

Two years later Lockhart recorded another meeting:

Gave luncheon to Kerensky at the Wellington. Discussed the various secret peace proposals during the war. Kerensky is convinced that had the Germans not known in advance and on that account made a deal with the Bolsheviks, Russia would have made peace with Turkey and Bulgaria in 1917 and Kerensky would still be in power. Kerensky swears that the negotiations were on the point of success. Kerensky also tells me that all the stories of his truculence towards the Emperor are untrue. He says the Empress said to him: "What a pity we had not known men like you before!"

And two years after that:

To the Dorchester at seven to see Mrs. Solomon, a friend of Kerensky. Kerensky is down and out; his money has come to an end; his paper has closed down. Mrs. Solomon says can I get him journalistic work not so much to bring him in money (he has friends who will not let him starve) but to save his moral self-respect. Eighteen years ago he could have had the front page of any newspaper in the world. Today, his value is nil. *Sic transit!*

During Gorky's final years in Sorrento, Moura came to the villa only as a guest. In 1927 the contract with Gosizdat was renewed, and although they were rather tight-fisted and Gorky had to ask Kryuchkov and Ladyzhnikov to apply pressure where it would do some good, his fear for the future, if not entirely dispelled, was in any event calmed. *The Life of Klim Samgin* was being printed in *Red Virgin Soil*, and Gorky had started making trips to Russia. He was now so thin that he stooped, and his legs barely supported him. The slightest effort exhausted him, and he slept little and badly. These journeys were enormously tiring and each time he would have to stop at the

Soviet embassy in Rome, where the ambassador was Dmitry Kursky, in order to rest and recover. And, of course, he would stop in Berlin, at the Hotel Palast on Potsdamer-Platz, where Andreeva and Kryuchkov shielded him from reporters. In 1930 he was so weak that he had to stay in Sorrento. That was the year when Andreeva and Kryuchkov were finally transferred from Berlin to Moscow, Andreeva having lost her high position as authorized representative of the film industry for the Trade Office, and Kryuchkov having lost his position as director of Mezhdunarodnaya Kniga. In Moscow they went their separate ways: she took charge of Craft Export, and was later made director of the House of Scholars (her next trip to Europe was in the mid-1930s "to purge Communists and Soviet officials abroad"). Kryuchkov became Gorky's official secretary and married the secretary to the editorial board of *Kolkhoznik*.

In the summer of 1932 Romain Rolland and Henri Barbusse were planning an International Anti-War Congress. On July 30 Gorky and numerous Soviet writers and fellow travelers co-signed a letter written by Barbusse protesting the impending imperialist war against the Soviet Union. The letter was addressed "To All Writers of the World, Friends of the USSR" and was sent to newspapers in Europe and America.

Barbusse energetically set about making the arrangements for the congress. After Paris, Brussels, Strasbourg, and Switzerland all turned him down, Holland agreed that the meeting could take place in Amsterdam. Back in May, when Gorky had signed the original appeal of the international committee, he had promised, despite his ailing health, to be present on opening day, now set for August 27.

Half ill, he left for Berlin with Shvernik[5] on August 24. At the

---

5. Nikolai Shvernik was head of the Soviet delegation at the congress. Between 1930 and 1944 he was first secretary of the All-Union Central Trade Union Council, and later first deputy chairman of the Presidium of the Supreme Soviet.

same time, Rolland was wiring Gorky from Switzerland to say that his doctors had forbidden him to make any public appearances and therefore he could not attend the congress. When Gorky arrived in Berlin, he wired Barbusse to inform him that Holland had refused visas to some of the Soviet delegation and he asked Barbusse to take appropriate measures.

Gorky himself remained in Berlin to protest the Dutch government's decision, and he stayed with the whole delegation at the old Hotel Palast for a few days, waiting to see how things turned out. His health, not helped by these annoyances, was deteriorating, his temperature rising, and the doctor told him to stay in bed. He summoned Moura from London. She came for several days, spending day and night at his bedside. On August 26, on the initiative of Willi Münzenberg, it was decided to move the congress from Amsterdam to Paris so that the Soviet delegation could participate. But the French government, like the Dutch, would not grant visas to the Soviet delegation as a whole nor to some of its individual participants. On August 26 Gorky wired Edouard Herriot, then head of the French government, asking him for emergency visas. On the 27th the congress opened in Amsterdam. The congress read aloud the declaration Rolland had sent from Switzerland, "War Against War," and elected Gorky and Shvernik to the presidium—in absentia. Gorky responded to this congratulatory telegram and learned that meetings were being held in factories, the Academy of Sciences, and other workers' collectives to castigate the Dutch government. The congress concluded on the 29th by electing a permanent international antiwar committee that included Gorky.

On August 30 the Communist newspaper *L'Humanité* announced that Gorky and the Soviet delegation would be issued French visas immediately, enabling them to attend the meeting in Paris that had been arranged by the French delegation to report on the Amsterdam congress. But Gorky did not go to Paris. Soviet sources claim that

French visas were sent to Gorky and Shvernik, on Herriot's insistence, but that Gorky did not feel it was right to abandon the Soviet delegation in Berlin. Others claim that it was Moura who would not let Gorky go to Paris and, with the help of his doctors, kept him in his bed in Berlin. He was much too ill and weak to travel to a meeting, to say nothing of speaking there, which would have been unavoidable. The speech Gorky wired to Paris, in Moura's translation, was read aloud at the meeting, after which the presidium of the meeting sent him a greeting. On that same day, September 2, he left for Moscow, arriving there on the 4th gravely ill. The morning of the following day he was taken to Gorki, a village outside Moscow, and on the 7th *Pravda* and *Izvestia* both ran his "Speech, Never Given."

Gorky returned to Sorrento for the final time in late October 1932. His last month in Moscow had been entirely dedicated to his anniversary—forty years of literary activity. The Moscow Art Theater now bore his name, and Nizhniy Novgorod as well as hundreds of factories, schools, academic institutes, and thousands of streets in cities and villages were renamed in his honor. Moura came to see him in Sorrento and stayed till Christmas. His two granddaughters, son, daughter-in-law, and the faithful Rakitsky were there also. In early spring they began to pack their things for the move to Russia. They were giving up Il Sorito, where the family had lived for eight and a half years, forever. Moura made one last trip back in March. Despite the fact that guests were staying in the villa up to the very last day, there was something that had troubled Gorky since 1926 and that he wanted to address. It was essential that it be handled by the most intimate family council—Gorky himself, Maxim, Timosha, Rakitsky, and Moura. This was the matter of Gorky's archives.

Some of his papers had been sent safely to Moscow back in 1926 and 1927. Gorky wanted his archives kept in the Pushkin House, the literary institute in Leningrad, and on January 13, 1926, he wrote a letter to Valentina Khodasevich: "Ask Mikhail Belyaev [an associate of the Pushkin House, Valentina's friend, and the brother of the well-known playwright Yury Belyaev], whom I should write to about transferring my archives to the Pushkin House."

About a thousand books from his library, which he had been accumulating in Italy since 1924 (the majority had been sent to him gradually from Russia), and the greater part of his letters and manuscripts, which were kept in boxes, had already been sent to Moscow via Berlin in 1928. There they were cataloged by associates of the Gorky Institute, who decided what to leave at the institute, what to transfer to the house on Kachalov Street in Moscow, and what to send to his dacha in Gorki. But there was yet another box in Sorrento that no one knew what to do with and that held letters and papers that could not be sent to Russia: they had to be put in safekeeping in Europe. Very little had been brought to Italy from the safe at the Dresden Bank; most of the papers had been collected in Sorrento.

The papers were of four types. First, there were the letters from émigrés (writers, mainly), with whom Gorky had corresponded over the years in Sorrento; most were from the early period, before 1926 and 1927, when Gorky took his sharp turn toward Moscow. Here were the letters of Vladislav Khodasevich, Marc Slonim, Vyacheslav Ivanov, Dmitry Mirsky (before he left for Russia), Fyodor Chaliapin, one letter from Andrei Bely (April 8, 1924), and one from Alexei Remizov (during the *Beseda* period); letters from émigrés less well known who had nothing to do with politics but had turned to him with various requests; and the letters of foreigners and vacillating young Russians abroad wondering whether they should go to Russia or not, what they should think about it, what was going on there, and how he viewed it all. Here one might include the letters of the first defectors, or dissidents, who escaped across the Finnish, Persian, Polish, Romanian, and Far Eastern borders and who wanted to give Gorky the latest news from the homeland and to open his eyes.

Second, there were letters from writers and scholars, actors and artists, who had come to Europe from the Soviet Union on a brief vacation or on business and had taken advantage of their time away to complain of the practices, or rather, malpractices, of the authorities in the homeland, and sometimes even of Stalin himself. Among them were letters from Isaac Babel, Konstantin Fedin, Mikhail Koltsov, Olga Forsh, Konstantin Stanislavsky and Vladimir Nemirovich-Danchenko, Vsevolod Meyerhold and Zinaida Raikh (who had been guests one summer in Sorrento), as well as others whom no one but Gorky knew: old friends and chance acquaintances who had found themselves outside Russia temporarily and had brought information to the writer in Sorrento about what was going on in his country.

Third were the letters from people with a political past who continued to argue with him despite his new orientation toward the Kremlin and his triumphal tours through Russia: some Mensheviks, like Galina Sukhanova, Nikolai Valentinov-Volsky, and Boris Nicolaevsky; a few right-wing Socialists, among them Ekaterina Kuskova, the veteran journalist and a childhood friend of Ekaterina Peshkova's, who was living in Prague and belonged wholly to the emigration but kept hoping until the end of her days to find some opportunity for reconciliation with the regime that had exiled her and others from Russia in 1922; or the journalist Mikhail Osorgin, who tried to assure both himself and everyone else that despite his collaboration with the émigré press and his lack of a work permit he was not an émigré and was ready to return the moment they let him; or Alexei Peshekhonov, who had moved from Prague to Riga and finally gone back to the homeland.

Last were the letters from Gregory Pyatakov, Alexei Rykov, and Leonid Krasin (and perhaps Trotsky as well, but that has not been established), who had come to Berlin, Paris, Ankara, Stockholm, and other capitals of the world, having broken out of the tight circle in which Stalin's consolidation of power had entrapped them. They wrote to Gorky, whom they knew personally, demanding that he raise his voice against tyranny and the flouting of Lenin's principles. These people with famous names included quite a few envoys and ambassadors affiliated with European governments, to say nothing of the Soviet plenipotentiaries in Italy, whom he knew personally. There were also several prominent bureaucrats traveling abroad on official business, such as Grigory Sokolnikov and Leonid Serebryakov. What was he to do with all this seditious correspondence, in and among which were scattered pages of notes Gorky himself had written about his meetings with these people, or copies of his replies to them? Maxim felt that all of this counterrevolutionary material should be burned here and now, right in the fireplace in Gorky's office (with its view of Vesuvius) or, even better, on the terrace in front of the house, under the guise of shooting off fireworks for some Italian holiday. But everyone else, Gorky included, was against that. They felt that the papers should be preserved. But whom could he leave them with? Whom could he trust? This was the problem at hand.

Moura took no part whatsoever in this dispute. She knew that there were two, and only two, people who could be entrusted with that box, and, being one of them, she felt that she had to hold her tongue. "I am an interesting [interested] party," she said, "so I'm going to sit here and keep quiet."

The first evening no decision was reached. But the next day it became clear that the other possible custodian would not do. This was Gorky's adopted son, Zinovy Peshkov, the one-armed hero of the first war and a general in the French army. It was he who had come to see Gorky in 1921 immediately after his arrival at St. Blasien from Petrograd, and later in 1925 he was a guest for a month at Sorrento. He was considered a member of the Peshkov family.

Two factors weighed against him: for all intents and purposes he was now French; and he had no permanent address. Actually, he did have an address, he had an apartment in Paris. But in the performance of his duty he might be living in Africa or traveling anywhere in the world (his last tour of duty was in a military-diplomatic post in Japan in 1950). According to rumors, he had an adoring girlfriend in every European capital—a Spanish countess, a French princess, an Italian duchess—who dreamed of marrying him. All this was rather silly, and Maxim joked about it, as did Gorky (although he believed every word Zinovy uttered), but Rakitsky was categorically opposed to storing such serious papers with a man who didn't know today where he would be tomorrow. Gorky was essentially on Nightingale's side, and in the end Maxim agreed that Titka should take the box. "I won't take a box," she said. "Give me a suitcase." And to this, too, everyone agreed.

Despite his cough and weakness, Gorky helped pack the books. Everyone pitched in, even Elena and Matilda, the daughters of Duke Serra di Capriola. Less than a year after Gorky's departure the two of them ran into Pavel Muratov in Italy, where he visited from time to time when he was living in Paris. They had known him since 1924, when he was Gorky's guest and had stayed at the Hotel Minerva, making friends with everyone. They told him how two months before Gorky's final departure his books were sent to Moscow, how the little granddaughters and their Swiss governess had left first, and how only later, after the Italian summer had already begun, Gorky, Maxim and his wife, and Nightingale had driven off in four carriages and two automobiles. The date was May 8, 1933. After saying goodbye to the servants and the dogs, they left for Naples accompanied by the writers Samuil Marshak and Lev Nikulin, who had been visiting them since mid-April. In Naples, Gorky and the members of his household—there were eight all told—boarded the *Jean Jaurès* and sailed for Odessa via Istanbul.

In April Moura left Sorrento for London with the suitcase full of Gorky's papers. On May 15 she arrived in Istanbul on the *Orient Express* and met the *Jean Jaurès* in port. On the 16th they all went to see the Hagia Sophia and on the evening of the 16th Moura said goodbye to Gorky on the shores of the Bosporus. That was the same spring she went with Wells to the PEN Congress in Dubrovnik and afterward to Austria, the spring when she was finally free and her future settled.

A new chapter in Gorky's life began that spring, too, his final Russian period: there was the aggravation of old illnesses and the appearance of new ones, fame throughout Russia, friendship with Stalin, vast plans to rewrite world literature starting with Homer, and, finally, the death of Maxim, the murder of Kirov, and his own demise.

Maxim's death in 1934 did not prevent two members of his family from turning up in Europe again the very next year. Maxim had died after an illness of only a few days, and rumors had reached Paris to the effect that he had been left alone, drunk, on a Moscow boulevard bench one raw May night; it was as if one of his drinking companions had desired his death and left him there to catch pneumonia. Hardly anyone believed that. Maxim was young, athletic, and healthy, and those who knew him well tried not to entertain such rumors, preferring to wait for an opportunity to find out the truth for themselves. There was little opportunity to do that in those days: contact with people in the Soviet Union was uncommon, letters rarely got through, and what did were mainly postcards, read up, down, and sideways by the censors. If someone did go to Moscow, it was not anyone in our circle. Once in a while we would hear: "Ehrenburg came from Moscow and said..." or "Babel's in Belgium right now, and he says...." But then early in the summer of 1935 an announcement appeared in the Russian papers saying that Ekaterina Pavlovna Peshkova and Nadezhda Peshkova (Timosha) were coming to London with a group of Soviet artists and planned to continue to Paris from there. Knowing that Ekaterina Pavlovna would probably see two of her oldest friends, I decided to find out where she was staying.

One was Ekaterina Kuskova, whom I've already mentioned, but

she was living in Prague and couldn't help me.[6] The other was Yuly
Martov's sister Lidia Dan, a member of the Menshevik Party. I called
her and said that I would like to see Timosha. She knew the state of
affairs in Gorky's house and advised me to go see Ekaterina Pavlovna
first, who was supposed to arrive before Timosha, and ask her permission to see her daughter-in-law. Such were the standing orders,
apparently. However strange it seemed to me that two grown women
could see each other only with the consent of a third, I followed Dan's
advice.

On a quiet street in Paris's seventeenth arrondissement, there is a
marvelous, peaceful little square called Saint-Ferdinand, and on it a
hotel by the same name. That block then was modest and genteel,
albeit elegant. It was often deserted, and there were no honking cars
or gaudy signs. When I arrived at the seemingly deserted hotel I
walked up to the third floor. Ekaterina Peshkova opened the door,
and I could see that she had guests, two young women: Vadim
Andreev's wife (and later the mother of Olga Carlisle) and her sister.
Ekaterina Pavlovna did not let me in and told me to wait downstairs.
I saw how she had aged: Maxim's death had seriously shaken this
hard, strong woman.

She called for me about twenty minutes later. She was alone and I
could tell that she was anxious for me to leave as quickly as possible.

---

6. Kuskova wrote me a long letter, which I quote here in part:

> Before this fall, Ekaterina Pavlovna had never come abroad for a visit without warn-
> ing us in advance. In recent years my husband and I, who know her well, have
> observed something abnormal in her moods. She wrote me last fall saying that despite
> her trip to Europe she was still suffering from "emotional depression." We had
> noticed it, too; when she came to see us about various matters that were on her mind,
> she got them all mixed up. In December a mutual friend...came to visit us in Prague.
> She confirmed that since Maxim's death E. P. had not been herself....Her "depres-
> sion" was made even worse by Gorky's exceptionally crude behavior at the funeral.

(1258 Khrebenka, Prague, May 27, 1935)

She gave me permission to see Timosha, who was still in London with Pavel Korin, whom Ekaterina Pavlovna called "a great artist—he's coming to Paris to finish his copy of the *Mona Lisa*"; his pupil, the artist Sofia Uranova, and some other artists whose names I didn't try to remember. Timosha was traveling with them, added Ekaterina Pavlovna, in order "to explain art to them—only realistic art, of course." We spoke for about five minutes, and I left. On a slip of paper she wrote: "Tuesday, four o'clock." That was the time I was to come.

So I went. And Timosha, just as young and attractive as ever, wearing a blue silk dress with white daisies, took me to her room on the fourth floor. I sat with her for about an hour. She betrayed neither joy nor embarrassment: she was as cold as ice, civil, and attentive; she asked questions that anyone in her place would have asked under the circumstances. But she did not ask about Khodasevich, and I did not ask about Gorky. I did, however, ask about Maxim, about his illness and death, and about his last few days. Looking to one side, she said, "Yes, you probably know everything from the newspapers." A little more than a year had passed since his death, but she spoke as if it had been five. She did not smile once the whole time, nor did I. Only when she asked, "Don't you want to go back home? I could arrange it for you," did I sense that it was time for me to go. We managed to avoid letting the conversation drift toward the subject of Valentina, who was now living in Moscow, and spoke instead of Moura, with whom Timosha had spent a week in London. She "helped buy me dresses," Timosha said, "now everything I have is new." I believe that Ekaterina Pavlovna had left Paris by then and had gone to Prague and would later meet Timosha in Berlin.

When I walked out into Saint-Ferdinand Square, I realized that I had made a mistake, and I regretted it immediately. Two weeks passed, and news came from Kuskova in Prague that Ekaterina Pavlovna had been to see her and had told her that she had gone to London with the aim of convincing Moura to turn over Gorky's archive, which had been entrusted to her two years earlier, so that it could be transferred to Russia. Moura had refused, and Ekaterina Pavlovna was angry with her.

During those years we were unable to draw certain conclusions from known facts that now, in light of what has happened, seem obvious. In the summer of 1935, Moura refused to let Gorky's archive be taken back to Moscow. In the spring of 1936 an attempt was made to steal Trotsky's papers from the house where he was living in Norway. Soon after that, pressure was put on Moura by someone who had come to London from the Soviet Union with instructions and a letter from Gorky: before his death he wanted to say goodbye to her. Stalin would provide a train car to meet her at the border, she would be taken to Moscow and then taken back to Negoreloe in the same train car. She was told to bring the archive with her, otherwise he would never see her again. The man who handed her the letter would accompany her from London to Moscow and back again.

This time she confided in Lockhart, and he was the only person to draw the proper conclusion: he answered her frankly that if she didn't give up the papers they would take them from her by force—by bomb, burglary, or at gunpoint.

Gorky had been ailing since the spring of this final year of his life. He was gravely ill, more so than ever. He was living in the Crimea, in Tesseli, and it was considered dangerous for him to go to Moscow, even in the summer. Meanwhile, in June 1935, a new congress was being organized, this time not "against war" but "in defense of culture." It was set for June 21, in Paris, and Gorky had been recruited for the presidium. Everyone was counting on his being there: André Malraux, André Gide (this was a year before he became disenchanted with the Soviet Union), Louis Aragon, Henri Barbusse, and Ilya Ehrenburg, who was then living in Paris.

The first of the Russians to arrive was Alexei Tolstoy. Gorky agreed to head up the deputation of Soviet writers invited to the congress and was writing his speech on the defense of culture, which he promised to read on opening day. He was even getting a foreign passport and joked with Fedin (in a letter dated June 4): "I have to pay a call on the women of Paris in my old age." But he did not leave Tesseli, despite the fact that the Paris evening paper *L'Intransigeant* announced on the 19th that Gorky had arrived in Paris. He did not go to Moscow until the 24th, in time for the arrival of Rolland and his wife, née Kudasheva, the former secretary to Pyotr Kogan, but was immediately confined to his bed with bronchitis.[7]

---

7. In the 1930s there existed in Parisian literary circles a strange distrust of certain women of Russian origin who had married French celebrities (young or not so young) from the world of letters, music, or the arts. It mattered little whether they were the legitimate wives of Romain Rolland, Louis Aragon, Paul Eluard, Fernand Léger or their mistresses. One always had the feeling on making their acquaintance that they had probably been sent by Moscow to attach themselves to these celebrities, with the principal mission of keeping these men of genius under Stalin's influence and preventing them from expressing critical opinions about him or changing their political position. Like Moura with Wells, there were Elsa Triolet, the wives of Eluard and Léger and many others, including Princess Maria Pavlovna Kudasheva. They were energetic, intelligent, elegant women who had chosen this dangerous profession fully aware of the possible consequences. Some of them used to go to Moscow, and would also entertain Soviet diplomats who happened to be in Paris and were charmed. They spoke French as well as they spoke Russian and above all kept their "domestic genius" under close surveillance. This is not the place to paint their portraits, but a few words must be said about Maria Kudasheva, who managed to get Rolland to marry her when he was sixty-eight years old (she was a little over thirty), after having gotten rid of his sister who had been living in his house in Switzerland. She surrounded Rolland with her Soviet friends and finally convinced him to take a trip to Moscow. According to Georges Duhamel, there was no doubt that she was working for Moscow. Kudasheva admitted to Duhamel's son that she had been "manipulated by the NKVD" (*Le Livre de l'amertume. Journal 1925–1956* [Paris: Mercure de France, 1983], 85, 417). She arrived in Paris in the 1920s after having been Kogan's secretary. Duhamel helped her to obtain a permanent residence visa (in Moscow she had solicited letters of recommendation from some high civil servants in the Ministry of Foreign Affairs). She quickly installed herself in Rolland's house and threatened suicide several times in order to make him marry her. She did not stint in her efforts to keep in her young and vigorous hands the old Nobel Prize winner whose health was failing. [Author's note added in 1987.]

Much was happening in Paris. On June 21, the opening day of the congress, the talented young French writer René Crevel killed himself, evidently coming to his desperate decision on political grounds. He left a suicide note with a political explanation for his act, which the organizers of the congress, in a state of near panic, did not allow to be read out loud.

The days were unusually hot. Men had to take off their jackets and sit in their shirtsleeves—a rare sight at the time. Only two remained true to tradition: Heinrich Mann (Thomas Mann's brother) and E. M. Forster kept their jackets on. In that heat (the thermometer rose as high as 40° C during the day) there were seven discussions in five days. On the second day there was an incident during André Breton's speech. He asked several questions: about Stalinism, about Stalin, about the system of government in the Soviet Union, and also about Victor Serge, the Trotskyite and French writer who by some miracle had recently managed to get out of the Soviet Union. But the questions raised by this former Communist who had left the Party, the leading Dadaist poet and founder of surrealism, went unanswered. Aragon and Ehrenburg would not yield the floor and they cut off people shouting responses from their seats. Malraux attempted to give the floor to Serge's friends, but they wouldn't let him. When Koltsov announced that Serge was mixed up in Kirov's murder, a hissing went up in the hall.

By the third day of the congress, the absence of Babel and Pasternak had begun to embarrass the presidium. Ehrenburg was losing his head. Gide and Malraux went to the Soviet embassy on rue de Grenelle to ask that Russia send some of its "more important and respected" writers to the congress. Ehrenburg sent a desperate telegram to the Writers Union in Moscow. Finally Stalin personally gave permission for Babel and Pasternak to attend, but they didn't get there until the last day of the congress. Pasternak arrived without luggage, so Malraux gave him a suit. Pasternak walked onto the stage wearing Malraux's suit, said a few words about how everyone should live in the country rather than the city, how you could pick flowers and not think about politics in the country, and how the more happy people there were in a country the better. After that he read a poem. Babel came out next and told a few anecdotes (he spoke French, beautifully). The congress concluded on June 29.

Gorky returned to Tesseli after Rolland's visit on September 25 and stayed through the winter. In May of 1936, he was so sick that the doctor and nurse who lived with him in Tesseli feared for his life and brought him to Moscow, believing he would get better care at the Kremlin hospital. On June 1 his condition was called critical, and on the 18th he died from cardiac arrest. He was cremated on the night of the 20th, and that same evening the urn with his ashes was bricked up in the Kremlin wall.

In her memoirs, Valentina Khodasevich complains that Kryuchkov would not let her into the house where Gorky was dying in Gorki, outside Moscow. Louis Aragon and his wife, Elsa Triolet, who had come from Paris, and Mikhail Koltsov, who was with them, were not even allowed onto the grounds by an armed guard who had been stationed at the gates. They sat in the car for a few hours and watched a car emerge from the gates driving the doctors away. It was the morning of Gorky's death. Aragon wrote about it in 1965 in *La Mise à mort* (*The Final Blow*), a book which has yet to be translated into Russian:

> A futile commotion over details, irritation, probably misunderstood instructions... The 18th of June, in front of the estate... An automobile. The driver argues with the guard, the chain on the gate is lowered. It's the doctor. Maybe after his visit we'll get our chance? Mikhail walks from the guard to us and back. Another hour passes. Mikhail manages to get close to the car as it pulls out. The doctor knows him. They discuss it.... Had I

known then that that doctor, as people later said and continued to say for twenty years, had taken part in a crime...that he was a murderer! Gorky was dead. There was nothing left for us to do but turn around and go back. Tears welled in Mikhail's eyes.... At the time no one knew yet, or even imagined, that this death, after a long illness, was a murder....

I didn't want to go to the funeral. The heat was such a horror, the road to the cemetery so long, all that walking and weariness.... Mikhail came to the hotel and begged, insisted. "Gorky so wanted to see you!"[8]...Finally we conceded. At first we walked together, then Mikhail was called aside, and Luppol and I continued on our own. He had been at the congress in Paris, in 1935, where we were all so surprised by Gorky's absence.... After they carried the body out of the Hall of Columns we crowded onto the square, and then they lined us up in rows.

Thus, in the old-fashioned style of "cinematic prose," with agitated ellipses, sketchy sentences, and an affected tone, the Socialist realist Aragon wrote about the doctor-murderer, and later, by the way, about the executed generals—Putna, Uborevich, Yakir, Kork, Eideman, Primakov, and Tukhachevsky. Koltsov told Aragon that

---

8. Aragon and Triolet deliberately delayed their arrival in Moscow for an important reason: in the spring of 1936, Ehrenburg, who had been close to Triolet since the 1920s, warned Aragon not to hurry to go see Gorky. Ehrenburg knew very well what was going on between Gorky and Stalin and did not wish to place Aragon and Triolet in a difficult and even dangerous position as a result of those "confidential matters," which may have brought Gorky to his deathbed. Gorky was certainly ready by then to tell them his grievances. So Aragon and Triolet stayed in London, then in Leningrad (at Lily Brik's) longer than was necessary. As has also been confirmed to me by a member of the family of her last husband, Lily Brik knew very well what she was doing. She was much more cunning than Ehrenburg, to say nothing of Koltsov, who was infantile...or was he just pretending to be naïve? Gide may also have been forewarned and made a point of not arriving too soon. [Author's note added in March 1988.]

they had all been traitors, and the famous poet and member of the French Communist Party believed him. How far Aragon was from his protest against the occupation of Prague by Soviet troops in 1968! How far from the confession he made in 1972: "My life is like a terrible game that I have utterly lost. I crippled my own life, warped it irrevocably." And how far from Triolet, who, a year before her death, wrote about their shared past: "My husband is a Communist. And it is my fault he is. I am a Soviet agent. I like to wear jewels, I belong to the highest society, and I'm a slattern."

In the early 1950s rumors circulated that Moura had gone to Moscow in June 1936, when Gorky's condition was hopeless and he wanted to see her one last time. Could he really have insisted that they give her a visa to Moscow, or—more significantly—that they give her permission to go back to London? What kind of guarantees were made? And could she have risked going?

Boris Nicolaevsky, who had so enjoyed the Saarow *pelmeni*, was the author of "The Letter of an Old Bolshevik" printed in 1936 in *The Socialist Herald*, and later, in 1965, of a book of essays, *Power and the Soviet Elite*. These writings played a prominent role in European and American Sovietologists' understanding of the corridors of power inside the Kremlin and the meaning of the Moscow trials. George Kennan said of them that they were "the most authoritative and important bit of source material on the background of the purges." The well-known American journalist Louis Fischer wrote of Nicolaevsky that "all of us who are Soviet specialists have sat at his feet," and Professor Robert Tucker, the author of a biography of Stalin, said, "For many in the present generation of Anglo-American scholars in Russian studies, Nicolaevsky has been and remains in the fullest sense a mentor."

Nicolaevsky was a historian, a member of the Russian Social Democratic Party (Menshevik), a collector of rare historical books and documents. For a while he oversaw Trotsky's archives in the

Slavonic Library in Paris (on rue Michelet) and had contacts with both international Social Democrats and prominent Bolsheviks visiting from the Soviet Union. He had answers to many questions, and once, in Vermont, in 1959, when he, Mikhail Karpovich, and I were visiting mutual friends, I asked him about something that puzzled me. In 1958, books devoted to Gorky's life and work were being published by the USSR Academy of Science Publishers. Some of the books contained excerpts from letters or from other documents that had once been taken to London. They were followed by a note saying that the originals were located in the Gorky Archive in Moscow. How could those documents have wound up in Moscow (at the Institute of World Literature) when Gorky gave them to Moura for safekeeping? That they had been given to Moura I knew from Pavel Muratov. Nicolaevsky replied that Moura had indeed taken them back to Moscow in June 1936, when Gorky asked Stalin to allow her to come say goodbye to him. Stalin gave his assent, but would only guarantee she would be allowed to leave the USSR on the condition that she bring the archive. I remember that Karpovich was horrified at Nicolaevsky's story and remained so for a long time.

Six years passed. In 1965, while speaking with Louis Fischer (my neighbor in Princeton), who was always eager to hear new information about Soviet Russia, I described for him my conversation with Nicolaevsky. Fischer asked me if I had written documentation for that conversation. Naturally, I didn't. He asked my permission to write to Nicolaevsky about it. He mentioned that in one of his last letters Nicolaevsky had asked Fischer if he knew anything about Gorky's archives. He showed me the letter dated December 14, 1965, from Menlo Park, California. In it was a question: "Do you know anything regarding the removal of Gorky's archives to Russia in April 1936? Do you know that that delivery exerted a great influence on Stalin's plans?"

Fischer's letter to Nicolaevsky as printed here is taken from a copy;

Nicolaevsky's letter, from the original. Both documents come from Fischer's archive in Princeton. Fischer wrote in English; Nicolaevsky in Russian.

> [Princeton]
>
> 11 January 1966
>
> Your reference to the removal of Gorky's papers to the USSR in April, 1936 is of tremendous significance. Is it possible that the papers contained damaging evidence—in Stalin's eyes—of the disloyalty to him of many Soviet leaders who might have complained to Gorky by letter? Who took Gorky's papers to Moscow and why?

Nicolaevsky wrote back immediately:

> Menlo Park, California
>
> 18 January 1966
>
> The story of Gorky's papers is a long one. Among them were Gorky's records of conversations he had had with Soviet writers and public figures who had come to see him. Gorky left them for safekeeping with his last wife (Mar. Ign. Budberg), née Benckendorff, the daughter of the last tsarist ambassador to England. In 1917–18 she had been in love with the well-known Bruce Lockhart ("Masha" in the latter's memoirs), and there is a lot about her in Peters's memoirs. Gorky set one condition: she must not surrender the papers to anybody. Even if he should demand they be sent to him in Moscow, she was to refuse. In 1935, when Gorky stood up on behalf of Kamenev, Stalin denied Gorky a visa to attend a writers' congress in Paris and demanded that he hand over the archive. Peshkova went abroad on Gorky's request, but Budberg refused to give up the papers (this I know from Kuskova, who at the time was still seeing and

speaking with Peshkova). The change in Budberg's position, according to certain information, was due to the influence of Lockhart, who then had a particular policy toward Moscow. Budberg arrived in Moscow in April of 1936. A special train car was waiting for her at the frontier, and from the train station she went straight to the sanatorium where Gorky was and where she met with Stalin and Voroshilov.... There are several more details, which are also interesting, but they would take too long to tell.[9]

Fischer was planning to be in London the next summer. He had heard about Moura from Lockhart and had seen her with Wells a few times. I asked him to telephone her, maybe invite her out for dinner, and ask her, in passing, whether she had been in Russia between 1921 and her trip there in 1958, when, as everyone knew, she went on Peshkova's invitation. Peshkova had written of her wish to resume friendly relations with her.

My question consisted of two parts: Was she in Russia in 1936, and did she see Gorky before his death?

But there could be no question of inviting Moura to a restaurant, she had long since stopped going out in the evenings. She was seventy-five years old, and she did not show herself in public, particularly in the mornings. Fischer had to go to her home "for a cup of tea." She was living in an apartment littered with souvenirs and knickknacks, and on the walls hung icons and photographs. She was very fat and had a hard time moving around, but he had no trouble steering the conversation toward Russia. To the first question she answered cate-

---

9. As usual, Nicolaevsky remembered the facts very well, but he did not retain the details over those thirty years. We know that she was not a relative of Ambassador Benckendorff, that she was called Moura and not Masha, and that in his story on the "Lockhart plot" (*Proletarian Revolution*, 1924) Peters mentions Moura only in one paragraph, which I cited in chapter three. Finally, as we shall see, she arrived in Moscow in June, not April.

gorically no. She did not travel to Russia between 1921 and 1958. To the second question, she answered yes; she had traveled from London to Berlin to see him when, a year before his death, in 1935, he had stopped there on the way to the congress in Paris. There he had fallen ill, and the doctors would not let him go any farther. She herself had insisted that he not go anywhere and that he return to Moscow as quickly as possible. She had spent four days with him.

"But that was in 1932, at another congress," I said.

"She spoke quite convincingly and at length. She said it was in 1935," Fischer replied.

Then I showed Fischer copies of *Pravda* and *Izvestia* from June 1935 with Gorky's greeting: "I'm deeply saddened that the state of my health has kept me..." And the notation: "Tesseli."

Gorky did not leave Russia after 1933, as Lydia Bykovtseva makes clear in *Gorky in Moscow*. According to Lev Nikulin's memoirs, Moura went to Moscow briefly, for about a week in June 1936. She had given Fischer a confusing answer counting on him not to remember the dates of the many congresses where the friendship between the Western world (its "progressive" part) and the Soviet Union was solidified. During the 1930s there were two or three every year. As Bykovtseva wrote in her book: "After 1933, the writer did not go abroad and spent the winter months in the Crimea." In *Moscow* magazine (no. 2, 1966), Nikulin declaims with false pathos: "When people ask us to whom *The Life of Klim Samgin* is dedicated, who this Maria Ignatievna Zakrevskaya was, we think about how her portrait stood on the table next to Gorky until his final days. She flew to him from a far-off country and was by his side in the last hours of his life."[10]

10. Volume 3 of the historical almanac *Minuvshee* (*The Past*), dated autumn 1987 (published in Paris by Atheneum, edited by V. Alloy), included some letters from Alexei Tolstoy to his third wife, Natalia Vasilyevna Krandievskaya. In one letter dated March 8, 1935, Tolstoy recounts at Gorky's house (in Gorki, outside Moscow) that he read to Voroshilov his opera libretto (*The Decembrists*) and his version of *Pinocchio*, and said: "Maria Ignatievna was

It is essential to note that at that time there was no regular air service or passenger planes between London and Moscow; "flew" is just the Lenin Prize laureate's fancy metaphor for "came by train." The title of his memoirs is *Words Not Spoken*, which gives an accurate idea of what we are condemned to read in its pages. But what Nikulin did not say the *Great Soviet Encyclopedia* did: there, in the list of European cities where Gorky's archives had once resided, is London.

She concealed her trip even to the very end of her life, repeating the version she had given Fischer in an interview for *Vogue* in October 1970. Disclosure of the secret Moscow trip could have led to the disclosure of the secret return of the archives to Gorky. In fact, however, they were handed over to Stalin, who, as Nicolaevsky suspected, took them away from her. Stalin, of course, could have managed without them in his preparations for the Moscow Trials, but there was probably something of use to him there. In his own way Lockhart had been right when he had told Moura to go. It would have been too dangerous for her to keep the Sorrento suitcase in her apartment. Someone could break in at night, as happened to Walter Krivitsky, or even during the day, as happened to Kerensky. Or they could gradually have wormed their way into her confidence, as they did with Trotsky, or spied on her to see when she had left the apartment so they could fit a key to the lock. In 1935 Moura had not yielded when Peshkova came to London to plead with her to part with the archive, but a year later she did. Could fear of a break-in and theft of the papers be behind this, or did she fear that Genrikh Yagoda, the chief of the secret police, might blackmail her? And if she did fear blackmail, then on

---

there (she leaves on the 10th). She's taking *Pinocchio* to translate into English, Slavka [B. Malakhovsky] is going to illustrate it." It was probably at this time that negotiations were under way for the repatriation of that portion of Gorky's archives he had entrusted to Moura and which Stalin acquired in 1936. [Author's note added in December 1987.]

what grounds? Could Peters have talked her into it, thereby saving his own head? In 1936 he was still at liberty, although out of favor. Could he have helped to put pressure on her, threatening to reveal their acquaintance, which might have begun even before she met Lockhart, when she became friendly with Hill, Cromie, and the others in Petrograd in January or February of 1918? And could he, protecting himself by mixing lies with truth, have let her know that he would slander her and "expose" the fact that he had sent her to British political intelligence unless she did what he demanded? And did this help Peters survive another two relatively peaceful years before he was executed, as indeed Yagoda was himself?

Or the explanation for her act lies somewhere else entirely. In 1935 Peshkova may have been acting independently, without Gorky's knowledge, and now Gorky himself was demanding from Moura what she had been entrusted with, giving her some reason to break her old promise not to return the papers even if he demanded them. There was another rationale as well: having the papers at hand could help him establish the guilt of his old enemies for past crimes, or, just the opposite, could shield someone close to him, perhaps saving them from hard labor and execution. Anything was possible, but one thing is certain: Moura did bring the archives to Moscow and they were taken away from her. Gorky never saw them. However, if she arrived in June (rather than April), then he would have been so badly off that the papers scarcely could have done him any good, and he may never even have asked her about them.[11]

If we accept the possibility that Gorky hoped to save someone close to him, it could mean that in the last year of his life Gorky did in

---

11. Along with the archive, she evidently surrendered her own "notes" as well. Did they amount to two pages or twenty, and when had they been written? They are mentioned only once in Gorky's *Complete Collected Works* (vol. 18 [Moscow: Nauka, 1973], 546). Later, in 1938, for no apparent reason, she sent a few more letters from Gorky to Wells to Moscow.

fact see the true horror of Stalin's terror, as several memoirists testify. Not only did he see it but he had decided to fight it, and for that he sought the weapons he would need. Supporting such a theory are reports of a later period describing how Gorky "couldn't even breathe" and was "trying to get to Italy." Kryuchkov had to have known Gorky's state of mind, and he may have informed Stalin about it—to save himself (more will be said later about his dual role). Nevertheless, the hypothesis of Gorky's natural death stands. His long years of poor health—since he was a young man—had brought him to that point. In a country like Russia, Kryuchkov could have been shot not for Gorky's murder, which he confessed to even though he did not commit it, but for informing on Gorky, after which he had to be got rid of as a witness to Gorky's moods. Or, on the contrary, because when he failed to inform the proper authorities about those moods, he subjected Stalin to the danger of being exposed by Gorky. Kryuchkov might also have been shot as a Chekist who had helped Yagoda conduct his murky affairs, or as Gorky's loyal and trusted agent of many years' standing. He could have been Yagoda's accomplice in Gorky's murder, just as he could have been the instrument of Stalin's will. One thing is certain: if Gorky died a violent death, the slightest push would have been enough to accomplish the deed. Since the summer of 1935 his illness had kept him at death's door.

In 1936 there were three archives in Europe that Stalin felt he needed, and he wanted to get control of them within a year. He did: the first, Trotsky's archive in Paris, he took care of by means of arson; the second, Gorky's, Stalin acquired by making a deal with the dying man; the third was seized by breaking into Kerensky's modest apartment in Passy, on the rue des Eaux. As far as I know, the French police never knew anything about this, and there was not a word about it in either the Russian or the French press. Not only was it not reported but even Kerensky's French friends didn't know anything: such was the victim's wish. Kerensky told me so himself.

Trotsky's widow, Natalia Sedova, recounted in detail how Trotsky's archive had been taken (see the book she wrote with Victor Serge, *The Life and Death of Leon Trotsky*). There were four raids in all. The first was in late 1932, on Principo, when a mysterious fire broke out in Trotsky's library; the books burned, but the papers were rescued.[12] Another was in 1933, at Saint-Palais (near Royan), where they were living at the time. The third was in the spring of 1936, in Norway, when an attempt was made to get into the house of Knudsen, who was sheltering them; and the fourth was in August 1936, in Paris. These four raids, which Stalin had organized, stand in sinister symmetry with the murders of Trotsky's four children, for which Stalin was either directly or indirectly responsible. Nina died of tuberculosis as a result of starvation. Zina committed suicide. Sergei was shot in Siberia, evidently in a prison camp. And Lev was poisoned in a Paris hospital after an operation. Trotsky, one of the last Russian Europeans, had lost everything before his skull was split open with an iron bar in 1940, in his house in Coyoacán, in Mexico City.

Here is what Sedova writes about the 1936 Paris raid:

> A part of Leon Davidovich's papers was deposited in the Institute of Social History at 7 rue Michelet, in Paris, where they had been entrusted to the Russian Social Democratic historian Boris Nicolaevsky. One night, professional burglars approached the building, cut through the service entrance with a blow torch, and stole all Trotsky's private papers.... The robbery bore all the marks of the OGPU, which obviously intended to make use of Trotsky's papers in preparing a more plausible tissue of fresh lies [for the Moscow Trials].

---

12. Jan van Heijenoort, the author of *With Trotsky in Exile*, believes Sedova was mistaken and that the fire occurred in March 1931.

Trotsky's personal papers were not the only things kept in this building—the archives of the Paris office of the Amsterdam International Institute of Social History were there as well. Nicolaevsky used to explain the break-in and theft of forty packets of papers by saying that Stalin needed material for the planned Rykov–Bukharin (Yagoda–Kryuchkov) trial, and wanted information about the contacts Bukharin had made when he was abroad in 1935.

6

SURVIVAL

> I love long life better than figs.
> *Antony and Cleopatra*, I, ii, 32

SHE STOOD AT Wells's side at the top of the broad staircase of the Savoy Hotel and greeted the arriving guests. She had a smile and something gracious to say to each of them, for herself as well as for him, because lately he had been rather angry and sullen, and something sarcastic had crept into the smile on that puffy face. The world was blatantly ignoring him—and going in exactly the opposite direction from the one he had prescribed. The PEN Club had arranged a formal reception in honor of Wells's seventieth birthday. In recent years it had become obvious to everyone that his writing was getting worse. He was losing prestige in literary circles and with the broader public that he had enjoyed just ten years ago (to say nothing of an even earlier period), and so his friends, primarily people of his own generation (he liked young people less and less), were holding this reception to lift his spirits. When Galsworthy died in 1933 Wells had become president of the International PEN Club, and now Moura was receiving guests as lady of the house.[1]

---

1. From the early 1930s to the early 1950s, Moura played a rather important role within the

255

The chandeliers were burning in the high-ceilinged hall, and the gilt on the furniture glittered. A month earlier Moura had been in Moscow, and now, saying just the right thing to each of the guests and enchanting them all with her art of knowing how to be and not to be, she was at the center of attention. In the wings a hurried, anxious discussion was taking place about where to seat her: should she really be next to the guest of honor? On the other hand, said others, whispering, she's done so much for the international club, ever since she turned up at the congress in Dubrovnik and charmed everyone. She tried so hard back then to get the members of the club to agree unanimously to invite Soviet writers to join; it would have been a triumph for world literature. Now it seemed awkward to seat her at a distance from the center table. Nothing had ever come of her efforts to bring Soviet writers into the PEN Club, but Wells hadn't had much success either when he had spoken about it with Stalin in Moscow in 1934.

Moura, however, who had been smiling and saying only nice things to everyone, slipped out unnoticed and went into the large adjoining hall where the tables had been set. She picked up her place card and inconspicuously moved it to a humbler seat, away from the Webbs and Shaw, J. B. Priestley, Artur Rubinstein, Lady Diana Cooper, and everyone else who crowded around Wells that evening.

When the champagne was served the speeches began. Wells responded with a long emotional speech of gratitude. He was radiant from all the compliments and recognition, from the applause and smiles. But he confessed that he realized his life was drawing to a close and that he felt like "a little boy at a lovely party, who has been given quite a lot of jolly toys and who has spread his play about on

International PEN Club, successfully barring Russian émigré writers from membership. She was supported by left-wing intellectuals in England and Europe, and also by English publishers such as Gollancz. [Author's note added in 1987.]

the floor. Then comes his Nurse. 'Now Master Bertie,' she says, 'it's getting late. Time you began to put away your toys.'"

He spoke of his future plans for an encyclopedia, which he meant to start working on shortly, and which would give people a chance to avoid the bloody catastrophe of revolutions and wars by showing them, through self-education, how to make life beautiful. He was his old self again, just as he had been for fifty years, profoundly pessimistic on the inside and full of faith in and hope for progress on the outside.

For years he had been trying to convince Moura to marry him, so one day she talked him into playing a practical joke on his friends, who for his own good, and perhaps even unselfishly, were also trying to persuade her to do so at long last. Moura sent out some thirty invitations to a wedding banquet, and the guests arrived. The English writer Enid Bagnold recalls this cheerful day in her autobiography:

> When he asked us to his wedding party in a Soho restaurant there was a long table at which we all sat. . . . I went up to Moura to congratulate her. She smiled up at me with calm. "I'm not going to marry him. He only thinks I am. I'm not such a fool. Marjorie [his daughter-in-law] can go on doing the housekeeping!"
>
> They appeared arm in arm when everyone had gathered. Congratulations, champagne, gaiety were all in order. But in the middle of the dinner Moura suddenly asked for the floor and stood up.
>
> "This has all been just a joke," she said. "We tricked you. We never got married today and have no plans to in the future."

Jokes like this distracted him from his constant anxiety about the future, his worries about illness, loneliness, and death, the future of mankind, not to mention the impending war, new weapons of destruction and extermination, and the triumph of world fascism.

But in recent years jokes had ceased to amuse him, and more and more frequently he would fall victim to fits of rage, saying—actually screaming in his shrill voice—malicious, unjust, and sometimes just plain childishly stupid things. When Thomas Hardy and Galsworthy were awarded the Order of Merit by King George V over Wells and Somerset Maugham, Wells shouted furiously, "I may be called a snob, but I've too much pride to take an Order which has been given to Hardy and Galsworthy."

Lockhart, who recorded that scene, added in his usual sincere and calm way, neither condemning Wells nor extolling him:

> Poor H. G.! The thirties tried him severely. He foresaw clearly the Nazi danger which so many failed to see. He became a prophet and a pamphleteer, and his new style of book did not sell as well as the great novels of his youth and middle age. . . . He was on the whole a true prophet, but he had a knack of rubbing even his best friends the wrong way.

Lockhart had gone down quite a different path by then. He had once been a good fellow and boon companion, a bit of an egoist with a taste for adventure, a spendthrift, a man who close to forty was still saying he hadn't yet found himself, and now he was a mainstay of Beaverbrook's newspaper empire and a personal friend of Edward VIII. People listened to what he had to say both in England and abroad. He knew everyone he needed to know, and when he thought about the looming war, which he did frequently, he could picture his own future role in the impending conflict.

He was a brilliant journalist. He knew Eastern Europe and the Balkans inside out, traveling there frequently. He also sent Moura there and had his own network of informers working for him. In London he was an habitué of the clubs where old friends who had once worked in the secret service of the Foreign Office, such as Walpole and

Maugham, were now well-known writers. He called on Mrs. Wallis
Simpson, Neville Chamberlain, and Eduard Beneš and was even a
house guest of Wilhelm II, whom he went to see in Doorn several
times. Through Benji Bruce and Karsavina he had entrée to theatrical
circles; through his former diplomatic colleagues he had access to top
officials in the Foreign Office and members of the government. And
through Lady Rosslyn he was a regular guest in the aristocratic homes
of London. His first book had brought him fame in Europe and
America, and the movie based on it ran for several years in theaters.

Lockhart's second book, *Retreat from Glory,* begins with an
account of how, after all his failures in Russia, he had nearly been
ostracized from respectable society; his career destroyed, he sought
refuge in Scotland, the land of his forefathers, where he went on a
fishing trip that turned into what he called his "vegetation in the
country," which lasted nearly a year. In his third book, *Comes the
Reckoning*, we find him at last returning to the Foreign Office and the
life that he had been preparing himself for essentially since he was a
young man.

He knew a great deal about Russia, but he was cautious in what he
said in articles about the country and its regime, and guarded in conversation. He learned about Kirov's murder hours after the event in
December of 1934, and knew, as he writes in his diary, "the real
story": "It was," Lockhart wrote, "an internal plot framed by the
OGPU who disliked the diminution of their power and blamed
Kirov's influence with Stalin for it." When Kirov was killed, not only
was a guard posted at Gorky's house in Tesseli (where he was living at
the time) within an hour after a telephone call (at the time Gorky
thought that the guard had been sent to protect him, but in fact he
had been instructed to hold Gorky under house arrest), but Yagoda
himself, the chief of OGPU, who at that time was intimate with
Gorky's daughter-in-law, was held for twenty-four hours on Stalin's
order. Stalin was afraid that detaining Yagoda any longer or ordering

his summary execution would be too damaging to Bolshevik prestige at home and abroad. Lockhart had no doubts that Nikolaev, who killed Kirov, had been hired by Yagoda, who in turn had been acting on Stalin's instructions. Lockhart got his information from Moura, who went to Vienna right after the murder with the express purpose of seeing Ekaterina Peshkova, who was en route to Europe from Moscow, to learn what had happened. After Moura's report, Lockhart wrote in his diary: "But although the [English] papers are full of the story now I could not get it published in my paper." He could not even print the fact that fourteen of Nikolaev's closest collaborators and friends had been shot with him, and some three thousand Communist Party members had been arrested. A hundred thousand people were deported in the Leningrad purge. This could have complicated relations between London and Moscow.

Lockhart's energy was so highly prized that in 1937 the Foreign Office invited him to take a permanent job there—in other words, to give up journalism and return to the very place that had thrown him out in November 1918.

So he agreed to return to government service, despite Beaverbrook's sincere and warm regrets. Lockhart was making the right decision: his natural talents, his intelligence, his ability to get along with people in high places, and his desire, which had been with him since his earliest years, to "serve his country," a desire which he had at one time failed to understand correctly and which had nearly finished him—all this gave him the right at age fifty to begin a new career, his fourth. Actually, his fifth. He organized his work in such a way that the Foreign Office claimed only a part of his time. The rest was taken up with trips to Eastern Europe.

Lockhart was in Bulgaria in 1938, a month before his old acquaintance Fyodor Raskolnikov, once the pride and joy of the Baltic fleet and the author of several books about 1917, was forced to leave his position as Soviet ambassador in Sofia. Stalin recalled Raskolnikov to

Moscow by personal letter, and he left the same day he received it (April 1)—not for Moscow, though, which was where his subordinates thought he was going, but for Paris. He took his wife and little girl, having decided to go into hiding when he learned from the Prague papers that Moscow had dismissed him.

Raskolnikov's first marriage, when he was a youth, had been to the well-known journalist and Communist Larisa Reisner, who was active in the civil war and died of typhoid fever in 1926. A Bolshevik hero of the early years of the revolution, Raskolnikov had belonged heart and soul to the Party since 1910, when he was only eighteen. In 1914 he was mobilized, and after the February Revolution he became comrade chairman of the Kronstadt Soviet. After October he was appointed deputy people's commissar of the navy. He fought against Kolchak, captured Kazan, commanded first the Volga–Caspian and then the Baltic fleet, and was twice awarded the Order of the Red Banner.

In the early 1920s Raskolnikov went into the diplomatic corps, serving as envoy to Afghanistan. He was appointed to the editorial board of *Red Virgin Soil* and later headed the office of theatrical censorship. During that period he put out two books of memoirs about his heroic battles against Kolchak and Yudenich and wrote a play about the French Revolution.

The friction between Raskolnikov and Stalin began over the execution of the Soviet marshals and the Moscow Trials. Nikolai Ezhov and Lavrenty Beria started to keep track of his movements, and en route to Paris, on April 5, 1938, Raskolnikov decided not to return to Moscow. He first took up residence in a hotel on Montmartre and later rented an apartment, where he hid for more than a year—as much from French and Russian reporters as from Soviet agents, who he feared might kidnap him.

On September 10, he went to Geneva for a meeting with Litvinov in order to "clarify his position." There was nothing Litvinov could do for him. On October 12, Raskolnikov answered the summons of the Soviet ambassador in Paris, Yakov Surits. They met on the rue de Grenelle (having taken certain precautions), and Surits accused Raskolnikov of having made an "unauthorized sojourn abroad"—and nothing else. He guaranteed Raskolnikov that he would not be harmed and advised him to return to Moscow.

On October 18, Raskolnikov sent a letter to Stalin declaring that his stay abroad was not voluntary but forced. He got no answer.

Finally, on July 17, 1939, he read a brief notice in *Poslednie novosti* (The Latest News), a Russian émigré newspaper in Paris) that he had been tried in absentia and sentenced to the "supreme measure of punishment."

At this time, Raskolnikov's play *Robespierre* was running at the Port Saint-Martin Theater in Paris. It was not a success. His money was coming to an end, evidently, and he was getting depressed. In July 1939, he and his family moved to the Riviera, but when he found out that he had been sentenced in Moscow he sent a letter to the editors of *The Latest News* entitled "How I was turned into an enemy of the people." The letter, published on July 26, says that efforts had been under way for more than a year to lure him back to Moscow, just as they had lured Karakhan by promising him a post in Washington, and Antonov-Ovseenko (who was in Spain), by promising him the job of People's Commissar of Justice. Both were shot when they returned to the Soviet Union:

> I prefer living in freedom on bread and water to innocently wasting away and perishing in prison without any chance to defend myself.... This decree [his sentence] sheds light once more on Stalin's justice, on the staging of the notorious trials, graphically demonstrating how countless "enemies of the people" are fabricated and what grounds are deemed sufficient for the Supreme Court to sentence a man to capital punishment.

During those weeks Raskolnikov's depression took a turn for the worse, forcing him to go to the hospital in Nice. At the end of August (the day after the Molotov–Ribbentrop pact was signed) he attempted to slit his wrists. He was saved. On September 12, ten days after World War II began, he took advantage of being left alone in his fifth-floor ward and threw himself out the window.[2] Death was instantaneous. His wife and daughter vanished that day, and no one knew what became of them. The official Soviet version was—and remains to this day—that Raskolnikov died of a heart attack.

Before committing suicide, however, Raskolnikov wrote a third letter to Stalin, dated August 17. Here are the most important declarations in it:[3]

> Stalin, you have proclaimed me an outlaw. By this act you have placed me on a level regarding my rights—or rather, my lack thereof—with all Soviet citizens who live as outlaws under your rule.
>
> On my part, I reciprocate in full: I hand back my ticket to the kingdom of "socialism" you have built, and break with your regime.
>
> The triumph of your "socialism" has put the people who

2. Madame Canivez (Raskolnikov by her first marriage) accepted the Soviet version of the death of her first husband: he had died of natural causes in the hospital in Nice. But it is notable that she never challenged the true version, which was advanced by two distinguished memoirists: Alexander Barmine, a Soviet diplomat in Greece, author of an autobiography *One Who Survived* (New York: Putnam's, 1945), who describes the poisoning of Raskolnikov by Stalin's agents; and Yury Annenkov, painter, filmmaker, memoirist, and novelist, who in his memoirs, *People and Portraits: A Tragic Cycle* (New York: Inter-Language Literary Associates, 1966), speaks about the suicide of Raskolnikov as an incontestable fact. [Author's note added in 1987.]

3. This letter was published in full in Alexander Kerensky's journal *Novaya Rossiya* (no. 71, October 1, 1939). Since then, it has been republished in Russian in *Materialy Samizdata* (1972) and *Ogonek* (no. 26, 1987).

built it behind prison bars. It is as far from true socialism as the tyranny of your personal dictatorship is from the dictatorship of the proletariat, but in your understanding, politics is a synonym for swindling and deceit. You practice politics without ethics, authority without honesty, socialism without a love of man.

What have you done with the constitution, Stalin?

Free elections frightened you. You saw them as a leap into the unknown threatening your own personal rule. You have trampled on the constitution as if it were a mere scrap of paper. You have turned elections into a pitiful farce of voting for one candidate, and the sessions of the Supreme Soviet are filled with ovations and hymns of praise in your honor. Between sessions you quietly liquidate any "wayward" deputies, thereby mocking their immunity and reminding them that you are the master of the Soviet land, not the Supreme Soviet.

You have done everything to discredit Soviet democracy, as you have discredited socialism. Instead of following the line marked out by the constitution, you crush the mounting dissatisfaction with violence and terror. You have gradually replaced the dictatorship of the proletariat with your own personal dictatorship and in so doing have brought in a new era, which will go down in the history of our revolution as a reign of terror.

You hide behind the slogan of "combating Trotskyite Bukharinist spies." But power did not come into your hands yesterday. No one could have assumed a position of authority without your permission.

Who placed the so-called enemies of the people in positions of the greatest responsibility in the state, the Party, the army, and diplomacy?

Joseph Stalin.

Who installed the so-called wreckers into the Party and Soviet apparatus?

Joseph Stalin.

Using dirty forgeries you have staged trials that surpass the medieval witch trials in the absurdity of their accusations, as you know from the textbooks you read in your seminary days.

You know that Pyatakov did not fly to Oslo, Maxim Gorky died a natural death, and Trotsky did not derail a train.

And as you well know, I was never a Trotskyite. On the contrary, ideologically I fought all opposition groups in the press and in Party meetings. Even now I do not agree with Trotsky's political positions, program, or tactics. But even though I disagree with Trotsky in principle, I still consider him an honest revolutionary. I do not and never will believe in his "deal" with Hitler or Hess.

You have slandered, dishonored, and shot men who were Lenin's long-standing comrades-in-arms: Kamenev, Zinoviev, Bukharin, Rykov, and others. Their innocence was well known to you. Before their deaths you forced them to confess to crimes they never committed and to wallow in dirt.

Where are the heroes of the October Revolution? Where is Bubnov? Where is Krylenko? Antonov-Ovseenko? Dybenko?

You arrested them, Stalin.

Where is the old guard? They are no longer among the living.

You shot them, Stalin.

You triumphantly proclaimed the slogan of promoting new cadres. But how many of those young men you brought up are already rotting in your torture chambers? How many of them have you shot, Stalin?

With the brutality of a sadist you have slaughtered the very cadres the country needed: you see them as a threat to your personal dictatorship.

On the eve of war you are destroying the Red Army, the country's pride and joy, the bulwark of her might.

You have beheaded the Red Army and the Red Navy. You have killed our most talented, battle-tested commanders, starting with the brilliant Marshal Tukhachevsky.

You have exterminated the heroes of the civil war who modernized the Red Army and made it invincible.

Right when the military danger is greatest, you continue to exterminate the army's leaders, mid-level officers, and junior commanders.

Where is Marshal Blyukher? Where is Marshal Egorov?

You arrested them, Stalin.

Under pressure from the Soviet people you have hypocritically resurrected the cult of historical Russian heroes like Alexander Nevsky and Dmitry Donskoy, Suvorov and Kutuzov, hoping that in the coming war they will help you more than your executed marshals and generals.

Hypocritically proclaiming the intelligentsia to be the salt of the earth, you have deprived writers, scholars, and artists of even a modicum of inner freedom.

You have gripped art in a vise, choking and extinguishing it. The savagery of the censors, who quail before you, and the understandable timidity of the editors, who answer for everything with their own heads, have led to the petrification and paralysis of Soviet literature. A writer cannot get published, a playwright cannot get his plays produced in the theater, a critic cannot express an opinion if it has not received the official seal of approval.

Following Hitler's example you have reinstated the book burnings of the Middle Ages.

I have seen with my own eyes the long lists sent out to Soviet libraries of books subject to immediate and unconditional destruction. When I was ambassador in Bulgaria, on the list I received of prohibited literature condemned to the flames I found my own book of historical reminiscences, *Kronstadt and Petersburg in 1917*. Opposite the names of many authors there was the instruction: "Destroy all books, pamphlets, and portraits."

You have denied Soviet scholars—especially in the humanities—the intellectual freedom without which creative work becomes impossible for anyone doing research.

Ignorant administrators are using fatuous intrigues, squabbles, and badgering to keep scholars from their work in the universities, laboratories, and institutes.

You have proclaimed prominent, world-renowned Russian scholars, the Academicians Ipatiev and Chichibabin, to be defectors, naïvely thinking to defame them, but by doing so you have only disgraced yourself by letting the whole country and the world know what is a mark of shame for your regime: the best scholars are fleeing your paradise, leaving to you your "blessed gifts" of an apartment, an automobile, and a ration card allowing them to eat in the Kremlin cafeteria.

Knowing that with our shortage of trained personnel, every cultured and experienced diplomat is especially precious to us, you have lured home and destroyed nearly every Soviet envoy, one by one. You have totally destroyed the apparatus of the People's Commissariat for Foreign Affairs.

"Father of Nations," you betrayed the vanquished Spanish revolutionaries, left them to the mercy of fate, and let other governments worry about them. The magnanimous rescue of human lives is not among your principles. Woe to the vanquished! You don't need them anymore!

Indifferent to the fate of Jewish workers, intellectuals, and craftsmen fleeing Fascist barbarism, you slammed shut the doors to our country, which in its vast territory could hospitably give shelter to many thousands of immigrants.

> Sooner or later, the Soviet people will make you take the defendant's bench as a traitor to socialism and the revolution, the chief wrecker, the true enemy of the people, the perpetrator of famine and of judicial forgeries.
>
> F. Raskolnikov
August 17, 1939

Soviet historians did not forget Raskolnikov. In 1964 a book about him came out in Leningrad written by a Party historian A. P. Konstantinov, who pays proper homage to the heroism of this sailor who was commissar of the Baltic fleet. The book tells the story of how he was taken prisoner by the English in 1919, when the English navy, despite Trotsky's protests, cruised near the entrance to the Gulf of Finland. The English, who had come to the Baltic as observers and to aid General Yudenich, captured Raskolnikov, took him to England, and later, after interrogating him in London, released him and returned him to Russia. The book, which came out eleven years after Stalin's death, goes on to say that Raskolnikov, who had died of a heart attack long before, had had his title of Hero of the October Revolution restored to him. His diplomatic career is recounted in four pages (out of 154), and his death in three lines. The heart attack is presented as having been the direct result of mental and emotional stress brought on by the "cult of personality."

Raskolnikov killed himself without leaving a suicide note. His wife appeared in Paris a week after her husband's death. She was a short blonde, very quiet, evidently still shaken by what had happened. I knew her, I saw her little girl, and so did many other friends and acquaintances of Ilya Fondaminsky, an editor of *Sovremennye zapiski* (*Contemporary Annals*), the leading émigré journal published in Paris. Fondaminsky put her up in his flat for eight months, then found work for her in the office of one of the Russian émigré organizations in the suburbs.[4] Her fate is unknown to me, but her daughter lived until 1986 and was a scholar at Strasbourg University in ancient Greek and Roman economic history.

I saw Moura for the final time in Paris in 1937. I had last seen her in 1932, when I had run into her by chance one evening in a deserted café near the École Militaire. I was sitting alone on the terrace having a cup of coffee. She did not notice me at first and sat down two tables away. We started talking. She was about forty at the time. She was thin and held herself very erect. Her face looked tired, but not from anything in particular—it had changed permanently. I immediately sensed that she was not in the least glad to see me. But this had nothing to do with me—she had come here to wait for someone, and a

---

4. There is one piece of evidence that sheds some light on the reason for Fondaminsky's sympathy for the widow of the Soviet diplomat and especially his little daughter. V. M. Zenzinov, a comrade of his from the SR and a close friend of Fondaminsky and his wife, wrote in his obituary of Fondaminsky (*Novy Zhurnal*, no. 18):

> After the dissolution of the Constituent Assembly by the Bolsheviks [January 18, 1918], Fondaminsky, like many others, had to go underground—first in Petersburg, later in Moscow, and finally on the Volga, in Kostroma Province, where he was compelled to go into hiding. Only a strange coincidence saved him from arrest and summary execution: F. Raskolnikov, the Bolshevik commissar for naval affairs, came to search the ship on which Fondaminsky was traveling. Raskolnikov showed what was either weakness or unexpected softheartedness: he took one look at him and walked right past.

That Raskolnikov recognized Fondaminsky there can be no doubt: under the Provisional Government Fondaminsky had been commissar of the Black Sea fleet, while Raskolnikov was commissar of the Baltic fleet. Was he that breed of Bolshevik that nails were made of, as the poet Nikolai Tikhonov put it in the 1920s? And that suggests the possibility that Raskolnikov told his wife that if anything happened to him, she could turn to the émigré Fondaminsky for help. Before calling Fondaminsky, the chief of the Sûreté Générale certainly must have asked Raskolnikov's widow whether she knew anyone in Paris who might vouch for her.

third person could only be in the way. We talked for all of a minute, and she looked from side to side distractedly the whole time. I paid and left. She did not try to stop me.

But our last meeting, five years later, was quite different. It was 1937, the centenary of Pushkin's death, there was an exhibit in Paris of his books and portraits of him and his contemporaries. In addition, the costumes for *The Golden Cockerel*, *Tsar Saltan*, *The Queen of Spades*, and *Eugene Onegin* were on display from the collection of Serge Lifar, who had inherited it from Sergei Diaghilev. When he needed money in the late 1920s, Khodasevich had sold Diaghilev his first editions of Pushkin, which he had been collecting since he was a young man. The collection had been brought by him from Russia in 1925, and here it was intact, in the old nineteenth-century bindings.

I went to the exhibit alone, but at the entrance I ran into Alexander Benois. He and I walked in together and looked at his drawings, which were hanging in the first room. When we walked into the second room I immediately spotted Moura standing next to Dobuzhinsky. There were not many people around. The four of us exchanged greetings. Moura said that she had come specially from London to see the exhibit. On her suggestion the London PEN Club was organizing a formal reception to honor Pushkin, and she wanted to talk to Lifar about the possibility of bringing some of the exhibits to London— "definitely your drawings, Alexander Nikolaevich," she said addressing Benois, "and yours, Mstislav Valerianovich," she said to Dobuzhinsky, addressing them with such affable courtesy that I suddenly saw her as she once had been. A few minutes later Benois and Dobuzhinsky walked away and we were left alone. I said to her what I had just felt: "You're the same as ever, you haven't changed at all." Her smile told me how nice it was to hear it. Then I said: "I'm still waiting for you to write your memoirs." This evidently surprised her, and a look of alarm crossed her face. She cocked her head to one side and looked me in the eye for a moment. Then quietly, and rather slyly, as if she were laughing to herself, she said, "I will never have any memoirs. All I have are memories."

Then she gave me her hand and, no longer smiling, walked away as naturally as if not a word had passed between us.

The third of the Moscow Trials dealt with the murder of Maxim Peshkov by Kryuchkov and Yagoda and the murder of Gorky by two well-known Moscow doctors, aided and abetted by Kryuchkov and Yagoda. The trial began in 1938 with the cases of Bukharin and Rykov, in the presence of foreign diplomats and correspondents. The defendants, it was announced, had all confessed to their crimes, beginning with Bukharin, who was accused of being a Japanese spy. (Trotsky, who at that time was already in Mexico, was accused of being in the service of Hitler.) The defendants meekly answered the questions put to them and then listened to the prosecutor's speeches and waited for the sentence. Only Nikolai Krestinsky, who had been ambassador to Berlin for nine years, and then deputy commissar of foreign affairs for five years, tried to protest, but he was quickly called to order. Yagoda was the only one of the accused to ask the court that he be questioned behind closed doors.

On the defendants' bench were the nineteen members of the so-called anti-Soviet right-Trotskyite bloc: Bukharin, member of the Comintern, the Central Committee, the Politburo, theoretician of Marxism-Leninism, and Lenin's close friend; Rykov, who succeeded Lenin as chairman of the Soviet of People's Commissars; Yagoda, the former commissar of internal affairs (the organ of state security, variously called the Cheka, OGPU, NKVD, KGB); Krestinsky, a former trade representative; Arkady Rozenholz, the former commissar of trade; professor of medicine Dmitri Pletnev; Lenin's one-time physician Lev Levin, who was well known to all of Moscow; Kryuchkov, Gorky's agent since the early 1920s; and eleven others.

Kryuchkov was born in 1889. Before World War I, he had graduated from St. Petersburg University law school. At the time of the revolution he was assistant to a barrister in Petersburg. He was a rather short, strong, thickset, balding blond. Nearsighted, he wore a pince-nez, and he was snub-nosed and pale. He had unusually hairy hands, on one of which he always wore a ring with a large and very valuable alexandrite, which Maria Andreeva had given him.[5] There were two opposing views of him at the time of his arrest. One was best expressed in the memoirs of Ilya Shkapa, who had worked for seven years for *Our Achievements* and other periodicals edited by Gorky (Shkapa was later arrested and exiled to Siberia for twenty-plus years and then rehabilitated after Stalin's death). He was in Gorky's home several times a week and knew both Gorky and his entourage well. He considered Kryuchkov to be Gorky's guardian angel, his thoughtful friend, who rationed Gorky's cigarettes, kept him from going out in bad weather, and politely sent away guests when he noticed that Gorky was tired. Kryuchkov was his nanny, and in the last year of his life Gorky really needed a nanny. In this capacity Kryuchkov never left Gorky alone, and Gorky himself, it must be added, had no wish to be left alone with his guests. Kryuchkov knew all his affairs better than Gorky did himself: he handled incoming calls and knew where that paper was Gorky needed or whether such and such a letter had been answered.

But the Russian émigré Mensheviks (Nicolaevsky, Abramovich, Aronson, Valentinov), as well as Khodasevich, thought that Kryuchkov had been planted by the OGPU, either immediately upon Gorky's first visit to Russia in 1928 or else even earlier, at the very beginning of Gorky's sojourn abroad, when Kryuchkov was "intermediary in Gorky's dealings with journals inside Russia and controlled his every

---

5. This was the same stone Alexander Tikhonov had brought Gorky from the Urals, where he worked as a mining engineer. Gorky had requested an alexandrite for a ring he wanted to give Andreeva, with whom his romance was just beginning.

step, allotting his time as he saw fit, and present at all his conversations with visitors." Khodasevich and the Mensheviks believed that Kryuchkov had killed Maxim—or helped to kill him—in order to do Yagoda a favor. At his trial Kryuchkov refused an attorney and admitted his guilt. Strictly speaking, he was accused of two crimes— the murder of Maxim and the murder of Gorky—but the trials were combined.

Kryuchkov confessed that he had killed Maxim for private, mercenary reasons—to get his hands on Gorky's legacy—and that he had acted at the instigation of Yagoda, who was a member of the "bloc of right-wing Trotskyites" and was acting on orders Trotsky passed on to him from Mexico. Kryuchkov also confessed to the much more serious crime, the murder of Gorky, saying that the "bloc of right-wing Trotskyites" had used him, through Yagoda, for their "counter-revolutionary purposes of conspiracy against the Soviet people, against the proletarian state." And all this came to pass because Kryuchkov had listened to Yagoda, who was in the service of that "insolent swine Trotsky."

Yagoda's confession was more restrained. From the very start he had wanted his crime (the murder of Maxim) to be considered personal, not political: he asked the court to question him behind closed doors. The U.S. ambassador in Moscow, Joseph Edward Davies, who had come to believe that Bukharin was indeed mixed up with Japan and Trotsky with Hitler, sat in the front row at the Moscow trials and later published his diary, *Mission to Moscow*, which was adapted for the screen with great success. He wrote: "That Yagoda was infatuated with young Gorky's beautiful wife...is generally accepted here as true." Indeed, it was generally known, both by those who were around Gorky in Moscow and by those who kept track of his life in Russia from abroad. Timosha and Yagoda's romance had begun between 1932 and 1934, when the family had taken up permanent residence in Moscow. Now, in court, Yagoda wanted to portray a

political assassination as a crime of passion. His request was hon-
ored, and he was questioned separately. But that did not save him. Of
the nineteen, the court sentenced eighteen to be executed. Professor
Pletnev, who at that time was nearly sixty-five, was given twenty-five
years in a concentration camp.

If doubts linger about whether Gorky was poisoned at all and, if he
was, by whom, there could be no such doubts regarding the nature of
Maxim's death. Not only was he young, healthy, athletic, and actively
making plans for a trip to the Arctic Circle to work on a geological
survey, but Yagoda's intimacy with his wife lends a sinister cast to the
last three years of Maxim's life. Perhaps during the last year of his life
Gorky, too, entertained doubts about Maxim's death, and perhaps
that circumstance helped open Gorky's eyes to the political reality
surrounding him. Nor should it be forgotten that Stalin now had in
his hands the Gorky archives that had been brought from London.
Stalin could read not only letters of complaint addressed to Gorky,
from which it was easy to guess what Gorky himself had been writing
to his correspondents, but also Gorky's own notes about what he was
reading and what he was thinking, and maybe even some reflections
on the literary policies that Andrei Zhdanov and Alexander
Shcherbakov had instituted in Russia.

In *Seven Years with Gorky*, Shkapa writes: "I'm very tired [Gorky
muttered to himself], it's like there's a fence around me I can't get
across." Shkapa had no comment, knowing full well that Gorky was
restricted to his Moscow–Gorki–Tesseli circuit. Citing his weak
health, the doctors would not let him choose the itineraries for his
trips. "Suddenly I heard, 'I'm surrounded...hemmed in...no going
back, no going forward! It's unreal!'"

Possibly his self-enforced silence and the depression accompanying
it, more than anything else (poison, tuberculosis, or age), brought
Gorky to his death. Shkapa writes that when he thought no one was
listening Gorky would mutter about how what they had really done

was take away his freedom, that he was under house arrest. He couldn't go where he wanted to go, couldn't see whom he wanted to see, couldn't say or write what he wanted to say or write. How had this happened? Nicolaevsky offers an answer in his "Letter of an Old Bolshevik."

Gorky and Stalin had a falling out soon after the assassination of Kirov on December 1, 1934. All that year Gorky had tried to use his status and his friendship with Stalin to soften the dictator, suggesting whenever they met or spoke by phone, that maybe he could ease up on the reins now that he possessed unlimited power and the whole world had recognized his genius. Gorky was especially dispirited by the hounding and persecution of old Bolsheviks, Lenin's comrades, among them Lev Kamenev, who was married to Trotsky's sister.

Kamenev had been Kirov's friend. Kirov was killed by the OGPU on Stalin's order, and Stalin saw a nest of enemies in the Gorky–Kamenev–Kirov triumvirate. Or maybe it was Gorky–Kirov–Kamenev. Both Gorky and Kirov had long agreed that the Party must finally be reconciled with "public opinion"—the word "intelligentsia" sounded too old-fashioned, anti-Party, and ambiguous. Through Ezhov, Stalin ordered David Zaslavsky, a close associate at *Pravda* who occupied one of the top spots on the paper, to write an article against Gorky, which he did. The article was crudely insulting to a man whose name had been given to streets in every city of the Soviet Union. Gorky demanded a passport to go abroad. He was refused. Stalin stopped calling and visiting. Relations were broken off.

According to one story, Stalin had Kryuchkov feed Gorky poison bonbons. Gorky had been preventing Stalin from liquidating the "old Leninist guard" and "the opposition," and Gorky's death untied Stalin's hands for the Moscow Trials. There is some contradictory circumstantial evidence for this theory but nothing definite; it remains a matter of conjecture. After 1945, Gorky's murder was mentioned in print very rarely, and after 1953 not at all.

We do have what Ekaterina Peshkova said to the American journalist Isaac Don Levine during his stay in Moscow in 1964. They
were old friends and he went to visit her. When he asked about
Gorky's death, she replied: "Don't ask me about it! I won't be able to
sleep a wink for three days and nights if I tell you."

The implication here is ominous but it does not clear up the mystery. It essentially tells us nothing, only that the strong, stern Ekaterina Peshkova had become a hysterical old lady. She had her chance
to testify, and she let it go by. When Levine next asked about Maxim's
death, she replied that he had died of pneumonia.

Lockhart kept close tabs on what was happening in Russia. He
went to Paris shortly before Moura's trip to Moscow, and, as was
often the case, she went there at the same time. She loved the Russian
restaurants and Russian food, not the ones where former generals
and governors accepted tips for clients checking their galoshes but the
simpler, poorer ones in the fourteenth or fifteenth arrondissement,
where Gypsy romances were sung to the accompaniment of a guitar
and by the end of the evening the crowd was singing along, where you
could have an especially bittersweet time recalling the Moscow nights
of 1918, the Gypsy Maria Nikolaevna, and those cabdrivers who had
taken her and Bruce to the outskirts of Moscow.

"Mr. Lokhar!" the drivers would shout to Lockhart. "Have a seat,
and I'll take you for a ride!" And off they would dash through the
dark streets. Later the drivers disappeared, too, when the horses were
slaughtered for meat.

In the Russian bars of Paris everything responded to Lockhart's
secret emotional needs in a way he himself didn't quite understand.
Music and the light affected him from the moment he walked into the
dingy, smoke-filled rooms. He and Moura, as he later recalled, rarely
spoke about the past: "Our gypsy days were over." He would go to
Paris in the late 1930s on his way to London from Prague or
Budapest; she would give him a call, and they would meet at a "Rus-

sian cabaret" at 72 rue Fondary. Sometimes they were joined by her sister Anna and her husband, or one of her old friends from tsarist times, maybe a friend of her brother's or of the late Mosolov's, or of some brilliant, dashing diplomat who now worked as a janitor, a night guard, or a bouncer in Paris.

In the run-down and half-dark cabaret, little lanterns were burning on the tables and people were drinking vodka and shedding a few tears over the past:

> The tall pianist, an émigré aristocrat, drew wonders from his cottage piano. There was a competent Caucasian guitarist. The requisite gypsy element was represented by a dignified old lady in a plain black dress with a faded white lace collar and a long necklace of imitation pearls. The voice was genuine, as good as any that I have heard, and, as she sang all the old favourites in that deep quivering contralto which is the special gift of the real *tsiganka*, the mist between the present and the far-off yesterdays rolled away. As a finale to a long session she sang to an old tune the song of the exiles, "Molis Kunak," Pray, warrior, pray that God will give you strength to return to your own country.
>
> The song, banned on the Paris radio in order to please the Soviet Government, was plaintive and in the dim light of the little cabaret very moving. I thought of Yesenin, the blond young peasant poet, whose brief flame of genius had flourished in Moscow during the early years of the revolution:

> > Pray, warrior, on a foreign strand,
> > Pray, warrior, for your native land...
> > Pray for those your heart holds dear,
> > May God protect them far and near.
> > And though in exile now we roam,
> > Deprived of native land and home,

Yet we believe the hour draws nigh
When the sun again will light our sky.

I looked at Moura. Her eyes were fixed on the ceiling, and there were tears in them. These gypsy songs did not help one to forget. They forced one to remember. And for Moura and for me there was no way back across the years.

Lockhart was in London in 1938 when the Munich Agreement was signed. Now Czechoslovakia had fallen into Hitler's hands, and Beneš and Jan Masaryk had fled to London. If Russia was Lockhart's destiny, then Bohemia had been his love ever since his youthful years when he had discovered those excellent fishing streams. After the war, when Beneš and Masaryk returned to Prague, the British government refused to appoint Lockhart head of the British diplomatic mission to Czechoslovakia. According to the old English tradition, he could not be a diplomat in a country to which he was so strongly attached. He wrote a book about Jan Masaryk after his suicide. That was all he could do to repay the country where he had been so well loved. For five years during the war, when they lived in England, Beneš and Masaryk were an important part of his life.

Lockhart left the *Evening Standard* in 1938. It was clear to him and those around him that the instant war broke out he would be called into the Foreign Office (Political Intelligence Department) to work at the Russian desk. His old friend Rex Leeper felt he would "bring that political department to life." Harold Nicolson assumed the same post for Eastern Europe, sharing responsibility with Leeper. Lockhart "found himself a bureaucrat once again," as he put it. In January 1939, seven months before the war began, he took a trip to America and reported back to London "a confidential memorandum for the Foreign Office regarding my impressions of the United States." By 1944 he had risen to the rank of director general of the

Political Warfare Executive, which was part of the Foreign Office and the Ministry of Information (but still under Churchill's direct control). He became close to his counterpart in the American intelligence service, the writer Robert Sherwood, who was head of the Office of War Information in Europe and author of numerous novels and plays. "We shared all our secrets," Lockhart later wrote, just as he had once shared secrets with Colonel Robins.

Before the war and the air raids began, Lockhart continued to have lunch at the Carlton Grill. In a wood-paneled room hung with candelabras, he dined with acquaintances and friends, from the Duke of Windsor to Soviet Ambassador Ivan Maisky, from Churchill to the German crown prince. Between luncheons with Moura, Lockhart went on meeting Kerensky there right up until war broke out. "Discussed [with Moura] the new Russian constitution in the light of my yesterday's conversation with Kerensky," Lockhart records:

> Moura maintains that Russia is going Liberal and that Russia and the democracies do stand together for the defence of the liberal spirit. This is only a half-truth.... Moura thinks the Right will win the civil war in Spain. So does Beaverbrook. I don't. H. G. is staying in London; he likes his new house in Regent's Park—Hanover Terrace. As pronounced by Moura it sounds like "Hangover Terrace." He has had five front teeth out— nothing wrong with them—just afraid they won't last as long as he intends to live.

Lockhart and Wells had helped Moura break into movie circles as an expert on Russian pictures. She had been working for some years now for Korda and Sam Spiegel, who later made *Lawrence of Arabia* and *Nicholas and Alexandra* with her aid. Since 1936 she had been on Korda's payroll and worked as his assistant for films on Russian topics. After 1941, when the Soviet Union was drawn into the war, he had a special need for an expert and adviser on Russia before and after the revolution. In Lockhart's (and Wells's) opinion, she fit the bill perfectly.

But Korda had little luck with his Russian films. *Catherine the Great* was not a success, and Moura, though she was considered an expert on Catherine's era and at the time was translating the empress's *Memoirs* from French into English, had been unable to rescue it; his 1948 *Anna Karenina* with Vivien Leigh was much weaker than the 1930s *Anna Karenina* with Greta Garbo; and *Knight Without Armour*, about the Russian Revolution, was a total flop. Nevertheless, Moura did not lose any prestige with the studio and continued to be the undisputed authority on matters Russian, not only during Korda's life but after his death as well, gradually extending her consulting work to the theater, assisting in the London productions of *Tovaritch*[6] (1963) and *Ivanov* (1966) with Laurence Olivier. At first Wells supported her efforts, recommending her to everyone as an expert on Russian history and modern life, and so did Lockhart, who was on good terms with Korda (although he was also known to call him a crook) and had been friendly with movie people ever since he had worked with Michael Curtiz. It is not surprising therefore that in the relatively circumscribed social circle of wartime London we run across Moura's name on guest lists for receptions given by the French and Czech governments in exile. However, she soon stopped attending the French gatherings because relations between André Labarthe, with whom she was working on *La France libre*, and General de Gaulle and his "official London headquarters" had seriously deteriorated.

She had been appointed the "eye of the Foreign Office" in the editorial offices of *La France libre* early in 1940, when French exiles in

---

6. *Tovaritch*, a comedy by Jacques Deval about the life of aristocratic Russian émigrés, ran in Paris from 1934 until the outbreak of the war.

London formed an association. She very quickly came to know many who had fled occupied Paris, beginning with Labarthe, the editor and publisher of *La France libre*, a review put out by the French resistance in exile. During the war years she acted as liaison between Lockhart's office and Labarthe's editorial office. She was also working in the French section of the BBC, where the director was Harold Nicolson, who noted in his diary after one of Moura's visits from London: "I talk to Moura until she goes by the evening train. It is a joy to have her here. She really is one of the most delightful people I have ever known."

Things were not going smoothly between Labarthe and General de Gaulle. Among the English, de Gaulle enjoyed neither sympathy nor popularity. But Labarthe, judging by what would be written about him by his contemporaries and also by the brilliant, interesting, and highly cultured review he published, was a remarkable man in many respects. In his diary Nicolson describes his qualities as a political figure, editor, and man:

> I dine with...Moura Budberg and André Labarthe. The latter tells us that people who escape from France come and see him, since it is his voice which they know and love on the wireless. He is a passionate and brilliant man, and I cannot help feeling that he represents France far better than de Gaulle. He is so happy at the success of his review. It is difficult for people like me (who really love France passionately) to know what to do. The split between de Gaulle and the intellectuals is very wide. The Carlton Gardens [de Gaulle's London headquarters] people are antipathetic to me. Yet de Gaulle is the great name.

Moura worked for Lockhart at *La France libre* for the duration of the war. Wells did not like de Gaulle and had no compunctions about saying so even in writing, but in Labarthe's review, where he published three articles in French, he held his tongue. The French in exile were divided into two camps: the rightists considered General de Gaulle the symbol of France and reconciled themselves to his difficult nature; the leftists considered him a quasi-Fascist and a potential dictator. Everyone knew that relations between the general and Churchill were one step away from a complete break, and by the end of the war they were practically nonexistent. Lockhart tried not to reveal his feelings toward the general. He needed to know what was going on inside both groups, de Gaulle's and Labarthe's, and he was well informed; it was his responsibility to deal with the liberals, and Nicolson's to deal with the conservatives from Carlton Gardens.

When he had his first mild stroke in 1942, Wells thought up an epitaph for himself: "God damn you all! I told you so!" He had had tuberculosis since his youth, and now he began to suffer from what was then called catarrh of the throat and catarrh of the stomach. His heart was ailing, and his prostate gave him trouble. He had long been assuring everyone that he had only one lung and one kidney left. Toward the end of his life his eyesight got so weak that Somerset Maugham started coming to read him the newspapers. "Is there anything about me?" Wells would ask. But there never was, and he often drifted off to sleep in the middle of a conversation. In 1945, a year before his death, there was no longer hope of improvement, and he lived out his final year on the threshold of death. From then on Moura and Wells were inseparable, she was always nearby, always around.

She was now fifty-three years old. The war had aged her, and she was starting to get fat. She ate and drank a great deal and was neglecting her figure. Someone had to be by Wells's bedside around the clock, and his two sons and Marjorie (his daughter-in-law), who had once officially been his secretary and housekeeper, were at his side constantly. Moura would read to him, and he would dictate to her the letters to be written in French and, sometimes, Russian. She did what she could to lighten Marjorie's duties, but over the years she had grown sluggish, and she now had translating work to do. There was not a lot of it, nor was it steady, but nevertheless it gave her the professional aura she considered essential.

Wells's house grew dark, dismal, and soundless. He did not always recognize Moura when she came to see him, and even when he did he was unable to express his happiness. Between one doctor's visit and the next there was nothing but waiting and silence. They had given up hoping long ago, and as a result somewhere deep down inside each of them lay the concealed wish that it would all end, that it would not go on for too much longer.

Both sons—Gip and Anthony—tried to keep him quiet and calm during his final months. Later, after his death, each attempted to justify Wells's state of mind in his own way. In his foreword to *The Last Books of H. G. Wells*, Gip, Wells's eldest son and a professor of zoology, tried to explain to the readers that when Wells wrote *Mind at the End of Its Tether* he was no longer the man, writer, thinker, or prophet his contemporaries had known.

Anthony, the son of Wells and Rebecca West, was less optimistic. In his analysis of Wells's last pronouncements, "The Dark World of H. G. Wells," published in *Harper's Monthly* in May 1957, he holds that, toward the end of his life, his father realized he had erred all his life in not realizing his potential as a writer and artist, priding himself instead on his sociological prose written for the good of mankind. "His final despair came not because he realized that the world was not a warm cozy place where everyone was making a comradely effort to achieve progress" but because "he saw that he had been wrong in turning away from artistry, art, creative prose"—precisely what Henry James had once rebuked him for. Instead Wells had stubbornly proclaimed himself a "journalist," resolved to enlighten people and change the world so that it might be a happier place for his having done so. He had been given talent, but he had not understood that talent places a responsibility on the artist to cultivate it. And his attempt to make mankind conscious of its imminent demise, to prevent that self-destruction—to become a universal prophet, in other words—had been insufficiently convincing.

Wells died on August 13, 1946. He would have been eighty years old the next month. On the 16th he was cremated. J. B. Priestley, who had once spoken at his anniversary, spoke at Wells's graveside about the "great seer of our time." After the cremation both sons (they were thirteen years apart) went to the Isle of Wight and scattered the ashes over the waves of the English Channel. In his will, drawn up shortly before his death, Wells declared that his money, literary rights, and house should be divided among his closest relatives—his children and grandchildren. His servants and friends were not forgotten. Moura was left a hundred thousand dollars.

How did Moura live through that inner hell that Wells carried within him and that tormented him so during those final years of his life? What did she feel being constantly next to him and seeing that strong, self-assured, willful, difficult man gradually destroyed body and soul? She left no oral or written record of her emotional state at the time. But there is one piece of indirect evidence which says something about the tenor of their affections in the last ten years of their life together and about the nature of her life after he was gone.

It is with good reason that Moura is referred to as Gorky's translator in notes to some of the documents relating to him. Over fifty years she translated several of his plays and several dozen stories, as well as other books, into English. But she lacked the professionalism she sought as a translator, both in what she chose to translate and in the quality of the finished product. It may seem strange, but it is impossible to say with certainty exactly how many volumes she translated after 1924, when she began working on Gorky's *The Judge* with Barrett Clark and on Gorky's *Fragments from My Diary* and *The Story of a Novel and Other Stories*. In 1926 she published an English translation of a novel by Sergeev-Tsensky. When things did not work out—"The Childhood of Luvers" (Pasternak), "The Enchanted Wanderer" (Leskov), and Chekhov's letters to Olga Knipper—it was disappointing, but she did not stay discouraged for long. This perhaps explains why a number of her translations were done in collaboration with a second translator, and others under the editorship of, or with a foreword by, a true professional. There is a certain insecurity in her translations, something amateur and haphazard about them. Her name was removed from several of her translations when they were reprinted: they had gone through so many changes and corrections that there was little left of her work. There were translations she signed Maria Zakrevskaya, others Maria or Moura Budberg, and still others Baroness Budberg. In several bibliographies (always incomplete) she is listed under the name Benckendorff.

Let us return now to the indirect evidence mentioned above. Among the miscellaneous books Moura translated was one called *The Drama of Einstein*, a title evidently calculated (by the translator) to attract the attention of the broader reading public. The author was a Frenchwoman named Antonina Vallentin who had written an entire series of "lives of great men." At one time she had been Wells's lover, and after his death she wrote a book about him called *H. G. Wells: Prophet of Our Day*. She was on the best of terms with Moura, and her book about Wells (the English translation was *not* Moura's) was doubtless written not so much with Moura's blessing as in close consultation with her. In none of the other numerous biographies of Wells is so much said about Moura, both quantitatively, in terms of pages devoted to her, but also qualitatively, in its illumination of her role in H. G.'s life. It is characteristic that Moura is never referred to by name in the book. That was, of course, according to her wish, part of the same quest for anonymity that had made her insist on changes in Lockhart's book twenty years earlier.

Vallentin's book is essentially a work of compilation and is not especially brilliant or original, though it was clearly written by an unquestionably intelligent and experienced woman. In it one sees how Moura supplied Vallentin with material on Wells's last year, evidently because she liked and trusted the author, and how Moura colored that material slightly with her own take on Wells as an individual and her role in his life. Just as in Lockhart's *British Agent*, Moura herself is disguised but her relationship to the hero is not. Vallentin has more to say about that than any other biographer of the creator of *The War of the Worlds*.

We see the picture as Moura wanted us to see it. She was trying to fix her place in the story of his life, in the context of his affairs with other women. The picture may not wholly correspond to reality, but it does give us an exact image of how Moura wanted to come down to us.

All her life Moura had been far from indifferent to her gestalt, to the image she carefully constructed around herself. That was one thing she would never leave to the whims of fate. She shaped it and gave it definite features, and in her heart of hearts she was probably happy that she had been able—from her earliest youth to her old age—to construct a myth that was her own and that helped her to live. In Vallentin's book, Moura comes across as infinitely devoted, kind, obedient, and modest, a woman who was the reflection, the shadow of the man for whom she felt only admiration. She was his guardian angel and muse simultaneously, diverting and consoling him.

Never for one moment, however, was his supremacy and her submission the real picture. For these two canny partners that would have been too simple, too flat and ordinary, a drearily conventional case of male superiority and female inferiority. The love between Wells and Moura was a play acted on the stage of a perfectly empty theater. The game was played for each other's benefit, and all the fire, energy, and inspiration connected with it amused and consoled them.

Wells had always felt that there should be no competition or "conditions to be met," but rather understanding, aid, and comfort. What she gave him was what he had been looking for all his life. Not stormy passions but sympathy, not willfulness and originality but a kind of complete subordination that would give joy equally to them both: to him as victor and champion in his hour of rest, to her as goddess who could give him that rest and thereby find her own fulfillment in body and soul, a goddess for whom everything becomes divinely possible and whose power knows no bounds.

Neither criticism nor competition, only support and agreement, without any of the "why" and "what for" questions that spoil happiness. Today he might play the world genius and demigod, and without a word she understood and performed the role at which he had barely hinted. Tomorrow he might want to play the child, and she would go along, as if she had always been only a mother to him. And if he wanted to imagine himself an old, sick, grumbling, half-senile, whining, forgotten grandfather, she would join in the game without hesitation. If the desire came over him to behave like a frivolous bon vivant in pursuit of a young woman, then she was right there, helping him in his role, acting as both director and prompter. Maybe his secret or even subconscious fantasies made the dominant chord in his relations with Moura this ritual in which he would take on one role after another, and that role (like the ritual itself) became his way of playing out those secret fantasies. Nothing had to be explained to her. She was always at the ready, always gentle and warm, always prepared to indulge any whim of his, any order. All he had to do was look at her and she knew what he expected. But mainly she assuaged all the hurt feelings and affronts, which with each passing year became more frequent and more cutting (no one remembered him or wrote about him, no one telephoned or invited him anywhere). If an insult hit too close to home, she made it disappear. She was a magician, she would not let them wound him.

There's an indubitable parallel between Wells's end and the death of that other writer of world renown and believer in progress. Like Wells, his popularity had waned and he could consider himself half forgotten: they still had names, but their books gathered dust on the shelves. Gorky's last year, which he spent in isolation in Tesseli, says something to us about *his* despair, whose origins were different from Wells's but no less strong. Ilya Shkapa's memoirs leave no doubt as to the depths of Gorky's disenchantment when he was brought to Moscow in June 1936, two weeks before his death. As with Wells, Gorky's illusions were all gone, and nothing remained but naked reality, with death the only way out. The question of whether he was poisoned—and if so by whom, or whether he died from tuberculosis and heart failure, or poisoned himself—loses its urgency: for Gorky, as for Wells, death was an escape and a release. In both cases we see their inability to grasp and accept the changes that had come about in the world during their lives, one spanning sixty-eight years, the other eighty. They fought for their convictions to the extent their powers and talent allowed, by methods that no longer seem terribly effective or exemplary. Everything on which their optimism had been based was destroyed, because from the beginning they had been sure there was a system, but it turned out there wasn't any, there was only "chance" and "necessity." Both reckoned that they and their teachers were the best minds in the world and therefore could not be mistaken. The shake-up and collapse of that structure proved fatal to them both.

Moura was fifty-four when Wells died. Twenty-eight years had passed since she had left Estonia in 1918 for revolutionary Petrograd, the city half starving, cold, and armed to the teeth; and from the day H. G. died to the end of her own life she had another twenty-eight years to live. But there is little left to tell about this second half of her life. For a few years, while England was undergoing postwar reconstruction, she lived utterly free (her son was a farmer on the Isle of

Wight and her daughter was married) and without any financial or other concerns in London, where old friends and acquaintances were gradually returning and where she knew every intersection and side street. The city had been hers since 1911; she belonged here and nowhere else, in this apartment, furnished with heavy furniture, with shelves reaching to the ceiling—many books and just as many papers, her own and others', English and Russian, letters and manuscripts, hundreds of letters, most of them unanswered because she was growing lazy and careless. The myth she had spent her whole life creating required no more freshening up or elaboration. She was a lonely, aging aristocrat who spoke in a bass voice, moved about very little, and never laughed at her own jokes, draped in heavy beads and wearing long, wide, dark skirts. She smoked cigars and peppered her speech with four-letter words (English ones, of course). She loved salty stories and had a store of piquant gossip about people in "high society"; at times she was not averse to arranging a liaison. She was a woman who belonged to a world that had long ago receded into the history of an imperial Russia that was no more.

Lockhart reassigned her in the 1940s when he asked her to work for him at *La France libre*. Paris, where she had traveled three or four times a year before the war, was now cut off, Eastern Europe as they knew it no longer existed, her Tallinn contacts were broken off, and the political life of the Russian emigration was at a standstill. He apparently needed Moura to serve less and less in her former capacity. One of Lockhart's diary entries before the start of the war touches on this. After another of their routine meetings—they lunched together at Jardin, a French restaurant in London—Lockhart writes: "She has just returned from Esthonia and is full of forebodings about Russia. She says Litvinov is now in trouble and that he may be the next to go. I doubt this, but nothing would surprise me today. Since Gorky's death and especially since Yagoda's arrest, she has been herself completely cut off by Bolsheviks."

This entry makes clear that after Gorky's departure for Russia in 1933 (and until 1938, when Yagoda was liquidated) Moura still had some rather durable ties to someone high up in the Soviet diplomatic hierarchy or the NKVD, and that the link ran through Estonia. She still went there almost as frequently as she ever did (whenever that was possible), although she didn't seem to have cause for doing so, since her children had lived in England for many years.

Who could have been her contact in Tallinn during those years (1930 to 1939), and who was the Soviet representative in Estonia then? Was it someone who had been close to Gorky, Kryuchkov, and Yagoda? Or was it someone she had known from the old days, through Krasin, Krimer, and Solomon? Or was somebody from nearby Latvia involved? In 1936 Peters was already out of favor but still at liberty. Could contact—seemingly innocent—have been established with a member of his circle? Could something like this have led to courier activities between London and Moscow? After the Moscow trials, such contacts must have been lost. Could it be assumed—only assumed, and even then with great caution—that she had some kind of link to Raskolnikov himself, who in 1930 was the Soviet representative in Estonia prior to his appointment in Sofia? In 1936 the Kremlin had already begun to consider Raskolnikov "suspect" and he was transferred to Bulgaria; in 1937 they started suggesting another transfer—first to Mexico, then to Czechoslovakia, Greece, Turkey. But he steadfastly refused their offers. The Soviet ambassador to Bulgaria was an old acquaintance Moura and Lockhart both knew well.

Moura used to see him with his first wife at the apartment on Kronverk (Raskolnikov and Larisa had known Gorky since 1915), after Raskolnikov had returned from London in 1919 as a prisoner of war. He had been captured by the English at the entrance to the Gulf of Finland, where they were observing the civil war between the Bolsheviks and General Yudenich. On the Hanko Peninsula in southwest

Finland there was a naval base, and after capturing Raskolnikov they took him to London, where he was questioned through an interpreter. This interpreter was none other than Bruce Lockhart, whom Raskolnikov first mistook for a Russian, so flawless was his accent (in his memoirs the commissar of the Baltic fleet calls Lockhart the "Blond"). Lockhart submitted his conclusions about Raskolnikov and suggested that the authorities exchange him for a few English prisoners of war recently captured by Red sailors. This was done, and thanks to Lockhart, Raskolnikov was set free. He was let out of prison a few days before being sent back to Soviet Russia: Lockhart put him up at a hotel and helped him buy suits and attend some London plays.

So it was, by a strange set of coincidences, that not only did Moura know Raskolnikov but Lockhart had played no small role in Raskolnikov's fate. Did Lockhart renew his acquaintance with the doubtless grateful Soviet diplomat on his visits to Sofia—where Lockhart went several times during Raskolnikov's tenure there—in February 1937 and February 1938?

Tallinn was the hub for Moura's correspondence with Gorky as long as he lived. But isn't it possible that even after his death her postal connection with Moscow and Gorky's family continued? There is no reason why it shouldn't have, after all. When Raskolnikov was transferred to Sofia, Moura could have tried to keep that channel open, and it is possible that the ambassador himself, who went to Sofia against his will, helped her in securing it. Did Lockhart take advantage of this channel for his own intelligence purposes? This explanation seems more likely than the suggestion that minor Soviet functionaries in Belgrade and Bucharest served as contacts with Moscow.

In Lockhart's journal he recorded news that Moura brought him from Tallinn, Berlin, Vienna, Paris, Italy, or London itself. One item was about Alexei Tolstoy, who had come to London for the Congress of Friendship with the USSR only the day before. Tolstoy told Moura that there was "a Cheka man following him wherever he goes." And it was she who first told Lockhart, among other gossip, that his own wife was filing for divorce.

Moura had no difficulty getting her British citizenship in the early 1930s. As a British citizen, she eventually was able to travel to Russia after the war, and not just once but at least four or five times. In any event we can confirm the following trips: she went in 1956 at the invitation of Ekaterina Peshkova, who was turning seventy-eight, so that after their long separation Moura could finally see her, and also see Timosha and her two daughters, Marfa and Darya. In 1958, Ekaterina Peshkova, with whom Moura stayed in Moscow, and Timosha took Moura down the Volga on a holiday. On that trip Moura brought some papers relating to Gorky that she still had (she had also sent others in 1938), and among them were several (but far from all) of Gorky's letters to Wells. She handed them over to the Gorky Archive.

Her third trip was in 1960, when Moura went to Moscow with a group of her London friends to visit Boris Pasternak and interview him at Olga Ivinskaya's flat. Ivinskaya would write colorfully about this visit in her memoirs:

> One day during this same last year of his life we were told that two Russian ladies who had long been living abroad wanted to visit BL [Boris Leonidovich Pasternak]. They had arrived in Moscow either as tourists or as correspondents of some big newspaper or other. One of them, Vera Trail, was the granddaughter of Guchkov, who had been minister of war in the Provisional Government, and the other was the no less celebrated Maria Ignatyevna Zakrevskaya (otherwise known as Countess Benckendorff, and also as Baroness Budberg). BL was particularly thrilled by the prospect of a visit from Maria Ignatyevna Zakrevskaya, a woman with an unusual and checkered past,

who had once been very close to Maxim Gorky and was the official widow of H. G. Wells.

BL invited the two ladies to have lunch with him at the Potapov Street apartment and began hectic preparations for their reception. He came in from Peredelkino at seven in the morning and went to his apartment in Lavrushinsky Street where he first summoned a barber, and then began phoning us. Ira was asleep near the phone when he woke her up with his first call at eight and asked for me. "Olya," he inquired anxiously, "do we have H. G. Wells?" I told him we had the two-volume edition. "Open it up and put it out in a place where it can be seen."

At half-past nine he rang again:

"And do we have Gorky? Just leave him lying around somewhere. One of his things is dedicated to Zakrevskaya!"

When he called a third time at eleven, Ira, robbed of her sleep, shouted out to me tearfully: "Mama, she's had a very long life. Just stay by the phone—'Classoosha' will phone ten times more." But he had to give up with the international adventurer who had supposedly been Maria Ignatyevna's first lover: we didn't have a copy of his memoirs.

We had a large jar of pressed caviar for the guests. I suggested we put it out on the table as it was, but BL said something about laying some small bowls to eat it out of. He was soon to discover how absolutely right I had been.

All spruced up, with his hair newly trimmed, BL duly arrived, to be followed shortly afterward by the two ladies— who for some reason preferred to walk up to the sixth floor of our apartment instead of using the elevator. It was easy enough for the younger of the two, but it was harder for the Baroness. Large and corpulent, she struggled for breath, refused to let BL help her off with her fur coat, and all the while searching persistently for something in her bottomless pockets. At last she produced a present for Boria: a large, old-fashioned tie—something she may well have inherited from H. G. Wells. But this was not all: after a further search she came up with yet another tie for Boria, and a pair of large gold-plated earrings for me.

Eventually our two guests got their breath back and took off their coats. BL, thanking them profusely for their gifts, invited them into the dining room, where the table was laid for lunch. They said the main purpose of their visit was to interview him. It was decided that they would conduct the interview over lunch.

Boria was most affable and courtly, talking about Wells, Gorky, and literature in general. The Baroness, taking no note at all of the books by Wells and Gorky, tucked into the pressed caviar for all she was worth. Between this and listening to Boria's gushing eloquence, the two ladies managed to get in some questions—all of which seemed to us completely absurd, for example: "What kind of jam do you like?" or "What color tie do you prefer?" BL decided that these questions were clearly meant in jest and responded with laughter, trying to get the conversation back to more serious topics, mainly literary ones.

When the two had departed, I suggested diffidently that their questions had been put in all seriousness, but Boria waved his hands in the air and laughed at me for failing to appreciate, in my ignorance, the Western sense of humor displayed in the conversation. How embarrassed he was a month or so later with the arrival of some British and American newspapers which informed their readers that the Nobel Prize winner Boris Pasternak liked strawberry jam best of all, wore ties with colored designs, and never touched black caviar.

Between 1960 and 1973, Moura went to Russia two or three more times, again staying with Peshkova and, after her death, Timosha. She was greeted quite ceremoniously (except for the first time, when her visit passed unnoticed); according to one eyewitness "they rolled out the red carpet." In 1973 her son retired at the age of sixty to Italy, liquidating all his assets. Moura was now a very sedentary eighty-two-year-old woman who still had a large circle of acquaintances.[7] She went out rarely, and mostly kept in touch with people by telephone, which she always had at hand. She did not hide the fact that to be able to "function," as she put it, she needed alcohol. In her big purse, which she kept close by at all times, there was always half a bottle of vodka, without which Moura wouldn't go anywhere. But even with it Moura sometimes grew weak and vague, drifting off, coming back only after another drink or two. Once the London police detained her at one of the department stores: she was walking out of the store without having paid for something she had picked up. This was ascribed to a strange forgetfulness that sometimes descended upon her. The money Wells had left her had come to an end, and after the incident at the store her London friends collected several thousand pounds for her, enabling her to get out of a tight spot. The few people who continued to see her frequently in the 1960s recall the huge helpings of food she could consume at one sitting and the vast amount of liquor she could put down. In 1970 she gave a long and detailed interview to *Vogue*. The reporter was Kathleen Tynan (who later wrote a book about President Ford's wife, Betty), the wife of the drama critic Kenneth Tynan, whose *Oh, Calcutta* was playing all over the Western world. Both Tynans were friends of Moura's.

---

7. After publication of the Russian edition of this work, I learned by a chance conversation that the famous English spy Guy Burgess, who worked for Moscow, was also a friend of Moura's, or at least an acquaintance, and came to see her when no one else was invited. As is known, the English police let Burgess, Donald MacLean, and Kim Philby, spies who were former students at Cambridge, escape. Two of them went to Moscow with their families and lived in or around the capital to an advanced age. [Author's note added in 1987.]

In the interview Moura told quite a lot about herself, unintentionally confusing some things and intentionally distorting others. She returned to the cultivation of her myth, embellishing it and amplifying its contours. She was a woman of decisive and brave character, the inspiration, adviser, and helpmate to great men of her century. She had only recently "done" Chekhov's *Seagull* for Simone Signoret, Vanessa Redgrave, and James Mason. She spoke about her own fantastic staying power and capacity for work, despite her arthritis and two operations, about the ability she had had ever since her youth to accept anything life threw at her, to get out of any tough spot, and to be surprised by nothing. Her wide face, the cheekbones more prominent now in old age, her serious gaze, and her masculine voice left no doubt that she was saying exactly what she thought. Her small apartment looked more 1870 than 1970: the antique velvet furniture, paintings, jars of sweetmeats, old photographs, bottles, dusty knick-knacks on étagères, and embroidered tablecloths; a tapestry with a portrait of Nicholas II and his family (a gift from Wells); and a small portrait of Gorky in oil (probably from Rakitsky's brush). In the interview she recalled her father's rococo house in Petersburg, where she had once lived and danced at cotillions. She touched on the story of her friendship with Lockhart, arrested by the Cheka under suspicion of plotting to kill Lenin, and the story of her own imprisonment when she tried to leave Petrograd without permission, and how she was eventually freed with Gorky's help. She mentioned her long years of friendship with Alexander Korda, who had given her a regular salary as a consultant in all his productions and whom she helped become what he was. She described how after Korda's death she collaborated with Sam Spiegel when he was making *Lawrence of Arabia*. In 1967, Larry (Olivier) produced her translation of *Three Sisters* with great success at his theater in London. She herself had also appeared from time to time (in silent roles), in such movies as *Nicholas and Alexandra*. She steered clear of politics, but she did say that she felt that the new émigrés coming out of the Soviet Union should have stayed in their homeland, that it was not patriotic to leave the place where you were born and become a citizen of another country.

Much in this interview sounded just as unlikely as the story of her forgetfulness in the department store, or her trip from Moscow to Estonia in 1918. The strength and determination she was so proud of were seen in a diaphanous, slightly artificial light that softened the sharp edges. But maybe her memory simply wasn't as good as it was in the old days, not as invincible and flexible, and maybe her imagination was now less masterful in its resolute twists and turns. The fairy tale created more than half a century ago was suddenly losing its flesh and blood in the English reporter's copy.

Born between 1890 and 1900, she belonged to a generation of Russians that was three-fourths destroyed—first by World War I, and then by the civil war. Many of those who did survive had perished in the Red Terror when they refused to accept the October Revolution. The rest, who accepted it, perished in the purges. Many émigrés, not knowing foreign languages, found themselves déclassé pariahs, and some never managed to get enough schooling to change their condition. Those born at the beginning of the final decade of the previous century were born too soon to accept a changing Russia, while those born at the end of that decade tried to adopt a Western life, and some of them succeeded. There were others, however, and quite a few, who ended their too-short lives in German death camps. The verb "to perish" in those days, both in Russia and in Europe, did not necessarily mean to die; it very often meant continuing to live, but devastated by war, prison, banishment, abandonment, poverty, loneliness, exile. Those born early were traumatized by their losses, and those born late never became strong enough to start a new life in the West, to change and grow up together with the new century. Like thousands of others, Moura would have perished had it not been for the fact that every day, every hour was a struggle and a challenge. She was heir, like millions of others, to the warped principles of the past, the crippling taboos and Victorian prejudices of the nineteenth century—she was a product of her class, meant to lead an easy, sated, idle, and pointless life; but then she was thrown into a world where everything was cracking and crumbling and being built, and where, over the next fifty years, new people, new ideas, new means of struggle and survival, of destruction and renewal, changed the world and made it younger. In this new world the outworn trappings of six or seven European monarchies collapsed and turned to dust. The idea of the "great powers" she had grown up with had vanished, and the "great men" either came to see their greatness as worthless or used it to destroy others like themselves.

Like everyone in her class, she would have to confront homelessness, fear, charity, madness, and suicide. All around her a tragedy on a historic scale had unfolded, the metaphor for which was her flight across the ice of the Gulf of Finland, from the Karelian tundra to Europe. But she didn't cling to her sweet and false past, didn't play the helpless parasite, didn't hide from the challenges fate handed her, and she didn't claim "female weakness" to try to justify the mistakes she made.

She concealed neither her age, nor her gross weight, nor her need for drink. Over the years she came to boast more and more about her famous lovers and famous friends, her fabulous ancestors who had received their titles from the hands of tsars, her beautiful grandmothers who were immortalized by poets. Groaning from her arthritis, she would lift her wide skirts and show her huge, swollen knees.

She grew up among people who lived (or pretended to live) for salvation in the life to come, who believed in its rewards. Then she had spent her life among people who lived for future generations, believing (or trying to believe) that the world was progressing toward a shining future for each and all. She herself lived for the moment, though, and that was the only way she knew how to live—for life itself, the only thing that had meaning for her.

In the fall of 1974 she moved to Italy, and two months later, on November 2, news of her death and a long obituary running two full columns were printed in *The Times* of London. It was entitled "Hostess and intellectual leader." She had been, according to *The Times*, at the center of London's intellectual, artistic, and social life for forty years. At various times she had "shared homes" with H. G. Wells, Maxim Gorky, and Sir Robert Bruce Lockhart, not hiding her relationships with them, which were known to everyone. She was an "author, translator, production advisor on plays, films, and television programs." In rare instances she had been an "occasional actress herself (mostly in striking silent parts)." She had been "a stage or costume designer, historical researcher and artistic codirector, publishers' reader of manuscripts in five languages, and during the Second World War managing editor of *La France Libre*," in the service of the Political Warfare Department of the Foreign Office.

Her body was brought to London from Florence, where her son still lived. The funeral took place on November 11 in the Russian Orthodox church. In the front row stood the French ambassador to London, M. Beaumarchais, and his wife, and behind them the English aristocracy as well as a few members of the Russian aristocracy, along with Moura's children and grandchildren. Altogether about fifty people attended.

She did not depart without leaving a fitting coda for her legend, which, like a musical coda, recapitulated the theme of her life. At the end of *The Times* obituary we find a story, hitherto untold, about how she was a direct descendant of Empress Elizaveta Petrovna by her morganatic marriage to Alexei Razumovsky. In 1742 a son was born to Peter I's daughter, and it was that son who initiated the Zakrevsky line.

This final joke of hers would have been appreciated by Till Eulen-spiegel, who, with a rope around his neck, ran out of time before he was able to pull off his last prank. She had waited fifty years to assure her listener that if he looked at her closely he would see in her face an undeniable resemblance to Peter the Great.

Princeton, 1978–80

Select Bibliography

Anonymous. *The Russian Diary of an Englishman, Petrograd, 1915–1917*. London: Heinemann, 1919.

Aragon, Louis. *La Mise à mort*. Paris: Gallimard, 1965.

——. "La Valse des adieux." In *Lettres françaises*, October 11, 1972.

Bagnold, Enid. *Enid Bagnold's Autobiography*. London: Heinemann, 1969.

Banks, Arthur, and Alan Palmer. *A Military Atlas of the First World War*. London: Heinemann, 1975.

Baring, Maurice. *The Mainsprings of Russia*. London: Nelson, 1914.

——. *The Puppet Show of Memory*. London: Heinemann, 1922.

Benckendorff, Count Constantine. *Half a Life*. London: Richards Press, 1954.

Benckendorff, Count Pavel Konstantinovich. *Last Days at Tsarskoye Selo*. Translated by Maurice Baring. London: Heinemann, 1927.

Beneš, Eduard. *Memoirs: From Munich to New War and New Victory*. Translated by Godfrey Lias. Boston: Houghton Mifflin, 1954.

Berberova, Nina N. *Histoire de la Baronne Boudberg*. Translated by Michel Niqueux. Arles: Actes Sud, 1988.

——. *The Italics Are Mine*. Authorized translation by Philippe Radley. New York: Harcourt, Brace and World, 1969.

——. *The Tattered Cloak and Other Novels*. Translated by Marian Schwartz. New York: Knopf, 1991.

——. *Zheleznaia zhenshchina: rasskaz o zhizni M. I. Zakrevskoi-Benkendorf-Budberg, o nei samoi i ee druz'iakh (Iron Woman: The Story of the Life of M. I. Zakrevskaya-Benckendorff-Budberg, About Her Herself and About Her Friends*). New York: Russica, 1981.

Besedovskii, Grigorii. *Revelations of a Soviet Diplomat*. Translated by Matthew Norgate. Westport, CT: Hyperion Press, 1977.

Blok, Aleksandr. *Sedoe utro* (*Grey Morning*). Peterburg: Alkonost, 1920. (Moura Budberg's copy is in the Kilgour Collection, Houghton Library, Harvard University.)

Browder, Robert Paul. *The Russian Provisional Government, 1917: Documents*. Selected and edited by Robert Paul Browder and Alexander F. Kerensky. Stanford: Stanford University Press, 1961.

Brown, John Mason. *The Worlds of Robert E. Sherwood: Mirror to His Times, 1896–1939*. New York: Harper and Row, 1965.

Buchanan, Sir George. *My Mission to Russia and Other Diplomatic Memories*. London: Cassell, 1923.

Buchanan, Meriel. *Petrograd, the City of Trouble, 1914–1918*. London: W. Collins, 1919.

Budberg, Baron Michael. *Russian Seesaw*. London: M. Hopkinson, 1934.

Bunyan, James, ed. *Intervention, Civil War, and Communism in Russia, April–December 1918*. Baltimore: The Johns Hopkins Press, 1936.

Bykovtseva, Lidiia P. *Gor'kii v Moskve 1931–1936* (*Gorky in Moscow 1931–1936*). Moscow: Moskovskii rabochii, 1968.

Calder, Robert. *W. Somerset Maugham and the Quest for Freedom*. London: Heinemann, 1972.

Churchill, Sir Winston. *The World Crisis, 1916–1918*. New York: Scribner's, 1927.

Clark, Barrett. *Intimate Portraits*. New York: Dramatists Play Service, 1951.

Conquest, Robert. *The Great Terror: Stalin's Purge of the Thirties*. New York: Macmillan, 1973.

Cumming, C. K., and Walter W. Pettit, eds. *Russian-American Relations, March, 1917–March, 1920*. Documents and papers compiled and edited [for the Foreign Policy Association]. New York: Harcourt, Brace and Howe, 1920.

Dallin, David J. *Soviet Espionage*. New Haven: Yale University Press, 1955.

Davies, Joseph E. *Mission to Moscow*. New York: Simon and Schuster, 1941.

Deacon, Richard. *A History of the British Secret Service*. London: Muller, 1969.

Degras, Jane T., ed. *Soviet Documents on Foreign Policy*. London: Oxford University Press, 1951–53.

Deutscher, Isaac. *Trotsky*. 3 vols. New York: Oxford University Press, 1954–63.

Dittmar, F. J., and J. J. Colledge. *British Warships, 1914–1919*. London: Allan, 1972.

Edel, Leon. *Bloomsbury: A House of Lions*. New York: Lippincott, 1979.

Fowler, W. B. *British-American Relations, 1917–1918: The Role of Sir William Wiseman*. Princeton: Princeton University Press, 1969.

Francis, David R. *Russia from the American Embassy, April, 1916–November, 1918*. New York: Scribners, 1921.

Futrell, Michael. *Northern Underground: Episodes of Russian Revolutionary Transport and Communications through Scandinavia and Finland, 1863–1917*. New York: Praeger, 1963.

Gerson, Lennard D. *The Secret Police in Lenin's Russia*. Philadelphia: Temple University Press, 1976.

Gorky, Maksim. *A Book of Short Stories*. Edited by Avrahm Yarmolinsky and Baroness Moura Budberg. New York: Holt, 1939.

———. *Fragments from My Diary*. Translated by Moura Budberg. New York: Praeger, 1972 [first published in 1924].

———. *The Judge* (a play in four acts). Authorized translation by Marie Zakrevsky and Barrett H. Clark. New York: R. M. McBride, 1924.

———. "Letters to Khodasevich." In *Harvard Slavic Studies* 1 (1953).

———. *The Life of a Useless Man*. Translated by Moura Budberg. Garden City, NY: Doubleday, 1971.

———. *Polnoe sobranie sochinenii: Khudozhestvennye proizvedeniia v dvadtsati-piati tomakh (Complete Works: Artistic Writings in Twenty-Five Volumes)*. Moscow: Nauka, 1968–76.

———. *The Story of a Novel, and Other Stories*. Authorized translation by Marie Zakrevsky. New York: Dial Press, 1925.

————. *Unrequited Love, and Other stories.* Translated by Moura Budberg. London: Weidenfeld and Nicolson, 1949.

Grenard, Fernand. *La Révolution russe.* Paris: A. Colin, 1933.

Harari, Manya. *Memoirs 1906–1969.* London: Harvill Press, 1972.

Hard, William. *Raymond Robins' Own Story.* New York and London: Harper, 1920.

Harriman, W. Averell. *America and Russia in a Changing World.* Garden City, NY: Doubleday, 1971.

Hart-Davis, Rupert. *Hugh Walpole.* New York: Macmillan, 1952.

Herzen, Aleksandr. *From the Other Shore.* Translated by Moura Budberg. London: Weidenfeld and Nicolson, 1956.

————. *The Russian People and Socialism, an Open Letter to Jules Michelet.* Translated by Richard Wollheim. London: Weidenfeld and Nicolson, 1956.

Hill, George Alexander. *Go Spy the Land, Being the Adventures of I.K. 8 of the British Secret Service.* London: Cassell, 1932.

Ivinskaya, Olga. *A Captive of Time.* Translated by Max Hayward. Garden City, NY: Doubleday, 1978.

Katkov, George. "German Foreign Office Documents on Financial Support to the Bolsheviks in 1917." In *International Affairs* 32, no. 2 (April 1956): 181–189.

————. *The Trial of Bukharin.* New York: Stein and Day, 1969.

Kennan, George F. *The Decision to Intervene.* Princeton: Princeton University Press, 1958.

————. *Russia Leaves the War.* Princeton: Princeton University Press, 1956.

Keun, Odette. "H. G. Wells, the Player." In *Time and Tide* 15 (1934).

Khodasevich, Valentina M. "Takim ia znala Maksima Gor'kogo" ("Maxim Gorky as I Knew Him"). In *Novy mir*, no. 3 (1968).

————. *Unpublished Letters to Nina Berberova.* Edited by Richard D. Sylvester. Berkeley: Berkeley Slavic Specialties, 1979.

Khodasevich, Vladislav F. *Belyi koridor* (*White Corridor*). Edited by Grigory Poliak, with commentary by Richard D. Sylvester. New York: Serebrianyi Vek, 1982.

———. "Gor'kii" ("Gorky"). In *Nekropol': Vospominaniia* (*Necropolis: Memoirs*). Brussels: Petropolis, 1939. (Written in 1937.)

———. "Gor'kii" ("Gorky"). In *Sovremennye zapiski* (*Contemporary Annals*), no. 70 (1940). (A different memoir written in 1938.)

Knox, Alfred William Fortescue. *With the Russian Army, 1914–1917.* London: Hutchinson, 1921.

Konstantinov, Aleksandr Petrovich. *F. F. Il'in-Raskol'nikov.* Leningrad: Lenizdat, 1964.

Korda, Michael. *Charmed Lives: A Family Romance.* New York: Random House, 1979.

Lenin, Vladimir Il'ich. *V. I. Lenin i A. M. Gor'kii. Pis'ma, vospominaniia, dokumenty* (*V. I. Lenin and A. M. Gorky. Letters, Reminiscences, Documents*). Edited by B. A. Bialik et al. Moscow: Nauka, 1969.

Levine, Isaac Don. *I Rediscover Russia.* New York: Duell, Sloan and Pearce, 1964.

Litvinov, M. M. "Transportirovanie oruzhiia v Rossiiu" ("Transporting of Weapons to Russia"). In *1905. Boevaia gruppa pri TsK RSDRP(b): stat'i i vospominaniia* (*1905. Operations Group of the Central Committee of the Russian Socialist Democratic Party (Bolshevik): Articles and Reminiscences*). Compiled by S. M. Pozner. Moscow: Gosizdat, 1927.

Lockhart, Sir R. H. Bruce. *British Agent.* New York: G. P. Putnam's Sons, 1933. (Published in London in 1932 by Putnam as *Memoirs of a British Agent.*)

———. *Comes the Reckoning.* London: Putnam, 1947.

———. *The Diaries of Sir Robert Bruce Lockhart.* Edited by Kenneth Young. Vol. 1, 1915–1938. New York: St. Martin's Press, 1973.

———. *Friends, Foes, and Foreigners.* London: Putnam, 1957.

———. *Giants Cast Long Shadows.* London: Putnam, 1960.

———. *Guns or Butter.* Boston: Little, Brown, 1938.

———. *Jan Masaryk: A Personal Memoir.* London: Dropmore Press, 1951.

———. *My Europe.* London: Putnam, 1952.

———. *Retreat from Glory.* New York: Putnam, 1934.

———. *The Two Revolutions.* London: Bodley Head, 1967.

———. *Your England.* London: Putnam, 1955.

Lockhart, Robin Bruce. *Ace of Spies*. London: Hodder and Stoughton, 1967.

Luxemburg, Rosa. *Listy do Leona Jogichesa-Tyszki (Letters to Leon Jogiches-Tyszka)*. Edited by Feliks Tych. Warsaw: Ksiazka i Wiedza, 1968.

MacCloskey, Monro. *Torch and the Twelfth Air Force*. New York: Rosen Press, 1971.

MacKenzie, Norman Ian, and Jeanne MacKenzie. *H. G. Wells: A Biography*. New York: Simon and Schuster, 1973.

Mal'kov, Pavel D. *Zapiski komendanta Kremlia (Reminiscences of a Kremlin Commandant)*. Moscow: Molodaia gvardiia, 1967.

Mandelstam, Nadezhda. *Hope Against Hope*. Translated by Max Hayward. New York: Atheneum, 1970.

Maugham, Robin. *Somerset and All the Maughams*. New York: New American Library, 1966.

Morgan, Ted. *Maugham*. New York: Simon and Schuster, 1980.

Mosolov, Aleksandr Aleksandrovich. *At the Court of the Last Tsar*. Edited by A. A. Pilenco. Translated by E. W. Dickes. London: Methuen, 1935.

Nabokov, Konstantin D. *The Ordeal of a Diplomat*. London: Duckworth, 1921.

Nicolaevsky, Boris I. *Power and the Soviet Elite*. Edited by Janet D. Zagoria. New York: Praeger, 1965.

———. *Revolution and Politics in Russia: Essays in Memory of B. I. Nicolaevsky*. Edited by Alexander and Janet Rabinowitch, with Ladis K. D. Kristof. Bloomington: Indiana University Press, 1973. (Contains an extensive list of Nicolaevsky's publications.)

Nicolson, Sir Harold George. *Diaries and Letters*. Edited by Nigel Nicolson. New York: Atheneum, 1966–68.

Noulens, Joseph. *Mon ambassade en Russie soviétique, 1917–1919*. Paris: Plon, 1933.

Orwell, George. "Wells, Hitler, and the State." In *The Collected Essays, Journalism, and Letters of George Orwell*. New York: Harcourt Brace Jovanovich, 1968.

Ould, Hermon. *The Book of the P. E. N.* London: A. Barker, 1950.

Parvus, Alexander. *Der wirtschaftliche Rettungsweg*. Berlin: Verlag für Sozialwissenschaft, 1921.

————. *Im Kampf um die Wahrheit*. Berlin: Verlag für Sozialwissenschaft, 1918.

————. *Le Socialisme ouvrier et la Révolution mondiale*. Olten: Troesch, 1919.

Pascal, Pierre. *Mon journal de Russie*. 4 vols. Lausanne: L'Age d'homme, 1975–82.

Ransome, Arthur. *The Autobiography of Arthur Ransome*. Edited by Rupert Hart-Davis. London: Cape, 1976.

————. *Six Weeks in Russia in 1919*. London: Allen and Unwin, 1919.

Ray, Gordon N. *H. G. Wells & Rebecca West*. New Haven: Yale University Press, 1974.

Reilly, Sidney George, and Pepita Bobadilla. *Britain's Master Spy: The Adventures of Sidney Reilly*. New York: Harper, 1933.

Robien, Count Louis de. *Journal d'un diplomate en Russie (1917–1918)*. Paris: A. Michel, 1967.

Rumbelow, Donald. *The Houndsditch Murders and the Siege of Sidney Street*. London: Macmillan, 1973.

Sadoul, Jacques. *Notes sur la révolution bolchévique. Octobre 1917–Janvier 1919*. Paris: La Sirène, 1919, and F. Maspero, 1971.

Sayers, Michael, and Albert E. Kahn. *The Great Conspiracy: The Secret War against Soviet Russia*. Boston: Little, Brown, 1946.

Schapiro, Leonard B. *The Communist Party of the Soviet Union*. New York: Random House, 1960.

Scharlau, Winfried B., and Zbynek A. Zeman. *Freibeuter der Revolution, Parvus-Helphand: eine politische Biographie*. Cologne: Verlag Wissenschaft und Politik, 1964.

Schurer, Heinz. "Alexander Helphand-Parvus—Russian Revolutionary and German Patriot." In *Russian Review* 18, no. 4 (October 1959): 313–331.

Serge, Victor. *Year One of the Russian Revolution*. Translated and edited by Peter Sedgwick. Chicago: Holt, Rinehart, and Winston, 1972.

Serge, Victor, and Natalia Sedova Trotsky. *The Life and Death of Leon Trotsky*. Translated by Arnold J. Pomerans. New York: Basic Books, 1975.

Sergeev-Tsenskii, Sergei Nikolaevich. *Transfiguration*. Translated by Marie

Budberg. Edited and with an introduction by Maxim Gorky. Westport, CT: Hyperion Press, 1973.

Shkapa, Ilya Samsonovich. *Sem' let s Gor'kim (Seven Years with Gorky)*. Moscow: Sovetskii pisatel', 1966.

Skirda, Alexandre. *Les Anarchistes dans la révolution russe*. Paris: Editions Tête de feuilles, 1973.

Solomon, Georgii A. *Among the Red Autocrats: My Experience in the Service of the Soviets*. Translated from the German edition. Edited and revised by Arno C. Gaebelein. New York: Our Hope, 1935. The Russian original is *Sredi krasnykh vozhdei* (Paris: Mishen', 1930).

Sukhanov, N. N. *The Russian Revolution, 1917*. Edited, abridged, and translated by Joel Carmichael. Princeton: Princeton University Press, 1984.

Tabori, Paul. *Alexander Korda*. London: Oldbourne, 1959.

Thomson, David. *The New Biographical Dictionary of Film*. New York: Knopf, 2002.

Trotsky, Leon. *My Life*. New York: Scribners, 1930.

Tyrkova-Williams, Ariadna. *Cheerful Giver: The Life of Harold Williams*. London: P. Davies, 1935.

Ullman, Richard H. *Anglo-Soviet Relations, 1917–1921*. 3 vols. Princeton: Princeton University Press, 1961–72.

Vallentin, Antonina. *H. G. Wells, Prophet of Our Day*. Translated by Daphne Woodward. New York: J. Day, 1950.

Van Heijenoort, Jean. *With Trotsky in Exile: From Prinkipo to Coyoacán*. Cambridge, MA: Harvard University Press, 1978.

Walpole, Sir Hugh. *The Dark Forest*. New York: George H. Doran, 1916.

———. *The Secret City*. New York: George H. Doran, 1919.

Webb, Beatrice Potter. *Beatrice Webb's Diaries, 1924–1932*. Edited by Margaret Cole. London: Longmans, 1956.

Wells, H. G. *Apropos of Dolores*. London: Cape, 1938.

———. *Experiment in Autobiography: Discoveries and Conclusions of a Very Ordinary Brain (since 1866)*. New York: Macmillan, 1934.

———. *Journalism and Prophecy, 1893–1946*. Compiled and edited by W. Warren Wagar. Boston: Houghton Mifflin, 1964.

————. *The Last Books of H. G. Wells*. Edited and with an introduction and appendix by G. P. Wells. London: H. G. Wells Society, 1968.

————. *The Open Conspiracy: Blueprints for a World Revolution*. London: Gollancz, 1928.

————. *The Secret Places of the Heart*. London: Cassell, 1922.

————. *The Shape of Things to Come: The Ultimate Revolution*. London: Hutchinson, 1933.

————. *World Brain*. London: Methuen, 1938.

Zeman, Z. A. B., and Winfried B. Scharlau. *The Merchant of Revolution: The Life of Alexander Israel Helphand (Parvus) 1867–1924*. London: Oxford University Press, 1965.

Index of Names

Abel, Rudolf (1902–71). KGB colonel arrested in the United States in 1957; exchanged for Gary Francis Powers in 1962, *60, 77*

Abramovich, R. A. (Raphael R. Abramovitch) (1880–?). Menshevik leader; emigrated to Berlin in 1920; journalist and historian; one of the editors (with Fedor I. Dan, David J. Dallin, and Yuri O. Martov) of *Sotsialisticheskii vestnik (Socialist Courier)*, first in Berlin, then Paris, then New York (1921–65), *272*

Adler, Bruno Fridrikhovich (1874–1942). Geographer; one of the editors of *Beseda, 177*

Afinogenov, Alexander Nikolaevich (1904–41). Soviet playwright, *224*

Aldanov, Mark Alexandrovich (1889–1957). Author of historical novels; emigrated to Paris in 1919, *49n, 94*

Alexander Nevsky, Grand Prince of Vladimir, Saint (1220–63). So named because he defeated the Swedes on the Neva River in 1240. A military decoration, instituted in his name by Peter the Great, was abolished in 1917, but revived in 1942. Sergei Eisenstein's film *Alexander Nevsky* (1938) was intended as anti-German propaganda, but when the Nazi-Soviet Pact was signed in 1939, Eisenstein was required to make a public declaration of his support for the treaty of friendship with Germany, *266*

Alexeev, General Mikhail Vasilievich (1857–1918). Chief of staff under Nicholas II, then supreme commander until June 1917. With Kornilov and Denikin created the White Army of the south in 1918 to oppose the Bolsheviks during the civil war, but soon died of pneumonia, *29*

Alksnis, Yakov Ivanovich (1897–1938). Commanding general of Soviet air forces (1931–37); executed in 1938; rehabilitated in 1957, *84*

Andreas-Salomé, Lou (1861–1937). Born in St. Petersburg. There are numerous writings by and about her: she wrote about Rilke; her letters to Freud have been published and discussed; and she wrote a book about Nietzsche and a memoir called *Looking Back*, *xiii*

Andreev, Vadim Leonidovich (1903–76). Writer and poet; Olga Carlisle's father. Fought with the French Resistance; became a Soviet citizen in 1946; served as Soviet representative to UNESCO. He was the son of Gorky's friend, the well-known writer Leonid Andreev (1871–1919), painter of the absurd and horrific, *238*

Andreeva, Maria Fyodorovna (1868–1953). Actress in the Moscow Art Theater; Gorky's common-law wife after 1903; Party member; personal friend of Lenin's. After the revolution was commissar of theaters and circuses for Petrograd (1918–21); appointed in 1921 to the Soviet Trade Office in Berlin; director of the House of Scholars in Moscow (1931–48), *96, 100–105, 109–110, 115–117, 124–125, 134, 138, 146–147, 158–160, 164, 167–170, 182, 196, 230, 272*

Antonov-Ovseenko, Vladimir Alexandrovich (1884–1939). Led seizure of Winter Palace, arrest of Provisional Government, and land expropriations (1919–20). Trotskyite. Ambassador to Czechoslovakia, Lithuania, Poland after 1924; during the Spanish civil war was Stalin's representative in Spain (1936). Arrested in 1937; shot in 1939; rehabilitated in 1956, *262, 282*

Aragon, Louis (1897–1982). Surrealist poet; Stalinist; liberal Communist after 1956. (*See* Bibliography), *240–245*

Aronson, Grigory Yakovlevich (1887–1968). Menshevik; author of memoirs about 1917. Émigré in Berlin (1920s), Paris (1930s), New York (after 1940). Became an American citizen; wrote for the New York Russian newspaper *Novoe russkoe slovo* (1944–57), *272*

Asquith, Herbert Henry (1852–1928). Liberal British prime minister (1908–16) forced out by Lloyd George, *39*

Axelrod, Pavel Borisovich (1850–1928). With Plekhanov, one of the first proponents of Marxism in Russia. Menshevik in 1903; supported the Provisional Government; emigrated to Germany; died in Berlin, *149*

Babel, Isaac Emmanuilovich (1894–1941). Soviet writer (*Red Cavalry*); arrested in May 1939; died in the camps; rehabilitated in December 1954, *234, 237, 242–243*

Bagnold, Enid (1889–1981). English novelist and playwright. (*See* Bibliography), 257

Balfour, Arthur James (1848–1930). British foreign minister (1917–19), *39, 43, 47*

Baliev, Nikita Fyodorovich (real name: Mkrtich Asvadurovich Balyan) (1877–1936). Creator, artistic director, and master of ceremonies of the famous Moscow cabaret the Bat (1908–20). Emigrated to Paris in 1920, creating new skits and miniature scenes for audiences in French as well as Russian. Took the theater to South America, Hollywood, and New York, but during the depression it became difficult to keep the theater alive; while seeking a venue and financial backing in New York, he had a fatal stroke in a taxi, *16*

Balmont, Konstantin Dmitrievich (1867–1942). Symbolist poet; emigrated to France in 1920, 24

Barbusse, Henri (1873–1935). Politically active French writer; published a book praising Stalin in 1935, *230–231, 240*

Baring, Maurice (1874–1945). Diplomat; man of letters; translator; press correspondent in Russia; author of books on Russia and Russian and French literature; editor (with notes by D. S. Mirsky) of the *Oxford Book of Russian Verse*. He dedicated his book *The Mainsprings of Russia* to H. G. Wells; the character Bailey in Wells's novel *Joan and Peter* (1918) is based on him. (*See* Bibliography), *6–9, 13–16, 21, 119–120, 143–144, 185, 214*

Bayley, Charles Clive (dates unknown). British consul general in Moscow (1913–15), *20*

Beaumarchais, Jacques Delarüe Caron de (1913–79). French ambassador to London (1972–77), *299*

Beaverbrook, Lord William Maxwell Aitken (1879–1964). Political conservative, press magnate; publisher of the *Evening Standard* from 1923 until his death, *34, 202, 205–206n, 209–210, 213, 258, 260, 279*

Bebel, August (1840–1913). German Social Democrat; leader of the Party after 1890; editor of *Vorwärts*, *149, 153*

Beletsky, Stepan Petrovich (1873–1919). Deputy interior minister (1915–16); shot by the Bolsheviks, 72–73

Bely, Andrei (Boris Nikolaevich Bugaev) (1880–1934). Writer and memoirist; symbolist theoretician, 49n, *169, 171, 175, 179, 233*

Belyaev, Mikhail Dmitrievich (1884–1955). Pushkinist; director of Pushkin House (1921–29); arrested in 1930; freed in 1933. Valentina Khodasevich's friendship with him began when she painted his portrait (reproduced in *Apollon* 8 [1916]), *232*

Benckendorff, Count Alexander Khristoforovich (1783–1844). Chief of gendarmes under Nicholas I, *2, 6*

Benckendorff, Count Alexander Konstantinovich (1849–1917). Russian ambassador to the Court of St. James (1900–17); "the first gentleman in Europe" (Maurice Baring, *The Puppet Show of Memory*), *2, 6, 8, 120, 248n*

Benckendorff, Ivan Alexandrovich (1882–1917). Embassy secretary in Berlin; Moura Zakrevskaya's first husband, *xv, 1–2, 8–12, 89, 108, 120, 128, 140*

Benckendorff, Count Konstantin Alexandrovich (1880–1959). Ambassador Benckendorff's son. Naval officer during the Russo-Japanese War; musician; farmed the Benckendorff estate near Tambov; called to duty with the Red Navy during the civil war; arrested by the Cheka but released. During NEP allowed to go to England, where he settled. Author of a valuable memoir about his life up to 1923. (*See* Bibliography), *6, 7*

Benckendorff, Pavel Ivanovich (1913–96?). Moura's son, *xvii, 9, 10, 42–43, 108–109, 122, 125–131, 143, 159, 166, 168, 170, 174, 183, 185, 189, 192, 196, 198–199, 206, 208, 217, 290, 295, 299*

Benckendorff, Count Pavel Konstantinovich (1853–1921). Ambassador Benckendorff's brother; marshal at the court of Nicholas II; author of a memoir about the Tsar and his family at Tsarskoye Selo in the spring and summer of 1917. (*See* Bibliography), *7*

Benckendorff, Tatiana ("Tania") Ivanovna (1915–2004). Moura's daughter. Married Bernard Alexander in 1940 in London. As Tania Alexander she published a memoir in London in 1987 entitled *Little of All These: An Estonian Childhood* (the American edition is entitled *Tania: Memories of a Lost World*), *xvii, xviii, 9, 10, 42–43, 108–109, 122, 125–131, 143, 159, 166, 168, 170, 174, 183, 185, 189, 192, 196, 198–199, 217, 289, 290, 299*

Beneš, Eduard (1884–1948). Czechoslovakia's foreign minister 1918–35; president of Czechoslovakia (1935–38 and 1945–48), and of the Czech government in England (1938–45). Resigned after Communist coup of February 1948. (*See* Bibliography), *190, 259, 278*

Bennett, Arnold (1867–1931). English novelist and playwright known for novels and stories set in provincial English towns, *13, 181, 210*

Benois, Alexander Nikolaevich (1870–1960). Russian artist, born in St. Petersburg; designer; art historian and critic; archivist and memoirist; founded World of Art group with Diaghilev and Bakst (1899–1904). After the revolution led efforts to preserve Russian art, took charge of museums, collaborated with Gorky at Universal Literature. Traveled to France in 1926, where he remained, continuing his artistic career, designing productions for the Paris Opera, Covent Garden, and other theaters, including new productions of works by Stravinsky and Ravel. Died in Paris, *92, 270*

Benois, Nikolai (Nicola) Alexandrovich (1901–88). Alexander Benois's son; designer at La Scala in Milan, *199*

Beria, Lavrenty Pavlovich (1899–1953). Chief of the Cheka in Georgia (1921–31), he replaced Ezhov at the NKVD in 1938, ending the Great Purge; arrested after Stalin's death; shot in December 1953. Repeatedly denied rehabilitation, most recently in 2000, *163, 261*

Bernstein, Eduard (1850–1932). Theoretician in the German Social Democratic Party; member of the Reichstag, *149*

Bernstorff, Count Albrecht Theodor (1890–1945). German Rhodes scholar (Trinity College, 1909); counselor at the German embassy in London (1922–33); antifascist; executed April 24, 1945, *212–213*

Berzin, Eduard Petrovich (1894–1938). Latvian Bolshevik and Chekist provocateur during the "Lockhart plot," *55–59*

Beseda (*Colloquy*). Literary and scientific review published in Berlin (1923–25) by Solomon Kaplun under the editorship of Gorky, Bely, Khodasevich, Bruno Adler, and Friedrich Braun (seven issues). Publication ceased when the Soviets would not allow it to be distributed in Russia, *164n, 177–178, 181, 193, 233*

Besedovsky, Grigory Zinovievich (ca. 1890–?). Soviet diplomat who defected to the West in 1930. Published two books in Paris, *Oui, j'accuse* (1930) and *Staline, "l'homme d'acier"* (1932); the former was translated into

embassy in St. Petersburg under Buchanan. Married the Russian ballerina Tamara Karsavina (1915), 23, 42, 259

Brusilov, Alexei Alexeevich (1853–1926). Commander in chief of Russian forces under the Provisional Government (June–July 1917); later served in the Red Army, 75

Bryusov, Valery Yakovlevich (1873–1924). Leading Moscow Symbolist poet, critic, novelist, 24

Bubnov, Andrei Sergeevich (1883–1938). As chief of the Red Army's political administration (1924–29), he purged the army of Trotsky's followers; as minister of public education (1929–37), he was instrumental in making Party history a subject in Soviet schools; arrested in 1937; shot in 1938 (some sources say 1940); posthumously rehabilitated, 265

Buchanan, Sir George (1854–1924). British ambassador to Russia (1910–18). (See Bibliography), 13–16, 18, 20, 23, 30, 45, 227

Budberg, Baron Nikolai ("Lai") (1895–1972). Baltic German nobleman; second husband of Moura Zakrevskaya-Benckendorff. They separated in 1922; in 1926 they were officially divorced by a Berlin court in the absence of both parties. Died in Rio de Janeiro, 2, 132–134, 138, 140, 143, 165, 168–170, 174, 176–177, 196, 247–248,

Bukharin, Nikolai Ivanovich (1888–1938). Bolshevik from 1906; dubbed "the favorite of everyone in the Party" by Lenin in his "Letter to the Congress"; leading theorist and advocate of NEP; allied with Stalin against Trotsky, Zinoviev, and Kamenev (1924–28), then leader of the "right opposition" to forced collectivization; member of the Central Committee until 1934, then editor of Izvestia; arrested in 1937; tried and executed in March 1938; formally rehabilitated in February 1988 and reinstated in the Party in June 1988, 254, 265, 271, 273

Bulgakov, Mikhail Afanasievich (1891–1940). Novelist and dramatist; master of philosophical and satirical fiction. His most famous work is The Master and Margarita, published twenty-five years after his death, 224

Burenin, Nikolai Evgenievich (1874–1962). Bolshevik, Gorky's friend; accompanied Gorky and Andreeva on their trip to America in 1906, 96

Burgess, Guy (1911–63). British double agent; fled to asylum in the Soviet Union in 1951, 295n

Christie, Mikhail Petrovich (1875–1956). Held posts in the Commissariat of Enlightenment (1918–26), including director of the House of Scholars in Petrograd; later deputy director of the Bureau of Science, *103, 109, 129*

Chukovsky, Kornei Ivanovich (Nikolai Vasilievich Korneichukov) (1882–1969). Literary historian, critic, translator, diarist; Russia's most popular children's author. London correspondent for the *Odessa News* (1903–5); head of the Anglo-American section of Gorky's Universal Literature (1918). Honorary Doctor of Letters, Oxford University (1962), *99, 103–104, 118, 129*

Churchill, Randolph Henry Spencer (1911–68). Winston Churchill's son and biographer, *213*

Churchill, Sir Winston Leonard Spencer (1874–1965). British statesman and prime minister during World War II. As war minister in 1919 was anti-Bolshevik and an advocate of intervention. Nobel Prize in Literature 1953. (*See* Bibliography), *34, 39, 84, 279, 282*

Chuzhak, Nikolai Fyodorovich (1876–1937). Left futurist; theoretician of "factographic" and utilitarian art, *224*

Clark, Barrett Harper (1890–1953). American writer on theater; translator; author of a memoir about Gorky. (*See* Bibliography), *xviiin7, 172–174, 191, 284*

Clemenceau, Georges (1841–1929). French statesman known as "the Tiger." War correspondent as a young man with Grant's army (1865). French premier (1906–9 and 1917–20); head of French delegation to peace conference, *31, 157*

Cooper, Lady Diana (1892–1986). British aristocrat and artist; wife of the ambassador to Paris (1944–47), *256*

Crevel, René (1900–35). Fellow traveler of surrealism and the French Communist Party. André Breton wrote: "René Crevel committed suicide at the end of the exhausting discussion with congress [for the defense of culture] organizers over giving me a chance to speak" (*Entretiens 1913–1952* [Paris: Gallimard, 1969]). Breton had insulted Ehrenburg, who had defamed the surrealists, *242*

Cromie, Francis Newton Allen (1882–1918). Captain in the British navy; commanded a flotilla of submarines in the Baltic on the eve of World War I. Assigned as naval attaché to Russia during the war. Close friend

Dmitry Donskoy, Grand Prince of Moscow (1350–89). Won the first victory over the Tatars on the Don in 1380; canonized in 1988, 266

Dobrolyubov, Nikolai Alexandrovich (1836–61). Protegé of Chernyshevsky; like him, revered by the radical intelligentsia. His articles on literature expounded the utilitarian concept of art (critical realism); this view of the function of literature, with its criticism of Russian life and belief in progress, led the way to Lenin's demand that literature should serve the interests of the Party (1905), and from there to "socialist realism" devised by Stalin, Zhdanov, and Gorky in 1932, *111*

Dobrowen, Issay Alexandrovich (1891–1953). Russian pianist; pupil of Konstantin Igumnov and Leopold Godowsky; composer and conductor. Emigrated in 1923 and made his career as a conductor in the United States, Europe (especially at La Scala), Stockholm, and his adopted country Norway, where he died, *106, 109, 175*

Dobuzhinsky, Mstislav Valerianovich (1875–1957). Painter and graphic artist; book illustrator; theatrical designer; memoirist. Emigrated in 1924 to Paris, where he worked three years at Baliev's Bat, but he also worked in theaters in Riga, Lithuania, and England; in 1939 he moved to New York, where his work included productions at the Met, *103, 112, 270*

Duddington, Natalie (née Ertel) (1887–1972). born in Moscow, lived in London. Translator of Russian fiction (Pushkin, Goncharov, Saltykov-Shchedrin, Merezhkovsky, Afanasiev's fairy tales), philosophy (Soloviev, Berdyaev, Lossky, Frank), history (Kliuchevsky), and poetry (Akhmatova). She was close to Constance Garnett, whom she served as amanuensis for twenty years, 24

Duhamel, Georges (1884–1966). French novelist and essayist; traveled to Moscow in 1927, 241n

Duke (*Duka*). Gorky's nickname. According to Berberova, the name comes from Pushkin's poem "Angelo" (1833), inspired by Shakespeare's *Measure for Measure*

Dukes, Sir Paul (1889–1967). Agent of the British secret service in Russia (1918–20), where he worked independently and reported directly to London; published a book about it in 1922 called *Red Dusk and the Morrow*. Lockhart knew and liked him (*Diaries*, November 1, 1935), *50, 56*

Dybenko, Pavel Efimovich (1889–1938). Commissar of the Red Navy (October 1917–April 1918). One of the judges who condemned Tukhachevsky in 1937; shot in 1938; rehabilitated in 1956, *265*

Dzerzhinsky, Felix Edmundovich (1877–1926). Of Polish gentry by birth; joined Socialist Democratic Party of Poland and Lithuania in 1895; imprisoned in Siberia several times, released by amnesty of February 1917. Founder (December 1917) and chairman of the Cheka; chairman of Supreme Economic Council (1924); Stalin's ally. "The most remarkable thing about him was his eyes. Deeply sunk, they blazed with a steady fire of fanaticism. They never twitched. His eyelids seemed paralysed. He had spent most of his life in Siberia and bore the traces of his exile on his face" (Lockhart, *British Agent*, 254), *25, 39, 41, 47, 54–55, 58–63, 67–68, 84, 102, 104, 125, 159, 182, 196–198*

Ebert, Friedrich (1871–1925). Leader of the German Social Democratic Party. Elected president of the German Republic by the national assembly at Weimar (1919). Suppressed Hitler's attempt to establish dictatorship in Bavaria in 1923, *151, 155, 157*

Edward VIII (1894–1972). Prince of Wales; succeeded George V as king in 1936; abdicated to marry American divorcée Wallis Simpson, becoming the Duke of Windsor; frequently mentioned in Lockhart's *Diaries*, *258, 279*

Egorov, Alexander Ilich (1883–1939). Soviet marshal (1935); shot in 1939; rehabilitated in 1956, *266*

Ehrenburg, Ilya Grigorievich (1891–1967). "Chameleon" writer and journalist, whose writings portrayed the dominant mood at a given moment; lived mainly abroad until 1941 as correspondent of *Izvestia*; soon after Stalin died, he became a leader of the literary "thaw," a word he used as the title for a novel (1954). He promoted the rehabilitation of authors destroyed by Stalin. Wrote important memoirs; as he had requested, his archives were transported to Israel clandestinely after his death, *33, 237, 240, 242, 244n*

Eichhorn, Hermann von (1848–1918). German WWI field marshal whose corps occupied Ukraine, where he was military governor (1917). Assassinated in 1918 in Kiev: "Donskoi, a young Moscow student and a member of the Social-Revolutionary Party, hired a cab and passing Eichhorn, threw a bomb" (Lockhart, *Diaries*, July 30, 1918), *54*

Eideman, Robert Petrovich (1895–1937). Professional officer trained in the tsarist military academy; Soviet general; commander of the Frunze Military Academy; shot in 1937; rehabilitated in 1957, 244

Ekaterina Pavlovna. *See* Peshkova, Ekaterina Pavlovna

Eliseev, Stepan Petrovich (?–1926). Wealthy financier; owner, before the revolution, of the mansion that became House of the Arts, 117

Elizaveta Petrovna (1709–61). Daughter of Peter I and Catherine I; empress of Russia from 1741; made a morganatic marriage to Ukrainian Cossack Alexei Razumovsky, who was made a count, 299

Eluard, Paul (1895–1952). French surrealist poet; member of the French Communist Party; friend of Picasso's and Ehrenburg's; his first wife was a Russian (E. D. Dyakonova), 241n

Ertel, Alexander Ivanovich (1855–1908). Russian writer whose novels portray the minor nobility and the intelligentsia, 24

Ezhov, Nikolai Ivanovich (1895–1939). Head of OGPU after Yagoda (September 1936–December 1938); organizer of the Great Purge; arrested in April 1939; shot. In 1988 the Supreme Court refused to rehabilitate him, 261, 275

Fedin, Konstantin Alexandrovich (1892–1977). Novelist, in the 1920s a leading fellow traveler (a term coined by Trotsky meaning writers who were not Party members but supported the regime); Stalin Prize 1949; secretary of Union of Writers after 1959, 234, 241

Fischer, Louis (1896–1970). American journalist and Sovietologist, 245–250

Fondaminsky, Ilya Isidorovich (pseudonym: Bunakov) (1879–1943). Socialist Revolutionary; in exile in Paris from 1906 to 1917 and again after 1919. Commissar of the Black Sea Fleet for the Provisional Government. One of the editors of the important émigré journal *Sovremennye zapiski* (*Contemporary Annals*, Paris, 1920–40). Arrested by the Nazis in 1941; perished in Auschwitz, 268–269n

Forsh, Olga Dmitrievna (1873–1961). Writer of historical novels based on documentary material, 234

Forster, Edward Morgan (1879–1970). English novelist and critic, 242

France, Anatole (1844–1924). French novelist and satirist, 135

Francis, David Rowland (1850–1927). U.S. ambassador to Russia (1916–18), 31–32, 35, 39–40, 87

Francis, Kay (1903–68). American film actress who was a star in the 1930s. Playing Moura in *British Agent*, she was, in David Thomson's words, "Lenin's [sic] perfectly groomed secretary" (*The New Biographical Dictionary of Film*), 207–208

Friede, Colonel Alexander V. (?–1918). Tsarist officer implicated in the "Lockhart plot"; shot in 1918, *88, 90*

Fürstenberg. *See* Ganetsky, Yakov Stanislavovich

Galsworthy, John (1867–1933). English novelist and playwright; first president of International PEN; Nobel Prize in Literature 1932, *13, 99, 135, 177, 181, 255, 258*

Ganetsky, Yakov Stanislavovich (alias: Fürstenberg) (1879–1937). Party Bolshevik of Polish origin (born: Hanecki); Lenin's ally; raiser and distributor of funds; held high posts in the Soviet State Bank, Foreign Commissariat, and Commissariat of Foreign Trade. Arrested in 1937 and shot. His son Lev, a diplomat in Rome, defected to the United States in the 1930s; his other son Evgeny, a diplomat in Berlin, was sent to the Gulag and released in 1955, *137, 156*

Garnett, Constance (1862–1946). Translator of Russian classics into English; writer Edward Garnett's wife, *24, 173*

Garstin, Dennis (Denys) (1890–1918). English painter Norman Garstin's son; novelist Crosbie Garstin's brother; graduate of Cambridge and captain in the British cavalry who spoke Russian and served on Lockhart's staff in Moscow in 1918. Close to Lockhart, Moura, and Hicks. Ordered to join General Poole in Archangel, where he was killed by a Bolshevik bullet, *21–22, 26*

Gide, André (1869–1951). French writer who reported his impressions of a trip to the Soviet Union in 1936 (*Retour de l'URSS*), which would have been insignificant had Gide not been a prominent fellow traveler of the French Communist Party, *210, 240, 242, 244n*

Gip. *See* Wells, George Philip

Glazunov, Alexander Konstantinovich (1865–1936). Russian composer. Lived in Paris after 1928, but was not an émigré; conducted concerts in Detroit and Boston in 1929, *13*

Gnedin, Evgeny Alexandrovich (1898–1983). Son of Alexander Parvus, from whom he was separated in 1904. Head of the German desk and press

classics and modern writers in translation (Mark Twain, H. G. Wells, Maupassant), with branches in Moscow, St. Petersburg, and Berlin. Gorky's close friend (Gorky was godfather to his oldest son); published Gorky's works. Left Russia in October 1921 with Gorky to set up business in Berlin, counting on hopes given him by Soviet officials that he would be able to sell his books in the USSR, but this did not happen. He gradually went bankrupt and died in debt in Paris, *103, 107, 109, 129, 139–140, 147, 167, 169, 171, 193*

Gumilev, Nikolai Stepanovich (1886–1921). Russian poet; Anna Akhmatova's first husband; shot for failing to denounce a friend who wanted to join a counterrevolutionary organization (*Novy mir* 12, 1987), *5, 106, 137*

Haldane, John B. S. (1892–1964). English scientist and professor of genetics. During the Spanish civil war, joined the Communist Party and remained a member until 1950, when he became disillusioned with Stalin's suppression of scientists. During his years in the Party he wrote frequently for the London *Daily Worker*, *223*

Hamsun, Knut (1859–1952). Norwegian novelist; Nobel Prize in Literature 1920, *220*

Hanecki. *See* Ganetsky, Yakov Stanislavovich

Harari, Manya (née Benenson) (1906–69). Artist, translator, publisher and founder of the Harvill Press. Born in St. Petersburg in a wealthy Jewish family who emigrated to England, where she grew up. Translated Ehrenburg's *Thaw* and several other books from Russian, including her translation with Max Hayward of Boris Pasternak's *Doctor Zhivago* in 1958. Author of memoirs. (*See* Bibliography), *227*

Hardy, Thomas (1840–1928). English poet and novelist, *258*

Hauptmann, Gerhart (1862–1946). German writer; Nobel Prize in Literature 1912, *135–136*

Heintse (Geintse), Maria Alexandrovna ("Molecule") (1902–1930). Physician; "adopted" by Gorky, who helped her go to medical school in Petrograd, where she met the artist Vladimir Tatlin and became his common-law wife, *101, 103, 105, 109–110, 115, 122*

Helfferich, Karl (1872–1924). Economist, banker, German ambassador to Moscow in August 1918, *54*

Hellens, Franz (1881–1972). Belgian writer who wrote in French; translated Esenin and Mayakovsky, *177*

Helphand (Gelfand). *See* Parvus, Alexander Lazarevich

Henderson, Arthur (1863–1935). English trade union leader; elected chairman of the Socialist International (1923), *18, 228*

Herriot, Edouard (1872–1957). French radical politician and writer; traveled to Soviet Russia in 1922 (*La Russie nouvelle*). France recognized the Soviet Union when he was foreign minister (1924–25), *231–232*

Hicks, Captain William L. ("Hickie") (?–1930). When Lockhart left for Russia on January 14, 1918, as agent of the British mission to the Communist government, Hicks was one of the members of the mission traveling with him (Lockhart, *Diaries*, p. 32). Remained a friend of Lockhart's and Moura's. Married Lyuba Malinina (Moscow mayor Chelnokov's niece), *21–28, 42, 47, 56, 58, 61, 64–69, 82, 85, 144, 185–188*

Hill, Captain George Alexander (later Brigadier) (dates unknown). Agent of the British secret service and associate of Sidney Reilly. Close to Lockhart, Moura, Hicks, and Garstin in Moscow; arrested in 1918; released when Lockhart and members of the British mission were deported to England. Author of a book about his service as a secret agent. (*See* Bibliography), *14, 50, 251*

Hoover, Herbert Clark (1874–1964). Chairman of several American war and famine relief commissions (1915–21); U.S. secretary of commerce (1921–24); U.S. president (1929–33), *105, 135*

Howard, Leslie (1893–1943). English actor; son of Hungarian immigrants. Played Lockhart in the film of *British Agent*. Though "central Europe haunted his features," Hollywood adopted him as "the epitome of class" (David Thomson, *The New Biographical Dictionary of Film*). His image assumed a patriotic mystique during the war when he was shot down on a government mission on a flight from Lisbon to London, *207–208*

Ipatiev, Vladimir Nikolaevich (1867–1952). Russian chemist, known for work on industrial catalytic reactions. On a business trip in 1927 remained abroad, finding work with an oil company in Chicago and at Northwestern University as a professor, *39, 267*

Ivanov, Vsevolod Vyacheslavovich (1895–1963). Soviet writer; fellow traveler in the 1920s, *224*

Ivanov, Vyacheslav Ivanovich (1866–1949). Symbolist poet; philologist; essayist; translator; settled in Italy in 1924; became a Roman Catholic in 1926, *24, 112, 199, 233*

Ivinskaya, Olga Vsevolodovna (1912–95). Pasternak's companion from 1946 until his death in 1960; inspiration for Lara in *Doctor Zhivago*. (*See* Bibliography), *292*

Jagow, Gottlieb von (1863–1935). German foreign minister (1913–16), *155*

Jogiches, Leon (pseudonym: Jan Tyszka) (1867–1919). Polish historian and journalist; Rosa Luxemburg's husband, *151*

Kalamatiano, Xenophon (?–1923). American secret agent in Russia; implicated in the "Lockhart plot"; sentenced to death in December 1918, but not executed; repatriated when American famine relief began in 1921, *50, 81, 88, 90*

Kamenev, Lev Borisovich (real name: Rozenfeld) (1883–1936). Old Bolshevik; journalist; literary critic; with Zinoviev, hostile to Lenin's policy of seizing power in October 1917; chairman of Moscow Soviet (1918–20); Politburo member (1919–25). At Lenin's death, led the Party with Zinoviev and Stalin, then went into opposition; expelled from and reinstated in the Party three times; arrested in December 1934; shot in August 1936 after the first Moscow Trial; rehabilitated in June 1988. Married to Trotsky's sister, Olga Davidovna Bronshtein, who perished with him, *20, 104, 247, 265, 275*

Kannegiesser, Leonid Samuilovich (1898–1918). Student and poet; assassinated Mikhail Uritsky on August 30, 1918; shot. In response to this assassination, the Cheka shot 900 hostages in Petrograd, *60, 67*

Kaplan, Dora (Fanya Efimovna) (1890–1918). Called Dora by the SRs, Fanny by the Cheka. A terrorist and Spiridonova's ally, she spent eleven years in tsarist prisons. Bitter at what she considered betrayal of Socialist principles by the Bolsheviks, wounded Lenin with two pistol shots on August 30, 1918, in Moscow; executed on September 3 by Malkov, *60, 67, 72, 110, 179*

Kaplun, Solomon Gitmanovich (real name: Sumsky) (1891–1940). Menshevik; director of Epokha in Berlin (1922–25); publisher of *Beseda*. Went bankrupt as a result of the Soviet refusal to admit *Beseda*; worked in Paris on an émigré newspaper until it was shut down by the German

Keun, Odette (1888–1978). Journalist; author; H. G. Wells's companion. (*See* Bibliography), *215, 216, 221*

Keynes, Lord John Maynard (1883–1946). British economist; married the ballerina Lydia Lopokova (1925), 23n

Khalatov, Artemy Bagratovich (1896–1938). Commissar for food supplies to the army (1918–22); chairman of the Committee for Improving Living Conditions of Academics (KUBU) during the period when Gorky was living on Kronverk; chairman of Gosizdat (State Publishing House) (1928–32), where he played a major role in establishing the system of political censorship; victim of the purges, *103*

Khodasevich, Valentina Mikhailovna ("Kupchikha") (1894–1970). Artist; Vladislav Khodasevich's niece; set and costume designer at Sergei Radlov's Theater of Popular Comedy (1920–22); head designer at the Kirov Theater of Opera and Ballet in Leningrad (1932–36). Author of memoirs about Gorky, Mayakovsky, and others: *Portrety slovami* (*Portraits in Words*) (Moscow: Sovetskii pisatel', 1987). (*See* Bibliography), *ix, 101–102, 104, 140, 167, 232, 243*

Khodasevich, Vladislav Felitsianovich (1886–1939). Poet and literary critic; Pushkinist; memoirist; left Russia in 1922 with Nina Berberova and remained in emigration in Paris after 1925. His memoirs of Gorky were written in 1936 after Gorky's death. (*See* Bibliography), *ix, x, xiv, xx, 1, 2–4, 24, 49n, 63, 78, 102, 105–107, 125, 145, 160–161, 166, 168–185, 193, 198, 233, 239, 270, 272–273*

Kholodnaya, Vera Vasilievna (1893–1919). Russian star of silent films, *16*

Khvostov, Alexei Nikolaevich (1872–1918). Interior minister (1915–16); arrested by the Provisional Government; shot by the Bolsheviks, *72*

Kirov, Sergei Mironovich (real surname: Kostrikov) (1886–1934). Named Party secretary in Leningrad after crushing of the opposition in 1926; assassinated December 1, 1934, probably with Stalin's complicity. His demise began a wave of terror that led to Ezhov's Great Purge of 1936–38, *237, 242, 259–260, 275*

Klyuev, Nikolai Alexeevich (1884–1937). Mystical peasant poet and revolutionary; arrested in 1933. Gorky intervened in 1934 to alleviate his fate, but was arrested again and died in the Gulag; rehabilitated in 1957, *224*

Knipper-Chekhova, Olga Leonardovna (1868–1959). Actress at the Moscow Art Theater; married Anton Chekhov (1901), *173, 285*

Knox, Sir Alfred William Fortescue (1870–1964). British military attaché to St. Petersburg 1914–18; liaison officer with the Russian army (1914–17). (*See* Bibliography), *15, 39*

Kogan, Pyotr Semyonovich (1872–1932). Literary historian; Marxist critic. Visited Gorky in Sorrento in 1927, *241*

Kolchak, Admiral Aleksandr Vasilievich (1874–1920). Led the anti-Bolshevik struggle in the civil war, established military rule in the Urals and Siberia; captured and shot in Irkutsk, *134, 261*

Kollontai, Alexandra Mikhailovna (née Domontovich) (1872–1952). First woman to serve in the Soviet government, as commissar of public welfare, and, from 1923 to 1945, first woman ambassador (Norway, Mexico, Sweden). Champion of women's rights and theorist of free love; author of *The Autobiography of a Sexually Emancipated Communist Woman* and *Love and the New Morality*. Pavel Dybenko's wife (1918–23). She sided with Stalin in 1927, *103, 190*

Koltsov, Mikhail Efimovich (1898–1940). Soviet journalist; Party member; *Pravda* correspondent (1922–38); editor of journals, including Gorky's *Za rubezhom* (*Abroad*) (1932–38). Books included a diary of the Spanish civil war and a life of Gorky. Arrested December 12, 1938; died in prison camp; rehabilitated in 1954, *163, 234, 242–244*

Korda, Sir Alexander (1893–1956). Hungarian-born British film director and producer, *226–227, 279–280, 296*

Korin, Pavel Dmitrievich (1892–1967). Russian artist, *225, 239*

Kork, Avgust Ivanovich (1887–1937). Trained as a tsarist officer, he fought with the Red Army during the civil war; as a Soviet general, held major army commands in Ukraine, Belarus, the Caucasus, central Asia, and Leningrad; joined the Party in 1927; purged in 1937 with Tukhachevsky, Uborevich, Yakir, and others; rehabilitated in 1957, *244*

Kornilov, General Lavr Georgievich (1870–1918). Commander in chief of the Russian army (July–August 1917); marched on Petrograd in September 1917 to prevent a Bolshevik coup but was arrested on Kerensky's orders. Escaped in December 1917; formed and led the first volunteer anti-Bolshevik units in the south (the "White army of the Don"); killed in combat, *18–19*

Korolenko, Vladimir Galaktionovich (1853–1921). Russian writer; defender of human rights and of the oppressed from the time of the pogroms to the Bolshevik terror, *147*

Koteliansky, Samuel Solomonovich (1880–1955). Ukrainian Jew who went to England on a research scholarship from Kiev University and stayed. Knew the Woolfs, Wells, D. H. Lawrence, Katherine Mansfield, and Constance Garnett; translated Chekhov, Gorky, and others into English, *118*

Koussevitzky, Serge Alexandrovich (1874–1951). Virtuoso double-bass player in the Bolshoi Theater Orchestra, later an eminent conductor. In 1905 he married a daughter of a rich tea merchant, which gave him the means to become an influential music publisher; published Stravinsky, Prokofiev, Rachmaninoff, and Scriabin, whose music he championed. Active as a conductor in Moscow and Petrograd during the revolutionary period. Left Russia in 1920 for Berlin, Rome, Paris; from 1924 until his death he was conductor and music director of the Boston Symphony and the summer festival at Tanglewood, *97*

Krandievskaya, Natalia Vasilievna (1888–1953). Poet; wife of A. N. Tolstoy from 1914 to 1935, 249n

Krasin, Leonid Borisovich (1870–1926). Engineer; clandestine bomb maker for Bolshevik action groups (1904–7), then director of the Russian branch of Siemens. Commissar of trade and industry in 1918, of foreign trade (1920–23); ambassador to Great Britain twice between 1920 and 1926 and to France in 1924, *103, 136, 152–153, 171, 234, 290*

Krestinsky, Nikolai Nikolaevich (1883–1938). Commissar of finance (1918–21); ambassador to Berlin (1921–30); deputy commissar of foreign affairs (1930–35); arrested in May 1937; shot in March 1938; rehabilitated in February 1988, *271*

Krimer, Friedrich Eduardovich (1888–?). Economist; worked on Gorky's newspaper *New Life*. Directed Arcos, the Anglo-Russian Cooperative Society, an official Soviet trading company chartered in London in 1920, *xviii*n7, *103, 136, 290*

Krivitsky, Walter G. (1899–1941). Chief of Soviet military counterintelligence in Western Europe; defected in 1939. Died mysteriously in a Washington hotel. Author of *In Stalin's Secret Service* (1939), *250*

Krivoshein, Alexander Vasilievich (1857–1921). Minister of agriculture (1908–15), he assisted in carrying out Stolypin's agrarian reforms (1906–11); resisted the Bolsheviks; emigrated to Western Europe after the civil war, *29*

Krupskaya, Nadezhda Konstantinovna (1869–1939). Lenin's collaborator and wife (beginning 1898); dealt with issues of education and propaganda after the revolution; in the opposition with Zinoviev and Kamenev (1925–26); went over to Stalin's side but remained in disgrace, *179, 181*

Krylenko, Nikolai Vasilievich (1885–1938). Chairman of the Supreme Tribunal in 1918; general prosecutor of the Russian Republic; commissar of justice of the Russian Republic beginning 1931, of the Soviet Union beginning 1936; arrested in 1937; shot; rehabilitated in 1955, *41, 73, 265*

Kryuchkov, Pyotr Petrovich ("Peppycrew," an acronym formed from the initials of his name) (1889–1938). As Andreeva's secretary and companion, he accompanied her in 1921 to the Soviet Trade Office in Berlin; worked in the Berlin office of Foreign Books (Mezhdunarodnaya Kniga), where he reported to OGPU; subsequently was assigned by Yagoda to be Gorky's secretary and to keep track of and report on the writer's activities. Arrested after Yagoda's arrest in 1937, he was accused of playing a role in the suspicious death of Maxim and of poisoning Gorky during his medical treatment; confessed to being a "hired murderer" of the "right Trotskyite gang"; sentenced to death on March 13, 1938, and summarily shot. Formally rehabilitated in 1988, *101, 104, 105, 109–110, 125, 134–136, 138–139, 141, 143, 147, 159–160, 162–163, 167, 169–170, 178–183, 192, 220, 224, 229–230, 243, 252, 254, 271–275, 290*

Kudasheva, Maria Pavlovna (1895–1985). Prince Kudashev's widow (he was killed during the civil war); secretary to Pyotr Kogan; married Romain Rolland in 1934; admitted to having been "manipulated by the NKVD," *241*

Kupchikha. *See* Khodasevich, Valentina Mikhailovna

Kursky, Dmitry Ivanovich (1874–1932). Commissar of justice and prosecutor general (1918–28); ambassador to Italy (1928–32), *230*

Kuskova, Ekaterina Dmitrievna (1869–1958). Important figure in the Constitutional Democratic Party; right-wing Socialist; political writer; exiled from Russia in 1922. Married to S. N. Prokopovich (1871–1955), a Freemason, minister of trade and industry in the Provisional Government. They lived in Berlin until 1924, then Prague, then Geneva after 1939, *197, 234, 237–239, 247*

Kutuzov, Mikhail Illarionovich (1745–1813). Supreme commander of the Russian army during the Napoleonic campaign, *266*

Labarthe, André (1902–67). Physician; in 1940 joined General de Gaulle in London, where he founded the monthly *La France libre, 280–282*

Ladyzhnikov, Ivan Pavlovich (1874–1945). Editor; Gorky's friend; acted as his literary agent and business manager; director of Kniga Publishers in Berlin, *97, 134–135, 138–139, 141, 143, 147–148, 152, 154, 157–163, 167, 169, 171, 178, 180, 183, 192–194, 226, 229*

Lai. *See* Budberg, Baron Nikolai

Lalaingue, Jacques de (dates unknown). Belgian diplomat in Moscow in 1917, *23*

Latsis, Martyn Ivanovich (real name: Jan Soudrabs) (1888–1938). High-level official in the Cheka; active in the collectivization campaign; arrested in 1937, sentenced and shot in 1938; rehabilitated in 1956, *58, 84*

Lavergne, General Jean (dates unknown). Head of the French military mission in Russia; military attaché in Petrograd, *31–33, 56, 58, 70, 73, 90*

Lawrence, David Herbert (1885–1930). English poet and novelist, *225*

Lawrence, Thomas Edward ("Lawrence of Arabia") (1888–1935). English officer; writer, *13*

Leeper, Sir Reginald ("Rex") (1888–1968). British diplomat; intelligence officer at the foreign office. Assistant to Lockhart during World War II at the Political Warfare Department; later, as Sir Reginald, was British ambassador to Greece, *20, 278*

Léger, Fernand (1881–1955). French artist, Communist. In 1927 he began living with his pupil Nadia Khodossievitch (1904–82; from Belarus, no relation to Khodasevich), better known as Nadia Léger; they were married in 1952. She was a loyal Communist whose paintings include portraits of leaders of the international Communist movement; she also painted a portrait of Gorky, *241n*

Lenin, Vladimir Ilich (Ulyanov) (1870–1924). Chairman of the Soviet of People's Commissars. (*See* Bibliography), *xi, 25, 32–35, 39–40, 47, 52–54, 58, 60–61, 67–70, 72, 74, 82, 91, 93, 95, 98, 101–107, 110, 115, 117, 121, 124–126, 138, 141, 145–156, 160–161, 166, 173, 178–180, 192, 198, 205, 209, 220, 227–228, 235, 265, 271, 275, 296*

Leontiev, Konstantin Nikolaevich (1831–91). Russian conservative writer and thinker; diplomat; became a monk in 1887, *46n*

Leskov, Nikolai Semyonovich (1831–95). Russian fiction writer, mostly of stories, admired for his originality, *133, 285*

Levin, Lev Grigorovich (1870–1938). Chief of medicine at the Kremlin hospital; Lenin's physician (1922–23); accused in 1938 of the medical assassination of Vyacheslav Menzhinsky, Valerian Kuibyshev, and Gorky. Shot; formally rehabilitated in February 1988, *271*

Levine, Isaac Don (1892–1981). American journalist. Born in Mozyr (Belarus) to a family with Zionist sympathies; came to the United States in 1911; worked for *The Kansas City Star* and the *New York Tribune*; covered the Russian civil war; became a columnist for the Hearst newspapers, *276*

Lifar, Sergei Mikhailovich (1905–86). Russian-born French dancer and choreographer; worked at the Opéra de Paris (1929–58), *270*

Lindley, Sir Francis Oswald (1872–1950). Diplomat in the British embassy in Petrograd (1915–18), *20, 23, 41*

Litvinov, Maxim Maximovich (real name: Meyer-Genoch Movshevich Wallach) (1876–1951). Bolshevik; manager of funds from "expropriations" (1906); settled in England in 1907, where he married Ivy Low (1916); arrested in retaliation for Lockhart's arrest, for whom he was exchanged in 1918. Deputy commissar of foreign affairs (1921–30), then commissar of foreign affairs (1930–39); replaced by Molotov in 1939 to allow Stalin to conclude the German-Soviet pact (not only was Litvinov against the pact, but Hitler objected to negotiating with a Jew); Soviet ambassador to the United States (1941–43). (*See* Bibliography), *20, 27, 51, 62, 80, 82, 85, 148, 163, 261, 289*

Lloyd George, David (1863–1945). British statesman; chancellor of the exchequer (1908–15); minister of munitions (1915–16); prime minister (1916–22), *17–19, 27–28, 39, 54, 88, 157, 205, 227*

Lockhart, Sir Robert Hamilton Bruce (1887–1970). British diplomat and journalist; consul general to Moscow (1912–17), then chief of the British mission; arrested and expelled in 1918. Commercial secretary at the legation in Prague (1920–22), then with the Anglo-Austrian Bank (1922–29). Columnist for Lord Beaverbrook on the *Evening Standard* (1928–37); author of numerous books. During the war (1939–45) worked at the Foreign Office in the Political Warfare Department. (*See* Bibliography), *xi, xii, xv, xvi*n, *1, 9, 14–35, 37–90, 108–109, 116, 125–128, 143–144, 185–191, 202–216, 226–229, 240, 247–251, 258–260, 276–282, 285–286, 289–292, 296, 299*

Lodi, Zoya Petrovna (1886–1957). Russian lyric soprano; highly esteemed as a singer of art songs, *199*

Lopokova, Lydia (Russian name: Lopukhova) (1891–1981). Russian ballerina with Diaghilev's Ballets Russes (1910–29); appeared in famous productions (*The Firebird* and *Petrushka*). Married the economist John Maynard Keynes in 1925 and was a prominent figure in British literary and dance circles, *23*n

Low, Ivy (1890–1977). English writer (published stories in *The New Yorker* in the 1960s); married Maxim Litvinov in England (1916). Taught English in Russia and reportedly tutored Stalin. Popular hostess in Washington during Litvinov's tenure as ambassador. After more than fifty years in Moscow, returned to England to live (1972), twenty years after her husband's death, *20*

Ludendorff, General Erich (1865–1937). German general; politician, *28–29, 54*

Lunacharsky, Anatoly Vasilievich (1875–1933). Critic; playwright; commissar of enlightenment (1917–29), *103–104*

Luppol, Ivan Kapitonovich (1896–1942). Nadezhda Peshkova's second husband. Literary historian; critic; editor of Gosizdat; head of the Gorky Institute of World Literature. Arrested 1940; died in the Gulag, *244*

Luxemburg, Rosa (1871–1919). Polish-born German revolutionary; assassinated during the Spartacist uprising. (*See* Bibliography), *149, 151–152, 155*

Lvov, Prince Georgy Evgenievich (1861–1925). Constitutional Democratic politician; president of the Provisional Government (March–July 1917); emigrated to France in 1920, *17*

Lykiardopoulos, Mikhail Fyodorovich ("Lyki") (1883–1925). Russian of Greek and English origin; translator; music and theater critic; secretary of Moscow Art Theater; linked to Russian and English secret services; died in London, *13, 24, 116*

Mackenzie, Sir Compton (1883–1972). English author of novels and autobiography, *13*

MacLean, Donald (1913–83). British double agent; took asylum in the Soviet Union in 1951, *295n*

Maisky, Ivan Mikhailovich (1884–1975). Menshevik, then Bolshevik (1920); Soviet diplomat (1922–46); ambassador in London (1932–43); diplomatic historian and author of memoirs, *279*

Maklakov, Vasily Alexeevich (1870–1957). Lawyer; journalist; a leader of the Constitutional Democratic Party; unaccredited Russian ambassador in Paris (1917–24); director of the Office for Russian Émigré Affairs under the French Interior Ministry; Freemason, *17*

Malevich, Kazimir Severinovich (1878–1935). Russian painter; one of the founders of abstract art (Suprematism), *110*

Malinina, Lyuba (dates unknown). Mikhail Chelnokov's niece; married Captain Hicks in 1918 and emigrated to England, *23, 82, 85, 144, 186*

Malkov, Pavel Dmitrievich (1887–1965). Commandant of Smolny, then the Kremlin, about which he wrote a memoir. (*See* Bibliography), *xv, 61, 64–67*

Malraux, André (1901–76). French novelist; author of *Man's Fate* (*La Condition Humaine*, 1933). Appointed minister of cultural affairs by de Gaulle (1959–69), *240, 242–243*

Mandelstam, Nadezhda Yakovlevna (1899–1980). Osip Mandelstam's wife; author of memoirs about the poet and his era. (*See* Bibliography), *196–197*

Mann, Heinrich (1871–1950). German writer; exiled to France in 1933; interned in 1940 but escaped to the United States, *242*

Manukhin, Ivan Ivanovich (1882–1930). Bolshevik; Gorky's physician; worked with the Political Red Cross; in 1920 was sent, thanks to Gorky, to the Pasteur Institute and remained in Paris, *114, 158*

Marchand, René (1888–?). Correspondent for *Le Figaro* in Russia; became a Communist, *32, 50, 73–75n, 80, 84*

Maria Fyodorovna. *See* Andreeva, Maria Fyodorovna

Marr, Nikolai Yakovlevich (1864–1934). Orientalist and linguist; author of controversial theories on the origin of languages, 223

Marshak, Samuil Yakovlevich (1887–1964). Poet and translator of English poetry; popular children's writer, *218, 223, 236*

Martov, Yuri Osipovich (1873–1923). Leader of the Menshevik Social Democrats; in emigration in Switzerland after 1920; editor of the *Socialist Courier, 156, 238*

Masaryk, Jan (1886–1948). Czech diplomat and Lockhart's close friend. Ambassador to London (1921–38); foreign minister in the Czechoslovak government-in-exile in London; committed suicide, or was pushed out a window, in Prague during the Communist coup in 1948. His father, the philosopher and statesman Thomas Masaryk (1850–1937), was the first president of Czechoslovakia, *190, 204, 278*

Mata Hari (1876–1917). Dutch femme fatale; accused of spying for Germany in World War I and executed by the French. Films based on her, often with a Russian twist to the plot, include *Mata Hari* with Greta Garbo and *Dishonored* with Marlene Dietrich as agent X-27, both 1931, *xiii*

Maugham, William Somerset (1874–1965). English novelist and playwright; secret agent in World War I, *13–14, 144, 170, 218, 258–259, 282*

Maxim. *See* Peshkov, Maxim Alexeevich

Mayakovsky, Vladimir Vladimirovich (1893–1930). Futurist poet; revolutionary; committed suicide, *171, 192*

Mendrokhovich (Mandro) (dates unknown). Russian arms dealer, *49*

Merezhkovsky, Dmitry Sergeevich (1866–1941). Poet; novelist; essayist; welcomed the 1905 revolution, rejected that of October 1917; emigrated to France in 1920, *13*

Meyerhold, Vsevolod Emilievich (1874–1940). Actor; director; producer; active before the revolution in the Moscow Art Theater and leading theaters in St. Petersburg; joined the Party in 1918; worked at the Theater of the Revolution, eventually forming his own theater based on "biomechanical" techniques of acting. Publicly refused to accept "socialist realism." Arrested in 1939; died in prison, *199, 234*

Mezhlauk, Valery Ivanovich (1893–1938). Commissar of heavy industry; theoretician of planned economy and chairman of Gosplan; shot in July 1938; rehabilitated in 1956, *84*

Miklashevsky, Konstantin Mikhailovich (1888–1943). Petrograd actor and writer who worked with Meyerhold in commedia dell'arte productions (1914–17) and at Sergei Radlov's Theater of Popular Comedy (1920–22), *169*

Miliukov, Pavel Nikolaevich (1859–1943). Historian; leader of Constitutional Democratic Party (1907–17); foreign minister in the first cabinet of the Provisional Government; emigrated to Paris in 1918; editor of Russian newspaper *Poslednie novosti* (*The Latest News*) (1920–40), *17*

Milner, Lord Alfred (1854–1925). British statesman; member of the war cabinet in 1918, *19*

Mirbach, Count Wilhelm (1871–1918). First German ambassador to the Soviets; assassinated in Moscow by Yakov Blyumkin, *45, 54, 60*

Mirsky, Dmitry Petrovich (Prince Svyatopolk-Mirsky, known in England as D.S. Mirsky) (1890–1939). Critic; historian of Russian literature. Guards officer before the revolution; emigrated to England in 1920; taught at London University; wrote articles and books, including influential two-volume *History of Russian Literature*. Joined the British Communist Party and returned to Soviet Russia in 1932 with Gorky's help. Arrested in 1937; sentenced to the Gulag where he died; rehabilitated in 1962. Recent publications about him include a biography by G.S. Smith, *D.S. Mirsky* (Oxford: Oxford University Press, 2000), *223, 233*

Molecule. *See* Heintse, Maria Alexandrovna

Molotov, Vyacheslav Mikhailovich (real name: Scriabin) (1890–1986). One of Stalin's first supporters and second only to Stalin after 1930. Chairman of the Soviet of People's Commissars (1930–41); replaced Litvinov at foreign ministry (May 1939); removed from Central Committee Presidium in 1957; expelled from the Party in 1962; reinstated in 1984, *160, 163, 263*

Morozov, Savva Timofeevich (1862–1905). Textile manufacturer; philanthropist; supplied funds for the Bolsheviks; committed suicide, *95, 102*

Mosolov, Lieutenant General Alexander Alexandrovich (1854–1939). High-level tsarist official. (*See* Bibliography), *12, 91, 98, 105, 108, 277*

Münzenberg, Willi (1889–1940). German Communist; follower of Lenin. Broke with Stalin after the Stalin-Hitler pact; assassinated in France, probably by the NKVD, *231*

Muratov, Pavel Pavlovich (1881–1950). Writer; translator (from French); military historian; art historian (Russian icons, Italian art); Khodasevich's close friend from 1906 and Berberova's from 1922. Sent out of Russia (1922); lived and wrote in Italy, Paris, and Ireland, where he died, 236, 246

Muravyov, Mikhail Artemievich (1880–1918). Left SR, tsarist colonel. Led defense of Petrograd against Kerensky in November 1917. Won Bolshevik confidence, commanded southern, then eastern fronts during civil war. Joined SR revolt of 1918, planned Czech asault of Ekaterinburg; shot while resisting arrest, 53

Mussolini, Benito (1883–1945). Italian fascist dictator (1922–43); assassinated by partisans, 174, 178, 199–201

Nabokov, Konstantin Dmitrievich (1872–1927). First secretary of the Russian embassy in London, then chargé d'affaires (1917–19); uncle of writer Vladimir Nabokov. (See Bibliography), 51–52

Nechaev, Sergei Gennadievich (1847–82). Fanatical anarchist who masterminded the murder of a fellow student; prototype for Peter Verkhovensky in Dostoyevsky's novel The Devils, 95

Nekrasov, Nikolai Vissarionovich (1879–1940). Constitutional Democrat; minister of railways in the Provisional Government; joined the Bolsheviks and worked in the administration of Soviet trade unions (1921–31); victim of the purges, 213

Nemirovich-Danchenko, Vladimir Ivanovich (1858–1943). Stage director; founder with Stanislavsky of the Moscow Art Theater, 234

New Economic Policy (1921–28). Aimed at restoring the economy by making concessions to private enterprise; followed by the Five-Year Plans, 126, 135

Nicolaevsky, Boris Ivanovich (1887–1966). Menshevik revolutionary; historian; emigrated in 1922 to Berlin, Paris, New York, and finally Stanford. Author and editor of numerous books and hundreds of articles about the revolution, its origins, its actors, its aftermath. The vast archive of documents he collected (the Boris I. Nicolaevsky Collection) is in the Hoover Institution at Stanford University in California. (See Bibliography), 94, 171–172, 234, 245–250, 253–254, 273, 275

Nicolson, Sir Harold (1886–1968). British diplomat; biographer; literary

Nicolson, Sir Harold (*continued*) journalist; diarist. (*See* Bibliography), *xvii, 170, 204, 206*n, *213, 278, 281–282*

Nightingale. *See* Rakitsky, Ivan Nikolaevich

Nikolaev, Leonid Vasilievich (1904–34). Kirov's assassin, *260*

Nikolaev, Mikhail Konstantinovich (1882–1947). A director of the Soviet firm Foreign Books (1923–30), *141*

Nikulin, Lev Veniaminovich (1891–1967). Soviet novelist; suspected of denouncing Babel and others, *218, 236, 249–250*

NKVD. *See* Cheka

Nostitz, Countess (dates unknown). Wife of General Nostitz, who was Clemenceau's representative in Petrograd in 1917, *23*

Noulens, Joseph (1864–1939). Finance minister in 1914; ambassador to Russia in 1917. (*See* Bibliography), *31–32, 35, 39–40*

OGPU. *See* Cheka

Oldenburg, Sergei Fyodorovich (1863–1934). Minister of education in the Provisional Government; Orientalist; permanent secretary of the Academy of Sciences (1904–29), *103*

Olivier, Laurence (Baron Olivier of Brighton) (1907–89). English actor, director; director of the National Theatre, *280, 296*

Osorgin, Mikhail Andreevich (real surname: Il'in) (1878–1942). Novelist; journalist; worked in Italy as a Russian correspondent (1906–16); arrested during the civil war; exiled from Russia in 1922; in Berlin (1922–23), after that in Paris, as literary editor on Kerensky's newspaper, *234*

Osten-Sacken, Count Nikolai Dmitrievich von der (1831–1912). Russian ambassador to Berlin, *9*

Oudendijk, W. J. (dates unknown). Dutch diplomat in Moscow (1918), *69*

Paléologue, Maurice (1859–1944). French ambassador to St. Petersburg (1913–17); author of memoirs, *31*

Parvus, Alexander Lazarevich (Helphand, Gelfand in Russian) (1869–1924). Russian-born German Social Democrat; became a millionaire in the war; supplied funds to the Bolsheviks with Yakov Ganetsky acting as intermediary. (*See* Bibliography), *148–163, 180, 192–193, 196*

Pascal, Pierre (1890–1983). Assigned to the French military mission in Petrograd in 1916; remained in Soviet Russia until 1933 as a Christian

Socialist and member of the French Communist group of Moscow. After returning to France, became a prominent Slavic scholar and translator. (*See* Bibliography), *82*

Pasternak, Boris Leonidovich (1890–1960). Soviet poet and prose writer who led the life of an "internal émigré." His early experimental story "The Childhood of Luvers" was written during the civil war and published in 1922; it portrays the first dawning of consciousness in a young girl. His novel *Doctor Zhivago* was published abroad in 1957; he won the Nobel Prize in Literature 1958, but was forced to refuse it; the novel was published in the Soviet Union in 1988, *242–243, 285, 292, 294*

Pavlov, Ivan Petrovich (1849–1936). Russian physiologist; author of works on conditioned reflexes; won Nobel Prize in Physiology 1904, *93, 97, 118*

Peppycrew. *See* Kryuchkov, Pyotr Petrovich

Peshekhonov, Alexei Vasilievich (1867–1933). Minister of food supplies in the Provisional Government (May–August 1917); exiled in 1922. Refused permission to return; in 1927 finally gained official status as an economic consultant to the Soviet government in Riga, where he died, *234*

Peshkov, Maxim Alexeevich (1897–1934). Gorky and Ekaterina Pavlovna Peshkova's son; died in Moscow under suspicious circumstances. His grave, with a life-size sculpture, is at Novodevichy Cemetery, *xvin3, 102, 271*

Peshkov, Zinovy Alexeevich (1884–1966). Yakov Sverdlov's older brother; Gorky's adopted son. As a Jew he had to be baptized to continue his schooling in Moscow; Gorky stood in as his godfather and gave him his surname and patronymic. In 1904 he left Russia for good; lived in New York, France, and Italy; fought in the French army during World War I. Naturalized French citizen (1923); joined the French Foreign Legion and served in Morocco in the 1920s and 1930s, during which period he made several visits to Gorky in Sorrento. Joined General de Gaulle in London in 1941; chief of French military mission in Japan (1945); ended his career in 1950 in Tokyo as general of the army corps. Buried at Sainte-Geneviève-des-Bois with heroes of the Resistance, *101, 141–142, 159, 167, 235–236*

naturalist writer who specialized in stories and essays about the poverty of peasants and workers and the growth of their political consciousness, *112*

Pogodin, Nikolai Fyodorovich (real name: Stukalov) (1900–62). Soviet playwright, *xv–xvin2*

Poincaré, Raymond (1860–1934). French statesman; president of the Republic (1913–20), *74, 84, 88*

Poole, Major General Frederick C. (1869–?). British commander of the Allied force at Archangel (May 1918). His authoritarian methods antagonized the Russians and his reckless plans displeased President Wilson. Recalled to London and replaced (October 1918), *38, 41, 45, 52, 55–58*

Powers, Gary Francis (1929–1977). American U-2 pilot captured by the Soviets in 1960 and exchanged for Rudolf Abel in 1962, *60*

Preobrazhenskaya, Olga Osipovna (1871–1962). Dancer in the Mariinsky Theater in St. Petersburg (1889–1917); emigrated to France in 1921 and directed a highly reputed dance school in Paris, *100*

Priestley, John Boyton (1894–1984). English novelist; essayist, *256, 284*

Primakov, Vitaly Markovich (1897–1937). Soviet general who held attaché posts abroad in 1925–30 (China, Afghanistan, Japan); in 1933–36 commanded army districts of the Caucasus, then Leningrad; arrested in August 1936, tortured, and sentenced by the same tribunal that condemned Tukhachevsky and others; shot; rehabilitated in 1957, *244*

Pushkin, Alexander Sergeevich (1799–1837). Genius of world literature; killed in a duel, *xx, 1–4, 6–7, 222, 270*

Putilov, Alexei Ivanovich (1866–1926). Russian industrialist, *29*

Putna, Vitovt Kazimirovich (1893–1937). Soviet general; military attaché to England (1934–36); recalled in 1936 and liquidated in the army purge in 1937; rehabilitated in 1957, *244*

Pyatakov, Georgy Leonidovich (1890–1937). Bolshevik since 1910; formed the first Soviet government in Ukraine in 1918; sided with Trotsky from 1920 but retained power on the Supreme Economic Council. Expelled from the Party in 1927 as a Trotskyite, then reinstated as deputy commissar for heavy industry; arrested in 1936; tried at the second Moscow Trial in 1937; shot; rehabilitated in June 1988, *234, 265*

Guardian (1916–24), and *The New York Times*, which published eighty of his dispatches in 1918. Married Evgenia Shelepina, Trotsky's former secretary. "Ransome was a Don Quixote with a walrus moustache, a sentimentalist who could always be relied upon to champion the underdog, and a visionary whose imagination had been fired by the revolution. He was on excellent terms with the Bolsheviks and frequently brought us information of the greatest value" (Lockhart, *British Agent*, 263). (*See* Bibliography), *23, 144*

Raskolnikov, Fyodor Fyodorovich (1892–1939). Deputy commissar of the admiralty (1918); commander of the Volga–Caspian fleet, then the Baltic fleet (1920); first ambassador to Afghanistan (1921–23); had responsibilities in publishing and culture (hostile to fellow travelers, which displeased Gorky); named ambassador to Estonia in 1930, then to Denmark and Bulgaria. Recalled to Moscow in 1938; refused to return after learning in the press of his removal. On the eve of his death, denounced Stalin's arbitrary rule. Ten days after World War II began, jumped out of the window of a hospital in Nice, *103, 260–269, 290–291*

Rasputin, Grigory Efimovich (1872–1916). Adventurer of peasant origin; healer; exercised an occult influence over Tsarina Alexandra Fyodorovna; assassinated by monarchists, *xiii*n, *9, 12*

Razumovsky, Count Alexei Grigorievich (1709–71). Husband of Empress Elizaveta Petrovna by morganatic marriage, *299*

Redgrave, Vanessa (1937–). English actress, *296*

Reilly, Sidney (alias of Georgy Relinsky) (1874–1925). British secret agent in Russia. (*See* Bibliography), *48–60, 63, 70–71, 79, 84, 90, 190*

Reinhardt, Max (1873–1943). Influential Austrian-born Jewish director associated with Expressionism and Berlin's Kleines Theater and others. Escaped to the United States in the 1930s, *148–151*

Reisner, Larisa Mikhailovna (1895–1926). Revolutionary; writer; combatant in the civil war; Fyodor Raskolnikov's wife, after 1922 Karl Radek's companion; died of malaria. According to Trotsky, she had "the beauty of an Olympian goddess, a subtle mind, and the courage of a warrior" (quoted in Max Hayward's notes to Nadezhda Mandelstam's *Hope Against Hope*, 412). (*See* Bibliography), *103, 261*

Salomé. *See* Andreas-Salomé, Lou

Saltykov-Shchedrin, Mikhail Evgrafovich (1826–89). Russian novelist and satirist, 97

Savich, Ovady Gertsovich (1897–1967). Writer; Hispanist; Ehrenburg's friend; lived for a long time in Paris, 33

Savinkov, Boris Viktorovich (1879–1925). SR terrorist; writer and poet; in 1918 created the Union for the Defense of the Fatherland and Freedom and organized an anti-Bolshevik uprising in Yaroslavl. Lockhart wrote of him: "he was a forcible speaker who could impress his personality on his listeners. At one time he entirely captivated Mr. Churchill, who saw in him a Russian Bonaparte" (*British Agent*, 179). Lured to Russia in 1924; died in Lubyanka prison, probably pushed out a window, *17, 29, 38, 41, 45–46, 50, 53, 55, 58*

Scheidemann, Philipp (1865–1939). Right Social Democrat; first chancellor of the German Republic (1919), *151, 155, 157*

Schmidchen (Jan Janovich Buikis) (dates unknown). Latvian Chekist, *55, 57–60, 73*

Scriabin, Alexander (1872–1915). Russian composer of genius who lived in Moscow, *13*

Sechenov, Ivan Mikhailovich (1829–1905). Russian thinker; founder of the Russian school of physiology, 97

Sedov, Lev (Léon) (1905–38). Trotsky and Natalia Sedova's oldest son; died in a Paris hospital, *253*

Sedov, Sergei (1909–38?) Trotsky and Natalia Sedova's youngest son; engineer; arrested in late 1934 or early 1935; disappeared in the camps, probably shot, *253*

Sedova, Natalia Ivanovna (1882–1962). Trotsky's second wife, *253*

Semyonova, Marina Timofeevna (1908–). Prima ballerina at the Bolshoi; married to Lev Karakhan. Retired as coach and repetiteur at age ninety-five, and received the President's Prize in 2004, *203*

Serebryakov, Leonid Petrovich (1890–1937). Deputy commissar for transportation (1921–22); member of the Left Opposition; shot after the second Moscow Trial (January 1937); rehabilitated in 1986; reinstated in the Party in 1987, *235*

Serge, Victor (Viktor Lvovich Kibalchich) (1890–1947). Socialist; writer.

Shishkov, Vyacheslav Yakolevich (1873–1945). Realist prose writer; fellow traveler in 1924; author of historical fiction about Siberia, *224*

Shkapa, Ilya Samsonovich (real name: Grinevsky) (1898–?). Writer and publicist, Gorky's associate; arrested in 1935; spent more than twenty years in the camps. Wrote a memoir about Gorky. (*See* Bibliography), *272, 274, 288*

Shklovsky, Viktor Borisovich (1893–1985). Russian theoretician of literature and formalism, *169, 175, 223–224*

Shvernik, Nikolai Mikhailovich (1888–1970). Chairman of the All-Union Central Trade Union Council (1930–44 and 1953–56); member of the Central Committee from 1925, *230–232*

Simpson, Wallis (Duchess of Windsor) (1896–1986). American divorcée; married Edward VIII in 1937, forcing him to abdicate; mentioned in Lockhart's *Diaries* after 1934, *259*

Sinclair, Upton (1878–1968). American novelist; journalist; Socialist Party politician; author of books protesting the abuses of capitalist industry, *135, 181, 225*

Slonim, Marc Lvovich (1894–1976). Youngest deputy (Socialist Revolutionary) in the Constituent Assembly in January 1918; emigrated in 1919 (Florence, Prague, Paris); in 1941 went to the United States, where he taught and published numerous books on Russian and Soviet literature, *233*

Smolny. Institute for Young Ladies of Noble Birth founded in 1764 in St. Petersburg, where the Bolshevik Party headquarters, including Lenin and the Petrograd Soviet, installed themselves at the time of the October Revolution, *18, 22–25, 32, 37, 68, 118*

Smuts, Jan Christiaan (1870–1950). South African politician; military man; philosopher; member of Lloyd George's war cabinet in 1917; prime minister of South Africa (1919–24), *19*

Sokolnikov, Grigory Yakovlevich (real name: Girsh Yankelevich Brilliant) (1888–1939). Commissar of finance (1922–26); vice-chairman of Gosplan; ambassador to England (1929–32); arrested in 1936; tried in 1937; sentenced to ten years in the camps, where he was reportedly killed by his cellmates; rehabilitated in August 1988 and reinstated in the Party, *235*

Stolypin, Pyotr Arkadievich (1862–1911). Russian statesman and prime minister who carried out agrarian reforms between 1906 and 1911. Assassinated by an SR terrorist who was also a police agent, *8*

Strong, Anna Louise (1885–1970). American journalist; pacifist; labor agitator from Seattle; moved to Moscow, was editor of the *Moscow News*, and lived there a long time. Stalin had her accused of espionage and deported. Moved to China, became a follower of Mao, and lived there until her death, *83*

Struve, Pyotr Berngardovich (1870–1944). Economist, philosopher; principal representative of "legal Marxism," then one of the leaders of the Constitutional Democratic Party; emigrated to Paris after the revolution, *45*

Sukhanov, Nikolai Nikolaevich (1882–1940). Menshevik; member of the Petrograd Soviet in 1917. Published his seven-volume *Notes on the Revolution* in Berlin (1922–23). Returned to Soviet Russia; condemned at the trial of the Mensheviks (1931); perished in the camps. His *Notes* were banned from the Stalin period until 1991, when they were republished in Moscow. (*See* Bibliography), *95*

Sukhomlinov, Vladimir Alexandrovich (1848–1926). General; war minister (1909–15), fired for corruption; emigrated to Finland in 1918, then Berlin, where he died, *79*

Sumsky. *See* Kaplun, Solomon Gitmanovich

Suvorin, Boris Alexeevich (1879–1940). Landowner; manufacturer; journalist; writer; publisher; son of Anton Chekhov's friend, the publisher Alexei Suvorin (1834–1912); sided with the Whites in the civil war; emigrated to Paris in 1920, *49, 101*

Suvorov, Count Alexander Vasilievich (1729–1800). Field marshal; considered the greatest general in Russian military history, *266*

Sverdlov, Yakov Mikhailovich (1885–1919). Chairman of Central Executive Committee of Soviets after the revolution (titular head of state). For a period in 1918–19 he was, along with Stalin, Lenin's closest collaborator, *101, 141*

Sytin, Ivan Dmitrievich (1851–1934). Famous Moscow publisher of affordable books for "everyman," *94*

Tatlin, Vladimir Evgrafovich (1885–1953). Constructivist painter; architect; designer, *105, 110, 171*

Thomas, Albert (1878–1932). French Socialist minister in charge of armaments and munitions (1914–17); sent to Russia in April–June 1917, *31*, *33*, *37*

Tikanova, Nina Alexandrovna (stage name of N. A. Tikhonova) (1910–95).Varvara Tikhonova and Alexander Tikhonov's daughter; ballerina and choreographer; premiere dancer in the companies of Ida Rubinstein, Ballets de Monte-Carlo, Ballets Russes de Nijinska, etc.; Chevalier des Arts et des Lettres 1986. Author of a memoir, *La jeune fille en blue* (Lausanne: L'Age d'homme, 1991), *100*

Tikhonov, Alexander Nikolaevich (1880–1956). Gorky's friend from 1903 and collaborator in all his publishing activities from 1914 to the end of Gorky's life; wrote memoirs about Gorky, *xviii*n7, *95*, *97–98*, *100–102*, *107*, *135*, *139*, *224*, *272*n

Tikhonov, Nikolai Semyonovich (1896–1979). Poet; literary official, *269*n

Tikhonova, Varvara Vasilievna (née Zubkova) (1884–1950). Married first to Anatoly Shaikevich; after their divorce (1909), Alexander Tikhonov's companion; also Gorky's unofficial wife before Moura came to Kronverk. After 1921 she and her children lived in Paris, *100–102*, *135*, *165*

Timosha. *See* Peshkova, Nadezhda Alexeevna

Tolstoy, Alexei Konstantinovich (1817–75). Lyric poet; novelist; playwright, *7*

Tolstoy, Alexei Nikolaevich (1883–1945). The "Red Count"; worked for General Denikin as a propagandist during the civil war; emigrated to Paris in 1918, then to Berlin, but was permitted to return to Russia in 1923. He became the principal writer of the Stalinist era and the war; exalted national values, *167*, *210*, *224*, *240*, *249*n, *291–292*

Triolet, Elsa (1896–1970). Novelist; Louis Aragon's companion beginning in 1928; sister of Lily Brik, Mayakovsky's unofficial wife, *241*n, *243–245*

Trotsky, Lev (Leon) Davidovich (Bronshtein) (1879–1940). Menshevik after 1903, then Bolshevik after 1917; commissar of foreign affairs (1917–18); war commissar (1918–25) who organized and led the Red Army during the civil war. In 1920 Trotsky, like Bukharin, defended the superiority of forced labor over free labor for the transition to socialism and the nationalization of the trade unions. Expelled from the Party in

Webb, Beatrice (née Potter) (1858–1943). English Socialist; diarist. (*See* Bibliography), *221, 256*

Webb, Sidney James (1859–1947). English Socialist; founder of the Fabian Society (1889) and of the Socialist weekly *The New Statesman* (1913). Sidney and Beatrice Webb traveled to the Soviet Union in 1932; became ardent Communist sympathizers (*Soviet Communism: A New Civilization?* [London: Longmans, Greene and Co., 1935]), *221, 256*

Wells, George Philip ("Gip") (1901–84). Oldest son of H. G. and Amy Catherine Wells. With his father and Julian Huxley, co-authored *The Science of Life* (London: Amalgamated Press, 1929), *117–118, 122–123, 127, 212, 282–283*

Wells, Herbert George (1866–1946). English journalist; novelist; author of futuristic novels, then of didactic works. (*See* Bibliography), *xi–xii, xv–xvi, xx*n, *8–9, 13, 16, 72, 115–123, 125, 126, 135, 143–144, 177, 185, 190, 216–221, 226, 237, 241*n, *248, 251*n, *255–258, 279–288, 292–296, 299*

Wells, Marjorie (dates unknown). G. P. Wells's wife; H. G. Wells's secretary, *257, 282–283*

West, Anthony (1914–87). Novelist; critic; H. G. Wells and Rebecca West's son, *212, 282–283*

West, Rebecca (real name: Cicily Fairfield) (1892–1983). British feminist; journalist; novelist; H. G. Wells's companion, by whom she had a son, Anthony, *212, 214–215, 283*

Wilhelm II (1859–1941). Emperor of Germany (1888–1918); abdicated after the armistice and lived in exile near Doorn in Holland. Lockhart was the first Allied journalist to interview him (1929), and he later visited him and corresponded with him, *xi, 9, 29, 140, 205, 259*

Williams, Harold Whitmore (1876–1928). London *Times* correspondent in Petrograd before the revolution; married Ariadna Tyrkova in 1911 in Constantinople, where they were both correspondents, *14*

Wilshire, Henry Gaylord (1861–1927). American Socialist; editor of *Wilshire's Magazine.* A sponsor of Gorky's 1906 visit to the United States that resulted in a scandal when Gorky and Andreeva were evicted from their New York hotel because they were not legally married. A wealthy early Californian: Wilshire Boulevard in Los Angeles is named after him, *116, 214*

Zhdanov, Andrei Alexandrovich (1896–1948). Succeeded Kirov in Leningrad in 1934 and was Stalin's mouthpiece on cultural policy. At the First Congress of Soviet Writers (1934) declared "socialist realism" to be the official Party doctrine in the arts. After the war led a campaign of denunciation and decrees aimed at writers and others accused of "poisoning" the minds of Soviet youth (Akhmatova, Zoshchenko, Pasternak, Eisenstein, etc.). His death, attributed to doctors, served as a pretext for a bloody purge of the Party in Leningrad by Malenkov and Beria, 274

Zhelyabuzhsky, Yury Andreevich (1888–1955). Film director, cinematographer, and screenwriter, who took part in filming Lenin in 1918; made numerous films and was a professor at the State Film Institute in Moscow; Maria Andreeva and Andrei Zhelyabuzhsky's son, 102

Zinoviev, Grigory Evseevich (1883–1936). Lenin's principal collaborator (1909–17); chairman of the Petrograd Soviet after the revolution (he lived in the Astoria Hotel); Gorky's personal enemy; chairman of the Communist International (1919–26). Allied with Stalin and Kamenev in 1923–24, then principal figure in the Left Opposition; arrested in December 1934; shot at the end of the first Moscow Trial in 1936; formally rehabilitated in June 1988, 25, 51, 74, 93, 95, 104–108, 110, 122, 126, 156, 161, 179, 265

Zweig, Stefan (1881–1942). Austrian Jewish writer; pacifist; visited Gorky in Sorrento in 1930; went into exile in 1935 to England. He and his wife committed suicide on a trip to Brazil, 177, 225

NINA BERBEROVA (1901–1993) was born in St. Petersburg. She and her companion Vladislav Khodasevich, later described by Vladimir Nabokov as the "greatest Russian poet of our time," lived in the household of Maxim Gorky for some years before emigrating to Paris. Khodasevich died in 1939, and in 1950 Berberova moved to the United States. She taught herself English and worked as a clerk in New York before becoming a professor of Russian literature at Princeton in 1963. In 1985, the novellas Berberova had written in the 1930s about Russian émigrés living in Paris were rediscovered by Hubert Nyssen, the director of the French publishing house Actes Sud, and he began a program of reissuing her works, which include *The Ladies from St. Petersburg*, *The Tattered Cloak*, *The Book of Happiness*, *The Accompanist*, and an autobiography, *The Italics Are Mine*.

MARIAN SCHWARTZ has been translating Russian fiction and nonfiction for over thirty years. Her work includes Edvard Radzinsky's *The Last Tsar*, Yuri Olesha's *Envy*, and many works by Nina Berberova.

RICHARD D. SYLVESTER is Professor Emeritus of Russian at Colgate. His writings about Russian poetry include essays on Khodasevich and Brodsky, and Tchaikovsky's *Complete Songs: A Companion with Texts and Translations* published by Indiana University Press. He began this translation of *Moura* in 1980 at the request of Nina Berberova.